HUMAN SEXUAL
INADEQUACY

Human Sexual Inadequacy

WILLIAM H. MASTERS
DIRECTOR

VIRGINIA E. JOHNSON
ASSISTANT DIRECTOR

THE REPRODUCTIVE BIOLOGY RESEARCH FOUNDATION
ST. LOUIS, MISSOURI

LITTLE, BROWN AND COMPANY
BOSTON

LIBRARY OF CONGRESS CATALOG CARD NO. 71-117043

ISBN 0-316-54985

FIRST EDITION

Fifth printing

Published in Great Britain
by Churchill/Livingstone, Edinburgh and London

PRINTED IN THE UNITED STATES OF AMERICA

PREFACE

If the first book from the Reproductive Biology Research Foundation, the preclinical text *Human Sexual Response*, is judged of value, there must be a second, a text incorporating clinical application of the basic science disciplines of physiology and psychology.

This clinical text has myriad shortcomings in concept and content—statistically limited and motivationally biased population, imperfect five-year patient follow-up, unproved alterations of basic concepts of psychotherapy, and inability to describe precisely subtleties so vital to effective treatment return are some examples. Certainly this report will be of little value unless concept and content are reinforced in the future by the success of a large number of dual-sex therapy teams in a variety of geographic areas throughout the world.

Human Sexual Inadequacy adds clinical experience with human sexual function and dysfunction to preclinical investigation. Knowledge in both areas provides a solid base from which to construct improved rapid-treatment programs for human sexual inadequacy.

For *prevention* of problems of sexual dysfunction, the plan for a multidisciplined approach can be evolved only from regularly recurring reports of investigative substance. Such is the Foundation's commitment to the future.

It is to be hoped that human sexual inadequacy, both the entity and this book, will be rendered obsolete in the next decade. We would like to contribute to the project.

W. H. M.
V. E. J.

St. Louis

v

ACKNOWLEDGMENTS

We are deeply indebted to the professionals who have worked with us, visited us, and have observed, considered, and criticized our concepts and techniques. Particularly are we indebted to our clinical and preclinical collaborators Sallie Schumacher, Richard Spitz, and Gelson Toro.

Barbara Koehler has been primarily responsible for collecting and cataloging the bibliography. It has been a time-consuming, well-conducted task.

Again Marilyn Harris of Washington University's Department of Medical Illustration has been our illustrator. We are indeed fortunate to have continued access to her talents.

Ayerst Laboratories and G. D. Searle & Co. supplied the sex-steroid products used in treatment of aging male and female patients, and International Flavors and Fragrances, Inc., the fragrances used in the special sense studies.

Finally, we express our sincere appreciation to Wanda Bowen and Shirley Shelley and to their entire secretarial staff for total cooperation in the preparation of the manuscript.

To these our friends and to all who have contributed, our respect and our gratitude.

W. H. M.
V. E. J.

CONTENTS

PREFACE   V

ACKNOWLEDGMENTS   vii

1. Therapy Concepts   1

2. Therapy Format   24

SECTION A
Concept of History-Taking   24
The History-Taker   28
Format of History-Taking   29
Outline of History-Taking   34
Comment on History-Taking   51
Procedure   53

SECTION B
Medical History   57
Physical Examination   58
Laboratory Evaluation   59

SECTION C
Roundtable Concept   60
Sensate Focus   67
Special Sense Discussion   75
Roundtable Goals   83

SECTION D
Instructions   85

3. Premature Ejaculation   92

4. Ejaculatory Incompetence 116

5. Primary Impotence 137

6. Secondary Impotence 157

7. The Treatment of Impotence 193

8. Orgasmic Dysfunction 214

SECTION A

Concept 214
Systems of Psychophysiological Influence 218
Background of Orgasmic Dysfunction 222

SECTION B
Primary Orgasmic Dysfunction 227
Situational Orgasmic Dysfunction 240

9. Vaginismus 250

10. Dyspareunia 266

Female Dyspareunia 266
Male Dyspareunia 288

11. Treatment of Orgasmic Dysfunction 295

12. Sexual Inadequacy in the Aging Male 316

13. Sexual Inadequacy in the Aging Female 335

14. Program Statistics 351

15. Treatment Failures 370

BIBLIOGRAPHY 393

INDEX 451

HUMAN SEXUAL INADEQUACY

I

THERAPY CONCEPTS

In any approach to a psychophysiological process, treatment concepts vary measurably from school to school and, similarly, from individual therapist to individual therapist. The Reproductive Biology Research Foundation's theoretical approaches to the treatment of men and women distressed by some form of sexual dysfunction have altered significantly and, hopefully, have matured measurably during the past 11 years. Current treatment concepts are founded on a combination of 15 years of laboratory experimentation and 11 years of clinical trial and error.

When the laboratory program for the investigation in human sexual functioning was designed in 1954, permission to constitute the program was granted upon a research premise which stated categorically that the greatest handicap to successful treatment of sexual inadequacy was a lack of reliable physiological information in the area of human sexual response. It was presumed that definitive laboratory effort would develop material of clinical consequence. This material in turn could be used by professionals in the field to improve methodology of therapeutic approach to sexual inadequacy. On this premise, a clinic for the treatment of human sexual dysfunction was established at Washington University School of Medicine in 1959, approximately five years after the physiological investigation was begun. The clinical treatment program was transferred to the Reproductive Biology Research Foundation in 1964.

When any new area of clinical investigation is constituted, standards must be devised in the hope of establishing some means of control over clinical experimentation. And so it was with the new program designed to treat sexual dysfunction. Supported by almost five years of prior laboratory investigation, fundamental

1

clinical principles were established at the onset of the therapeutic program. The original treatment concepts still exist, even more strongly constituted today. As expected, there were obvious theoretical misconceptions in some areas, so alterations in Foundation policy inevitably have developed with experience.

C O N J O I N T   M A R I T A L · U N I T   T H E R A P Y

A basic premise of therapeutic approach originally introduced, and fully supported over the years by laboratory evidence, is the concept that there is no such thing as an uninvolved partner in any marriage in which there is some form of sexual inadequacy.

Therapeutic technique emphasizing an one-to-one patient-therapist relationship, effective in treatment of many other psychopathological entities, is grossly handicapped when dealing specifically with male or female sexual inadequacy, if the sexually dysfunctional man or woman is married. Isolating a husband or wife in therapy from his or her partner not only denies the concept that both partners are involved in the sexual inadequacy with which their marital relationship is contending, but also ignores the fundamental fact that sexual response represents (either symbolically or in reality) interaction between people. The sexual partner ultimately is the crucial factor.

If treatment is directed separately toward the obviously dysfunctional partner in a marriage, the theoretically "uninvolved" partner may actually destroy or negate much therapeutic effort, initially from lack of knowledge and understanding and finally from frustration. For example, if little or no information of sexual import, or for that matter, of total treatment progress reaches the wife of the impotent husband, she is in a sincere quandary as to the most effective means of dealing with the ongoing marital relationship while her husband is in therapy. She does not know when, or if, or how, or under what circumstances to make sexual advances, or whether she should make advances at all. Would it be better to be simply a "good wife," available to her husband's expression of sexual intent, or on occasion should she take the sexual initiative? During actual sexual functioning should she maintain a completely passive, a somewhat active, or a mutually participating role? None of these questions, all of which inevitably arise in the mind of any intelligent woman contending with the multiple anxieties and the performance fears of an impotent husband, find answers in the inevitable communication void that develops between wife and husband when one is isolated as a participant in therapy.

Of course, an identical situation develops when the wife is non-orgasmic and enters psychotherapy for constitution of effective sexual function. It is the husband that does not know when, or if, or how, or under what circumstances to approach her sexually. If he approaches his wife in a physically demanding manner, she reasonably might accuse him of prejudicing therapeutic progress. If he delays or even restrains expression of his sexual interest, possibly looking for some signal that may or may not be forthcoming, or hoping for some manner of behavioral guideline, he may be accused of having lost interest in or of having no real concern for his sexually handicapped wife. Not infrequently he also is accused (probably with justification) of being a significant contributor to his wife's sexual dysfunction. But if no professional effort is made to explain his mistakes or to educate him in the area of female sexual responsivity, how does he remove this continuing roadblock to his wife's effective sexual function?

Methods of therapy using isolation techniques when approaching clinical problems of sexual dysfunction attempt to treat the sexually dysfunctional man or woman by ignoring half of the problem—the involved partner. These patient-isolation techniques have obliterated what little communication remained in the sexually inadequate marital unit *at least as often* as the techniques have returned effective sexual functioning to the distressed male or female partner.

It should be emphasized that the Foundation's basic premise of therapy insists that, although both husband and wife in a sexually dysfunctional marriage are treated, the marital relationship is considered as the patient. Probably this concept is best expressed in the statement that sexual dysfunction is indeed a marital-unit problem, certainly never only a wife's or only a husband's personal concern.

DUAL-SEX THERAPY TEAMS

Definitive laboratory experience supports the concept that a more successful clinical approach to problems of sexual dysfunction can be made by dual-sex teams of therapists than by an individual male or female therapist. Certainly, controlled laboratory experimentation in human sexual physiology has supported unequivocally the initial investigative premise that no man will ever fully understand woman's sexual function or dysfunction. What he does learn, he learns by personal observation and exposure, repute, or report, but if he is at all objective he will never be secure in his concepts because he can never experience orgasm as a woman.

The exact converse applies to any woman. By repute, report, observation, and by personal exposure in and out of bed, she too learns to conceptualize male sexual functioning and dysfunctioning, but she will never fully understand the basics of male sexual responsivity, because she will never experience ejaculatory demand nor seminal fluid release.

Since it soon became apparent in the laboratory that each investigator needed an interpreter to appreciate the sexual responsivity of the opposite sex, it was arbitrarily decided that the most theoretically effective approach to treatment of human sexual dysfunction was to include a member of each sex in a therapy team. This same premise applied in the clinical study provides husband and wife of a sexually dysfunctional marital unit each with a friend in court as well as an interpreter when participating in the program.

For example, it helps immeasurably for a distressed, relatively inarticulate, or emotionally unstable wife to have available a female cotherapist to interpret what she is saying and, far more important, even what she is attempting unsuccessfully to express to the uncomprehending husband and often to the male cotherapist as well. Conversely, it is inevitably simpler for any wife to understand the concerns, the fears, the apprehensions, and the cultural pressures that beset the sexually inadequate man that is her husband when these grave concerns can be defined simply, effectively, and unapologetically to her by the male cotherapist. The Foundation's therapeutic approach is based firmly upon a program of education for each member of the dysfunctional marital unit. Multiple treatment sessions are devoted to explanations of sexual functioning with concentration on both psychological and physiological ramifications of sexual responsivity. Inevitably, the educational process is more effectively absorbed if the dual-sex therapy teams function as translators to make certain that no misunderstandings develop due to emotional or sexual language barriers.

THERAPISTS' ROLE AND GUIDELINES

If there are to be dual-sex therapy teams, what roles do the individual cotherapists play? What guidelines do they follow? What therapeutic procedures ensue? What should be their qualifications as professionals in this sensitive, emotionally charged area? These are all pertinent questions, and, as would be expected, in some cases they are difficult to answer. The major responsibility of each cotherapist assigned to a marital-unit problem is to evaluate in depth, translate for, and represent fairly the member of the distressed marital unit of the same sex. This concept should not be taken to suggest that verbal or directive interaction is limited to wife and female cotherapist or to husband and male cotherapist—far from it. The interpreter role does not constitute the total contribution an individual cotherapist makes in accepting the major responsibility of sex-linked representation. The male cotherapist can provide much information pertaining to male-oriented sexual function for the wife of the distressed marital unit; and equally important, female-oriented material is best expressed by the female cotherapist for benefit of the husband.

Acute awareness of the two-to-one situation frequently develops when a sexually distressed marital unit sees a single counselor for sexual dysfunction. For example, if the therapist is male and there is criticism indicated for or direction to be given to the wife, the two-to-one opposition may become overpowering. Who is to interpret for or explain to the wife matters of female sexual connotation? Where does she develop confidence in therapeutic material, if she cannot express her concepts adequately to the two males in the room? Exactly the same problem occurs if the therapist is female and contending with a sexually dysfunctional marital unit. Who interprets for or to the husband?

A dual-sex team avoids the potential therapeutic disadvantage of interpreting patient complaint on the basis of male or female bias. Experience has established a recognizable pattern in the various phases of response by a female patient to questioning by a male cotherapist. As a rough rule of thumb, unless the distress is most intense, the wife can be expected to tell her male therapist first what she wants him to know; second, what she thinks he wants to know or can understand; and not until a third, ultimately persuasive attempt has been made can she consistently be relied upon to present material as it is or as it really appears to her. With the female cotherapist in the room, although the wife may be replying directly to interrogation of the male cotherapist, during the first exposure to questioning she routinely is careful to present material as she sees it or as she believes it to be, for she knows she is being monitored by a member of her own sex. The inference, of course, is that "it takes one to know one." The "presence" usually is quite sufficient to remove a major degree of persiflage from patient communication.

When the sexually dysfunctional male patient is interviewed by a female therapist, it is extremely difficult to elicit reliable material, for cultural influence inevitably will prevail. Many times the male tells it as he would like to believe it is, rather than as it is. His ego is indeed a fragile thing when viewed under the spotlight of untempered female interrogation. Not infrequently his performance fears, his anxieties, and his hostilities are magnified in the face of his concept of a prejudiced two-to-one relationship in therapy, when he presumes that his wife has the advantage of the therapist's sexual identity.

The participation of both sexes contributes a "reality factor" to therapeutic procedure in yet another way. It lessens the need for enactment of social ritual designed to gain the attention of the opposite-sex therapist, an unnecessary diversion which often produces biased material in its effort to impress.

These hazards of interrogation and interpersonal misinterpretations can be bypassed through use of the dual-sex team. Certainly, during history-taking there is a session devoted to male cotherapist interrogation of the wife and female cotherapist interrogation of the husband (see Chapter 2), but in each instance within the method there is built-in protection to avoid the previously mentioned pitfalls. First, the husband has had an extensive discussion with the male cotherapist the previous day (as has the wife with the female cotherapist); thus, the pattern for same-sex confrontation and information interchange has already been introduced, concomitantly establishing greater reliability of reporting. Second, both members of the sexually disturbed marital unit are aware that four persons are committed to a common therapeutic goal and that all parties will be brought together the next day for the "roundtable" discussion (see Chapter 2). Hence, any tendency of the patient to provide the cotherapist with inaccurate clinical material in the opposite-sex interrogative session usually is curbed in advance by the dual-sex team environment and the previously described progression of the treatment program.

Equal partner representation in a problem of sexual dysfunction is a particularly difficult concept to accept for those patients previously exposed to other forms of psychotherapy. When either partner has been accustomed to being the principal focus of therapy, he or she finds it strange indeed that neither partner holds this position. Rather it is their interpersonal relationship within the context of the marriage that is held in focus.

An additional fortunate therapeutic return from the presence of both sexes within the therapy team is in the area of clinical concern for transference. There always is transference from patient to therapist as a figure of authority. There is no desire to avoid this influence in the therapeutic program, but, beyond both patients' and therapists' need to establish the authority figure, every effort is made in the brief two-week acute phase of the therapy program to avoid development of a special affinity between either patient and either cotherapist. Instead of generating emotional currents, especially those with sexual connotation, from one side of the desk to the other, the therapeutic team is intensely interested in stimulating the flow of emotional and sexual awareness between husband and wife and encourages this response at every opportunity.

For example, if the team were to observe the wife becoming

intensely attentive to the male cotherapist, directing all questions to him, accepting or even prompting answers only from him—in short, replacing the husband with the cotherapist as the male figure of the moment—the team would take steps to counteract this distracting, potentially husband-alienating trend. The male cotherapist would begin to direct questions only to the husband, and all material pertinent to the wife (even including basic information pertaining to male sexual response) would be presented by the female member of the team until it was obvious that the wife's incipient tendency to establish special interpersonal communication with the male cotherapist had been counterbalanced by team intervention. Attempted recruitment of special rapport with the female cotherapist by the husband is handled in a similar manner. To create further emotional trauma for either sexually insecure marital partner by encouraging or accepting such alignment, however deliberately or naïvely proffered, is not only professionally irresponsible, but also can be devastating to therapeutic results.

It cannot be emphasized too vigorously that the techniques of transference, so effective in attacking many of the major psychotherapeutic problems over the years, are not being criticized. The Foundation is entirely supportive of the proper usage of these techniques as effective therapeutic tools. However, from the start of the clinical program, the Foundation has taken the specific position that the therapeutic techniques of transference have no place in the acute two-week attempt to reverse the symptoms of sexual dysfunction and establish, reestablish, or improve the channels of communication between husband and wife. Anything that distracts from positive exchange between husband and wife during their time in therapy is the responsibility of the therapeutic team to identify and immediately nullify or negate. Positive transference of sexual orientation can be and frequently is a severe deterrent to effective reconstitution of interpersonal communication for members of a marital unit, particularly when they are contending with a problem of sexual dysfunction.

THERAPEUTIC PROCEDURES

In therapeutic procedure involving the dual-sex teams, the control within the team rests primarily with the silent cotherapist during treatment sessions. The silent cotherapist is literally in charge of each therapeutic session. He or she, as the observer, is watching for and evaluating levels of patient receptivity to therapeutic concept and to the educative and directive material presented by the active cotherapist. The silent cotherapist's role is to define, if possible, degrees of understanding, acceptance, or rejection of material and to identify immediate areas of concern in either member of the dysfunctional marital unit.

The silent observer really acts as the coach of the team. As soon as it is apparent that there is need for a situational change of pace, that the individual subject under discussion can be presented in a different, possibly more acceptable or understandable manner, or that it requires further clarification, the roles reverse and the cotherapist functioning previously as the observer, fortified and advantaged with the salient features of patient reaction to the ongoing situation, becomes the active discussant. The previous discussant then assumes the role of observer. And so roles change back and forth as indicated by patient responses or the immediate need for a particular sex-linked definition or explanation of material. Much of the patient's reaction can be identified by the observer that cannot be immediately apparent to any individual therapist simultaneously attempting to direct therapy and to evaluate levels of patient receptivity. In the finite cooperative interaction between mutually confident cotherapists in any dual-sex therapy team, the currently dominant partner influence at any particular time is not being exercised by the one that is talking, but by the one that is observing.

Inevitably any sexually dysfunctional marital unit has, as one of its fundamental handicaps, insecurity in any and all sexual matters. How often have the sexual partners asked themselves if they are really "complete" as individuals? Has their functional efficiency been diminished in stressful situations other than in bed? How do their patterns of sexual response compare to those of their peers? How can a particular sexual situation or any confrontation with material of sexual content be handled without awkwardness or embarrassment? The cotherapists encounter a multiplicity of these problems to which they can respond by holding up a professional "mirror" and helping the marital partners understand what it reflects. With the nonjudgmental mirror available, constructive criticism can be accepted in the same non-prejudiced, comfortable manner in which it must be presented. With this educational technique of reflective teaching, the distressed marital unit can be encouraged to take that first step that ultimately presages success in therapy for sexual dysfunction. The step consists of putting sex back into its natural context.

Seemingly, many cultures and certainly many religions have risen and fallen on their interpretation or misinterpretation of one basic physiological fact. Sexual functioning is a natural physiological process, yet it has a unique facility that no other natural physiological process, such as respiratory, bladder, or bowel function, can imitate. *Sexual responsivity can be delayed indefinitely or functionally denied for a lifetime.* No other basic physiological process can claim such malleability of physical expression.

With the advantage of this unique characteristic, sexual functioning can be easily removed from its natural context as a basic physiological response. Everyone takes advantage of this characteristic every day as he rejects or defers untimely or inappropriate sexual stimuli in order to comply with the social requirements of the moment. Religions have found dedicated support from those willing to sacrifice their functional physical expression of sexuality as a devotion to or an appeasement for their god or gods. If the natural physiological process of human sexual response did not encompass this completely unique adaptability, the sacrifice of denying one's sexual functioning for a lifetime could never have been made.

But the individuals who involuntarily take sexual functioning further out of context than any other are those members of marital units contending with inadequacy of sexual function. Through their fears of performance (the fear of failing sexually), their emotional and mental involvement in the sexual activity they share with their partner is essentially nonexistent. The thought (an awareness of personally valued sexual stimuli) and the action are totally dissociated by reason of the individual's involuntary assumption of a spectator's role during active sexual participation.

It is the active responsibility of therapy team members to describe in detail the psychosocial background of performance fears and "spectator" roles. This explanation is best accomplished by the cotherapist of the same sex as that of the individual whose performance fears are to be discussed. Again, education is the basis for therapeutic success, and the dual-sex team can best present this information by following a sex-linked guideline.

FEARS OF PERFORMANCE

Regardless of the particular form of sexual inadequacy with which both members of the marital unit are contending, fears of sexual performance are of major concern to both partners in the marital bed.

The impotent male's fears of performance can be described in somewhat general terms. With each opportunity for sexual connection, the immediate and overpowering concern is whether or not he will be able to achieve an erection. Will he be capable of "performing" as a "normal" man? He is constantly concerned not only with achieving but also with maintaining an erection of quality sufficient for intromission. His fears of sexual performance are of such paramount import that in giving credence to or even directing overt attention to his fears, he is pulling sexual functioning completely out of context. Actually, the impotent man is gravely concerned about functional failure of a physical response which is not only naturally occurring, but in many phases involuntary in development. To oversimplify, it is his concern which discourages the natural occurrence of erection. Attainment of an erection is something over which he has absolutely no voluntary control. For, as described in Chapter 7, no man can will, wish, or demand an erection, but he can relax and allow the sexual stimulation inherent in erotic involvement with his marital partner to activate his psychophysiological responsivity. Many men contending with fears for sexual function have distorted this basic natural response pattern to such an extent that they literally break out in cold sweat as they approach sexual opportunity.

Not only does the husband contend with fears of performance when impotence is the clinically presenting complaint, but the wife has her fears of performance as well. Her constant concern is that when her husband is given adequate opportunity for sexual expression, he will be unable to achieve and/or maintain an erection. She has grave fears for his ability to perform under the stress of the psychosocial pressure which both partners have unwittingly contrived to place upon this natural physical function. Additionally, wives of impotent men are terrified that something they do will create anxiety, or embarrass, or anger their husbands. All of these crippling tensions in the marital relationship are gross evidence that two people are contending with sexual functioning unwittingly drawn completely out of context as a natural physical function by their fears of performance.

An exactly parallel situation can be a factor in female sexual inadequacy. Fifty years ago in this country the nonorgasmic woman was led (or under the pressure of propriety, forced) to believe that sexual responsivity was not really her privilege. Sexual pleasure was considered an unnatural physical response pattern for women, and any admission of its occurrence was unseemly to say the least.

The popular magazines, with their constant consideration of the subject, have brought to the nonorgasmic female a realization that in truth she is a naturally functional sexual entity. Unfortunately they have also provided her with real fears of performance by depicting, often with questionable realism, the sexual goals of effectively responsive women. Her frequently verbalized anxieties when she does not respond to the level of orgasm (at least a certain percentage of time) are: "What is wrong with me?" "Am I less than a woman?" "I certainly must be physically unappealing to my husband," and so on. These grave self-doubts and usually groundless suspicions are translated into fears of performance. *It should be restated that fear of inadequacy is the greatest known deterrent to effective sexual functioning, simply because it so completely distracts the fearful individual from his or her natural responsivity by blocking reception of sexual stimuli either created by or reflected from the sexual partner.*

Therapy concepts place major emphasis on the necessity for familiarizing the marital partner of a dysfunctional patient with details of the fear component. There must always be real awareness of the fears of performance by the marital partner attempting to support his or her mate in the distress of sexual inadequacy.

The husband of the nonorgasmic woman may well have his own fears of performance. He worries about why he, as a sexually functional male, cannot give her the "gift" of response. Why is his wife nonresponsive to his sexual approaches? What really is wrong when he cannot satisfy her sexual needs? The husband's fear of performance when dealing with a nonorgasmic wife reflects anxieties directed as much toward his own sexual prowess as to his wife's inability to accomplish relief of sexual tensions. It is the influence of our culture, expressed in the demand that he "do something" in sexual performance, that gives the man responsibility for the woman's sexual effectiveness as well as his own. If his wife is nonorgasmic, more times than not he worries about his inadequate performance rather than lending himself with personal pleasure to the mutual sexual involvement that would lead to release of his wife from her dysfunctional status. Together, these frightened people manage to take not only sexual functioning from its natural context, but also keep it in its unnaturally displaced state indefinitely.

One of the most effective ways to avoid emphasizing the patient's fears of performance during any phase of the therapy program is to avoid all specific suggestion of goal-oriented sexual performance to the marital unit. Regardless of the length or the intensity of the psychotherapeutic procedures, at some point the therapist usually turns to his or her patient and suggests that the individual should be about ready for a successful attempt at sexual functioning. Immediately the fears of performance flood the psyche of the individual placed so specifically on the spot to achieve success by this authoritative suggestion. Rarely is this suggestion taken as an indication of potential readiness for sexual function, as intended, but usually is interpreted as a specific direction for sexual activity. If there is a professional suggestion that "tonight's the night," the individual feels that he has been told by constituted authority that he must go all the way from A to Z, from onset of sexual stimulation to successful completion. In many instances, regardless of the duration or effectiveness of the psychotherapeutic program, the fears of performance created by this authoritative suggestion for end-point achievement are of such magnitude that sensate input is blocked firmly, and there will be no effective sexual performance regardless of the degree of motivation. Removal of such goal-oriented concept, in any form or application, is necessary to secure effective return of sexual function. This can be achieved by moving the interacting partners, not the dysfunctional individual, on a step-by-step basis to mutually desirable sexual involvement (see Chapter 2).

COMMUNICATION

Four-way verbal exchange is maintained at an open, comfortable level during therapy. First, communication is developed across the desk between patients and cotherapists. Within a few days, verbal exchange is deliberately encouraged between patients.

The cotherapists are fully aware that their most important role in reversal of sexual dysfunction is that of catalyst to communication. Along with the opportunity to educate concomitantly exists the opportunity to encourage discussion between the marital partners wherein they can share and understand each other's needs. If the therapy team functions well, its catalytic role in marital communication, which initially is of utmost importance, becomes a factor of progressively decreasing importance over the two-week period. If the catalytic role is well played, the marital partners will be communicating with increasing facility at termination of the acute phase of therapy; by then communication between the marital partners should be well established.

The ultimate level in marital-unit communication is sexual intercourse. When there is marital-unit complaint of sexual dysfunction, the primary source of absolute communication is interfered with or even destroyed and most other sources or means of interpersonal communication rapidly tend to diminish in effectiveness. Again, this loss of warmth and understanding is frequently due to fear and/or lack of comprehension on the part of either marital partner. The wife is afraid of embarrassing or angering her husband if she tries to discuss his sexually dysfunctional condition. The husband is concerned that his wife will dissolve in tears if he mentions her orgasmic inadequacy or asks for suggestions to improve his sexual approaches. Usually the failure of communication in the bedroom extends rapidly to every other phase of the marriage. When there is no security or mutual representation in sexual exchange, there rarely is freedom of other forms of marital communication.

It should be made abundantly clear, in context, that Foundation philosophy does not reflect the concept that sexual functioning is the total of any marital relationship. It does contend, however, that very few marriages can exist as effective, complete, and ongoing entities without a comfortable component of sexual exchange.

With detailed interchange of information, and with interpersonal rapport secured between marital partners, the dual-sex therapy team moves into direct treatment of the specific sexual inadequacy brought to its attention. After roundtable discussion (see Chapter 2), the team anticipates that both partners in the distressed marital unit will have become reassured and relatively relaxed by the basic educational process and will have established a significant step toward effective communication. Treatment approaches to specific sexual dysfunctions will be discussed separately under appropriate headings in subsequent individual chapters.

QUALIFICATIONS OF PROFESSIONAL COTHERAPISTS

From a professional point of view, formal training contributes little of positive value if a specific discipline is emphasized to a dominant degree in the treatment of sexual dysfunction. It is current Foundation policy to pair representatives of the biological and behavioral disciplines into teams of cotherapists. From a purely practical point of view, there is obvious advantage in having a qualified physician as a member of each team. This disciplinary inclusion avoids referring embarrassed or anxious marital units to other sources for their vitally necessary physical examinations and laboratory (metabolic function) evaluations. The behavioral member provides invaluable clinical balance to each team with his or her particular contribution of psychosocial consciousness. Many combinations of disciplines should and will be used experimentally as representative individuals are available, complying with the Foundation's basic concept of a member of each sex on each team.

The Foundation is constantly looking for professionals with the individual ability necessary to work comfortably and effectively with people in the vulnerable area of sexual dysfunction. There must be an established research interest; this requirement is peculiar to the Foundation's total research program but is unnecessary for purely clinical programs. There also must be an expressed interest in and demonstrated ability to teach, for so much of the therapy is but a simple direct educational process. Not a negligible requirement is the willingness to make a commitment to a seven-day week or its equivalent. Most important, the individual must be able to work in continual cooperation with a member of the opposite sex in what might be termed a single-standard professional environment. Team dominance by virtue of sex-linked or discipline-linked status by either cotherapist would tend to dilute their mutual effectiveness in this particular psychotherapeutic design.

Finally, individual members of any dual-sex therapy team, if they are to concentrate professionally on the distress of the marital units complaining of sexual inadequacy, must be fully cognizant and understanding of their own sexual responsivity and be able to place it in perspective. They must be secure in their knowledge of the nature of sexual functioning, in addition to being stable and confident in their own sexuality, so that they can in turn be objective and unprejudiced when dealing with the controversial subject of sex at the fragile level of its dysfunctional state. Many men and women who are neither personally secure in nor confidently knowledgeable of sexual functioning attempt the authoritative role in counseling for sexual inadequacy. There is no place in professional treatment of sexual dysfunction for the individual man or woman not culturally comfortable with the subject and personally confident and controlled in his or her own manner of sexual expression.

The possibility for disaster in a therapeutic program dealing with sexual dysfunction cannot be greater than when the therapist's sexual prejudices or lack of competence and objectivity in dealing with the physiology and psychology of sexual functioning become apparent to the individuals or marital units depending upon therapeutic support. If the therapist is in any way uncomfortable with the expression of his or her own sexual role, this discomfort or lack of confidence inevitably is projected to the patient, and the possibility of effective reversal of the marital unit's sexual dysfunction is markedly reduced or completely destroyed.

TIME COMMITMENT AND SOCIAL ISOLATION

At onset of the program, marital units were requested to devote three weeks of their time to the therapeutic program. This concept of time commitment was maintained for the first two years of this clinical research program. Evaluation of experience made clear that three weeks was simply too long for a marital unit's comfortable commitment of time away from home and, from the standpoint of therapy demand also was an unnecessarily extended period. Therefore, the outer limit of time demand became two weeks and has remained so for the last nine years.

An important clinical contribution to effective therapy in sexual dysfunction can be made by scheduling marital-unit partners on a continuum; all units in the acute phase of the treatment program are seen daily (seven days a week) during their two weeks in the Foundation's intensive educational program.

One of the therapeutic advantages inherent in the two-week phase of rapid education and/or symptom reversal is the isolation of the marital-unit partners from the demands of their everyday world. Approximately 90 percent of all marital units treated by the

Foundation are referred from outside the St. Louis area. These people are regarded and treated as though they were guests. Every effort is made to insure their enjoyment of a "vacation" during time spent in the city. Care is taken to familiarize them with the geographic area and supply up-to-date information regarding restaurants, areas of interest, amusement, educational potentials, etc.

Inevitably they rekindle, in part, their own communicative interests when there is no child crying, no secretary reminding of business commitments, or no relatives or friends inadvertently intruding. With this isolation from social demand, opportunity develops for a closeness or a unity that almost always is missing between marital partners facing crises of sexual dysfunction. This arbitrary social isolation certainly is an important factor supporting the effectiveness of the therapy program. Under these circumstances protected from outside pressures the marital partners frequently accept for the first time the Foundation's basic premise that "there is no such thing as an uninvolved partner in any marriage distressed by a complaint of sexual inadequacy."

Yet another advantage of the social-isolation factor is its effect upon the sexual interest of both marital partners. With the subject of sex exposed to daily consideration, sexual stimulation usually elevates rapidly and accrues to the total relationship. This specific psychophysiological support is indeed welcome to the cotherapists dealing with the blocking of sexual stimuli in individuals distressed by sexual inadequacy. To help develop a level of sexual interest for the marital unit which is realistic to their life style, vacations from any form of specific sexual activity are declared for at least two 24-hour periods during the two weeks, in a system of timely checks and balances. However, daily consideration of sexual matters and social isolation continue to give maximum return to this facet of the psychotherapy.

It might be held as part of this therapeutic concept that patients must have the opportunity to make those mistakes which reveal factors contributing to their particular distress. This means of learning is particularly important in reversing sexual dysfunction. In this interest, the patients are told that the cotherapists are not interested in a report of perfect achievement when they are following directions in the privacy of their own bedroom. The cotherapists are interested in marital-unit partners making their usual errors of reaction and interaction as they involve themselves in situations that provide opportunity for natural response to sexual stimuli. If the mistakes then are evaluated and explained in context, the educational process is infinitely less painful and more lasting. There are significant advantages in this technique. When mistakes are made, they are examined impartially and explained objectively to the unit within twenty-four hours of their occurrence. Additionally, they are discussed within the context of the misunderstanding, misconceptions, or taboos that may have led to or influenced their occurrence initially.

There is yet another specific advantage in daily conferences. If the distressed unit waits a matter of days after mistakes are made before consulting authority, the fears engendered by their specific episode of inadequacy or "mistake" in performance increase daily in almost geometric progression. In such a situation, alienation between partners is a common occurrence. By the time the next opportunity for consultation arises, a great deal of the effectiveness of prior therapy may have been destroyed by the takeover of the "fears." Fears of performance do not wait a few days or a week until the next appointment; in the meantime, the marital-unit partners, separately or together, must use their own methods of coping. Most often this will be withdrawal of sexual or total communication, which places them further away from altering the sexual distress than before therapy was initiated.

When patients do not make mistakes during their acute phase of treatment, the cotherapists arrange for them to do so. It is inevitably true that individuals learn more from their errors than from their ability to follow directions effectively on the first attempt. If marital partners reverse their sexual dysfunction and fully understand, through comparison with episodes of failure, why and what made it possible for them to function effectively, the probability of reduplicating the success in the home environment is increased immeasurably.

As evidence of the advantage to the therapeutic program of the unit's social isolation, those marital units referred to the Foundation from the St. Louis area require three weeks to accomplish symptom reversal rather than the standard two weeks for those living outside the local area. It is difficult to isolate oneself from family demands and business concerns if treatment is being carried out in the environment in which the couple lives. For this reason it has been found more effective to see patients referred from the St. Louis area on a daily basis for the first week, thereafter five times a week, and to assign a total of three weeks to accomplish reversal of symptomatology. Partners in sexually distressed marriages who cannot or do not isolate themselves from the social or professional concerns of the moment react more slowly, absorb less, and communicate at a much lower degree of efficiency than those advantaged by social retreat.

The Foundation's request for two weeks' withdrawal from daily demands, at first rather an overwhelming suggestion to most patients, pales into insignificance when compared to the isolation demands engendered by necessary hospitalization for acute surgical or medical problems. When the marital unit's presenting complaint is one of sexual inadequacy, it should constantly be borne in mind that there is not only the equivalent of two distressed people but also an impaired marital relationship to be treated.

REFERRAL FROM AUTHORITY

In order to establish at least a minimum of patient screening, at onset of the clinical treatment program no units were accepted in therapy unless the complaining partner in the marital unit (e.g., the impotent male or the nonorgasmic female) had a history of at least six months of prior psychotherapeutic failure to remove the symptoms of sexual dysfunction. Very soon this proved to be a poorly contrived standard, of little screening value. As should have been apparent at onset, there was no secure way of establishing the functional effectiveness of the prior therapeutic program. How determined and well oriented was the therapist? How cooperative or fully responsible was the patient? After two years this original standard was abandoned in favor of that currently in effect.

A reasonably effective method of screening has been substituted by requiring that no patients be accepted at the Foundation unless they have been referred from authority. As authority, the Foundation accepts physicians, psychologists, social workers, and theologians. Beyond screening the patients for appropriate referral to the Foundation, the referral source further is asked to provide available details of psychosocial background relevant to the marital-unit sexual dysfunction. A telephoned report is made to the referring authority describing marital-unit progress (or lack of it) during or immediately following the acute phase of treatment at the Foundation. Well-informed authority then can provide a most important reinforcement for newly acquired patterns of sexual interaction for the marital unit once removed from the Foundation's direct control by termination of the acute phase of therapy.

In many instances, patients in established psychotherapeutic programs have been referred for removal of symptoms reflecting a somewhat broad area of distress in which sexual inadequacy is only a part. After their two weeks at the Foundation, these marital units are, of course, returned to referring authority to continue their established treatment programs. Obviously, the referring authority, before continuing in therapy with his patient, is briefed in detail as to the marital unit's response to its Foundation exposure.

The screening process as currently constituted has several aims, all obviously selective in nature. Primarily, control which prevents referral of major psychopathology is presumed. In other words the psychoneurotic is acceptable, but not the psychotic.

It should be emphasized that the reversal of symptoms of sexual inadequacy in psychoneurotic patients is indeed a significant portion of the Foundation's objectives. Acceptance of this role by the Foundation is based on the premise that the reversal of particularly troublesome sexual symptoms may speed the progress of a psychoneurotic patient within the greater context of his established and broader-based psychotherapy. However, the majority of the marital units contending with sexual dysfunction do not evidence psychiatric problems other than the specific symptoms of sexual dysfunction. Sociocultural deprivation and ignorance of sexual physiology, rather than psychiatric or medical illness, constitute the etiologic background for most sexual dysfunction. Therefore, when a marital unit is properly educated in sexual matters, and their specific symptoms are reversed, there is no need for further psycho-therapy, unless extensive duration of the distress has created psychosocial complications no longer directly related to the sexual dysfunction.

Other areas of selective screening for information vital to the therapeutic program center on such questions as: (1) Are both members really interested in reversing their basic dysfunctional status? If one member of the unit simply has no interest whatso-ever in reversing the symptomatology of sexual dysfunction in the marital relationship, the unit probably needs legal rather than medical or behavioral advice. The chances of reversing the sexual dysfunction under the circumstances of total disaffection for a marital partner are negligible. (2) What, if anything, is known of the marital unit's adjustment or maladjustment to its social com-munity? (3) Do the referred members of the marital unit under-stand the programs, procedures, and policies of the Foundation? If not, it is suggested that the local authority, quietly briefed in advance by the Foundation's professional staff, present the in-formation in more specific detail to his patients. (4) What is the marital unit's basic financial picture? Should the Foundation offer the patients an adjusted fee scale or free care?

FOLLOW-UP COMMITMENT

The original research premise emphasized the fact that positive reversal of symptoms of sexual inadequacy during the acute phase of the treatment program was not of great import. If there were to be any clinical claim for positive effect in the Foundation's concentrated approach to symptom reversal, the clinical results would have to be judged in retrospect over a significant period of time, not at the termination of the acute phase of therapy. Therefore, the policy of five years of follow-up for marital units after termination of the rapid-treatment phase of the program became an integral part of research standards. Failures to reverse symptoms are, of course, considered most significant.

Little of clinical value can be established for any therapeutic program, regardless of length of its ongoing treatment phase, if the results are not evaluated in long-term follow-up after termination of the acute phase of therapy. The abiding guide to treatment value must not be how well the patients do under authoritative control but how well they do when returned to their own cognizance without therapeutic control. This result finally must place the mark of clinical failure or success upon the total therapeutic venture.

Individual members of marital units seen in treatment must agree to cooperate with five years of follow-up after termination of the acute phase of the therapy program. They fully understand the Foundation's basic premise that success in reversal of the symptoms of sexual dysfunction means little during the two weeks of intensive treatment, unless the symptom reversal is maintained for at least the first five years after separation from direct Foundation influence. Success in maintenance of symptom reversal for this length of time does provide some sense of permanency in the continuing effectiveness of the marital unit's sexual functioning.

Those marital units whose acute treatment phase was judged inadequate or a failure arbitrarily have not been placed in the five-year follow-up program. This type of follow-up would indeed have been a study of major importance, but such continuing interrogation certainly could have interfered seriously with other clinical approaches designed to relieve the unit's problems of sexual dysfunction.

The therapy concepts and clinical procedures depict basic methodology of cotherapist interaction, first, between team members, and second, directed toward husband and wife of the sexually dysfunctional marital unit. Jules Masserman has so aptly described psychotherapy as "anything that works." This "works" in a healthy percentage of cases.

2

THERAPY FORMAT

SECTION A

CONCEPT OF HISTORY-TAKING

The prevalent error in taking a sex history arises from the assumption that a "sex" history is a thing of meaning apart from a medical and psychosocial history reflecting the individual as a whole person. Even for purposes of structured social survey, significant material rarely is developed by sexually oriented questions uncorrelated with other aspects of an individual's existence. An unfortunate though understandable by-product of the cultural residual of Puritan ethic (or any other "sex is sin" concept), the separation of sex from consideration of the total of human existence has become an unwitting habit. Beyond investigation of its obligatory role in reproduction, sex is all too often studied outside its natural context. In truth, when taken out of context of the total being and his environment, a "sex" history per se would be as relatively meaningless as a "heart" history or a "stomach" history.

History-taking in the rapid-treatment method of psychotherapy currently presented for professional consideration is not designed to provide a statistical review of the patient's sexual experiences. Such a limited view immediately removes sexual functioning from its natural context, an error accomplished all too readily without professional support by the dysfunctional patient with his or her fear of sexual performance. Rather, Foundation sex-history-taking is structured to develop material within a chronologic framework of life-cycle influences, which reflects sexually oriented attitudes and feelings, expectations and experiences, environmental changes and practices. History-taking certainly must provide information sufficient to define the character (etiological background, symptom onset, severity and duration, psychosocial affect) of the present-ing sexual dysfunction. Equally important, history-taking must contribute knowledge of the basic personalities of the marital partners and develop a professional concept of their interper-sonal relationship adequate to determine (1) changes that may be considered desirable, (2) personal resources and the depth and health of the psychosocial potential from which they can be drawn, and (3) marital-unit motivation and goals (what the marital partners actually expect from therapy).

Changes, as discussed here, represent alterations or adaptations in patterns of personal behavior and the development of mutual interaction between marital partners which permits sexual response to evolve as a natural function. Alterations or adaptations of be-havior are considered desirable only if they can be developed within the context of the sexual value system of the individual marital partners involved, and if they support or enhance individ-ual participation within the marital relationship.

A sexual value system is derived from sensory experiences indi-vidually invested with erotic meaning, which occur under the choice of circumstances and the influence of social values which make them convertible to and acceptable as sexual stimuli. *Sexual value system* is intended to convey a broader concept than can be described by the term *cathexis* when applied to an expres-sion of sexuality. Definition of the specific dynamics of the indi-vidual's sexual value system (SVS) during initial history-taking often can be used to provide a baseline for early therapeutic progress. However, elaboration of the system should not be allowed to interfere with a well-paced development of the total history. Rather than pursuing details of these sexual require-ments, which may not be within the patient's conscious awareness at this early stage of interrogation, the program design contains specific provision for later development of relevant material. By direction, each member of the marital unit is provided opportunity to define his or her own sexual value system. Subsequently, this material can be described during regular therapy sessions and ap-plied by the cotherapists to support psychosexual redirection (see Section D).

The desirability, perhaps the necessity, of introducing behavioral redirection on the basis of established personal social values is obvious. It would provide the only reasonable therapeutic framework available to the brief time span afforded this form of psychotherapy. However, personal social values as they develop often are based upon the concept of a dishonorable role for sexual functioning; and social value systems operant with the presenting distress may include conscious or unconscious rejection of all that has sexual connotation. The cotherapists always must bear in mind the fact that alteration of an established value formation that has been reinforced by years of psychosocial adaptation may be less tolerable to the individual than the dysfunction itself. Unless basic sexual and social value concepts can be adapted in support of behavioral change through an educative process, newly constituted sexual effectiveness has little chance of long-continued maintenance after the marital unit returns to its own environment.

Effective sexual functioning developed during the treatment program despite a negatively invested sexual value system might be somewhat comparable to a situation in which adequate sexual function can be achieved (without therapeutic assistance) only on vacations or under circumstances which have either a festival quality or a once-in-a-lifetime aspect. In such instances, sexual responsivity would be vested in factors primarily reflecting social or sexual requirements that rarely are present in daily living or even adequate to ongoing sexual expression.

Contrary to widely held beliefs, a single instance of successful sexual function, or even situational relief of sexual function, does not carry a built-in assurance of permanency. This is due to the infinite varieties of random eroticism and the rigid psychosocial controls with which many individuals invest their sexuality in a complex system which presumes to grant "permission" to function sexually. This means, simply, that when "system-granted permission" breaks down, a single successful episode of sexual functioning seldom assures a future sexual effectiveness, since it usually is achieved under circumstances unrelated to or without understanding of the environment reflective of prior sexual failures. The sexual myths and misconceptions contributed by scientific limitations of the past and the cultural potpourri of sex-related fears of both past and present have contributed to this human sexual dilemma.

Nevertheless, details of specifically successful sexual events should be drawn from the patient's own experience during history-taking. They may provide the definitive bit of insight into the individual's sexual requirements upon which to build a bridge to attainable goals. Frequently, it is only a small step from the pattern that sustains sexual dysfunction to one that will remove the blocking mechanism and allow natural "unfolding" of sexual response within the larger context of an existing interpersonal relationship. For these reasons, individual social and sexual value systems should be well defined within the history before the members of the marital unit are given any specific physical direction which they must carry out together (see Section C).

In this, as in many methods of psychotherapy, the goal of symptom removal often provides the purpose to which a psychosexual-social history is directed. However, it must be reemphasized that the complaint of sexual dysfunction does not necessarily represent underlying psychopathology. It is possible to define those cases where sex-related inadequacy merely reflects too little sexual knowledge and/or unrealistic expectations in regard to sexual function. In these situations, sexual dysfunction consistently reflects the sexual partners' inability to communicate with one another. It frequently demonstrates inability of either or both marital partners to express their sexual identity without embarrassment, frustration, or fear of rejection. Most of them have never been able to share knowledge of those things that are sexually desired and those that distract from sexual responsivity.

In such situations, sexual dysfunction may not be the symptom but the "disease" itself. Such is the depth of the identity-related value given to effectiveness of sexual function by an incredible number of people, that to convey to sexually dysfunctional patients a concept of "sexual abnormality" is to risk creating psychopathology where only inadequate knowledge of natural sexual function and/or lack of marital-unit communication currently exist.

Therefore, history-taking for the purpose of reversing sexual problems should not be biased by professional assumption of existent psychopathology. Such bias may influence the structuring of questions to a degree that communicates prejudice in authoritative approach to a patient already fearful of revealing an unaccept-

able facet of his or her sexual character. This fear may result either
in the patient's masking of crucially important facts at history-taking or in the interrogator's loss of patient confidence. If either or
both marital partners do evidence specific psychopathology, an expression of bias during history-taking can signal the patients to
alter their verbal response patterns accordingly, and valuable material may be lost. History-taking, even in cases that indicate early
referral for definitive psychiatric care, is improved by maintaining
at all times an unbiased approach.

THE HISTORY-TAKER

In taking a sexual history the interrogator should (1) convey
an aura of comfort with the subject (and respond without embarrassment to unfamiliar material), (2) reflect factual knowledge
when it is appropriate, and (3) create an atmosphere free of
discernible prejudice toward the sexual values, ideas, or practices
discussed by the patient. The fact that these requirements rarely
are achieved with real consistency by professionals in the field
must be acknowledged as a major factor in the clinical failure of
various techniques of psychotherapy directed toward reversal of
sexual dysfunction.

A state of self-control and self-scrutiny must be maintained by
cotherapists in order to refrain from projecting emotional residuals
of personal conflicts. Psychosexual stability as well as freedom
from sexual prejudice are not only desirable qualities but also
actual requisites for individuals working in this professional area.

Authoritative, interested, and emotionally detached questioning
can impart the nature of the catalytic role the cotherapists intend
to assume during the program. This detached but concerned attitude helps to contain sexually invested, emotionally sensitive
material within the interactive potential of the marital partners.
It also emphasizes the cotherapists' commitment to the total of
the marital sexual relationship and underscores the fact that there
never is a primary cotherapist commitment to a specific marital
partner. Time limitations inherent in the two-week maximum

period for the rapid-treatment program do not permit cotherapists' acceptance of sexually implicated transference which may interfere either by design or by coincidence with the feelings, attitudes, or exchanges between marital partners. Transference, especially that which has obvious sexual implication, cannot be handled responsibly within the time limitation and is redirected as soon as it is recognized by use of techniques inherent in the dual-sex team approach (see Chapter 1).

Countertransference, especially as it seeks to satisfy a cotherapist's personal goals, may influence the establishment of unrealistic or unattainable goals for a marital-unit. It is most important that each cotherapist learn to identify those patients whom he or she tends either to overvalue or to underestimate as adaptable to certain types of direction. When a male-female team conducts the treatment program, this area of countertransference has little opportunity for development except during the one-to-one history-taking sessions. By design, team interaction will minimize or eliminate specific elements of countertransference crucially detrimental to the marital relationship or to a positive prognosis for therapy (see Chapter 1).

FORMAT OF HISTORY-TAKING

A basic format for taking a psychosexual-social history has been established for the rapid treatment of human sexual inadequacy during dual-sex team psychotherapy. However, this format is sufficiently flexible to serve a variety of clinical situations by progressive development of material in desired areas of interest until the required level of information is obtained. For instance, the basic history-taking technique may be used to screen patients for purposes of referral or to establish their suitability to a particular program of psychotherapy. This screening function usually requires less depth of historical content than that necessary for the Foundation's specific program for reversal of sexual inadequacy.

The marital unit available to history-taking at the Foundation already has been screened (at least superficially) by referring authority before acceptance in the rapid-treatment program. As a specific baseline for therapy, individual psychosexual-social histories are taken by the male-female team of cotherapists that will remain with the particular marital unit for the duration of the rapid-treatment program. Following termination of the 11 years of statistical control currently reported (December, 1969), therapy design will be altered to evaluate effectiveness of a system involving interchange of team personnel during the two-week treatment program, while maintaining uniformity of directive content and technique.

Introductory Session. The team of cotherapists and the marital unit meet, usually for the first time, during a brief (approximately 10 to 15 minutes) intake interview. The couple is formally welcomed and their immediate procedural commitment to the therapy program is outlined.

First, the marital unit is informed that all sessions, conjoint or individual, are recorded. The Foundation maintains a maximum control of security and tape storage. All microphones are in full view in each interview area.

It is explained that every therapy session is recorded both for patient and therapist advantage. The patient's personal security is protected by removing the necessity (through recording) for dictating involved, professional records of each session. The less material that must be dictated and typed in any controlled operation, inevitably the more security is achieved. Cotherapists are assisted several ways by a well-functioning centrally controlled recording system: (a) a tremendous amount of professional time is conserved if dictated comment for each therapy session is avoided; (b) the therapist is free to observe patient reaction to controlled questioning rather than being involved in and distracted by note-taking; and (c) no professional's recall is as effective as tape playback, to answer retrospectively questions of patient attitude or specific historical detail.

Second, the format of the history-taking that occupies the marital partners for the first two days of the program is explained, together with a passing description of the busy third day's medical history-taking, physical examination, general and metabolic laboratory evaluation, and roundtable session.

Third, husband and wife are requested not to discuss with each other questions asked or content of individual answers given until after the roundtable session on the third day. This approach permits professional consideration of each marital-unit partner as an individual before the therapy is focused primarily upon the marital relationship.

It also is helpful to create a mutual awareness of the fact that each partner is given simultaneous opportunity to describe sensitive or controversial material in response to detailed questioning. The mere fact that both marital partners are interviewed simultaneously inevitably tends to insure integrity of reporting.

Fourth, the old canard that patients referred for sexual inadequacy must appear as study subjects in the physiology laboratory is quietly dismissed. All patients are assured that nothing could be further from the truth. It is explained succinctly that men and women complaining of any form of sexual dysfunction would not qualify to appear as study subjects in the laboratory, nor would the cotherapists dream of exposing sexually dysfunctional patients to a physiological laboratory evaluation.

Fifth, by way of specific physical direction, the marital unit is requested to refrain from overt sexual activity until otherwise directed. This assumption of authoritative control over the marital unit's sexual functioning is established during the intake interview so that subsequent therapeutic direction can take into consideration individual need for sexual release. In order that concerns of marital-unit sexual tensions be handled by appropriate direction, history-taking on Day 1 should identify the occasion of the most recent ejaculation for the husband and the last sexual activity leading to an orgasmic level of response for the wife.

Sixth, it is reemphasized that patients are accepted only if they come for sexual therapy as members of the marital unit and are mutually committed to the Foundation's premise that there is no such thing as an uninvolved partner in a marriage where sexual dysfunction exists. However, history-taking should first delineate each partner as an individual sexual entity before contemplating problems of marital interaction. It also is desirable to establish each individual partner's impressions and feelings about the nature of the marital unit's sexual distress before the individual viewpoint can be prejudiced or significantly edited through exposure to the marital relationship's established "corporate" philosophy.

Technique.   By deliberate design the male cotherapist takes the initial definitive history from the husband, while the female cotherapist simultaneously elicits similar historical material from the wife. This basic format encourages marital-partner rapport with the cotherapist of the same sex. In alignment, the same cotherapists will define and interpret material reflecting sex-oriented attitudes and activity, when such sex-linked representation or interpretation is appropriate later in the overall design of therapy.

As a team the cotherapists first are committed to develop material with which to establish a diagnostic and prognostic assessment of the specific sexual inadequacy and the state of the marital relationship within which the dysfunction has occurred. Thereafter, history-taking, in addition to collecting pertinent material, must support the cotherapists' primary professional role as catalysts (1) to marital-partner understanding of the presenting sexual dysfunction and its probable causes; (2) to natural patterns of effective sexual function; and (3) most important, to communication. Interpersonal communication initiated on the first day between cotherapist and marital partner of the same sex and encouraged by the contrasexed interrogation of the second day is further stimulated on the third day at the roundtable discussion between cotherapists and the marital unit, and then gradually shifted to direct exchange between husband and wife later in the course of therapy.

History-taking provides an opportunity to initiate communication and it is also the way to begin the marital partners' process of attitudinal change. Within the format of questioning in depth, the interrogator can make the incomparably important therapeutic contribution of creating a climate of comfort with the subject of sex, first by the manner and tone of voice employed, and then by introducing a vocabulary that is both appropriate to the educational status of the marital partners and emotionally uncharged. The process whereby both the subject matter and the terminology can have the emotional charge removed depends entirely upon the cotherapists' continuing expression and aura of comfort and authority with sexual material.

The history-taker (of the same sex as the marital partner being interrogated) developing the basic history on Day 1 is responsible for chronological accuracy. This portion of the total sexual history is developed within an outlined framework of life-cycle influences and events and marked by the chronologic progression of education, occupation, and recreation. Accounts of dating, courtship(s), marital commitment(s) and reproductive history provide a chronologic basis for identifying specific patterns of sexual behavior and establishing sexual preferences. The identity of those people that have made meaningful contributions to or have influenced the formation of both the social and sexual value systems should be underscored and their contributing role evaluated.

Detailed information is drawn from tangential questioning, within the established format of the Day 1 interview (between the same-sex patient and cotherapist), directed toward:

1. Random events having special and/or sexual meaning for the individual
2. Sexual content of expectations, dreams, and fantasies
3. Those events, often traumatic in nature, occurring outside the usual life-cycle expectations, such as incest, illegitimate pregnancies, abortions, rape, infidelity, etc.

While developing information, questioning never should be pursued to the point of patient discomfort merely to attain chronologic precision. The flow of information should be structured mentally by the cotherapist, for notes taken in the patient's presence (even when recording facilities are unavailable) obviously would tend to distract both patient and cotherapist.

The arbitrarily structured interrogation should create a pattern of organization for the cotherapist within which a history can be developed and more easily retained. The structured interview holds a series of specific questions related to outlined categories which are considered basic to the psychosexual-social history required by the program. To elicit the categories of information needed, there are "kinds" of questions that can be used with relative reliability to lead the patient into a contributing memory pattern. However, the questioning format should never be rigid, and the history-taker (unencumbered by the necessity of keeping a written record) should remain free to follow imperative suggestion, interesting but random comments, or psychophysiological signals of danger areas arising from facial expressions and general demeanor of the patient.

In this manner the baseline of required facts can be augmented, clarified, colored, supported, or inspected. With a structured interview to fall back on but not to be dominated by, the interrogator has yet another advantage: when a train of thought is terminated or there is no apparent need for further elaboration of a specific subject, the cotherapist has the flexibility to return to the questions that remain unanswered in the outline.

DAY 1

OUTLINE OF HISTORY-TAKING

For purposes of the Foundation's rapid-treatment program, an outline of psychosexual-social history-taking has been developed. Pertinent material is not necessarily obtained in the exact sequence given nor are questions to be phrased in identical fashion to those listed below, since many of these questions may be answered during other lines of questioning.

This is only an outline for a chronologic history-taking procedure. In it related questions often are grouped beneath a "root" question which may be used to direct interrogation toward a specific category of material. Placement of a question in secondary positioning does not imply lesser importance of information requested, but signifies that this material frequently may be elicited by or included in a narrative initiated by the "root" question.

A structured interview suggests rigidity in therapeutic approach. Nothing could be more disastrous when dealing with the sensitive areas of sexual dysfunction than any semblance or even any concept of rigidity of thought or action in history-taking on the part of the cotherapists. This outline is presented for professionals as a point of departure *only*.

THE HISTORY-TAKING OUTLINE

I. PRELIMINARY BASELINE

An effective means of initiating the interrogation is to request an individual vignette or thumbnail sketch of the nature of the presenting distress. Subsequent interrogation can follow a relatively specific format based on whether the presenting distress is self- or partner-oriented or whether both marital partners are contending with problems of sexual dysfunction.

1. (*if partner-oriented*) What significance does the problem have with regard to your own sexual function?

2. (*if self-oriented*) How does the problem affect your partner's sexual function?

3. (*if dysfunction is present in both partners*) Which problem do you recall as having developed first?

4. How have you, as a marital unit, handled the problem(s) to date?

5. What is your concept of effective sexual function
   a. for a woman?
   b. for a man?

6. (*wife*) Under what circumstances have you been orgasmic, if ever? Describe the feelings (physical) that you associate with the experience.

7. (*husband*) Has your wife ever been orgasmic? Under what circumstances?

8. (*husband*) Have you ever had erective or ejaculatory difficulties? If so, describe.

9. (*wife*) Have you ever noted erective or ejaculatory difficulties on your husband's part? If so, describe.
   (THERAPIST: Degree of factual accuracy and/or sexual misinformation in answers to questions 6, 7, 8, and 9 should be evaluated on basis of maximum professional expertise with subject matter.)

10. By what means, other than intercourse, have you sought to bring sexual pleasure to your partner in the marriage? Describe results.

11. By what means has your partner attempted to bring sexual pleasure to you? Describe results.

12. What is your concept of appropriate male and female roles in marriage?
    a. In the marital bed?
    b. In social aspects of daily living?
    c. In other aspects of marriage?

13. How do you think your (husband, wife) would answer these questions?
14. What forms of contraception have you used, if any?
15. Are there children of the marriage?
     a. If so, were the children desired? Planned?
     b. How do the children affect your relationship with your (wife, husband)?
     c. How do the children affect your (wife's, husband's) response to you?

(COTHERAPIST: Focus should be directed to any correlation, positive or negative, between spontaneously presented vignette at onset of interrogation and content of answers to above questions. Every effort should be made to form some idea of the marital unit's philosophy and life-style while acquiring the baseline information from which to determine complementary direction of questioning during balance of history-taking.)

II. STATISTICS OF PRESENT MARRIAGE

1. Is this your first marriage?
     a. If not, give chronology of past marital history.
     b. Was/were the sexual relationship(s) satisfactory in this/these prior marriage(s)?
     c. If so, briefly give reasons for divorce(s).
     d. If not, give details of sexual incompatibility.
     e. Give number of children, if any, born to past marriage(s).
2. Is this the first marriage for your partner?
     a. If not, give number of marriages and children, if any.
     b. What do you know of reasons for divorce(s)?
3. What is the duration of the present marriage?
4. Have you ever been separated for long periods of time during this marriage (by military service, illness, etc.)?
5. How long after first meeting did you marry?
6. How long did the courtship last before formal engagement or agreement to marry?
7. Describe type and quality of any sexual encounters with your (husband, wife) prior to marriage. How did you react to these experiences?

8. Describe the first sexual encounter within the marriage.

9. How satisfactory has the sexual component of your marriage been when compared to other areas of the marriage?

10. Identify children of this marriage, if any, by age, sex, and sibling succession.

11. If no children, has there been a problem of sterility? Describe.

12. (*wife*) What is your husband's occupation?
    a. Does he enjoy his work?
    b. Do you live in a way which you both enjoy?

13. (*husband*) Does your wife work outside the home?
    a. If so, do you approve or object?
    b. If so, what is her occupation?

14. How much, if any, extramarital sexual activity has occurred on your part during this marriage? Discuss.

15. To your knowledge has there been any extramarital sexual activity on the part of your (husband, wife)? Discuss.

16. Do you and your (husband, wife) have similar social and educational backgrounds? Describe.
    a. If not, amplify differences.

17. Do you share the same religion?
    a. If not, amplify differences

Life-Cycle Influences and Events

III. CHILDHOOD (into adolescence)

1. What is your age?

2. Where were you born?

3. Was your home broken by death, divorce, or other causes?
   a. If so, with whom did you live?
   b. For how long?

4. How many times do you remember moving, if at all, prior to going away to school or leaving home to live elsewhere?

5. What was your childhood impression of the socioeconomic status of your family?
   a. Retrospectively what was the status?
   b. What was your father's occupation? Describe.
   c. Did your mother work outside the home? Describe.

6. In what religion, if any, were you raised?
   a. Was this your mother's or your father's religion, or were they of the same faith?
   b. How committed to their religion were your parents?

7. Identify any of the following which significantly influenced your childhood and adolescent years:
   a. Religion
   b. Ethnic background
   c. National origin or ancestry
   d. Regional or community mores and social standards
   e. Quality of parents' personal values

8. Describe the general atmosphere of your home environment.

9. Were you allowed to ask questions about or discuss sexual topics?

10. Approximately how old were your parents when you were born?

11. Are they still living? Together?

12. Had either had a previous marriage?
   a. If not now living together, a subsequent marriage?
   b. If a subsequent marriage, age of current spouse?

13. What is your impression of your parents' current relationship to each other?
   a. Your childhood impression of their relationship?
   b. Your impression of their relationship during your childhood in retrospect?

14. Do you have brothers and sisters? Were any other children raised in your home by your parents?
   a. If so, indicate origin, sex, chronology, and age in relation to your own.
   b. Which sibling were you closest to in interests? In affection?

15. Was affection shown freely by your parents to one another?
   a. To you and your brothers and sisters, if any?
   b. Between you and your brothers and sisters, if any?

16. Did you have any special friends before you reached high school age?
   a. Your own age?
   b. Adults?

17. Did you have a close relationship with other family members (grandparents, aunts, uncles, etc.) during this time?

18. Do you recall playing any sex games as a child?
    a. Or "doctor" or "house with babies" games?
    b. If so, were you ever caught or punished?
    c. Did you ever have an opportunity to see animals involved in sexual activity? Having their young? Any special reaction?

19. Did you ever watch anyone else, accidentally or otherwise, involved in sexual activity?
    a. If so, were they children or adults?
    b. Your parents?
    c. Do you recall your reaction?

20. When do you recall first having any pelvic (genital) feelings that were pleasurable?
    a. Were they in connection with any particular thoughts, activities, or situations?
    b. If so, did you have any specific reaction or feeling about them?

21. At what age did you first experiment with masturbation or with any kind of solitary activity which produced a (genital) feeling of pleasure?

22. With what frequency did you pursue this activity?

23. With what frequency do you use masturbatory release now? Earlier in your marriage?

24. Do you summon specific fantasies when you masturbate? Describe.

25. Do you summon particular images or fantasies during intercourse? If so, describe.

26. Do you dream? Often? About sexual situations? Describe.

27. As a child, when did you first experiment sexually, if ever, in the presence of another person? Describe.
    a. If so, with the opposite sex?
    b. Your own sex?
    c. If this took place when you were older, how old?

(COTHERAPIST: Regardless of "childhood" emphasis expansion of information regarding sexual feelings, adult values (operational or controlled), and specific details of early sexual conditioning can be developed at this time, if reflective approach to interrogation is used following a comfortable line of questioning established during Questions 17–27.)

IV. ADOLESCENCE (into teenage years)

1. Which parent did you feel closest to? Why?
2. To whom did you prefer to take your problems? Why?
3. With whom did you prefer to share exciting, important things? Why?
4. (*wife*) When did you start to menstruate?
   a. Had menstruation been factually and comfortably described to you well in advance?
   b. By whom?
   c. Was the subject freely discussed with your friends?
   d. Did you, and they, consider onset of menses a "coming of age" to be anticipated, or as something to be dreaded?
   e. Have you ever had any menstrual difficulties? If so, describe.
   f. By what term do you refer to menstruation?
5. (*husband*) How old were you when nocturnal emissions began?
   a. Did this frighten you?
   b. Did your (mother, father) ever make an issue of the emissions? If so, describe.
6. Did you have special friends in your school years?
   a. Mostly girls? Boys?
   b. Reasonably well-divided between girls and boys?
   c. Did you attend coeducational or sex-segregated school(s)?
7. What was your favorite pastime or recreation?
8. When did you learn "where babies actually come from" and how they are conceived?
   a. How did you learn?
   b. Do you recall how you reacted to the information?
9. When did you put the "whole picture" together (menses for the female, erection for the male, intercourse, conception, delivery, etc.)?
10. At what age did you start to date? In groups? On single dates?
    a. Did you usually steady-date? At what age?

b. Prior to high school, what was the most popular recreation shared on a date?

c. During high school?

11. In what kind of petting (making out) did you participate? Describe.

   a. On most all dates, or only with certain individuals?

   b. Manipulation of genital area of partner? Partner's manipulation of your genital area?

   c. Any other specific form of stimulation other than intercourse?

   d. Ever to intercourse?

      (1) If so, describe first occasion.

      (2) If so, what means of contraception was used (if any)?

      (3) Who accepted the responsibility of contraception?

   e. Under what circumstances did intercourse usually occur?

   f. How much pleasure and freedom from concern accompanied the experience?

   g. Were you ever suspected or caught? Punished?

V. TEENAGE YEARS (through high school and into college)

1. What is the extent of your education?

   a. High school?

   b. College?

   c. Postgraduate or professional?

   d. Vocational?

2. Were you a good student? Describe.

   a. Do you like to read?

   b. If so, have you acquired much of your sexual information by reading? What sources?

3. Were you popular with schoolmates or your particular social group?

4. Did you participate in many activities?

   a. In high school? Describe.

   b. In college? Describe.

   c. Outside school? Describe.

5. How well did you get along with your parents during high school years?

   a. After graduating from high school?

    b. Prior to marriage?

    c. (*if they are still living*) How do you get along with your parents now?

6. Describe the social and emotional climate of your home during your teenage years.

7. What was the family's position in the community?

8. Did you work during high school or college? If so, describe.

9. Did you work summers when going to school?
    a. If so, describe.
    b. If not, what types of activities did you take part in?

10. When did your first homosexual opportunity occur? Describe.

VI. PREMARITAL ADULTHOOD

1. Were you ever engaged to be married or seriously involved in other courtships before meeting your present (husband, wife)?
    a. If so, briefly describe the chronology and degree of relationship(s).
    b. Why was it (were they) terminated?

(COTHERAPIST: If there is early indication of an extensive dating and/or sexual history involving many individuals, request that the patient choose the most meaningful relationships (either positive or negative in nature) or those personally considered the most crucial to own life.)

2. What business or professional experience did you achieve after attaining highest level of formal education?
    a. Give brief description.
    b. Describe level of personal interest.
    c. Describe level of success.

3. Describe
    a. social interests
    b. leisure-time activities

4. What is your concept of your facility with interpersonal relationships during these years?

5. Were you living at home or separately?
    a. Give reasons.
    b. Describe your relations with parents during this period.

6. What was the distribution of friends?
   a. Male
   b. Female

7. Intellectual interests if any? Describe. Put in perspective.

8. Describe sexual interests, heterosexual and/or homosexual.

VII. AT MARRIAGE

(COTHERAPIST: Structure the following questions to correlate with answers provided during II. Statistics of Present Marriage.)

1. Describe briefly the circumstances and chronology of the first meeting and subsequent courtship.

2. What attracted you most to your (husband, wife) leading to your selection of (him, her) as a marriage partner?

3. Is that quality still present as you see (him, her) today?

4. What were your expectations regarding sex, lovemaking, intercourse, etc. before marriage?
   a. Were these expectations fulfilled at some point within the first year of marriage?
   b. If not, describe.

5. Describe briefly the setting and circumstances of your wedding.
   a. Describe your honeymoon or first two weeks of marriage.
   b. Describe sexual difficulties, if any.

6. How frequently do you recall having intercourse during the first month of your marriage?
   a. The first year of marriage?
   b. Did you enjoy this frequency level?
   c. If not, what frequency would you have preferred?

7. What is the usual incidence of intercourse now (times per week)?

8. If present dysfunction has occasioned withdrawal from sexual activity, what was the average frequency (times per week) prior to withdrawal?

9. What has had the most influence on when or how often or under what circumstances you and your (husband, wife) have intercourse?

10. Who usually chooses the time for lovemaking?

11. Does lovemaking always lead to intercourse? If not, give percentage estimate.
    a. Does coital activity usually grow out of shared moments of mutual emotional understanding, or is it scheduled?
    b. Does coition seem to occur from habit or a sense of duty?

12. Do you have a preference for a particular time of day and situation for lovemaking? Describe. When lovemaking includes intercourse?

13. Do you feel free to express your sexual desire at any time and anticipate warm receptivity?
    a. Do you usually encounter a similar level of response?

14. Describe the situation or kinds of situations which you find sexually most desirable.
    a. Describe the situation you find the most stimulating.

    b. Does this also represent the time(s) when you reach the highest or most fulfilling level of sexual response you ever achieve?

15. Do you tell your (husband, wife) what pleases you most sexually?
    a. What pleases you most otherwise?
    b. What displeases you sexually?
    c. What displeases you most otherwise?

16. In what areas or on what subjects do you feel you and your (husband, wife) agree most?

17. Do you spend spare time together or separately?
    a. Doing what?
    b. Is this a satisfactory arrangement for you?

18. Do you confide in one another?

19. Do either or both of you have a sense of humor?
    a. Do you use the sense of humor when "everything" goes wrong?
    b. Is humor used during sexually oriented situations?

20. Do you get along well (or badly) with most members of your partner's family?

Does your partner get along well (or badly) with your family?

21. What trait, behavior pattern, or habit does your (husband, wife) have that tends to diminish your sexual feeling (desire) for (him, her)?
    a. What trait diminishes your feeling for (him, her) in non-sexual situations?

22. Do you still find your marital partner attractive?

23. What do you want most in the way of attitude, behavior, etc., from your (husband, wife) that (he, she) does not provide you now?

24. What attitude, behavior, etc., do you receive from your (husband, wife) that you value most?

25. If there are children
    a. do you think of (him, her) as a good (father, mother)?
    b. how does (he, she) treat the children?

VIII. PERCEPTION OF SELF

1. (*wife*) Do you feel attractive at this point in your life?
   a. Were you a pretty child?
   b. Did you feel attractive during the courtship which led to this marriage?

2. (*husband*) Do you feel attractive?
   a. Would you like to change anything about yourself?

3. Do you feel you are attractive to your (husband, wife)?

4. What do you feel is your greatest attribute as a person?
   a. To your (husband, wife)?
   b. To your children, if any?

5. What is your greatest contribution or grace in social situations?

6. How would you describe your sexual identity?
   a. Does it please you?
   b. Are you comfortable with it?

(COTHERAPIST: Sensate focus is the basis for effective sexual expression. By using the following outline, but amplifying a response with every opportunity, you should develop a working baseline concept of your patient's emotional structure and sensual concepts.)

IX. SPECIAL SENSES (awareness of and response to sensory stimuli)

Touch

1. Is the dimension of touch meaningful to you? (For example, do you explore surfaces with your fingers to see whether they are smooth, patterned, rough, etc.?)
   a. Do you ever touch your marital partner in a similar manner for your own tactile pleasure?
   b. If yes, does he or she accept your touch with pleasure?
2. Do you usually find yourself abstractly petting small children or animals that come within your immediate range?
3. Do you and your (husband, wife) use body contact frequently to express your feelings to one another?
4. If so, what form does the body contact usually take?
5. Which of the following represent your most frequent reasons for using body contact:
   a. Affection or desire for affection
   b. Identification or a need to be "recognized" by partner
   c. Reassurance or a desire for reassurance
   d. Comfort or solace
   e. Affirmation of "belonging" for self? for partner? mutual?
   f. Sexual desire or sexual gratification through touch
6. Does your (husband, wife) desire or initiate this type of communication more than you do?
7. Do you ever find touching irritating? Does your partner?
8. Do you ever find touching embarrassing? Does your partner?
9. Do you find certain types of touch impossible to abide? If so, describe.
   a. How do you react when they are introduced?
10. Do you usually establish some form of body contact in social communication (i.e., a kiss, embrace or other physical form of greeting)? Occasionally?
    a. Are you receptive or embarrassed when someone greets you in this manner?
11. What do you find to be the most sexually stimulating type or dimension of touch, or what do you think it might be (area of body and manner in which it is introduced)?

    a. Can you answer this question in regard to your marital partner?

    b. Do you have a pattern of mutually exchanging back rubs, massaging tired muscles, etc.? If so, describe.

12. Does body contact, being held or touched, help you to
    a. relax and fall asleep?
    b. overcome depression or sadness?

13. Do you feel the need to be physically close or to be held after intercourse?
    a. Does your partner express a similar need?

14. How do you react when your expressed desire for body contact is ignored or denied?

15. Which do you actually enjoy more, if either: (1) expression of feeling through touch and body contact? or (2) intercourse?

16. What is the most comforting or pleasing kind of tactile expression you can recall from your childhood? Who was responsible for conveying it?

Vision

17. Do you think your marital partner is physically attractive? Was this a primary factor in his or her choice as a marital partner?

18. Is your visual pleasure in your marital partner enhanced when he or she is especially well-groomed or excitingly dressed?

19. Does either of you wear special kinds of clothing during love-making and sexual activity?

20. Do you enjoy watching your partner?
    a. On special occasions?
    b. When (he, she) is talking to others?
    c. When (he, she) is absorbed in some interest?
    d. When he or she is undressed?

Olfaction

21. Are you particularly aware of odors? Extremely sensitive to them? If so, describe.

22. Which of the following have the most pleasant connotation for you? Choose and describe.
    a. Food-related odors?
    b. Odors related to out-of-doors (smoke, cut grass, leaves, hay, earth, the sea, etc.)?
    c. Flowers?
    d. Scented products?
    e. Others?

23. Is your pleasure in this particular odor related to a specific experience or occasion that you can recall?

24. Do you associate any particular odors or fragrances with occasions, places, or people during your childhood? Describe whether they were pleasant or unpleasant.
    a. During your teenage years?
    b. Related to dating and courtship? Courtship that led to this marriage?
    c. During your marriage?

25. Do you associate any particular odors with pleasure? Displeasure? Discomfort? If so, do you recall why?

26. Have you noted any major change in your awareness of odors since you have been married?
    a. Any major changes in your preferences for scented products?
    b. In either odor awareness or preference since development of sexual dysfunction?

27. Do you regard certain categories of fragrance as masculine and others as feminine? If so, describe.
    a. Do you like your (husband, wife) to use scented products? If so, which of the following categories do you prefer: straight floral (lilac, lily, etc.), or floral bouquet; citrus; spicy; exotic (Oriental); "outdoor" scents like mossy, pine, leather, etc.?
    b. Is your preference related to an experience or occasion?

28. What odor emanating from and familiar to your home pleases you most?

29. Do you enjoy the smell of your marital partner's body with-

out the addition of scented products? Better than when fragrance has been added?

30. Do you enjoy the smell of a clean baby?

31. Are you particularly aware of body odors and fragrances of other persons?
    a. Who are strangers?
    b. Who represent something which you do not like or approve of?
    c. Who are connected pleasantly to your life?

32. Do you now relate specific odors or fragrances to specific occasions or environments? If so, describe.

33. When faced with fear or anger in your partner, are you aware of any specific odor?

Audition

34. Do extraneous sounds or noises tend to intrude upon your pleasure in whatever you are doing? Specifically during sexual activity?

35. Does music play a particularly important role in your life? In that of your marital partner?

36. Do you (together with your marital partner) ever add the dimension of music to your sexual enjoyment? If so, describe.

37. What types of music do you prefer?

38. Do you play a musical instrument? If so, describe.

39. Do you use music as a form of tension release?

40. Does your (wife's, husband's) voice please you? Displease you?

41. Do you do important work with radio or television turned on?

X. AGING POPULATION

(COTHERAPIST: These questions should be used only in addition to general material outlined above; they are designed to provide a point of interrogative departure *only*.)

1. What is the current state of the marriage?
   a. What are your "feelings" for your partner?
   b. What is your partner's response to you?

   c. What in your marriage is of mutual interest?
   d. Do you spend leisure time together?

2. How have your sexual attitudes altered in recent years?
   a. Those of your partner?
   b. Those of your friends?

3. How have your sexual patterns altered?
   a. Frequency of intercourse?
   b. Difficulties with intercourse?
   c. Responsivity with intercourse?
   d. Your partner's responsivity or difficulties with intercourse?

4. How have your social attitudes changed?
   a. Residual "double standard" concepts?
   b. Your religious viewpoints?
   c. Your political viewpoints?
   d. Your partner's social attitudes?

5. (*husband*) Are you regularly employed?
   a. Nature of employment?
   b. Fulltime? If not, describe.
   c. What other professional interests?

6. (*wife*) What are your interests outside the home?
   a. Are you employed? If so, describe.
   b. What percentage of your time is spent outside the home?

7. What are your family commitments?
   a. Children still living at home? Describe level of time demand.
   b. Relatives that demand share of time? Describe.

8. What is your state of physical health?
   a. Describe generally.
   b. Any specific difficulties? Describe.
   c. Previous surgery? Describe. Pelvic surgery (male or female)?
   d. (*wife*) Menopausal symptoms?
      (1) How much distress? Describe symptoms.
      (2) Sex hormone replacement? If so, describe.
   e. Maintenance dosage of any form of medication? If so, describe.
   f. Partner on maintenance medication? If so, describe.

9. What hobbies or other areas of interest?
   a. Those of your partner?
   b. Do these outside interests enhance or substitute for marital communion?
   c. Your partner's opinion?
10. What are the specific interests that bring you to treatment at this time?
    a. Did you or your partner initiate treatment demand?
    b. What changes would successful treatment make in your marriage?
    c. What changes in you as a personality?
    d. What changes in partner as a personality?

XI. GENERAL MATERIAL

(COTHERAPIST: The following material should be developed with chronologic significance within this interrogative framework as indicated by content of answers to questions and general demeanor of patient at the time question is answered.)
1. Major environmental changes, nature and effect.
2. People: attitudinal influence, contributing to social and sexual value systems.
3. People: sexual influence, contributing to sexual value system.
4. Random events of sexual significance.
5. Events of sexual orientation, outside life-cycle expectations:
   a. Incest
   b. Illegitimate pregnancy
   c. Abortion
   d. Rape
   e. Infidelity
   f. Homosexuality
   g. Random (other)

DAY 1

COMMENT ON HISTORY-TAKING

The listed questions are typical of those that should be asked to develop a working knowledge of the individuals who come as partners in a marital unit requesting reversal of sexual inadequacy. Their individual values, ideas, attitudes, and feelings about the marital relationship must be defined early in interrogation (Days 1 and 2). These personal sexual and social value systems, once defined, remain real and meaningful factors throughout the therapy. However, they must not be permitted to preempt therapeutic focus at the expense of marital interaction.

More valuable than detailed accounts of the sexual dysfunction are broad historical scans which bring to the surface crucial feelings and stimulate recall of past events which reveal, in turn, the quality of the marital relationship within the framework provided by personalities involved.

Many questions listed will not have to be asked, because answers will be contained in narratives growing out of responses to earlier questions. Others may not be pertinent to the direction the history is taking or appropriate to the specific life-style of the particular marital unit or the nature of the sexual dysfunction.

All questions can be asked either in sequence or at random; evolved from outlined life-cycle or marital-history segments when appropriate; or developed under direct, deliberate control by the interrogator. Choice of specific interrogative techniques (reflective, direct, etc.) should be based on the quality of comfort and ease of interchange which can be created between cotherapist and patient. Use of any specific interrogative technique must take into consideration its potential effectiveness in producing the particular information required.

Regardless of the type or degree of questioning employed, it would be presumptuous to assume that sufficient material could be obtained in a two-day interrogative procedure to establish chronologic accuracy and yet consistently reflect the patient's intended nuance of meaning and his or her sexual and social value systems. For this reason patients are instructed at onset of therapy and reminded time and again to call attention *at the moment noted* to any error in fact, misinterpretation of material, or any confusion of content on the part of the cotherapists. History-taking then becomes a continuously evolving process, never static in format, for the duration of the rapid-treatment program.

The marital-unit "corporate" history as a viable entity remains open to further additions, subtractions, and reinterpretations throughout the unit's treatment phase, but is especially open to patient inspection during the roundtable on Day 3 (see Section C). Free-flow history-taking becomes less a requirement after the roundtable, when the cotherapists summarize their views of the basic cause and effect of the sexual dysfunction as reflected in the historical material obtained. After this summation point, past history is of secondary import to consideration of the marital partners in their current status of a shared sexual relationship.

The use of historical material after accumulation is educative in purpose. The principal responsibility of the educational approach during the rapid-treatment period is to clarify and support understanding of the cause and effect of the dysfunction, and to provide opportunity for comparison between old behavior patterns which supported the sexual inadequacy and new ones which encourage the establishment of effective sexual function. After old patterns are highlighted and security of partner cooperation is established, the old must be set aside at least until some reliability in return of sexual facility is achieved. At termination of the rapid-treatment program, with sexual functioning hopefully established, the past history can be put in proper perspective.

DAY 2

PROCEDURE

Day 2 interrogative sessions are structured by the cotherapists upon review of material accrued from each marital partner during Day 1 history-taking. Interrogation is directed toward further clarification of specific historical content in the first day's information gathering. No personality evaluation is attempted at this early point in the treatment program. Brief abstracts of the marital partners' personal histories are exchanged to improve identification and smooth the process of Day 2 exchange between members of the therapy team and the marital unit.

The Day 2 history-taking session is conducted by the female cotherapist with the husband and the male cotherapist with the wife of the marital unit. It is structured upon review or abstract of material accrued from each marital partner during Day 1 history-taking. At first, Day 2 is specifically controlled by the interrogator to clarify areas of doubt or uncertainty about the material collected during the first day's interview with the marital spouse. On Day 2, second coverage is desirable of those areas in which (on Day 1) a severely prejudiced presentation or even deliberate omission of pertinent material is suspected, or reluctance to discuss a particular subject has been obvious. Specific review on the second day with the marital spouse may yield a totally new concept or an important volume of material, particularly if the first day's reluctance to communicate has been sex-linked.

There are many psychosexual response patterns that a woman cannot bring herself to tell another woman, and there are those areas which she is not comfortable discussing with a man during the interrogative sessions. The same response patterns obviously apply to men. Yet these repressive response patterns are entirely individual, rarely predictable along obvious, culturally set lines, and usually can be identified and relieved by either cotherapist in order to provide freedom of informational exchange, if the interrogator remains aware of the potential for omission of such material.

However, since both partners are made fully aware of the simultaneous nature of their mutual questioning, they usually are stimulated to make available pertinent material in a more cooperative manner. With the advantage of this environmental demand for freedom in information exchange, there is little of major import that escapes professional notice, unless there has been prior marital-unit agreement that they will withhold specific information. This mutual repression of pertinent material may indeed escape the cotherapists' notice on Day 1 and Day 2, but usually there is some discrepancy noted in portions of information or an obvious uneasiness evidenced in a specific area long before the rapid-treatment program is terminated. The repression of material pertinent to marital-unit sexual responsivity becomes particularly apparent when natural progression of treatment is stymied. Professional experiential sensitivity soon focuses on the area of informational discrepancy.

Beyond specific structuring to review the sexual partners' information or misinformation, the second day of history-taking should be used to add color and depth to the individual histories obtained and discussed the previous day. Sex-linked impressions developed the first day should be objectively reviewed during the contrasex interviews and new impressions accepted and evaluated. Random or previously omitted subjects can be pursued fully, once marital-unit chronology has been established. The second day provides opportunity to inspect individual marital-partner motivation for change by seeking answers for such professional concerns as: (1) Was some form of coercion present for either partner in the decision to seek therapy? (2) Is there a deep sense of marital duty involved which does *not* include sexual giving or even may hide a deeper sense of rejection of sexuality per se? If this sense of "marital duty" takes the place of basic interest in mutual participation in therapy, it may be accompanied by insufficient personal investment in the marriage or even total inability to make any investment of self.

Taking the history of the marital partner the previous day gives special meaning to answers to such questions as (1) What do you want from this therapy program for your husband (or wife)? (2) How do you perceive your marital partner's interest in the sexual part of your marriage? (3) What do you think he (or she) wants most from you? Reported material pertaining to the marital partner supplied by his or her family members (or past events as related by family members or friends) and retained by the husband (or wife) being interrogated can add another dimension to understanding, when applied to accounts given on Day 1 as personal experience. The purpose in this type of Day 2 questioning is not so much to "check" material as to contemplate the historical background within the different frame of reference of the marital partner.

Questions that reveal whether the patient sees the sexual dysfunction as a physical complication of psychosocial interaction, an emotionally induced problem, or purely of physical origin fit well within the second day of history-taking. Obviously, Day 2 can also provide the opportunity for the interrogators to ask the questions which simply were not covered on Day 1, either through lack of time or from oversight.

Until after the roundtable discussion, the marital partners are requested to avoid any form of physical sexual expression and to refrain from discussing the contents of both Day 1 and Day 2 interrogations with one another. As a result, the first two days at the Foundation can be portrayed to the patients as a period without pressures, and with only the natural, slightly apprehensive anticipation of interrogative procedures. Care must be taken, however, to integrate the patients into the social and educational opportunities the community affords. The two days of interrogation can be a period of tension-filled, disagreeable interaction between marital partners simply because there is a restless void to fill during the remainder of the days and nights when not involved with Foundation procedures.

Every effort is made to help the marital unit create and maintain a pleasant relaxed atmosphere, especially until after the roundtable session of the third day. The Foundation places responsibility for maintaining a comfortable, relaxed attitude not only with the cotherapists but upon staff management as well. During the interrogative period specifically, but certainly for the balance of the time committed to the rapid-treatment program, the perceptive capacity and social facility of members of the office staff who greet, direct, and inform the patients of places of interest to visit, good restaurants to patronize, educational and entertainment opportunities to enjoy, and social advantages to pursue make a real contribution to the overall success of the marital unit's two weeks with the Foundation. If the office staff has a vested interest in the overall effectiveness of the treatment program, an infinitely more stable, warm, and receptive concept of Foundation personnel is expressed to the dysfunctional marital unit.

Day 3—the roundtable discussion—institutes specific involvement of the marital unit in the therapeutic regimen, and free time becomes potentially less a problem.

SECTION B
DAY 3

Listed below are forms used on Day 3 of the Foundation's rapid-treatment program. They cover the medical and the physical examination and laboratory procedures used for the sexually dysfunctional marital partners.

These are but outline forms. If any evidence of pathology develops, a detailed evaluation is launched immediately.

While the incidence of a physiological etiology of sexual inadequacy is obviously very low, there is never any excuse for treating a physiological dysfunction as a psychological inadequacy.

MEDICAL HISTORY

Date _____

Name _____ Age _____ Occupation _____

Address _____

Referral source _____

Sexual History

Marital status _____ Length current marriage _____

Previous marriages _____

Pregnancy history _____ Difficulties _____

Contraceptives used _____

Frequency coitus _____ times/week.   % Orgasmic response _____

Difficulties _____

Previous work-up and results _____

Therapy to date _____

Review of Systems

Skin _____

HEENT _____

Breasts _____

MEDICAL HISTORY (*Continued*)

Review of Systems

Cardiorespiratory _____

Gastrointestinal _____

Genitourinary _____

Central Nervous System _____

Endocrine _____

Past History

Childhood diseases: Measles____ Rubella ____ Mumps ____ Chickenpox ____

    Whooping cough ____ Scarlet fever____ Rheumatic fever _____

Major illnesses: Diabetes ____ Hypertension ____ Coagulation disorders ____

    Kidney disease ____ Congenital defects _____

Venereal disease _____

Hospitalization _____

Surgery _____

Injuries _____

Medication _____

Tobacco _____ Alcohol _____ Drugs _____

Diet _____ Allergies _____

Family History

Mother _____ Father _____

MGM _____ PGM _____

MGF _____ PGF _____

Siblings _____

Others _____

Familial disorders and diseases _____

PHYSICAL EXAMINATION

GENERAL

B.P. ____ Temp. ____ Pulse ____ Resp. rate ____ Wt. ____ Ht. ____

General _____

PHYSICAL EXAMINATION (*Continued*)

GENERAL (*Continued*)

Skin _____

Head and eyes _____

Ears, nose & throat _____

Thyroid _____

Chest _____ Breasts _____

Cardiovascular _____

Abdomen _____

Extremities _____ Lymph nodes _____

Neurologic _____

Comments _____

REPRODUCTIVE ORGANS

Male

Penis _____ Testes _____

Rectal _____ Prostate _____ SVs _____

Comments _____

Female

External genitalia _____ Outlet _____

B & S glands _____ Vaginal mucosa _____

Cervix _____ Corpus _____

Adnexa _____ Rectal _____

Comments _____

LABORATORY EVALUATION

Complete Blood Count

Hemoglobin
Hematocrit } Anemia

White blood cells
Differential } Infections, bone marrow and lymphatic tissue disorders

VDRL Syphilis

PBI (protein bound iodine)
TBI (Thyroxine bound iodine) } Thyroid function
T_4 (serum thyroxine)

LABORATORY EVALUATION (*Continued*)

SMA-12 Screening Test

Calcium	Bone metabolism, parathyroid function
Inorganic phosphate	Bone metabolism, parathyroid function
Glucose	Diabetes (2-hour postprandial test)
Blood Urea Nitrogen (BUN)	Kidney function
Uric acid	Gout
Cholesterol	Arteriosclerosis, thyroid function
Total protein	
Albumin	
Globulin	Nutritional evaluation, liver function
A/G ratio	
Total bilirubin	Liver and gallbladder function
Alkaline phosphatase	Bone metabolism, liver and gallbladder function
Lactic dehydrogenase	
Serum glutamic oxalacetic transaminase	Myocardial metabolism, liver function

Vaginal Cytology

Morphology	Cancer
Endocrinology	Sex hormone level
Infection	Bacterial, fungal, or trichomonal infections

Elective

1. 5-hour glucose tolerance test for impotent males
2. Serum testosterone levels for all sexually dysfunctional male patients over 50 years of age regardless of the specific complaint
3. Detailed endocrine evaluations as indicated for either male or female patients
4. ECG and chest plate as indicated

SECTION C

DAY 3

ROUNDTABLE CONCEPT

On Day 3, after the scheduled physical examinations and laboratory evaluations of both marital partners, cotherapists and marital partners join in a roundtable discussion. This conjoint session follows a total of four individual history-taking sessions totaling approximately seven hours in time demand, an average of two hours by each cotherapist during Day 1 and one and one-half hours each during Day 2 of history-taking.

The term *roundtable* is used to convey the fact that the four principals (marital partners and cotherapists) are together in clinical session for the first time since the brief intake interview on Day 1, and that a professional summation of pertinent clinical material accrued during the two days of history-taking will be presented and discussed. This discussion is structured to relate individual and marital histories (and any physical or metabolic finding of significance) to the presenting sexual dysfunction. The roundtable provides the cotherapists the opportunity to correlate basic knowledge of human sexual function and dysfunction with their impressions and interpretations of the personal, marital, social, and sexual histories obtained. Marital-unit partners are requested to interrupt the recapitulation and interpretation of their psychosexual-social histories whenever either partner disagrees with professional concept, feels there is factual misunderstanding, or that lack of clarity exists in the presentation. Interruption is encouraged so that the specific material may be evaluated and, if indicated, revised in context. There is a natural hesitancy to take issue with authority, so patients must be repetitiously reminded of this requirement.

Also mentioned repetitively is the fact that the marital unit's ongoing sexual, social, and medical history is an evolving body of material never rigidly maintained in support of first impression, or of "fact-as-heard" by either cotherapist. The historical material is always subject to addition, subtraction, or clarification if either marital partner identifies or suggests professional misinterpretation or misinformation.

Within this historically established framework of probable cause and reported effect, the presenting sexual dysfunction is further correlated with an authoritative explanation of contributing factors. When pointing out to marital partners the existing sexual myths and misinformation in their concepts of sexual functioning, the unrealistic sexual expectations, failure in communication, nonserving individual or mutual behavior patterns, and specifics in the personal histories serving as etiological agents in the dysfunction, the most effective of therapeutic tools available to the cotherapists is employed. This therapeutic technique is the use of the "mirror" of unprejudiced objectivity held to reflect the sexually dysfunctional marital unit's patterns of personal interaction. A fundamental concept of the Foundation's program of rapid treatment for sexual inadequacy is the premise that objective, controlled, knowledgeable communication between therapists and sexual partners can develop a nonjudgmental evaluation of the sexually dysfunctional individual's prejudices, anxieties, and inadequacies to the educational advantage of both marital partners.

By holding up the mirror of professional objectivity to reflect marital-unit sexual attitudes and practices, and by recalling constantly that the marital *relationship* is the focus of therapy, information necessary for marital-partner comprehension of the sexually dysfunctional status can be exchanged rapidly and with security. With objectivity in and control of sexual material evidenced by both members of the therapy team, parallel personal security and sexual confidence will tend to develop for husband and wife afflicted by a dysfunctional sexual status. When the partners in the sexually inadequate relationship can see themselves as they have permitted the cotherapists to see them, when they can have their rationales for sexual failure and their prejudices, misconceptions, and misunderstandings of natural sexual functioning exposed with nonjudgmental objectivity and explained in understandable terms with subjective comfort, a firm basis for mutual security in sexual expression is established.

It must be emphasized that material identified by the cotherapists during history-taking sessions but not shared by one partner with the other is never disclosed or discussed during the roundtable, or on any occasions during therapy, without the specific permission of the individual from whom it originates. If marital-unit knowledge of this confidential material is considered by the cotherapists to be crucial to reversal of the sexual dysfunction, any decision to reveal information in such areas as premarital sexual experience, extramarital sexual experience, abortion, illegitimacy, incest, homosexuality, or other emotion-invested topics would be discussed at length with the involved partner. The degree to which the confidential information would be considered decisively pertinent to reversal of the marital unit's sexual inadequacy would be analyzed carefully. Should the involved partner decide that the information is inadmissible, either because he or she does not agree with specifically expressed professional opinion—or agreeing completely, simply cannot tolerate the introduction of controversial material—the cotherapists would, of course, comply with the individual's stand on the matter.

In this situation, a professional decision must be made in the best interests of the marital unit and its individual members, either to continue or to terminate the projected course of therapy. The rapid-treatment form of therapy is so dependent upon partner exchange of vulnerabilities that continuation of therapeutic procedure depends largely upon identification of stable elements in the marital relationship sufficient to support professional circumnavigation of the inadmissible information. If an adequately stable marriage is not defined by authority, termination of therapy is indicated. Every effort should be made to give an unrevealing, reasonable explanation for termination that would attempt to protect the marriage at current levels of psychosexual functioning. Return of the marital unit to the original referral source or cooperative referral from that authority to yet another form of psychotherapy would be attempted.

Returning to the roundtable sequence that has *not* encountered the "pressure point" of inadmissible material, there is a philosophical factor in this form of therapy that must be emphasized at outset to the marital unit involved. The marital partners, as a unit, must be able to accept with conviction that neither the husband nor the wife is regarded by Foundation personnel as *the* patient, regardless of the basic source of the sexual dysfunction. Both marital partners must understand that the cotherapists are committed by Foundation dictum to concern for the marital relationship primarily and to the individual marital partner's problems secondarily. This concept of the *marital relationship* as the patient can be highlighted with clinical justification.

Most marital partners, coping with sexual inadequacy without concept of how or why the dysfunction developed, feel that they are either victims or culprits of some deliberate breach of physical adequacy. This defensive reaction may carry with it a sense of self-depreciation, accompanied by an intense need to justify personal value as an individual. When marital partners with understandably beclouded self-images attempt to develop a one-to-one relationship with either cotherapist to the exclusion of their spouses, they are usually seeking approbation and ego support in the professional mirror. Failing at partner exclusion, they may at least try to establish a personally advantaged position with the cotherapists. Especially prone to seek a self-advantaged position in the rapid-treatment program are those marital partners accustomed to the traditional one-to-one relationship of more formalized psychotherapy.

It is infinitely more graceful and authoritatively more secure if the concept of one-for-all is well established at roundtable discussion before these individuals attempt to establish such special relationships. Potential alienation of authoritative control arises not only from the "divide and conquer" patient when effort is made to restrict this response, but from the other marital partner as well when the phenomenon of marital-unit loyalty emerges. Frequently an awareness of professional disciplinary devices results in the second partner's coming to the defense of the one necessarily being reminded forcefully that the marital unit's therapy goals must be mutually shared. Possible loss of valuable treatment opportunity can be avoided by early establishment of confidence and rapport between patients and cotherapists on a four-way basis.

There is, however, one positive, although separate, form of alignment possible. This specifically one-to-one alignment occurs when a patient and therapist conjointly attempt to explain or clarify an obscure sex-linked point not fully understood or accepted by the other marital partner. Actually, the roundtable formula specifically encourages these patterns of interaction as a mark of this form of psychotherapy. The husband and wife of the distressed marital unit have "friends in court," repetitively emphasized by the presence of a team member of the same sex. But it also must be made quite clear that no partner, regardless of prior psychotherapeutic conditioning, will have a disproportionate amount of the therapeutic concentration directed specifically toward him or herself.

As a further step in patient education during the roundtable discussion, the spectator role involuntarily assumed by both members of a sexually dysfunctional marital unit is identified in specific detail by the cotherapists. A clear example is provided by describing the reactions of the impotent male approaching sexual opportunity as follows: Apprehensive and distracted by his fears of performance, he usually forcefully initiates some form of physical sexual expression, and immediately takes a further step toward total sexual dysfunction by trying to will his sexual response, thereby removing sexual function from its natural context.

As sex play is introduced and mutual attempts made by marital partners to force an erective response, the impotent husband finds himself a spectator to his own sexual exchange. He mentally is observing his and his partner's response (or lack of it) to sexual stimulation. Will there be an erection? If and when the penis begins to engorge, how full will the erection become? When erection is obtained, how long will it last? The involuntary spectator in the room demands immediate answers for these questions from the anxious man in the bed, so intensely concerned with his fears of sexual performance. Rather than allowing himself to relax, enjoy sensual stimulation, and permit his natural sexual responsivity to create and maintain the erective process, he as a spectator demands instant performance. In the spectator role, a dysfunctional man completely negates any concept of natural sexual function. He cannot conceive of involuntary sexual responsivity sustaining an erection as a natural physiological process on the same natural plane as that of his involuntary respiratory responsivity sustaining his breathing mechanism.

Not only is there at least one spectator in the impotent male's bedroom, frequently there are two. For the wife, who is physically attempting to provide her husband with an erection, simultaneously may be mentally occupying an equal position of watchfulness, critically observing the apprehensive male's level of sexual responsivity. Is there to be an erection? If so, how full an erection? Will it be usable? Will it be maintained? Is she stimulating her husband satisfactorily? If he obviously isn't responding, what could she be doing that is wrong? All these questions arise when, in her spectator role, the wife quietly observes the progress of the particular sexual episode in her marriage. Is it any wonder the wife of the impotent male usually is not fully sexually responsive herself, even when the occasional sexual opportunity presents? Even in the immediacy of sexual opportunity, she frequently is psychologically caught in the corner observing the physical proceedings rather than physiologically tied to the bed totally involved with her own mating.

Neither partner realizes that the other is mentally standing in an opposite corner, observing the marital bedding scene in a spectator role. Both partners involuntarily distract themselves in their spectator roles, essentially uninvolved in the experience in which they are involved, to such an extent that there is no possibility for effective sexual stimuli to penetrate the impervious layers of performance fear and involuntary voyeurism.

Neither of these two spectator roles could or would be played by marital partners if it were not so easy to pull sexual functioning out of context by taking advantage of its unique physical response patterning of delaying indefinitely or denying for a lifetime a natural physiological process.

When these presumably hidden response patterns of spectator-role involvement are presented to the distressed marital unit, and discussed in detail by the cotherapists, rapport is established jointly as patient comprehension dawns. For the first time, responsible marital partners turn to each other to confess their mutually anxious, involuntary participation in spectator roles in the marriage bed. As a result, communication—based on the catalytic stimulus derived from a realization of shared apprehension and mutual need—is opened between these sexual partners possibly for the first time in their marriage.

The method of psychotherapy of the Foundation draws from the theoretical premise that human sexual response is constituted by two totally separate systems of influence. In discussing the etiology and definition of the presenting distress during the roundtable session, the cotherapists describe these biophysical and psychosocially based systems within the range of marital-unit understanding. Certainly it is vital that the cotherapists themselves conceptualize as realistically as possible the whole of human sexual experience. Similarly, a reasonable clinical concept also can provide the marital partners with a frame of reference for understanding the existence of their sexually inadequate status and how it developed. Many aspects of dysfunction become easier to interpret within the theory of interdigitating biophysical and psychosocial systems that coexist naturally and have the potential but not a biological demand to function in a complementary manner. Dysfunction can be more clearly comprehended as failure of one or both systems to contribute positively to psychosexual input.

The present status of female sexuality historically reflects adaptations to the omission of sociocultural support. As the result, the etiology of female sexual dysfunction usually demonstrates a wide variety of contributing factors. Therefore, it was felt that the theory of interdigital systems of influence in human sexual response could best be discussed within the framework of orgasmic dysfunction. Therefore, Section A of Chapter 8 contributes this material.

DAY 3
SENSATE FOCUS

The objective mirror-holding technique of the roundtable, while carefully structured to protect and sustain individual partners and their interpersonal relationship, occasionally produces the marital unit's first confrontation with the realities of their sexual distress. Before roundtable definition by the cotherapists, marital partners usually are frozen into patterns of self-sacrificing endurance, fear of hurting, or inability to understand or analyze the circumstances of their dysfunction. Rarely have they faced or shared together their individual sexual feelings or even mutually discussed the problem of their sexual dysfunction objectively beyond agreeing to seek consultation with authority. If roundtable confrontation develops into an overwhelming experience, the marital partners are encouraged by the cotherapists to establish a mutually supportive basis for further discussion and urged to continue this discussion together in the privacy of their own quarters. When roundtable confrontation has been overwhelmingly intense or even psychologically traumatic, specific direction for physical interaction is withheld until the following day. If, as usual, after twenty-four hours of shared introspection the marital pair have reasonably adjusted to the newly acquired insight into their presenting distress, Day 4 then is used to begin the directive sequence of sensate focus routinely scheduled for Day 3.

With reasonably effective pretherapy screening, the depth of experience described above is unusual. Usually the cotherapists encounter interested participation in discussion by the marital unit during the roundtable. Often to the relief of both partners, the cotherapists' summary of the causes and effects of the sexual dysfunction constitutes a reinforcement and clarification of their own previously agreed-upon interpretations. The marital partners simply had not been able to achieve objectivity in a sexual context, nor had they known what to do about their dysfunction, even if they correctly had analyzed etiology of onset.

Frequently paralleling the duration of sexual distress in a marriage is the displacement of the tensions created by the dysfunction to other facets of the relationship. These prejudiced interpersonal reactions are given authoritative consideration and ultimately even may require a major focus of therapy.

Even in those instances of total marital-unit agreement with content of the roundtable discussion, the husband and wife are encouraged to maintain an attitude of healthy skepticism toward future therapeutic procedure. It is vital that marital partners be willing to take direction in order to reconstitute their sexual experiences to those of a more positive nature, but it serves neither patients nor cotherapists if husband and wife become servile to direction and unquestioning of opinions expressed by the cotherapists.

The marital partners must continue while in therapy to represent positively their own social and sexual value systems and their own preferences in life-style. It is especially helpful if they continue to question what they are taught. Adaptive change or reorientation of behavior patterns always must be sought *within the context* of the marital partners' life-style as they have formed it or wish it formed. Their motivated, well-defined expression of personal feelings and preferences, established during history-taking on Day 1 and Day 2, functions as a guide to appropriate educational context for the cotherapists. Concomitantly, freedom to describe sexual feelings and performance provide the marital unit with repetitive opportunity for "trying on" and "trying out" authoritative direction and information that provides or suggests new patterns for social-sexual interaction. Authoritatively suggested sexual transactions between the partners, tried and found appropriate by them for inclusion into their ongoing total relationship, will have acquired some degree of familiarity and security with which to replace the old dysfunction-related patterns by the time the unit terminates the treatment program.

There must be a first set of specifically oriented physical instructions from the cotherapists. But any specific physical direction that carries with it the connotation of sexual expression initially will stimulate in both husband and wife a sense of trying to be natural and spontaneous on order (an impossible attainment) or may create for the marital unit an impression of someone peering over their collective shoulder. This semiembarrassment of the sexual partners with their obvious lack of spontaneity when following professional directions diminishes and all but vanishes by the second or third directive session. Especially does all self-consciousness disappear when the unit first becomes aware of positive evidence of change from dysfunction. However, some concept of artificiality may surface from time to time thereafter, depending principally upon the social climate of the patients' formative years. Motivation for change certainly will preempt most culturally inspired reticence in overt sexual expression.

Treatment progression for the marital partners during Days 3, 4, and 5 usually follows a relatively constant pattern of physical direction, regardless of the presenting distress, and is based upon the following research premise: subjective appreciation of sexual responsivity derives return from positive pleasure in sensory experiences that, in turn, derive their individual meaning and value from the patient's psychosocial sexual background.

Although it is a natural physiological function, sexual responsivity can be sublimated, delimited, displaced, or distorted by inhibition of its natural components and/or alteration of the environment in which they are operant. As examples: (1) If sexual function is honored as a natural process, but sublimated deliberately for sufficiently valued reasons, a high degree of tolerance to sexual tensions may exist with grace and without distortion. (2) If sexual function is rejected or denied an honorable or even acceptable role psychologically, yet actively sustained physically in spite of the rejecting value system, the result may be acquired sexual dysfunction. (3) If sexual function is undiscovered or unrealized because a natural, sequential development has been put aside, removed from context, or held in abeyance without sustaining expectations, the result may be primary sexual unfulfillment and/ or psychosexual confusion.

The first and last generalized categories are frequently reflected in the distresses presented by members of marital units referred to the Foundation. Although the first category essentially exemplifies a successful religious commitment, it also is found in marital relationships based upon religious orthodoxy. The second category, not as frequently seen in consultation, usually is exemplified by a single marital partner, while the spouse may have had the advantage of a more objective sexual environment during developmental years.

Two weeks does not allow time for finite analysis or appreciation of individual levels of psychosexual development, nor is such considered necessary for reversal of sexual dysfunction. Authoritative direction structured around use of the common denominator of sensory experience is employed in reversal of the presenting sexual distress. Selection of this particular factor was based upon the assumption that memory of pleasure in sensate experience probably represents the only *psychological* constant in human sexual response, since all other psychological investment is organized into a highly individualized matrix for every human being. (Other constants in sexual response are of genetic or biological origin.) On this premise an opportunity is provided by professional direction for all patients to experience the equivalent of a developmental point of sexuality, representing as nearly as possible the beginning of socialization of sexual feeling. It provides marital-unit partners with an opportunity to appreciate, or to develop and appreciate, personal receptivity of sensate focus.

The cotherapists describe the role that sensory appreciation plays in sexual response as a medium of social exchange vested primarily in touch. This premise of sensate value is based upon a cultural tendency. Communication intended to give comfort or solace, convey reassurance, show devotion, describe love or physical need is expressed first by touch. Olfactory, visual, or auditory communication generally serves as a reinforcement of the experience. The marital partners learn that sexual function is not just a physical expression. It is touch, smell, sound, and sight, reflecting how men or women as sexual beings show what they feel and think, that bring responsive meaning to the sexual act. These factors are as important to the male as to the female.

Touch, however, becomes the primary medium of exchange by initial cotherapist direction accompanied by encouragement for supportive experiences of an olfactory and a visual nature. (Other sensate foci often are described by the marital partners as their awareness develops but are not given specific attention in the therapy program.)

In order to introduce the advantages of sensate focus to the marital partners, they are asked to take two segments of time between termination of the roundtable discussion (Day 3) and the next projected therapy session on Day 4. It is suggested that the timing of episodes arises from a natural sense of warmth, unit compatibility and/or even a shared sense of gamesmanship. These time segments are not to be chosen by the clock unless clock-schedule living is an established life-style for both marital partners. Duration of each session is to be determined by this formula: The partners are to continue for whatever period of time gives pleasure or is appreciated as opportunity for discovery and pleasure, but never to a point of physical fatigue or procedural disenchantment for either partner. An authoritative directive currently reaching cliché status is, "A rewarding five minutes is worth much more than a stressful half-hour," but it still remains a relatively good rule of procedure.

In each session, physical procedure is to be as follows: In the privacy of their living quarters, marital partners should be unclothed, with a minimum of emotional or physical weariness, stress, or tension. Clothing can be an enhancing artifact to sexual interaction but it also can be a distraction in the presence of either partner's shyness, awkwardness, or embarrassment. Two people contending with the distress of sexual dysfunction need to avoid any environmental circumstance or physical procedure that may contribute to misunderstanding or awkward interaction. Hence, clothing should always be removed prior to any specific physical interaction carried out by direction during the two-week period, or at least until both marital partners have regained personal security in physical communication.

Cotherapists arbitrarily name one marital partner to approach the other first (thus removing still another roadblock to physical initiation or interaction), and ask that he or she introduce manual touch to the spouse. Drawing from roundtable discussion and cotherapist suggestion, and aided by specific direction from the recipient partner as to interest in specific body area and intensity of touch desired, the "giving" partner is to trace, massage, or fondle the "getting" partner with the intention of giving sensate pleasure and discovering the receiving partner's individual levels of sensate focus. If neither partner has any idea of physical preference, a gentle trial-and-error approach is suggested. Perhaps initially this seeking approach may be preferable for all men and women, whether or not they have previously established sensate preferences.

At this time, and until otherwise directed, neither partner is to approach or touch the genital area of the other nor should the wife's breasts be approached. There is to be no specific "sexual" stimulation, and neither this session nor any other is to culminate in specific physical sexual expression until otherwise suggested.

In this system of direction, sexual responsivity is broken down component by inherent component, and gradually (by days) each, in turn, is given opportunity to be appreciated individually. Introduction by either partner of the pressures of sexual performance by goal-orientation to end-point release (ejaculation, orgasm) is verbally discouraged. The rules of mutual exchange in sensate focus are simple. The recipient has only the responsibility to protect the "pleasuring" partner from committing an error which discomforts, distracts, or irritates. There is no requirement to comment upon that which is pleasurable by word, or even by "body English" unless the verbal or nonverbal communication is completely spontaneous.

For most women, and for many men, the sensate focus sessions represent the first opportunity they have ever had to "think and feel" sensuously and at leisure without intrusion upon the experience by the demand for end-point release (own or partner's), without the need to explain their sensate preferences, without the demand for personal reassurance, or without a sense of need to rush to "return the favor."

The partner who is pleasuring is committed first to do just that: give pleasure. At a second level in the experience, the giver is to explore his or her own component of personal pleasure in doing the touching—to experience and appreciate the sensuous dimensions of hard and soft, smooth and rough, warm and cool, qualities of texture and, finally, the somewhat indescribable aura of physical receptivity expressed by the partner being pleasured. After a reasonable time, as indicated by previously described formula, the marital partners are to exchange roles of pleasuring (giving) and being pleasured (getting), and then repeat the procedure in similar detail.

If, as observed by the cotherapists during the directive period of the roundtable, description of the dimensions of sensate exchange and its related interaction elicits a somewhat uncomprehending response from the marital unit, a reflective approach is introduced which inspects the husband's and wife's basic pleasure and freedom to enjoy similar, less-personal experiences. The marital partners are asked whether they consider the dimension of touch or feeling to be something that they instinctively (automatically) seek in their perception of paintings, surfaces, small children, or any living thing appropriate to their life-style ("touch" here does not have a specifically sexual connotation). They are further asked whether or not they enjoy the warmth of sitting, sleeping, or being close to one another in situations of privacy. Other reflective questions may be indicated and may inquire into the marital partners' reaction to shaking hands, their physical methods of showing emotion, if any, etc. Any positive content in their answers is referred back to the context of the previously given "touch" directions to develop a familiar frame of reference. Then the marital partners are asked to explore in privacy the opportunity presented by the instructions.

Sexual dysfunction is marked by specific levels of sensory deprivation that have origin in fear and apprehension of sexual situations, denial of personal sexual identity, rejection of partner or circumstance of sexual encounter, or lack of sexual awareness often lost originally through emotional or physical fatigue or preoccupation. Even if previously established, appreciation of sensate focus can be lost through lack of opportunity for expression or subjection to personally disagreeable experience. Sensate foci may have been negated or totally rejected as a part of sexuality (sexual identity) by prevailing attitudes or psychosocial trauma. It also is possible that sensate focus never has been discovered by some— at least not without accompanying distortion.

Introduction of the sensate focus by mutual touch in the context of considerable verbal and nonverbal communication, expressly without pressure to "make something happen" sexually, was first introduced to marital units presenting symptoms of sexual dysfunction over eleven years ago. Rather than seeking to refine or achieve sophistication of concept, the Foundation has chosen to retain the format as introduced at the original, uncomplicated level. Sensate focus, when explored without overt performance pressures, becomes something which marital partners can shape and structure as they mutually desire. Sensate focus then becomes theirs, not something that has been systematized for them. Only the first and possibly the second opportunity at mutual sensate exploration seems artificial. It is approximately at this point in therapy, just as the marital partners begin to develop mutual pleasure in the physical exchange, that the cotherapists begin their gradual withdrawal from their assumed role of bridge or catalyst to marital-unit communication.

Regardless of the careful explanation of the sensate focus concept with its accompanying authoritative contraindication of sexual activity per se, most marital partners will expect some sexual goal to be presented as a final instruction on Day 3. The Foundation's concept that sexual responsivity indeed grows from many transactions, erotic and otherwise, that occur in the context of human need—that sexual responsivity is not something one can will and thereby achieve—is not always easy to understand. The feeling that sensate pleasure at best represents indolence and at worst, sin, still permeates society sufficiently to influence the affectional, sexual patterns of many marital relationships, although most marital partners would intellectually deny conformation to such concept.

Some marital partners even feel guilty in accepting pleasure when it is deliberately sought, feeling that pleasure is permissible only when it is "accidental." For those who rarely, if ever, have given as much attention to the quality of their marital sexual functioning as they have to planning meals or buying clothes, the first simple directions for sharing an opportunity to touch and feel (within the context of all that the specific marital relationship represents) is an adequate beginning. Sensual pleasure is something to absorb gradually from positive experience, not to be accepted as an authoritarian directive. These husbands and wives may find reassurance in the quotation from Will and Ariel Durant, "Man's sins may be the relics of his rise rather than the stigmata of his fall."

Before Day 3 is terminated, a final reminder always is given not to touch genital areas and the wife's breasts and not to pursue specific sexual activity until otherwise directed. The marital unit is then released to investigate together the variables and the pleasures of sensate focus.

DAY 3
SPECIAL-SENSE DISCUSSION

Sensations aroused in skin and internal organs often cannot be classified because knowledge of the neurophysiological mechanisms involved remains incomplete. Certainly, special meanings given to these sensations vary directly with the number of individuals to whom they occur—and possibly as frequently as they occur. The psychosocial context within which feelings are perceived and the biophysical condition of the perceiver characterize the sensory experience and give it import of the moment. There-fore, arbitrary clinical isolation of each sensory category as pre-sented in this text is indeed theoretical.

Touch.   As described in the preceding discussion, Sensate Focus, the dimension of touch was chosen to provide the sensory experience most easily and appropriately available to marital partners as a medium for physical exchange in reconstituting natural responsiv-ity to sexual stimuli. The sense of touch not only is a primary com-ponent of psychosexual response but it is also considered a most meaningful form of psychosocial communication in this and many other societies. The familiarity with which touch is customarily, often spontaneously, used to greet, show affection, comfort, reas-sure, etc., gives this medium of sensate expression exceptional value for bridging the chasm of physical restraint in, or actual withdrawal from, sexual interchange so often present between marital partners contending with sexual dysfunction.

The experience of touch (both giving and receiving) also pro-vides a medium for developing appreciation of other sensate foci in the sexual partner's conscious pattern of response. This partner interaction in turn encourages the expression of natural sexual functioning.

Since sexual stimuli essentially represent experience in excitation of the senses made erotically significant by the individually con-ditioned sexual-value system, the cotherapists suggest specific phys-ical interaction involving the appropriate sensory and verbal com-munication that may produce these sensate experiences. In their directions to the marital unit, the theoretical isolation of each sensory influence is employed as a means of making the instruc-tions understandable (i.e., touch, smell, sight as separate experi-ences). These "exercises" are designed to free sexually dysfunc-tional individuals from inhibitions that deprive them of an op-portunity to respond naturally to sensory experience.

As has been suggested, the experience of touch and feeling carries a built-in opportunity for appreciation of other forms of special sensory excitation. For example, when the responses of olfaction and vision are related (by action or recall) to a pleasur-able experience of physical and emotional interaction, another dimension is added to the marital partners' mode of mutual expression. As a husband or wife, by direction, initially explores his or her own feelings as well as those of the partner's, discovery is made of specifics that translate into pleasurable, sexually invested experiences.

Subsequent reflection of marital-unit reactions, discussed during the therapy sessions, provide the cotherapists with a reliable impression of the partners' ongoing physical and emotional receptivity to one another. When this impression is correlated with facts and impressions provided by both the individual and the marital histories, a broader concept of individual requirements for the establishment of mutual responsivity is available for use in directing progression of therapy.

Sensory awareness and its communication to another person can be extremely difficult for those who have not had the opportunity to develop sensate orientation gradually, under circumstances in which the experience was valued and encouraged, or at least not negated. The high degree of self-education that takes place in learning to perceive this form of enjoyment is at times difficult to appreciate. The educational process, as initiated in therapy by the sensate "exercises," permits gradual modification of negative reactions to sensory stimuli so that learning occurs through return from positive experience. Positive experiences themselves depend upon marital-unit adaptation to patterns of interactive behavior developed by mutual understanding and melding of individual requirements.

Rejection of sexual identity, concern for personal unattractiveness, or similar attitudinal errors often are responsible for negative reactions to the sexual stimuli directly obtainable from the natural sensory experience of touch. To help bridge the gap of awkwardness, reticence, or possibly even initial rejection of sensory appreciation, another level of sensate focus has been introduced to the sexually dysfunctional marital units parallel in time with the direction for touch. This individual sensate focus is the potentially pleasurable dimension of olfaction.

In an early phase of the clinical research program, areas of specific concern for marital partners' ease and pleasure during their initial self-conscious attempts to follow therapy direction came to the attention of the research staff. There was practical clinical concern relative to roughness or dryness of patients' hands that distracted the individuals attempting to convey the sensate experience of touch and feeling. Several marital units commented that they had attempted to correct the situation by using commercial creams or lotions. However, there were distractions. The reports often underscored concerns for the stickiness of commercial materials or individual complaints that the lotions were too cooling or had an astringent effect when used during the sensory exercises.

At this same time, the Foundation was committed to a conjoint research venture with another investigative interest on the influence of odors on human experience, specifically odors possibly affecting sexual pleasure. The general study, tentatively designed to identify residuals of an olfactory signal system (if any) still operant in human sexual response, could not be structured without proper instrumentation for physiological and biochemical measurement. Therefore, its activation has been delayed.

Structuring such a study in human sexual response requires extensive preliminary information. Although animal studies have yielded many exciting clues, to date few are translatable to human application. This fact led to a pilot effort designed to elicit subjective reactions to the use of scented products and to establish preferences for representative odors and fragrances.

The primary research population was composed of 100 randomly selected marital units admitted to the therapy program for sexual dysfunction. It was anticipated that their participation in the treatment program might conceivably be enhanced by the optional introduction of fragrance.

A comparable population of marital units, individually and collectively reporting their sexual relationship to be both effective and enhancing to the total of their marriage, comprises the clinical control group. The basic psychosexual-social history was recorded routinely from both members of all marital units (see Section A). As this pilot study was activated, emphasis was placed on that section of the history pertaining to awareness of sensory stimuli.

Fragrances were placed in a medium of a special moisturizing lotion to serve a dual purpose. First, the research team was interested in establishing preferences, if any, in fragrance categories that might tend to enhance or signal sexual responsivity. Second, a moisturizing lotion was formulated to increase the quality of touch by avoiding irritation by dry, rough hands in the touch and feeling component of the sensate-focus exercises.

The specific choice of moisturizing lotion unwittingly served a twofold purpose. First, the use of moisturizing lotions provided the cotherapists with a unique method for defining and helping marital-unit partners identify and work through a variety of negative, in-depth feelings regarding their sexuality. Second, a subtle, early clinical indication of unanticipated treatment failure may have been stumbled upon inadvertently in this preliminary investigation into olfaction. These two entirely separate returns from investigative effort, one primarily diagnostic and the other of a therapeutic nature, will be described individually.

Initially to be considered is the opportunity provided by use of moisturizing lotions for dysfunctional men and women to work through negative, in-depth feelings regarding their sexuality. For example, in reports of their visceral reaction to sexual intimacy, a number of marital partners revealed concepts of rejection of the pelvic organs or of contamination by reproductive fluids that lowered sexual receptivity for either or both husband and wife. These feelings may have centered on the wife's revulsion by the seminal fluid or rejection of the penis per se, or on the husband's adverse reaction to the vaginal environment and/or to the vaginal lubrication. Those with such negative feelings had essentially corroborating histories, detailing primary influences of sexual negation, rejection, or trauma.

Other inhibitions in areas of physical communication revealed by the introduction of the moisturizing-lotion medium were less complex and were found similarly in marital units to whom the product was not made available. In these situations the contribution of the lotion medium was more therapeutic than diagnostic. In many marital units, particularly those in which religious orthodoxy was a factor, a wife may have been pleased by being touched pelvically, but direct handling of the husband's penis was all but impossible. In several similar situations, a most important clinical contribution was returned from use of the lotions. The moisturizing lotions were found to serve as a permissible medium of physical exchange wherein the act of applying the lotion introduced at authoritative direction provided the necessary "permission" to touch—to give or receive tactile pleasure.

Essentially, the use of a lotion gave the marital-unit member who could not touch his or her partner's genital areas a pleasant medium with which to work, while growing accustomed to exchanging with the marital partner a freedom to touch and to hold that heretofore had been a psychosocially forbidden form of mutual involvement. Subsequently, this freedom to touch pelvically moved rapidly to the next stage—comfort with the "feel of pelvic fluids" (seminal fluid or vaginal lubrication).

Classic comment reflecting the contribution of the moisturizing lotions has been made by two different women, stating in effect, "When ejaculation finally occurred during a touch-and-feeling episode, for the first time I felt no shock or revulsion. The ejaculate seemed just like the lotion I had been using to play with." Previously, neither of these women had ever allowed themselves to watch the ejaculatory process or to look at or touch the seminal fluid. They significantly related to the moisturizing lotion as a "permissible medium for physical exchange."

As will be noted in more detail in Chapter 11, sexual responsivity often "rides piggyback" on other intensely felt emotions connected with giving and receiving. Again, the use of a moisturizing lotion as a medium through which giving and receiving can be mutually exchanged has come to represent much more than massaging tired muscles or exploring sensory pleasure. This form of sensate pleasure has represented a totally new experience for many marital partners. It often initiates their first *deliberate* expression of an undemanding sexual exchange.

As a second return from the use of moisturizing lotions, an intriguing clinical signpost may be developing. The pattern of individual patient reaction to use of these lotions may constitute an early indication of markedly treatment-resistant cases. However, it is entirely too early to make any definitive claim for the existence of a previously unsuspected clinical signpost. Preliminary findings are reported to encourage further evaluation by other treatment centers. If there is significant investigative return, the entire olfaction program will be reported in a separate monograph dealing with the subject when the program is completed.

Among the 100 marital units that have been exposed to the use of moisturizers there have been 18 units that reported lack of interest in use of the medium or voiced serious objection to employing the prescribed moisturizing lotion in either giving or receiving sensate pleasure as conveyed during the touch exercises. They stated that such procedures were juvenile, undignified, unmeaningful, or that they got nothing from the lotion.

Among these 18 marital units rejecting the use of moisturizing lotions in the touch exercises, there were 5 units of bilateral partner and 13 of unilateral partner sexual inadequacy. The failure rate to reverse the symptoms of sexual dysfunction in this small segment of the population was staggering. In the 5 units with bilateral dysfunction, there were only three immediate reversals of sexual distress out of a total of 10 possible clinical successes. Among the 13 units with unilateral partner involvement, there were 12 failures to reverse the sexual inadequacy during the rapid-treatment program. In each of these 12 instances of treatment failure, that member of the marital unit (man or woman) denying interest in the use of the moisturizing lotion was the sexually dysfunctional member.

It must be emphasized that 16 of these 18 marital units objected only and specifically to use of any artificial medium in the course of their "touch experiences" but did not object to the "touch" form of sensate focus. In no instance were these 18 marital units represented together or individually in the group reporting preference for natural body odors over fragrance usage in sexually oriented situations.

Thus, out of 23 individual cases of sexual dysfunction (18 marital units), Foundation personnel failed to reverse symptoms of the distress in 19. This failure rate is more than 400 percent above the expected overall 20 percent failure rate (see Chapter 14). It is possible that negative patient receptivity to the introduction of moisturizers into the sensate-focus exercises of touch may provide to Foundation personnel a clinical indication of complex adaptive patterns of sexual behavior that may be extremely difficult to resolve.

Obviously, it is far too early to take any definitive stand on the matter. The control series is presently under review, but the staggering statistical association between lack of facility with or interest in use of moisturizers on the third day of the program and the incidence of ultimate failure of therapy at the end of the two-week rapid-treatment program must be mentioned even in an admittedly empirical manner. Since these statistics have no investigative validity to date, no further comment will be made. For a general statistical review of the rapid-treatment program see Chapter 14.

Olfaction. What of the reactions to the fragrance incorporated into the medium of moisturizing lotion? Patients were provided with unscented material as well as that which offered a selection of fragrances representing general categories of scent. By commercial assignment, some were considered to be male-oriented and others to have female connotation.

As previously described, the medium was introduced as a potential enhancement of the touch exercises by direction given at the end of the roundtable session. If a particular fragrance proved objectionable or occasioned any distress to either partner, the unscented material was substituted during the particular time period. A different fragrance category was chosen at random and introduced daily. After each of the individual categories of fragrance had been experienced once and personal reactions reported, subsequent choice was marked by marital-unit preference.

In addition to the unperfumed lotion there were nine fragrance categories represented in the moisturizer-lotion medium introduced concomitantly with direction for the sensate-focus exercises. Four were popularly conceptualized as being of "feminine" orientation, all of them bouquets: floral; a mossy green; a floral, woody blend; and oriental. The remaining 5 fragrance categories were considered "masculine": lavender bouquet; modern ambery, sweet bouquet; citrus bouquet; fresh citrus plus woody, floral bouquet; and a sharp fragrance with balsamic notes.

Based upon available data, individual preferences for particular fragrance categories have correlated only with personal experiential material elicited during history-taking. Within the concept of this form of psychotherapy, however, any expressed fragrance preference would be maintained, altered, or extended subject to further adaptive or learning opportunities. In certain instances the material reflects the preference as an integral component of an established sexual value system. However, information obtained within the investigative design is considered only as a basis for conjecture, to be used in planning future research direction.

One of the primary contributions made by fragrance use in the therapy program resulted from its stimulation of another of the major senses, adding further encouragement and dimension to individual sensate experience.

Of interest is the fact that those individuals and/or marital units who reported a preference for the use of fragrance in sexually oriented situations (as opposed to a stated preference for natural body odors), also reported a personal concept that use of fragrance per se carried erotic implication.

There is a tremendous undeveloped potential for clinical contribution of the special senses in support of treatment for human sexual dysfunction. Material as reported emphasizes the developmental status of this phase of the overall program.

DAY 3
ROUNDTABLE GOALS

1. Reflect from the patients' own accounts of personal and marital histories (Day 1 and Day 2) those attitudes, beliefs or misbeliefs, sexual practices, and factors of background and environment seen as probable correlates to the presenting distress of the specific sexual dysfunction.

2. Employ the "mirror" of professional objectivity and knowledge of sexual function and dysfunction to indicate the personal behavior patterns of each partner that have contributed specifically to loss of sexual understanding and generally to loss of unit communication.

3. Initiate an educational process describing the nature of effective sexual functioning by emphasizing and explaining:

(a) That sexual functioning is a natural physiological process.

(b) The impossibility of employing the goal of end-point release in sexual expression as a means to overcome basic sexual dysfunction.

(c) That sexuality is a dimension of personality (being male or female) expressed in every human act.

(d) That sex or sexual functioning is specific sexual activity (masturbation, intercourse, partner genital manipulation, etc.).

(e) The profound role played by fears of performance (felt by either sex) which specifically grow from lack of knowledge of effective sexual functioning and lead to a spectator's role.

(f) The sexual myths, misconceptions, and prejudices that have been defined in the material shared by the marital unit with the cotherapists.

(g) The fact that individual sexual preferences may differ because marital partners are two different personalities, have two different sets of attitudes, and often bring two different social, ethnic, and religious backgrounds to the relationship.

(h) That sexual patterns, habits, and values desirable to both partners usually have to be developed or identified by mutual effort.

(i) That cotherapists' interest will be focused upon gradual development of pleasurable sexual interaction by means of those elements of sensate focus meaningful to and understood by both sexual partners.

(j) That sexual effectiveness will be evolved from this gradual sensory appreciation and not from goal-oriented sexual performance.

(k) That "mistakes" generally are even more contributory to the progress of therapy than successes during the marital unit's attempts to follow the Foundation's authoritative directions.

(l) That the marital relationship remains the focus for therapeutic attention during the rapid-treatment program rather than either of the marital partners.

SECTION D

DAY 4
INSTRUCTIONS

Inevitably, therapeutic procedure on Day 4 as in all remaining days in therapy, is at least in part devoted to discussion of the marital unit's success or failure in following the specific instructions presented during the previous daily session. This session first requires verbal interchange that will reveal the degree of emotional rapport between marital partners. It is necessary, before continuing therapeutic procedure, to know whether or not the partners followed directions to exchange knowledge of themselves, of their feelings toward one another, and continued to "try on" the professional summation of their histories given on the previous day.

The cotherapists must constantly be aware of the current level of marital-unit motivation to continue the scrutiny of their sexual relationship and must also anticipate the direction of their personal enthusiasm. Has an increased feeling of warmth and closeness of personal relationship begun, or has confrontation within the relationship revealed deep personal animosities, possibly partner rejection, or even heretofore unknown emotional disabilities? If partners can be encouraged to be amused at their own foibles and exchange mutual compassion for error, a major communication breakthrough is at hand.

Day 4 provides the opportunity to reassure, to explain further the nature of sexual responsivity, and to emphasize the "friend in court" role of the cotherapist of the same sex. For many men and women the initial Day 3 exercise in sensate focus has proved to be delightful. Husband and wife have had an opportunity, perhaps for the first time during their marriage, to share physical giving of pleasure without the pressure of real or implied sexual goals. They have been able to enjoy each other without the fear of failing in the inevitable sexual performance demand, because any form of overt sexual expression was specifically contraindicated by authority. The usual marital-partner reaction is one of anticipation for the next step in direction.

It is a meaningful part of the Foundation's therapeutic concept that "mistakes" must be made in order to learn, even those that occur during the simplistic marital-unit exercise in sensate focus. They provide an opportunity for the cotherapists to point out and explain patterns of physical interaction that are nonserving to the unit. An educational process evolves from the direction-discussion technique, with the crucial positive factor provided through the step-by-step evolvement of sexual expression developed by the unit in the privacy of their bedroom. Cotherapist consideration of reported progress or stalemate in unit responsivity during these private learning opportunities indicates the area of therapy direction for the subsequent day.

The basic instruction, always part of Day 4 as well as other days, is to repeat the previous sensate-focus opportunities before following any other physical directions. In this manner, sensate-focus concept becomes a secure part of the marital unit's personal interchange. They learn that an expression of the innate desire to touch is not necessarily an immediate invitation to bed.

The second day of touch and feeling, like the first, is carried out within the context of the total relationship expressed by continuing discussion of attitudes, values, and vagaries of mutual behavior by the marital partners during any period of time peripheral to physical activity. The second sensate session provides continuing opportunity to develop mutual signal systems, a combination of verbal and nonverbal communication, through which individual feelings, reactions, and preferences of sexual importance may be shared and understood.

Authoritative direction encourages specific communication by suggesting that the recipient of the sensate "pleasuring" go beyond Day 3 limitation of responsibility, which required only protection of partner from unwittingly initiating sensate displeasure. For Day 4, the recipient is asked to add the dimension of active participation in the reception of sensate pleasure by placing his or her hand lightly on that of the partner giving pleasure, to indicate personal desire for change in pressure, rate of stroking, or area of touch.

As a means of introducing security for nonverbal control of sensate focus on Day 4, the cotherapists continue the marital unit's education in general sexual responsivity along the following lines.

The most unfortunate misconception our culture has assigned to sexual functioning is the assumption, by both men and women, that men by divine guidance and infallible instinct are able to discern exactly what a woman wants sexually and when she wants it. Probably this fallacy has interfered with natural sexual interaction as much as any other single factor. The second most frequently encountered sexual fallacy, and therefore a constant deterrent to effective sexual expression, is the assumption, again by both men and women, that sexual expertise is the man's responsibility. In truth, no woman can know what type of sexual approach she will respond to at any given opportunity until faced with absence of a particularly desired stimulative factor. How can a woman possibly expect any man to anticipate her sensual pleasure, when she cannot accomplish this feat with consistency herself? How can any man presume himself an expert in female sexual response under these circumstances?

Spontaneous sexual expression which answers the demand to be sexually needed and gives freedom for comparable male and female interaction, is universally the most stimulating of circumstances. Here the signal systems lead each partner toward and into the specifics that are desirable at a particular time. It is development of signal systems competent to deal with the response requirements (communication) toward which the cotherapists gradually direct the marital unit. Of course, individual preferences will rapidly become known and will repetitively produce the desired pleasure and stimulation. However, to record mentally these preferences and execute them by the numbers, either partner for the other, is to change the freedom of natural interaction back to one of stereotyped performance. The point is that sex removed from the positive influence of the total personality can become boring, unstimulating, and possibly immaterial.

Day 4 direction specifically includes touch directed to the genital areas and wife's breasts. However, authoritative direction for unit interaction still should include limitation of sexual interaction. The touch directed to the genital areas and breasts is to be offered and received without introduction of goal-oriented, demanding, stimulative effort intended to produce ejaculation or orgasm. This Day 4 session is designed only to extend the marital unit's experience with sensate pleasure to the whole-body response without the pressures of sexual performance intruding upon either partner's enjoyment of self-discovery.

At this time the cotherapists should be certain that both husband and wife are thoroughly familiar with the opposite sex's pelvic anatomy. While the man's external pelvic viscera are obvious, the woman's external pelvic anatomy frequently is a complete puzzle to her male partner. Figures 1 and 2 can be used to

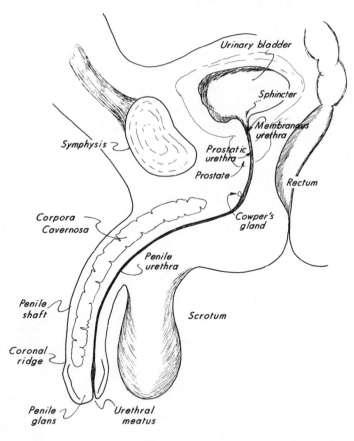

FIGURE 1

Male pelvic anatomy.

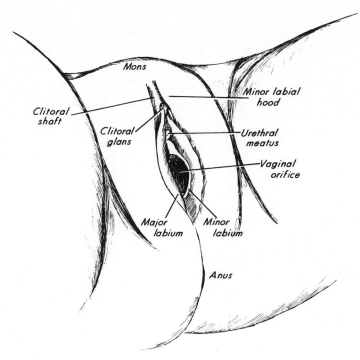

FIGURE 2

Female pelvic anatomy.

discuss anatomical placement with both husband and wife. However, if there is the slightest evidence that the husband is not really confident in his knowledge, his wife should provide him the opportunity to see and to know her external pelvic anatomy.

Any level of sexual responsivity spontaneously developing in this unpressured, nonperformance-oriented situation is, of course, the ultimate purpose of the exercises. This spontaneous expression of sexual tension will become the basis for continuing development of natural, effective sexual function, as subjective expression and objective description by the marital partners reflects its progression during the following days in the program.

As the cotherapists control the Day 4 discussion, they should employ such questions as, "What, if any, degree of erection (husband) or lubrication (wife) did you notice while you were 'pleasuring' one another yesterday?" Questions should be asked in a manner which neither requires nor suggests the need for a positive answer. In this way, directive questioning can be used to introduce awareness of how natural sexual responsivity actually develops from sensate focus. When patient answers are quietly interpreted in the light of professional concepts of the basics of human sexual physiology, this material can be the basis for understanding that sexual response is a spontaneous result of physical interaction between sexual partners meeting the requirements of their sexual value system but that such reactions simply do not develop on order.

Although each of the progressive steps in sexual involvement between husband and wife will introduce a separate component of the total of sexual responsivity, patients must be reminded that the fact of their introduction in the manner of a pleasant "game" does not indicate that these sexual components are temporary in nature. As each new dimension of touch and feeling is appreciated during the sensate-focus period of concentration, these new sensual pleasures must be included to a greater or lesser degree in future occasions of sexual interaction. Again, sensual pleasures should never be introduced by clock or check list but must be inherent in all sexual activity, because these steps are natural components of human sexual responsivity.

Day 4 directions should also include encouragement of more verbal communication, but verbalization should be of spontaneous inclination, never forced. When pleasured, the husband or wife may wish to express his or her pleasure in some manner of verbal release. If so, the individual should be encouraged in this desire. However, it is not uncommon for men and women who have never felt free to express themselves unconstrainedly sexually to find verbalization during sexual activity to be unnatural and distracting. To force verbal communication is to add the potential of further self-consciousness and lack of spontaneity.

Directions for the interim period between Days 4 and 5 should indicate, as before, that two episodes of time should be spent as in the first experience with touch and feeling. Each partner is to introduce unit interaction on one of the occasions. Turns of unspecified duration are to be taken in each episode of time. This length of physical activity should be determined as before by the formula of "continue to the extent of pleasure, but do not fatigue (either physically or emotionally) either partner."

With the termination of Day 4 in the basic treatment program, attention must be turned to the specific varieties of sexual dysfunction that serve as presenting complaints of patients referred to the Foundation for treatment. For the specifics of treatment of the individual sexual inadequacy, and the format for subsequent days' therapy direction, reference is made to the chapters dealing with the variations of human sexual inadequacy. In every instance, the treatment chapters will presume established marital-unit familiarity with the concept of and approaches to sensate focus.

3

PREMATURE EJACULATION

From a clinical point of view it is extremely difficult to define the syndrome of premature ejaculation. Most definitions refer specifically to the duration of intravaginal containment of the penis. For teaching purposes a genitourinary service in a medical center has described a premature ejaculator as a man who cannot control his ejaculatory process for at least the first 30 seconds after penetration. In similar vein a hospital psychiatric service has described the premature ejaculator as a man who cannot repress his ejaculatory demand for one full minute of intravaginal containment.

More realistically, a definition of premature ejaculation should reflect sociocultural orientation together with consideration of the prevailing requirements of sexual partners rather than an arbitrarily specific period of time. On occasion, 30 to 60 seconds of intravaginal containment is quite sufficient to satisfy a woman, if she has been highly excited during precoital sex play and is fully ready for orgasmic release with the initial thrusts of the penis. However, during most coital opportunity, the same woman may require variably longer periods of penile containment before attaining full release of sexual tension.

While readily admitting the inadequacies of the definition, the Foundation considers a man a premature ejaculator if he cannot control his ejaculatory process for a sufficient length of time during intravaginal containment to satisfy his partner in at least 50 percent of their coital connections. If the female partner is persistently nonorgasmic for reasons other than rapidity of the male's ejaculatory process, there is no validity to the definition. At least this definition does move away from the "stopwatch" concept.

The male's level of concern for an uncontrolled ejaculatory pattern and the concomitant depth of his female partner's sexual frustrations tend to increase in direct parallel to the degree of their formal education. For instance, grade-school or early high-school dropouts rarely request relief from premature ejaculation. In this sociocultural setting the man generally dominates the pattern of sexual function within the marital unit, and his sexual satisfaction is the major concern. Rapidity of ejaculation is not considered a sexual hazard, and in fact may provide welcome relief for the woman accepting and fulfilling a role as a sexual object without exposure to or personal belief in the concept of parity between the sexes in the privileges and the pleasures of sexual functioning. Rapid release from sexual service frequently is accepted as a blessing by women living in the restrictive levels of this sub-culture's inherent double standard. Of course these women are free to enjoy orgasmic expression if it develops, but neither partner usually considers it the man's responsibility to aid or abet woman's sexual responsivity. (It should be noted that Foundation studies have been extremely limited in material of cross-cultural or racial significance.)

The complainee in the marital unit contending with an established pattern of premature ejaculation usually is the female partner. If the male ejaculates regularly during premounting sex play or during attempts at mounting, or even with the first few penile thrusts after intravaginal containment, there rarely is opportunity for effective female sexual expression. Time and again women's sexual tensions are elevated by precoital sex play, further edged by the additional stimulation of the penetration process, only to be confronted with almost instantaneous ejaculation and subsequent loss of penile erection. There is a high level of female frustration, particularly when this male response pattern is repeated routinely time after time.

Sexual histories recorded from prematurely ejaculating males have a consistently familiar pattern. Variations on the basic theme are reflected by the man's age and, in some instances, the circumstance in which his initial sexual adventures were experienced. For the premature ejaculator now in the over-40 age group, the history of first coital experience is usually that of prostitute exposure. In the days of the prostitution houses, prior to the advent of the call-girl era, the accepted pattern of prostitute function involved satisfying the male's sexual tensions as rapidly as possible. Indeed the more rapid the customer turnover, the higher the financial return. Twenty-five to forty-five years ago, when the neophyte first gathered his courage to follow sociocultural demand that he "prove his manhood," he was subjected, often unexpectedly, to the frequent prostitute insistence that he complete the act as soon as possible. The sooner the male would mount and the faster he could ejaculate, the more pleased the prostitute. It took only two or three such house visits (frequently just the initial visit was sufficient) to establish the young man's commitment to self-centered expression of sexual need with its resultant physical pattern of rapid intromission and quick ejaculation. As the inexperienced male became conditioned to this pattern of sexual functioning, a life-time of rapid ejaculatory response might be established.

As the years passed and with them the "houses," the young male's first sexual opportunities with girls in his peer group frequently took place in the back seats of cars, lovers'-lane parking spots, drive-in movies, or brief visits to the by-the-hour motels. Coital connection established in these semi-private situations under the pressures inherent in dual concern for surprise or observation resulted in both coital and ejaculatory processes encouraged toward rapid completion. In these situations there usually is as little male concern for the female partner's sexual release as there was for that of her professional counterpart in previous years. Thus a pattern of rapid completion of the male sexual cycle is established by sociocultural demand, and again it only takes two or three such pressured exposures for potential conditioning of the young male to a pattern of premature ejaculation.

Yet another technique of teenage sex play encountered in the background of the premature ejaculator is frequently recorded in the histories of young men during their early years of sexual encounter. In this situation teenagers pet extensively and then the male mounts in a male superior position, clothes relatively in place, and pantomimes intercourse without any attempt at vaginal penetration until he is stimulated to ejaculation by the friction engendered by this pseudocoital process. This sex-play technique does preserve virginity and above all else does protect against unwanted pregnancy. Yet, young men repeatedly enjoying this form of premarital sex play are exposed to premature ejaculatory patterning, because value is given preeminently to accomplishing male sex-tension release as rapidly as possible with the full cooperation of the female partner. Of course, thought seldom is given to the sex tensions that develop in these young women serving as ejaculatory release mechanisms.

Yet another procedure that is popular with both married and unmarried groups is the withdrawal technique during coital connection. With this approach sex play terminates in active coital connection, but the man withdraws as he reaches the stage of ejaculatory inevitability and ejaculates outside the vagina. With this release pattern there is no necessity for the man to learn ejaculatory control. With coital partners using the withdrawal technique as a means of contraception, the usual sexual sequence prescribes participation in sex play to a plateau level of male excitation, a rapid mounting process with a few frantic pelvic thrusts, and then abrupt withdrawal, which satisfies the male with an ejaculatory episode and protects the female from pregnancy. Usually both partners fall into the psychosexual trap of ignoring at onset any concept of male responsibility for aiding female tension release.

This practice serves to encourage and ultimately to condition a rapid ejaculatory response upon the sexually inexperienced young man and to physiologically and psychologically condition both partners to the concept that the vagina is only to be used fleetingly as a stimulant for male ejaculatory pleasure. The anxious female partner, worried that the male may not withdraw in time, rarely has the opportunity to think and feel sexually, so any experience of orgasmic tension release would be coincidental. In every situation, ranging from the impatience of the prostitute to the contraception-oriented withdrawal techniques, total emphasis is placed on the presumed male prerogative of freedom of sexual expression without responsibility for his partner's sexual response. The old double standard of male sexual dominance is perpetuated by the concept of rapid and effective release of male sexual tensions provided by a female companion who services a man without expecting or receiving comparable sexual prerogatives from her sexual partner.

Despite strong cultural beliefs to the contrary, masturbatory practices, regardless of frequency or technique employed, have not been identified historically as an etiological factor in the syndrome of premature ejaculation. After all, in the usual male masturbatory sequence there is no female companion negating her own birthright of functional sexual demand in order to provide her male partner with tension release.

When the established premature ejaculator contemplates marriage, there may be "engagement-period" expression of concern by the wife-to-be for his sexual patterning. However, there usually is the expression of faith by both partners that the lack of ejaculatory control will be resolved with the new wife's understanding and cooperation and the continuity of the sexual exposure inevitably engendered by the privilege of marriage.

There is no way of knowing how many men who ejaculate prematurely in the first few months or even first year or two of marriage develop in due course reasonably adequate ejaculatory control, because these temporarily beleaguered marital units do not seek consultation. However, probably hundreds of thousands of men never gain sufficient ejaculatory control to satisfy their wives sexually regardless of the duration of marriage or the frequency of mutual sexual exposure. Unfortunately, all too few of these marital units ever seek professional direction.

Men and women have relatively stereotyped reactions when they are husband and wife in a unit contending with the syndrome of premature ejaculation. Some men simply cannot be touched genitally without ejaculating within a matter of seconds. Others will ejaculate immediately subsequent to observation of an unclothed female body or while reading or looking at pornographic material. Many others ejaculate during varying stages of precoital play. However, most men who ejaculate prematurely do so during an attempt at intromission or during the first few full strokes of the penis subsequent to intravaginal containment.

The uninformed wife's reaction to a husband with an established problem of premature ejaculation also is relatively type-cast. During the first months or years of the marriage the usual response is one of tolerance, understanding, or sympathy, with oft-voiced expressions of confidence that the problem will be overcome with patience, love, and mutual cooperation. With due passage of time and with her husband's rapid ejaculatory tendency not only continuing, but frequently becoming worse, the wife's sexual frustrations rise to the surface. She verbalizes her distress by accusing her husband of just using her as an object for sexual release; in short, of being selfish, irresponsible, or simply of having no interest in or feeling for her as an individual. These wifely complaints are legion, couched in individually self-expressive terms but reflecting in general rebellion at being used sexually rather than loved sexually. The "just being used" is the part most difficult for wives to accept.

Although marital-unit complaints of premature ejaculation have been referred to the Foundation after as brief an interval as one year of marriage, generally this particular syndrome is not presented for therapeutic reversal until after five to twenty years of marriage. Usually the problem is ignored or tolerated by the wife until children are born. With distractions provided by the demands of the new family, the prematurely ejaculating husband is accepted. But once a family of desirable size has been achieved, and the youngest has reached some level of independence, the wife's sexual frustrations, enhanced by her increasing psychosocial freedom as the children mature, reach the breaking-point. She spotlights the problem by (1) insisting on professional guidance for herself, (2) demanding that her husband seek professional help, (3) enjoying sexual release provided by another partner, male or female, or (4) any combination of these three potentials.

In general, psychotherapeutic support for the wife of a premature ejaculator is palliative at best. There is no way to alleviate the main source of irritation when dealing professionally with her sexual problems in a one-to-one method of psychotherapy. Nor has psychotherapy directed specifically toward the problem of premature ejaculation been particularly successful, because there has not been widespread professional knowledge of clinical techniques available to teach ejaculatory control. At best, the wife, by seeking other coital partners, can only double her levels of frustration, if she realizes comparatively through successful sexual experience with other men the inadequacies of her own husband's sexual performance. Conversely, she may find herself unresponsive in extramarital coition, possibly from feelings of guilt or from conditioned repression of her own sexual responses through years of contending with her husband's rapid ejaculatory pattern. Many women have sought psychosexual release in homosexual experience under these circumstances.

Before acknowledging loss of all hope of successful sexual functioning, the members of the marital unit individually or together try any number of physical dodges to avoid the usual rapid ejaculatory termination of their sexual exposures. The most consistently employed homemade remedy is the "don't touch" treatment. The husband requests that his wife not approach his genital area during their precoital play. Instead, both partners concentrate their attention on stimulating the female partner almost to the point of orgasm. Of course, there is concomitant male stimulation coming from observation of his wife's obvious "pleasure response" to his sexually stimulative approaches. Finally, if and when the wife attains a high level of sexual stimulation, there is an episode of hurried penile penetration with the husband vainly trying to distract himself from the sexually stimulating experience of intromission.

Various procedures for distraction are employed by the anxious husband. He fantasies such nonsexual material as work at the office, an unbalanced family budget, an argument with a neighbor, a fishing trip, counting backward from one hundred, etc. When the fantasy material has been proved ineffectual, the next step is to initiate some form of physical distress. The husband may bite his lip, contract the rectal sphincter, pinch himself, pull his hair, or use any other means of physical distraction. All techniques, subjective or objective, are designed, of course, to enhance ejaculatory control by reducing the level of the sensate input during the coital process.

The wife meanwhile is thrusting frantically in a vain attempt to achieve orgasmic release before her partner ejaculates. The rapid transition from the mutually agreed upon "don't touch" approach in precoital play to a rushed mounting episode and immediate contention with a demanding, thrusting, highly excited woman usually provides sufficiently forceful stimuli to initiate ejaculation before the wife possibly can obtain sexual release.

When all distraction techniques fail, the warmth of the marital unit's interpersonal relationship slowly ebbs away.

As the wife's level of cold personal disinterest reflecting her sexual frustration increases, and denunciations (verbal or silent) of her husband's sexual dysfunction continue, the next step taken by the now anxious, self-effacing husband, "the man who just can't get the job done," is one of slow but definite withdrawal from the unit's established frequency of sexual contact. Usually this action is temporarily acceptable to his frustrated wife. His withdrawal from sexual exposure continues despite the fact that the one thing the premature ejaculator cannot tolerate and still maintain any semblance of control is increasing periods of sexual continence. He frequently sleeps on the sofa or in another room; she visits her family and stays longer than planned, or simply refuses sexual contact for increasing periods of time. The longer the periods of continence, regardless of source, the more rapid and severe the husband's ejaculatory response on those rare occasions when sexual contact is permitted. Granted that the premature ejaculator may exhibit little significant control at the usual once- or twice-a-week rate of exposure, yet he certainly will have no control at all when the coital exposures are reduced to once, twice, or thrice a month.

Over a period of years with no obvious improvement in her husband's sexual performance, the wife loses confidence in her partner's consideration for or appreciation of her as an individual, and concomitantly some degree of confidence in herself as a woman.

When demands for effective sexual performance are continuously verbalized or acted out by the female partner over an extended period, the complication of erective inadequacy may appear (see Chapter 6). The husband, questioning his own sexual prowess time and again, abetted in this frightful concern by his wife's specific verbal derogation of his masculinity, frequently is enveloped by anticipatory fears of performance whenever sexual expression is imminent. These fears of performance, when combined with techniques for avoiding direct penile stimulation during precoital play and his wife's obvious disinterest in active sexual functioning, not only make the man increasingly conscious of his inadequacies of sexual performance but also raise psychologically crippling questions as to his very maleness.

In short, all these factors plus his fantasy patterns of trying to distract himself from subjective pleasure during active sexual functioning finally place the man in the spectator role in his own marital bed (see the discussion in Chapter 2). There is a slow transition from the role of physical self-distraction during coition to that of a fear-ridden spectator at his own sexual performance. Thus, the husband assumes the psychological stature of a secondarily impotent male * with all of the well-established concerns for sexual performance and the constant retreat to a spectator role.

Time and time again premature ejaculators of many years' standing not only lose confidence in their own sexual performance but also, unable to respond positively while questioning their own masculinity, terminate their sexual functioning with secondary impotence. This stage of functional involution is, of course, the crowning blow to husband and wife as individuals and usually to the marital relationship.

In the clinical progression of moving toward secondary impotence from an established pattern of premature ejaculation, there is an intermediate step that frequently can be underscored by careful history-taking. A man transitionally may become such an uncontrolled premature ejaculator that he episodically will ejaculate with partial or minimal erection. Occasionally the ejaculatory process may develop totally without penile erection. This syndrome of seepage of seminal fluid, reflecting little ejaculatory pressure, usually is accepted by the distressed marital unit as the ultimate in masculine humiliation. The obvious next step in male sexual inadequacy is complete secondary impotence.

There is no surety of progression toward secondary impotence from the syndrome of premature ejaculation. Most rapid ejaculators probably remain so without ever developing secondary impotence. They have little awareness of or no basic concern for the sexual needs of their female partners, and there is little or no ques-

* A composite history describing the natural progression from premature ejaculation to secondary impotence has been included in the detailed discussion of the latter subject in Chapter 6, page 161.

tioning of their own masculinity. In contrast, there is an increasingly large number of men with lack of ejaculatory control who, questioning the effectiveness of their sexual function and accepting their share of responsibility for their wives' sexual pleasure, create fears of performance which move them inexorably toward secondary impotence.

As opposed to other forms of both male and female sexual dysfunction, in premature ejaculation no specifically related environmental background, religious orientation, or pattern of parental dominance could be delineated from the histories of the marital units referred to the Foundation for treatment. The first few ejaculatory experiences predispose a man to the development of premature ejaculation regardless of his prepubertal and postpubertal environmental background.

As more sex information becomes available, as more acceptance of a single standard of sexual expression for man and woman develops in our culture, the sense of shared responsibility for female sexual release is assuming equal stature with, and presumably soon will supplant, the time-honored concept of the woman's subservient role in her mate's sexual gratification. With both a sense of responsibility and sufficient knowledge of effective sexual function must come major sociocultural improvement in the male capacity for ejaculatory control.

TREATMENT OF PREMATURE EJACULATION

The most important step in the treatment of the premature ejaculator is taken during the roundtable discussion (see Chapter 2). The marital unit must be and is assured unequivocally that a complaint of premature ejaculation can be reversed successfully. If marital partners are not so traumatized by the multiplicity of prior failures that they lose all interest in each other as individuals or as sexual partners, and if there is full cooperation from the female partner and an inherent interest in pattern reversal, there is negligible chance of therapeutic failure to reverse the male's rapid ejaculatory tendencies.

Before becoming too involved in therapeutic techniques for ejaculatory control, it might be well to review briefly the two stages of man's orgasmic experience. The first stage, termed "ejaculatory inevitability," is an interval before seminal fluid emission; the male feels the ejaculation coming and can no longer control the process. This first stage is specifically a 2- to 4-second time interval created by regularly recurring contractions by the prostrate gland and questionably the seminal vesicles. When any man reaches the stage of ejaculatory inevitability he cannot control his ejaculatory demand. Once started, the male moves through both first and second stages of his orgasmic experience without voluntary control. With the stage of "ejaculatory inevitability" comes loss of voluntary control of the total ejaculatory process.

The second stage of the male orgasmic process has onset with involuntary expulsion of seminal fluid content from its collection point in the prostatic and membranous portions of the urethra throughout the length of the penile urethra and culminates with expulsion of the seminal fluid bolus from the urethral meatus.

During the sensate-focus phase of the therapeutic program (see Chapter 2), when direct approach is first made to the pelvic organs, the wife is encouraged to employ any acceptable form of effective pelvic stimulation. This is, of course, in direct opposition to the usual marital-unit pattern of "don't touch," when relating to the wife's approach to her husband's genital organs. It is the no-touch concept that therapists wish to avoid.

When the male is approached pelvically, stimulative techniques are best conducted with the wife's back placed against the headboard of her bed (possibly supported with pillows), her legs spread, and with the husband resting on his back, his head directed toward the foot of the bed, with his pelvis placed between her legs, his legs over hers, so that she may have free access to his genital organs (Fig. 3). In this particular position the wife, responding to therapeutic direction with full understanding of the male performance fears involved, should approach her husband directly to encourage penile erection. As soon as full erection is achieved, the "squeeze technique" is employed. The concept of a direct approach to the premature ejaculator's pelvic organs in an

FIGURE 3
Training position for ejaculatory control.

attempt to teach control was first introduced by James Semans.

The "squeeze technique" develops when the female partner's thumb is placed on the frenulum, located on the inferior (ventral) surface of the circumcised penis, and the first and second fingers are placed on the superior (dorsal) surface of the penis in a position immediately adjacent to one another on either side of the coronal ridge (Fig. 4). Pressure is applied by squeezing the thumb and first two fingers together for an elapsed time of 3 to 4 seconds. If the man is uncircumcised, the coronal ridge still can be palpated and the first and second fingers correctly positioned. An approximation of frenulum positioning must be estimated for thumb placement. In either event, using an artificial model, cotherapists should make sure that the anatomical orientation so necessary to effective use of this technique is absolutely clear to both husband and wife. If there is any residual confusion on the wife's part as to the anatomical specifics of the squeeze technique and ejaculatory control does not develop, professional explanation and direction is presumed at fault.

Rather strong pressure is indicated in order to achieve the required results with the squeeze technique. As the man responds

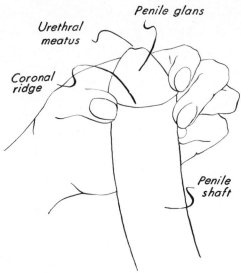

Penile glans

Urethral
meatus

Coronal
ridge

Penile
shaft

FIGURE 4

Demonstration of "squeeze technique."

to sufficient pressure applied in the manner described, *he will immediately lose his urge to ejaculate.* He may also lose 10 to 30 percent of his full erection. The wife should allow an interval of 15 to 30 seconds after releasing the applied pressure to the coronal ridge area of the penis and then return to active penile stimulation. Again when full erection is achieved the squeeze technique is reinstituted. Alternating between periods of specifically applied pressure and reconstitution of sexually stimulative techniques, a period of 15 to 20 minutes of sex play may be experienced without a male ejaculatory episode, something unknown to the marital unit in prior sexual performance.

There may be some wifely apprehension as to the amount of pressure that may safely be applied to the penis without eliciting physical distress from her husband. The amount of pressure necessary to depress a man's ejaculatory urge would be somewhat painful if the penis were in a flaccid state, but causes no similar level of discomfort when the penis is erect. If the wife still expresses concern over application of pressure, the husband should place his fingers over hers and apply sufficient pressure through her fingers to guide her to the required result. Showing his wife the degree of pressure that can be applied without resultant physical distress relieves her concern for his welfare and in turn improves the unit's level of nonverbal communication.

As stated, pressure should be applied with the squeeze technique for a period of no more than 3 to 4 seconds. If a positive clinical result is to be returned, it will be apparent in the loss of the husband's ejaculatory urge within this brief period of time.

Experience suggests that the male be brought to a low level of sexual excitement and depressed from his incipient ejaculatory urge with the squeeze technique four or five times during the first training session.

Aside from obvious control improvement, the greatest return from use of the squeeze technique is improved communication both at verbal and nonverbal levels for the marital unit. At first the wife applies pressure at her husband's direction, but soon his levels of sexual excitation become obvious to her, and she learns to apply the squeeze technique by observing his reactions to sexual stimuli.

Obviously the basic therapeutic concept involved in the squeeze technique is to enable the premature ejaculator to establish objectively a state of sexual excitation that he not only can identify but also can maintain indefinitely without ejaculation. He must be able to delay voluntarily that level of sexual excitation from which he cannot withdraw, the stage of ejaculatory inevitability. For most premature ejaculators, prior to experiencing physical response to the squeeze technique, any significant level of sexual stimulation usually has resulted in a quick leap toward ejaculatory inevitability. Once in the first stage of orgasmic experience, a man cannot be diverted or stopped from a total ejaculatory response.

As the result of the first day's exposure to the squeeze technique, the husband's fears for ejaculatory control and the wife's for her husband's inadequate sexual performance will be somewhat abated. Following the typical "healthy skepticism" concepts of the therapy program (see Chapter 2), husband and wife, while employing the squeeze technique, demonstrate for each other that complete cooperation, under proper therapeutic direction, can establish ejaculatory control. This self-demonstration of ejaculatory control markedly improves unit confidence and certainly is

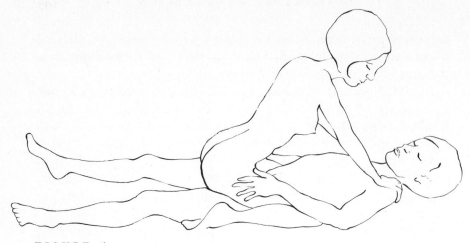

FIGURE 5

Female-superior coital position.

a major step toward reestablishing communication and terminating the cold war between the marital antagonists.

Establishing security of response relative to the squeeze technique is but the first step in a therapeutic progression that moves from onset of successful ejaculatory control under manipulative influence to a controlled coital process. Usually two or three days of marital-unit cooperation are necessary to establish full ejaculatory control with the squeeze technique under manipulative conditions.

The next step in progression of ejaculatory control involves nondemanding intromission. The male is encouraged to lie flat on his back and the female to mount in a superior position, her knees placed approximately at his nipple line and parallel to his trunk (Fig. 5). The nearer the two individuals are to the same height, the nearer the woman's knees should be placed to the nipple line. If the wife has the shorter trunk, she should place herself somewhat below the nipple line. If the wife has the longer trunk, her knees should be just above the nipple line. In this position, leaning over her mate at a 45-degree angle, she is comfortably able to insert the penis and then to move back on, rather than sit down on the penile shaft.

After bringing her husband to full erection and employing the squeeze technique two or three times for his control orientation, the wife then should mount in this specifically described superior position. Once mounted, she should concentrate on retaining the penis intravaginally in a motionless manner, providing no further stimulation for her husband by thrusting pelvically. Her physical restraint enables the husband to become acquainted with the sensation of intravaginal containment in a nondemanding, therefore nonthreatening, environment. No longer does he respond to the subconscious concept that his wife is ready to force his ejaculatory process to an unhappily rapid conclusion by overt physical expression of her own sexual desire.

For the established premature ejaculator the ultimate of sexual stimulation occurs with the mounting opportunity and during the first few seconds of intravaginal containment. If the man with inadequate control has not ejaculated prior to intravaginal penetration he will do so in short order, once penile containment has been accomplished, when there is any suggestion of active pelvic thrusting on his wife's part. When his wife cooperates fully in the superior coital position and in the sexually nondemanding fashion of penile containment described above, she enables her husband to concentrate on the concepts of ejaculatory control elicited by the squeeze technique and additionally to become accustomed to the stimulative effect of intravaginal containment.

When the husband's level of sexual excitation threatens to escape his still shaky control, he should immediately communicate this increased sexual tension to his wife. She then can elevate from the penile shaft, apply the squeeze technique in the previously practiced manner for 3 or 4 seconds, and reinsert the penis, again providing full vaginal containment without the added stimulus of pelvic thrusting. The specifically described female-superior coital position makes pelvic elevation from the penile shaft physically easy for her so that the squeeze technique can be applied rapidly to the proper area of the penis, if threatened loss of ejaculatory control develops.

In subsequent days, with some degree of performance reliability established for penile containment in the female-superior position, the husband is encouraged to provide just sufficient pelvic thrusting to maintain his erection. Again the wife is requested to maintain the specifically fixed superior position without active pelvic thrusting. If man and woman lie together with the penis in intravaginal containment without either partner providing some degree of pelvic thrusting, the man will tend to lose his erection after a short period of time, just as the woman will note marked reduction in the rate of lubrication production. This physiological evidence of reduction in sexual tension is, of course, due to the fact that both marital partners become distracted by any long-continued state of sexual inactivity, losing focus on the sensate pleasure inherent in the principle of quiet vaginal containment.

It should be emphasized to the marital unit that success in ejaculatory control in the female-superior position is but another psychophysiological step toward effective coital functioning in any desired coital positioning. It is an important psychological step in providing further relief for both husband's and wife's fears of performance. With a "healthy skepticism" attitude encouraged by authority, both members of the marital unit develop insight into the fact that they are accomplishing their own "cure." Through their physical cooperation and increasingly effective verbal and nonverbal communication, ejaculatory control is developing. Proof positive of improved control develops by the second or third day's exposure to the female-superior coital position in that 15 to 20 minutes of intravaginal containment without untoward ejaculatory demand is a relatively routine accomplishment.

Yet another important factor coming into focus at this stage in the development of the husband's voluntary ejaculatory control is the cooperative wife's level of sexual responsivity. Indeed many women married to premature ejaculators have never been orgasmic in the marriage, and most of those women that have been orgasmic in the marriage have obtained this release through manipulative or oral-genital techniques rather than coital opportunity.

Marital-unit attention obviously has been focused upon the male partner for the first few days of the therapeutic program, yet the wife may have experienced an elevation of sexual tension far superior to levels she might have anticipated. There are many reasons for this sex tension increment, the most prominent of which should be considered in some detail.

First, during the sensate-focus phase of the therapy, there is mutual "pleasuring" (see Chapter 2). Usually her levels of sexual responsivity elevate rapidly under these most advantageous conditions. There is physical closeness and holding, development or redevelopment of communication, and markedly increased warmth of understanding between husband and wife. Many of the misconceptions, fallacies, or even the taboos relating to the marital unit's prior sexual interaction have been faced, examined, explained in depth, and, to a major degree, reversed or mutually accepted during daily interviews with the cotherapists. There is no environment more conducive to marked elevation in the levels of female sexual response than that occasioned by the concept that something is happening of a positive nature to reduce or eliminate the marital unit's sexual dysfunction. As both husband and wife cooperate in the pleasuring opportunity, the increasing warmth of their interpersonal relationship is a hopeful support for the emotionally insecure woman that the wife of a premature ejaculator usually becomes after years of sexual frustration.

Second, during the manipulative phase of the squeeze technique there concomitantly is further increase in the level of female sexual tension. When the wife provides controlled play for her husband and observes both the physical pleasure she provides and his obvious delight in progress toward ejaculatory control, these reactions are reflected as positive and highly stimulative biophysical and psychosocial influences (see Chapters 2, 8). In short order the wife finds herself highly excited sexually and strongly motivated toward orgasmic release.

Third, although the wife is instructed to avoid pelvic thrusting, the initial period of intravaginal penile containment provides her with the simultaneous opportunity to feel and think sexually, not infrequently for the first time in her marriage. The sensate pleasures of nondemanding penile containment have not been available to her in view of the marital unit's basic sexual dysfunction. When there has been sufficient ejaculatory control to accomplish penetration, the actual act of physical connection usually has been followed immediately by the wife's straining demand for tension release. Alternatively, if past sexual patterning has forced her to lie quietly after penetration in the vain hope of avoiding forcing her husband to ejaculation, the entire psychosexual experience of coital connection has been focused on his battle for ejaculatory control rather than on providing her with any expression of freedom to enjoy personal sexual responsivity. Contending with a husband fighting a constant battle for ejaculatory control not only engenders severe sexual frustration for the wife but also over the years produces in her a distinctively negative attitude toward sexual expression.

Fourth, when in the female-superior coital position with intravaginal containment of the penis and even with controlled restriction of pelvic movement, the wife has been directed simply to feel and think sexually and to enjoy the sensation of vaginal distention. Following these suggestions, the proprioceptive pressures created by intravaginal containment of the erect penis are subjectively anticipated and appreciated. The wife gains almost as much from this stage in the exercise of ejaculatory control as does her husband.

Thus, the combination of subjective relief of fear for her husband's inadequacy of sexual performance plus the opportunity to feel, think, and relate sexually are enormously stimulating to the female partner.

As her partner's control increases, female pelvic thrusting can be encouraged, initially in a slow, nondemanding manner, but soon with full freedom of expression. Once sexual tensions, built from both freedom for biophysical-system response and growing confidence in the psychosocial elements of the unit's interpersonal relationships, are released to be enjoyed at will, orgasmic expression becomes a natural potential.

The final phase in the voluntary development of ejaculatory control is entered as the marital unit is encouraged to convert the female-superior position to that of the lateral coital position (see Fig. 10, Chapter 11). In the lateral coital position there is a maximum opportunity for male ejaculatory control. As the husband's sexual tensions elevate, he can withhold active pelvic thrusting yet provide a full controlled erection with which his wife can continue to express her own sexual demands and against which she can relieve her sexual tensions. In the lateral coital position the woman uniquely has complete freedom of pelvic movement in any direction. There is no pelvic or chest pinning, or cramping of leg or arm muscles. She can respond to her own tension demands as she sees fit, confident that this coital position provides her husband not only with high levels of subjective sexual pleasure but also with the best possible physical opportunity for ejaculatory control. After becoming secure in the multiple protection the position affords and in the anatomies of leg and arm arrangement (see Chapter 11), most marital units employ lateral coital positioning by choice in at least 75 percent of their coital opportunities.

Yet another reason for emphasizing the female-superior and the more effective lateral coital positioning is that the most popular position in our culture, the male-superior positioning, presents the greatest difficulties with ejaculatory control. If the coital connection is to be brief with both partners obviously wishing rapid pelvic thrusting to release of their high levels of sexual tension, coital positioning does not matter. But if there is desire to prolong the connection either for mutual pleasure or because the female partner needs more opportunity to feel and think sexually, the male-superior position, which places the greatest strain on ejaculatory control, should be avoided when possible.

On every occasion, before female-superior coital position is established and then possibly converted to a lateral mounting arrangement, a comfortable period of precoital sex play is encouraged. The wife should employ the squeeze technique at least two or three times before penetration is attempted. It takes a significant period of time to alter an early imprinting of the pattern of rapid ejaculation. However, in the two-week treatment program, sufficient competence in ejaculatory control can be developed to alleviate mutual fears of performance, obviate the spectator role, and provide all the opportunity necessary for continued improvement in control subsequent to release from the acute stage of therapy.

Before the marital unit leaves the Foundation, the cotherapists emphasize the fact that problems of ejaculatory control continue to a minor degree for at least the subsequent year. Several techniques to encourage continuing success in ejaculatory control are described for marital-partner benefit. The unit is reminded that after returning to the demands of their everyday world, regularity of sexual exposure is of primary concern. For the first six months the squeeze technique should be employed on at least a once-a-week basis prior to coital opportunity; the remainder of the unit's sexual opportunities during the week are encouraged to develop in a natural, unconstrained fashion. This approach provides the man with the necessary means for transition from a controlled sexual experience to a completely extemporaneous opportunity.

It is also suggested that the couple take advantage of the wife's menstrual period each month to provide at least one session of 15 to 20 minutes devoted specifically to male sexual stimulation with manual manipulation and repetitive application of the squeeze technique for control of the ejaculatory process. Ejaculatory control techniques usually are indicated for a minimum of six to twelve months after termination of the acute phase of therapy. During the routine follow-up discussions after termination of the unit's acute phase of treatment (see Chapter 1) decision to terminate use of the squeeze technique is made by professional evaluation of the degree of control during the unit's spontaneous matings.

It also is important to emphasize that if circumstances lead to separation of marital-unit members for a matter of several weeks, coital exposure after the marital unit is physically reunited may find the male returning to his role as a premature ejaculator. Obviously, the procedure in this situation is to reemploy the squeeze technique for several consecutive coital exposures. If constituted with warmth and understanding, ejaculatory control will return rapidly. With adequate warning of the possibility of these complications, a more relaxed concept of freedom of sexual approach is possible for marital units contending with severe premature ejaculation.

Innumerable approaches to the treatment of premature ejaculation have been described, discarded, or conducted with varying levels of professional acceptance. Hypnotic suggestion, both in natural and drug-induced states of receptivity, has been a popular approach to the problem. There has been widespread acceptance of anesthetic creams and jellies prescribed for application to the erect penis theoretically to reduce neurogenic end-organ sensitivity to the stimuli of manipulation or vaginal containment. Specific drug preparations, tranquilizers, barbituates, etc., have been prescribed in an effort to dull male sensitivity to stimuli in general and to stimuli of sexual content in particular. Many men have tried with varying degrees of success to lower their natural sexual tension levels by ingestion of sizable quantities of alcohol before anticipated sexual encounter.

And so it goes. Frantic men consume a never-ending list of potions, nostrums, and poisons, all designed to reduce rapidity of ejaculatory response, all curiously directed to a male's sexual functioning alone without regard for his partner's involvement. Any form of sexual inadequacy is a problem of *mutual* involvement for partners in a marriage. With a wife's full cooperation, her willingness to learn and to apply the basic principles of ejaculatory control, and the warmth of her personal involvement expressed openly to her mate, reversal of this crippling marital distress is essentially assured.

As further support of this argument for the necessity of involvement of the wife in the resolution of a well-established premature ejaculatory pattern, it should be pointed out that the squeeze technique is not effective if done by the male attempting to teach himself control. If a man manipulates his penis to erection and then applies the squeeze technique to control an imminent ejaculatory response, he usually can halt the natural progression of sex tension increment and successfully depress his ejaculatory urge. However, once this man returns to the stimulation of a heterosexual relationship, it is as if he had made no prior solitary attempts at control. What is obviated by solitary attempts to learn ejaculatory control is the fact that with a female partner the individual male cannot entirely set the pace of sexual functioning, nor can he entirely deny the sexual stimuli absorbed from the obvious psychosexual involvement of his marital partner.

In the past 11 years 186 men have been treated for premature ejaculation. There have been 4 failures to learn adequate control during the acute phase of therapy. Adequate control is defined as sufficient to provide orgasmic opportunity for the sexual partner during approximately 50 percent of the coital opportunities. The failure rate is 2.2 percent.

Three of the failures were with marital units; and one was with a man previously divorced because of his premature ejaculatory pattern, who brought a replacement partner to the treatment program (see Chapter 5).

In two of the four instances there was no real motivation on the part of the male partner to learn ejaculation control. These men had accompanied their nonorgasmic wives as a cooperative venture, but when they learned that they were in fact contributing to their wives' sexual dysfunction they refused further cooperation. They simply could not accept a reversal of their deeply ingrained double standard of sexual function.

There is no specific explanation for the two remaining failures to control the premature ejaculatory tendencies of the men involved. Both units were fully cooperative but the techniques simply did not work. One of these men, 64 years old, was the only failure among 19 men 50 years or older treated for premature ejaculation.

A brief note of clinical warning is in order. After learning to control a premature ejaculatory tendency, 23 of the marital units treated by Foundation personnel were confronted by a brief period of secondary impotence just before or shortly after termination of the acute phase of therapy.

Most marital units, delighted with the significant improvement in sexual functioning, enter a period of marked frequency of coital connection as compared with their sexual exposure rate just before visiting the Foundation. Sometimes the male partner simply cannot meet the suddenly elevated frequency demand and encounters an episode of erective failure. He only has to have one such experience before all his fears of performance flood his consciousness. What new form of dysfunction is this? Has the treatment caused it? His initial anxiety reaction is of serious proportion. The thought that he was sexually satiated for the moment never occurs either to the concerned husband or his sexually enthusiastic wife. Care must be taken by authority to warn couples of the possibility of a transitory experience with impotence, as they are adjusting their overwhelming pleasure with their newfound sexual function to the practicality of the male's level of sexual responsivity. With prior warning the marital units take an episode of impotence in stride, even laughing at the concrete evidence of their sexual greediness. Without adequate warning, a persistence of symptoms of secondary impotence is possible, for the fears of performance and spectator roles return to their dominant position before adequate explanation of the distressful event is available.

In brief, the problem of premature ejaculation is uniquely one that can be resolved effectively and permanently. For successful resolution of the problem, a man needs some understanding of the origin of distress, a knowledge of techniques to establish control, and, above all else, a cooperative, involved sexual partner.

4

EJACULATORY
INCOMPETENCE

Ejaculatory incompetence is a specific form of male sexual dysfunction that can be considered either primary or secondary in character. From diagnostic and therapeutic points of view, it is easier and psychophysiologically more accurate to consider this form of sexual inadequacy as a clinical entity entirely separate from the classical concepts of impotence. In the spectrum of male sexual inadequacy, symptoms of ejaculatory incompetence should be assessed clinically as the reverse of premature ejaculation.

A man with ejaculatory incompetence rarely has difficulty in achieving or maintaining an erection quality sufficient for successful coital connection. Clinical evidence of sexual dysfunction arises when the afflicted individual cannot ejaculate during intravaginal containment. Frequently this inability to ejaculate intravaginally occurs with first coital experience and continues unresolved through subsequent coital encounters. Some men contending with the dysfunction of ejaculatory incompetence experience such pressures of sexual performance that they may develop the complication of secondary impotence. If this natural progression in dysfunctional status occurs, the man with ejaculatory incompetence parallels the man with premature ejaculation.

There have been 17 males seen in therapy in the last 11 years with the complaint of ejaculatory incompetence. Fourteen of these men were married and with their wives sought relief from this specific distress. One man had been divorced for 18 months, and another was seen seven months after a year-old marriage had ended in annulment. The remaining man had never married. Twelve of these men, including the two males with divorce or

116

annulment in their backgrounds, had never been able to ejaculate intravaginally during coition with their wives. One of the 12 men had ejaculated intravaginally with another woman outside of marriage, and a second man ejaculated effectively in homosexual encounters. The single man had two engagements and numerous sexual encounters in his background, but had never been able to ejaculate intravaginally.

The remaining four men, all married, had no historical difficulty with coital function before or during marriage (marriages ranging from 6 to 21 years' duration) until a specific episode of psychosocial trauma blocked their ability to ejaculate intravaginally. Thereafter they were unable to maintain ejaculatory effectiveness within the marriage, but one of the four men could and did ejaculate with female partners outside of marriage.

Hence, the possibility arises of considering the dysfunction of ejaculatory incompetence as either primary or secondary in character. Actually, this form of sexual dysfunction has been encountered so infrequently that the clinical entity does not warrant separation into delimiting categories at this time. In view of the relative rarity of this form of ejaculatory incompetence, skeletonized clinical pictures of the 17 men referred for treatment will be presented. Hopefully, clinical identification will become easier with a broader concept of etiological background.

Of the 12 men never able to ejaculate intravaginally with their wives, five were tense, anxious products of severe religious orthodoxy: one of Jewish, one from Catholic, and three with fundamentalist Protestant backgrounds.

The Jewish man was of orthodox belief. One night, at the age of 24 years, totally breaking with traditional behavior for the first and only time in his life, he not only forced physical attention upon, but tried to penetrate a young woman somewhat resistant to his approach. She stopped him with a plea that she was menstruating. He was devastated with this information, left her company as soon as physically possible, and never saw the woman again. As a result of this experience the subsequent two years were spent in psychotherapy.

Four years later, this man married a young woman of similarly restrictive religious and social background. The courtship was severely chaste. In the marriage both husband and wife rigorously adhered to orthodox demands for celibacy within menstrual and postmenstrual time sequences. Every coital experience was potentially traumatic because, even with full erection and long-continued coital connection, the husband was unable to ejaculate intravaginally. His concept of the vagina as an unclean area had been reenforced by his traumatic premarital sexual experience. Such was his level of trauma that during marital coition, whenever the urge to ejaculate arose, the mental imagery of possible vaginal contamination drove him to withdraw immediately. A marriage of eight years had not been consummated when this marital unit was seen in therapy. During the two years before therapy, this man experienced an increasing number of instances of erective failure with coital opportunity as his fears for sexual performance increased.

A 36-year-old man referred to the Foundation was one of six siblings in a family devoted to Catholic religious orthodoxy. Two of his sisters and one brother ultimately committed their lives to religious orders. At the age of 13, he was surprised in masturbation by his dismayed mother, severely punished by his father, and immediately sent to religious authority for consultation. Subsequent to his lengthy discussion with the religious adviser, the semihysterical, terrified boy carried away the concept that to masturbate to ejaculation was indeed an act of personal desecration, totally destructive of any future marital happiness and an open gate to mental illness. He was assured that the worst thing a teenage boy could do was to ejaculate at any time. This youngster never masturbated nor experienced a nocturnal emission again after the shocking experience of being surprised in autostimulation.

Twelve years later with marriage, these fears for and misconceptions of the ejaculatory process were sufficient to deny him such experience. Whenever he was stimulated toward ejaculatory response by active coital connection, prior trauma was sufficient to deny him release. He continued without ejaculatory success for 11 years of marriage. Finally, as evidence of secondary impotence developed, the marital unit was referred for evaluation.

The three men with fundamentalist Protestant backgrounds provided such individual variations that no single etiological factor was found for the ejaculatory incompetence. Arbitrarily, one history has been selected to provide balance to the chapter, but either of the remaining two histories would be as representative.

Both parents of a man, 33 years old when seen in therapy, were of extremely puritanical family backgrounds and of deeply restrictive religious beliefs. Their religious dogma was a mass of "thou-shalt-nots," declared or implied. As little communication as possible with the outside world was the procedure of choice on Sundays. He was an only child. With one exception, the subject of sex was never mentioned in the home. All reading material was censored before it was made available to the boy. Neither mother nor father were ever observed in any stage of undress by their son. Total toilet privacy, including locked-door demand, was practiced, and swimming or athletic events that might terminate in public showers were forbidden due to the possibility of physical exposure to his peers. For the same reasons, he was never allowed to visit a friend's home overnight.

At age 13, the first occasion of nocturnal emission was soon identified by his mother. His father whipped him for this "sin of the flesh," and thereafter his sheets were checked daily to be sure that he did not repeat this offense.

He was not allowed to participate in heterosexual social functions until age 18, and then, returning from the most chaperoned of dating experiences, he was quizzed in minute detail by both mother and father as to the young lady's actions in order to be sure no effort had been made to entice their son into any overt form of sexual expression.

Although there were sufficient family funds, and the young man had very effective grades, college attendance was restricted to a small home-town college so that he could continue to live at home, avoid the debasing influence of dormitory life, and be available for a full day of church-oriented activity on Sundays.

The one exception to the taboo status for all material of sexual connotation, as mentioned, was a diatribe launched by his father when the son was 18 years of age. His father decried any pleasurable return from sexual function as a major sin, explaining that the ejaculate was dirty, equally degrading to both men and women, and that coition should only occur when conception was desired. It also was pointed out that no good woman would dream of having intercourse unless conception specifically was the goal.

Finally, a young woman 27 years old, socially acceptable not only to the now 26-year-old man, but far more important, to the rigid standards of his family, married him after an extremely chaste and thoroughly chaperoned nine-month courtship, during which three brief episodes of handholding were highlighted as the total of their premarital sexual experience.

On their wedding night, when the penis entered the vagina easily, the young man was surprised and shocked because he had been told by friends and by the minister before the ceremony that intercourse was always very painful to the virginal bride. He withdrew immediately and questioned his wife relentlessly as to the possibility of past sexual exposure. Finally, under duress, she admitted intercourse with a young man she was engaged to marry three years before she met her husband. He was gravely distressed to learn not only of the existence of the previous engagement but also that the male in question had actually ejaculated intravaginally when pregnancy obviously had not been desired. How a good woman, represented by his wife, could possibly have permitted such a transgression was inexplicable to him.

The honeymoon was one of mutual anguish. Forgiveness for past sins was repeatedly implored by the wife and finally conceded by the husband approximately two months after marriage. During the emotional bath of the reconciliation scene, the tearful young couple moved together toward the bed. Vaginal penetration again was easily accomplished, but the young husband could not ejaculate intravaginally. Time and time again successful coital connection was established, but ejaculation was impossible. His concern was for prior contamination.

During the following seven years the wife became multiorgasmic during coition, much to her husband's initial concern, for he felt such obvious sexual pleasure on his wife's part might be evidence that her previous sexual exposure had left some scar on her character. Actually, as time passed he began to enjoy her frequent, rather intense, response pattern. However, despite an estimated average of 15 to 30 minutes of intravaginal containment with most coital experiences, there was consistent failure to ejaculate intravaginally.

Noteworthy in the remaining two cases of religious orthodoxy are the few following facts. One of the men handicapped in sexual performance by strict adherence to fundamental Protestantism developed symptoms of erective inadequacy after three years of marriage. The three marriages averaged seven and one-half years' duration before the marital units were seen by authority. Two of these units were referred initially for conceptive inadequacy rather than ejaculatory incompetence.

Three men offered dislike, rejection, or open enmity for their wives as sufficient reason for failure to ejaculate intravaginally. In the first instance, the man married a distant relative whom he found totally objectionable physically. The advantages of the marriage were of monetary and social import. It probably mattered not whom the man married, as his sexual commitment was of homosexual orientation. He was able to function coitally with his wife from an erective point of view, but after penetration he was repulsed rather than stimulated by her demanding pelvic thrusting and delighted in denying to her the ejaculatory experience.

After six years of marriage and continuation of his homosexual commitments, he decided that children should be a part of his marriage's image to the community. But the established pattern of voluntary restraint was so strong that he could not ejaculate for conceptive purposes. After three years of involuntary ejaculatory constriction and a total of nine years of marriage, the unit was seen in treatment. The presenting complaint was not a request for relief of the ejaculatory incompetence nor for treatment of the homosexual commitment, but rather was for the concerns of conceptive inadequacy.

In the second instance, the marriage was of convenience, with no respect, interest, or admiration for the woman involved. Intercourse was initially considered an unpleasant duty by the husband, to be indulged in reluctantly and only when confrontation no longer could be avoided. The husband was so physically repulsed by his wife that, although erections were maintained, he rarely reached sufficient levels of sexual tension to approach ejaculation. On those few occasions when ejaculation seemed imminent, he would arbitrarily terminate coital connection to deny his wife consummation of the marriage. His great pleasure was to pretend he had ejaculated and then to enjoy her frustration when she ultimately discovered that he had not succumbed to her driving demand to consummate her marriage. He was consistently involved with other women outside of marriage with, of course, no ejaculatory difficulty. Despite her full knowledge of the degree of her husband's rejection of her as a person, she still wanted her marriage to survive, and the unit was referred for therapy.

The final unit depicting rejection of the wife as an individual resulted from the marriage of a 28-year-old man and a 25-year-old woman who had been raped as a teenager by 2 Negroes. She had not told him of the episode until their wedding night. Why she chose this particular time to confide in her virginal husband she could not say. He was overwhelmed by the story. He considered her contaminated, and, although there were a few episodes of coition, he could not ejaculate intravaginally. Their six-year marriage, unconsummated by intravaginal ejaculation, ended in divorce. Eighteen months after the legal separation, the husband was referred by his local physician because he could not ejaculate intravaginally with subsequent sexual partners. His rejection of intravaginal ejaculation had carried over to other women. Of interest is the fact that his former wife joined him as a replacement partner (see Chapter 5). This unit is reported in the marital-unit statistics.

There have been two examples of male fear of pregnancy among members of marital units seeking relief from ejaculatory incompetence.

One, a 19-year-old boy, had impregnated a girl of whom he was very fond. A criminal abortion was performed under the most brutal of circumstances and massive infection resulted. The girl was ill for many months, almost losing her life. Ultimately, she would have nothing to do with the man who had caused her pregnancy and who had insisted upon the abortion that nearly cost her life. Since he had insisted upon the abortion rather than accept marriage as a face-saving mechanism, his levels of guilt knew no bounds.

Five years later in another community and with another girl, a marriage was established. When attempting consummation, the husband found himself completely unsuccessful in ejaculating intravaginally and continued to be so for the next three years until seen in therapy. His was an overwhelming fear of causing pregnancy and of the possibly unfortunate complications thereof. Contraceptive practices offered him no real sense of security. His wife's mere suggestion of raising a family was sufficient to produce a severe anxiety attack. Since his wife had no knowledge of the historical onset of her husband's pregnancy phobia, she presumed personal rejection as the primary factor in his ejaculatory incompetence. The marriage was headed for legal separation when husband and wife were seen in therapy.

One man simply did not want children. His wife, although giving verbal support to his rejection of parenthood, would not practice contraception for religious reasons nor allow her husband to take contraceptive precautions. Consequently, he voluntarily refused himself the pleasure of intravaginal ejaculation in the early years of the marriage. In due course he found no difficulty with control and eventually could not respond with ejaculation to masturbatory practices. Although the marriage existed 11 years before professional aid was sought, and coital connection was generally one to three times a week, this man initially would not and ultimately could not ejaculate intravaginally.

The final example, not one of fear of, but of rejection of pregnancy, has a familiar clinical orientation. Inevitably, there has to be the expected clinical picture of a totally dominant mother essentially choosing a wife for her only son.

The mother had been in full control of the son's every major decision until his marriage. Following his parents' legal separation, the son's father was never in the home. Throughout his teenage years his mother insisted upon total control of his social commitments. She chose his school, his college, and his clothes. She also chose his female companions by the simple expedient of being so abhorrent to those she did not approve that they soon sought other company. Time and again she embarrassed her son by her obvious demand for dominance. He grew to hate his mother but lacked the courage to let her know his level of rejection. Particularly was he careful not to offend her too deeply, for she controlled a considerable amount of money and he was all too aware of the advantages this could bring.

Finally, there was a girl, grudgingly acceptable to his mother, that he could tolerate, so at age 27 he became engaged and in short order married the girl whom he knew only as a quiet companion who never objected to anything he wanted to do. Presumably, her contrast to his mother was her only redeeming grace in his eyes.

His constant fantasy was of revenge upon his mother. Since she had been coyly describing her anticipation of becoming a grandmother, he vowed she would be frustrated in this one area, if no other. There would be no children.

The thought never occurred to him that his wife might be frustrated, feel rejected, or fail to endorse his plan for revenge upon his mother. However, after marrying him she began to express her own requirements. After two and one-half years of increasing levels of mutual antagonism, the marital unit was referred to the Foundation for treatment. Several episodes of erective failure had developed during the last six months of the marriage. The man's severe levels of distraction, created by the ambiguity of his commitments, were obvious. The nonejaculatory pattern was one of first withholding voluntarily and then being unable to ejaculate on demand.

One man was single at the time of therapy, although he had been previously married for approximately one year. His marriage was annulled. His basic distress was simply that of fear of performance. Strangely, the performance fears did not arise from failed experience (he was a 29-year-old virgin at marriage), nor were religious, family, or homosexual influences of particular moment. He had been particularly insecure and introverted as a teenager. Dating was not attempted until 19 years of age and was rarely enjoyed thereafter. Social interchange was a rarity with either male or female companions. His postgraduate degree was in Library Science, and in his obvious withdrawal from social reality books were his companions.

He met and married a 33-year-old woman with an almost identical background of withdrawal from social participation. The gavotte-like courtship consumed three years and confined sexual expression to kissing and handholding. Although widely read on the subject of sexual functioning, the man had only attempted masturbatory release a half-dozen times in his life and had failed to ejaculate on two of these occasions. His guilt feelings about masturbation in general, and his grave concern with the two failed masturbatory performances in particular, tended to reduce any interest in overt sexual functioning. Since he had a fairly regular pattern of pleasurable experience with nocturnal emission, his comparison of these two experiences led him to believe that he was inadequate in ejaculatory function when under the stress of conscious sexual stimulation.

The wedding night and a subsequent year of repetitive attempts at coital functioning proved him right in his assumption—that he could not ejaculate with penile containment and under the stress of overt sexual stimulation. His wife took the fact of his ejaculatory incompetence to reflect personal rejection of her as a woman and, after a year of marriage, sought and was granted an annulment. His last attempts at sexual performance before the annulment were reported as partial or complete erective failures.

Seven months after termination of the marriage the man was referred for treatment. He was treated successfully with the aid of a partner surrogate (see Chapter 5). (The specifics of treatment approach are similar to those of all other incompetent ejaculators and are considered later in this chapter.)

A single male, age 31, was seen in therapy with a history of ejaculatory incompetence dating from age 18; he was surprised by the police in a local "lovers' lane" parking area while being manipulated to ejaculation by a young woman. The girl's terror and his overwhelming embarrassment and fear of public exposure left an indelible residual. Although actual exposure did not occur, he was unable to ejaculate intravaginally through two subsequent engagements and numerous other coital opportunities. He had no homosexual history. Since he had been on the verge of ejaculating when surprised, he thereafter was always frozen by fear of observation when a similar level of excitation developed.

When seen on referral to the Foundation, he was voluntarily accompanied by a young woman to whom he was married a few days after termination of the acute phase of therapy. Since this is a unique situation, this couple has been listed in the general statistics as married rather than considered as a man with a replacement partner. They had planned to be married as soon as therapy proved successful and the possibility for future pregnancy was established.

Four of the 17 men referred for ejaculatory incompetence could and did ejaculate intravaginally both before and during marriage until a specifically traumatic event, psychosocial in origin, terminated their facility for or interest in intravaginal ejaculation.

In the first instance, after six years of marriage the husband unexpectedly encountered his wife committing adultery. Her partner had just ejaculated and was withdrawing as the husband entered the bedroom. The traumatic picture of observing seminal fluid escaping his wife's vagina was his first fixed observation of activity in the bedroom. Forgiveness was begged and in time conceded. But when marital-unit coition was attempted, the mental imagery of seminal fluid escaping the vagina was sufficient to depress the husband's ejaculatory interest. He could not live with the concept of his seminal fluid mingling even symbolically with her lover's ejaculate.

In the second instance, husband and wife were surprised in the primal scene by their two children, ages six and eight, bursting into the bedroom. They were in active coital connection without clothes or the protection of bedding. The husband, just in the act of ejaculating, could not stop. The children's observation of the continuing coital connection was infinitely more disturbing to him than to his wife. He was devastated by the interruption. For the next nine years, whenever ejaculation was imminent, no matter how well-locked the door, the fears of interruption and observation were such that this man could not ejaculate intravaginally.

In the third instance, after 12 years of marriage and two children the wife insisted upon having a third child, which the husband neither wanted, nor personally felt was indicated for psychosocial and financial reasons. For nine months he controlled his ejaculatory urge whenever his wife, following her menstrual calendar, insisted upon coital connection. Finally, agreeing to his terms for continuance of effective sexual function in the marriage, his wife instituted contraceptive protection to avoid pregnancy. However, ejaculatory incompetence had been established, and the husband continued incapable of intravaginal ejaculation during the subsequent four-and-a-half-year period before seeking consultation.

Finally, in a marriage of just over 21 years' duration, the husband had established a strong attachment to another woman and was having regular intercourse outside of marriage. His mistress made him aware that she had suffered through a previous illegitimate pregnancy and constantly expressed serious concern for any risk of conception; so he accepted the responsibility for contraception and chose to use condoms routinely. On one occasion the condom ruptured just as he was ejaculating. The young woman's initial screams of protest when she became aware of his transgression and the hysterical evidence of the severe levels of her pregnancy phobia were major blows. They never met again. His traumatic reaction to her total rejection of him personally was of such magnitude that he was no longer able to ejaculate intravaginally with his wife. The memory of his failed commitment to contraceptive protection was so vivid and his sense of loss so painful that whenever ejaculation was imminent he would stop thrusting or withdraw. His wife had no concept of the cause for the major reversal in his established pattern of sexual behavior and took his state of voluntary ejaculatory incompetence as evidence of personal rejection. After four years of mutual misunderstanding they sought professional support.

There is a multiplicity of factors that can force development of ejaculatory incompetence. In addition to the primary influence of religious orthodoxy, male fear of pregnancy, or lack of interest in or physical orientation to the particular woman are major etiological factors. The usually underlined etiological factors of unopposed maternal dominance or homosexual orientation were present but quite in the minority in this small series.

Frequently, one particular event, one specifically traumatic episode, has been quite sufficient to terminate the individual male's ability to, facility for, interest in, or demand for ejaculating intravaginally. Occasionally a man may lose ejaculatory facility subsequent to a physically traumatic episode, but usually the only trauma is psychological.

Thus, ejaculatory incompetence, the clinical opposite of premature ejaculation, is indeed a specific dysfunctional concern separate from impotence. Since current conceptualization of this sexual dysfunction varies considerably from prior approaches, the clinical entity has been documented exhaustively.

A sidelight to the clinical picture of ejaculatory incompetence is the level of orgasmic response of the female partner. In some instances, grossly misinterpreting the causal factors in their husband's sexual dysfunction, wives have felt personally rejected when husbands could not or would not ejaculate; yet most of these women, despite a real concept of personal rejection, have known many occasions of multiorgasmic response during their marriages. Even those wives rejected by their husbands as physically unappealing occasionally were multiorgasmic during their coital opportunities.

Two of the four wives whose husbands had no problem in regularity of ejaculatory response during marriage prior to the specifically traumatic episode that turned them into incompetent ejaculators were multiorgasmic before the destructive experience. All four wives were multiorgasmic after onset of their husband's pattern of ejaculatory incompetence.

The major exception to the pattern of full female response in marital units contending with ejaculatory incompetence developed, as would be expected, in the five marital units with religious orthodoxy as a background. Only two of the five wives reported occasional orgasmic return during coition, regardless of frequency or duration of coital exposure, and neither of these women described multiorgasmic experience.

Seven marital units with the psychosocial complaint of ejaculatory incompetence initially were referred to the conceptive-inadequacy section of the Foundation in the past 22 years. Four of the seven units have conceived by artificial-insemination procedures, using the husband's seminal fluid produced by masturbatory techniques. They were not treated for the clinical symptoms of ejaculatory incompetence. Three of the seven units have conceived during routine coital exposure after therapy for their sexual dysfunction.

As previously stated, the incompetent ejaculator presents clinical symptoms that are on exactly the opposite end of the ejaculatory continuum from those of the premature ejaculator (see Chapter 3). The premature ejaculator usually has no difficulty in achieving erection during the initial years of his distress. His concern has to do with maintaining the erection before, during, and for a significant period after the mounting process. He may become so excited sexually during precoital sex play that he may ejaculate before any attempt is made to insert the penis into the vaginal barrel; or the stimulation inherent in the actual act of penetration may suffice to cause ejaculation. If the premature ejaculator should survive these two precipices in sexual adventure, usually the ultimate in stimulative activity for any male, the onset of female pelvic thrusting will stimulate an ejaculatory response in but a few seconds.

The premature ejaculator never encounters difficulty with the actual ejaculatory process. His area of concern is in controlling this process for a sufficient length of time to allow his female partner opportunity for orgasmic expression.

The only physiological parallel between the incompetent ejaculator and the premature ejaculator is that neither has any difficulty in achieving an erection. As opposed to the premature ejaculator, the incompetent ejaculator can maintain an erection indefinitely during coital sex play, with mounting, and not infrequently for a continuum of 30 to 60 minutes of intravaginal penile containment. The incompetent ejaculator's only sexual difficulty arises from the fact that he cannot or will not ejaculate during periods of intravaginal containment.

The two variants of ejaculatory dysfunction each demonstrate one correlation with the classic concepts of impotence, but their causations are diametrically opposed. The premature ejaculator frequently loses his erection during or immediately after penetration, as does the impotent male. However, the premature ejaculator's loss of erection usually is on a physiological basis (postejaculation), while the impotent male's erective loss is primarily psychogenic in character. The incompetent ejaculator's inability to ejaculate intravaginally is usually on a psychogenic basis. The impotent male does not ejaculate intravaginally on a physiological basis; he usually cannot physically accomplish intravaginal ejaculation when he has no erection.

Thus, on the opposite ends of the spectrum of male sexual dysfunction there is the volatile male, the premature ejaculator, and the nonreactive individual, the incompetent ejaculator. Neither of these entities should be confused with the basic concerns of primary or secondary impotence either from theoretical or practical points of view, or when dealing with the restrictive clinical approaches to diagnosis and treatment.

TREATMENT OF THE INCOMPETENT EJACULATOR

Treatment of ejaculatory incompetence follows the basic approach described for treatment of premature ejaculation (see Chapter 3). Once marital-unit interest in sensate focus has been secured, the next step is direct approach to penile stimulation. Instead of using the squeeze technique to avoid ejaculatory response as with the premature ejaculator, the female partner is encouraged to manipulate the penis demandingly, specifically asking for verbal or physical direction in stimulative techniques that may be particularly appealing to the individual male. Care should be taken to employ the moisturizing lotions described in Chapter 2 to avoid penile irritation.

The first step in therapy for the incompetent ejaculator is for his wife to force ejaculation manually. It may take several days to accomplish this purpose. The important concept to project to both unit members is that there is no rush. The mere act of ejaculation accomplished with the aid of the female partner is a long step in the right direction. Once he has ejaculated in response to any form of stimulation acceptable to her, the male no longer will tend to withdraw psychologically from her ministrations. When she has brought him pleasure, he identifies with her (not infrequently, for the first time in the marriage) as a pleasure symbol rather than as a threat or as an objectionable, perhaps contaminated, sexual image.

Three of the 17 men had never been able to masturbate to ejaculation before entering therapy. For the remainder, masturbation had been the major form of sexual tension release, but the men had infrequently included their wives as contributors to their release mechanisms (4 of 17). By denying their wives the privilege of participating in the ejaculatory experience, even if occasioned manually, they further froze the possibility of a successful sexual relationship.

As might be expected, some of the wives had no real interest in relieving their husbands through means other than successful coital connection. Although only three men constrained their ejaculatory processes to frustrate their wives, many more were accused of this motivation by their partners. Since ejaculatory incompetence is a relatively rare clinical entity, few members of the general public have heard of it. When wives did not understand that their husbands were involved in a form of sexual inadequacy, as evidenced by their ejaculatory incompetence, they were reluctant to participate in any sexual approach designed, in their minds, only as a means for male relief.

The tremendous advantage of dealing with both members of the marital unit in approaching the concerns of sexual dysfunction has no better example than in treating ejaculatory incompetence. If one dealt only with the husband, and the wife received her information second-hand, if at all, her rebellion would continue in a large percentage of cases. For the husband to suggest specific manipulative techniques at the direction of his therapist does not carry the weight of authority or enlist the degree of wifely cooperation that an adequate explanation can elicit when given to both members of the marital unit as equal participants in the therapeutic program. Inevitably, since education is always the procedure of choice, the marital unit must be dealt with directly. When these techniques of direct confrontation are employed, the wife's cooperation improves immeasurably.

Once the wife has been made fully aware of techniques that simultaneously tease and stimulate her husband, great variation is available in measures to relieve the problem of ejaculatory incompetence. As a first step, the husband should be encouraged to approach his wife sexually in order to provide her with release from sexual tensions accrued during the stimulative sessions she has conducted for her husband. The basic "give-to-get" principles described in Chapter 1 on therapy concepts stringently apply to the concerns of the incompetent ejaculator. He must feel not only the stimulation of his wife's sexual approach, but, in addition, he must be stimulated sexually by her obvious pleasure responses to his direct sexual approaches. Every possible advantage should be taken of this multiplicity of sexually stimulative physiological and psychological influences in order to achieve regularity of ejaculation for males faced with ejaculatory incompetence.

After establishing competence in ejaculatory function with masturbatory techniques, the next step toward intravaginal ejaculatory response is in order. Male partners are stimulated to a high degree of sexual excitation by their wives' direct physical manipulation of the penis. As the male closely approaches the first stage of orgasmic return (the stage of ejaculatory inevitability), rapid intromission of the penis should be accomplished by the wife in the female-superior position (see Chapter 3). She should continue penile stimulation during the attempted intromission.

Once the coital connection is established, a demanding style of female pelvic thrusting against the captive penis should be instituted immediately. Usually this teasing technique is sufficient to accomplish ejaculation shortly after intromission. If the male does not ejaculate shortly after intromission under the designated circumstances, pelvic thrusting should cease. The wife should terminate the coital connection and return to the demanding manual stimulation. As the husband, now conditioned to masturbatory response, reaches the stage of ejaculatory inevitability, he should notify his wife. She should remain in the female-superior position while demandingly manipulating the penis, and from this positional advantage quickly reinsert the penis into the vagina at her husband's direction. It matters not if she is a little too late in her intromission efforts. If the stage of inevitability has been reached and some of the ejaculate escapes during the intromissive process the first few times the technique is employed, there is no cause for concern. Even if but a few drops of ejaculate are accepted intravaginally, the mental block against intravaginal ejaculation will suffer some cracks. Every partial success at intravaginal ejaculation should be underscored in a positive fashion, and the obvious therapeutic progress should be emphasized in all discussions with the distressed marital unit. In short order most of the ejaculate will be delivered within the vagina and the husband's mental block neutralized or removed.

With the first intravaginal ejaculatory episode, the marriage has been consummated. This is a moment of rare reward for the wife of any man suffering from ejaculatory incompetence. Some wives referred to the Foundation have waited more than ten years to consummate their marriages. Their levels of psychosexual frustration during these barren years are beyond comprehension, despite their relative facility at multiorgasmic release of sexual tensions during their coital patterning.

Whether or not the wife is particularly stimulated sexually at this stage of the therapeutic program is of little or no importance. She has had her moments in the past of pure tension release, and she has much to gain if her husband's ejaculatory block can be obviated. The important fact is that the unit, with full communication, works well together. With proper application of effective stimulative techniques, the incompetent ejaculator usually has been enabled to consummate his marriage.

After three or four such episodes of rapid intravaginal penetration as the male is ejaculating, confidence in intravaginal ejaculatory performance will have been established. Then every effort is made to increase female partner involvement by including a period of voluntarily lowered levels of male sexual excitation before coital connection is initiated. In this way, a lengthened period of intravaginal penile containment is encouraged, for it has a specific purpose. The male's fears of continuing as an incompetent ejaculator have been dimmed or negated, both in view of his recent intravaginal ejaculatory success and the fact that he is controlling his ejaculatory response voluntarily to accommodate and not frustrate his wife. Needless to say, her fears for his facility of sexual performance disappear even more rapidly than do his performance concerns after the initial episode of intravaginal ejaculation.

The male usually experiences high levels of sexual excitation in the therapeutic sequence as opposed to feeling very little sexual interest during prior experience with involuntary ejaculatory incompetence. Taking advantage of his pleasure in these subjective changes and acceptance of the therapeutic program as devoted to his psychosexual security, every professional effort should be directed toward reconstitution of the marriage on a healthy, communicative basis.

Weaponry necessary to reinstitute the destroyed channels of communication within the marriage is described, and its usage is supported by direct exchange between cotherapists and patients at every session. The most effective communication of all, a functional marriage bed, has been made immediately available and the security of intravaginal ejaculatory response has been established for both partners. The fact of an ongoing consummated marriage in itself immeasurably facilitates marital communication.

Five men diagnosed as incompetent ejaculators developed symptoms of secondary impotence as their ejaculatory dysfunction continued without symptomatic relief over an average period of eight years. Three of the five men were handicapped by the psychosocial dominance of severe religious orthodoxy. Symptoms of erective incompetence also developed for the man refusing ejaculatory experience to his wife in order to prevent the possibility of pregnancy and accomplish revenge against a dominant mother. The man whose marriage had been annulled because he was afraid to bring himself to ejaculate intravaginally, was the fifth male with symptoms of impotence developing as an involuntary component to longstanding ejaculatory incompetence.

Inevitably, when impotence develops as a complication of either premature ejaculation or ejaculatory incompetence, the concerns of the impotent state must be treated before those of the ejaculatory dysfunction. When therapy for the impotent state is successful and erective adequacy is secured, the individual male again returns clinically to his prior status as premature ejaculator or incompetent ejaculator. These symptoms of sexual dysfunction must be treated in their turn, but always secondary to the primary attack on the state of impotence.

In all five instances, the symptoms of impotence developing secondary to those of an incompetent ejaculator were relieved with application of standard therapeutic techniques (see Chapter 7). Again, it is interesting to note the parallel between premature ejaculation and ejaculatory incompetence when existent for long periods of time. When a man's sexual competence is questioned over an extended period by a woman demanding sexual satisfaction, symptoms of ejaculatory dysfunction may retrogress toward impotence under the pressure of fears of performance.

RESULTS OF TREATMENT

There were three episodes of failure to reverse the symptoms of ejaculatory incompetence among the 17 cases referred to the Foundation. This is a failure rate of 17.6 percent, which certainly should be improved with more experience in dealing with this relatively rare syndrome.

The first failure was that of the orthodox Jewish male overwhelmingly traumatized in his premarital years by his one fall from grace during which he sexually approached a menstruating woman. The symptoms of secondary impotence that had developed after years of ejaculatory incompetence were relieved during therapy and have since continued under control, but he has not been able to ejaculate intravaginally. His haunting fear of vaginal-menstrual contamination and his reflex response of ejaculatory rejection could not be neutralized.

The second marital unit to fail to reverse the symptoms of ejaculatory incompetence was that of the husband surprising his wife in the physical act of adultery. Subsequently, whenever attempting to ejaculate intravaginally, he was faced with the vivid but castrating mental picture of the lover's seminal fluid escaping his wife's vagina. Therapeutic effort could not reduce the rigidity of this man's concept of the intravaginal ejaculatory process as a personally demeaning event. To ejaculate intravaginally during coition with his wife carried with it an implication that he was voluntarily mixing his seminal fluid with that of his wife's lover. He could not, or would not, forgive and forget.

The final clinical failure to reverse the symptoms of ejaculatory incompetence involved the man with no personal regard for, no interest in, and no feeling for his wife. His refusal to ejaculate intravaginally was a direct decision to deprive her of the pleasure of consummating the marriage. This man historically had numerous successful sexual encounters outside marriage. This unit had escaped the culling protection of the screening process described in Chapter 1. They should not have been seen in therapy, as there really was no specific ejaculatory dysfunction. This was only a case of a man's complete rejection of the woman he married. Once the depth of the husband's personal rejection of his wife was recognized, the unit was discharged from therapy. Divorce was recommended to the wife, but her immediate reaction was to hold on to her concept of a marriage.

Of interest is the fact that of the 17 men with ejaculatory incompetence, there were only 3 cases in which steps toward legal separation were taken, and in one of these 3 cases therapy reunited the marital partners. One of the men had been divorced for a period of eighteen months before both former husband and wife agreed to be seen as a unit in therapy. His wife remarried him shortly after termination of a successful therapeutic experience. This marital unit currently has two children.

The man with a year-old marriage plagued by the symptoms of ejaculatory incompetence leading to an annulment was treated with the aid of a partner surrogate (see Chapter 5). This man ultimately married another woman, and for the past three years has conducted himself as a sexually functional male in a successful marriage.

Four of the five men with religious orthodoxy as an etiological handicap acquired intravaginal ejaculatory function. Follow-up records report pregnancies for three of these five marital units. There was no increase in the levels of sexual responsivity of the three nonorgasmic wives in this group.

Two of the three units with male rejection of his female partner as the primary factor in the development of ejaculatory incompetence were reversed in therapy. Of interest in this group is the marital unit with the homosexually oriented husband. Once intravaginal ejaculation was accomplished, the husband continued to function effectively in this manner with his wife while also maintaining his own homosexual commitment with her full knowledge and consent. There have been two children born of this marriage.

Three of the four men developing ejaculatory incompetence after years of successful sexual functioning in marriage were returned to effective ejaculatory performance during therapy. These marriages have continued in a successful vein after terminaton of the acute phase of the therapy. One pregnancy has ensued.

It is obvious that the incompetent ejaculator can be treated effectively if both husband and wife wish reversal of this clinical dysfunction. This clinical syndrome of ejaculatory incompetence will be explored in depth in years to come as more material becomes available. Previously, ejaculatory incompetence has been considered a variant of erective inadequacy. Now there is sufficient knowledge to categorize the syndrome as the direct counterpart of premature ejaculation. Neither of these forms of ejaculatory dysfunction should be considered an integral part of the clinical picture of impotence because neither is necessarily associated with erective incompetence.

5

PRIMARY IMPOTENCE

For clinical purposes the primarily impotent man *arbitrarily* has been defined as a male never able to achieve and/or maintain an erection quality sufficient to accomplish successful coital connection. If erection is established and then lost under the influence of real or imagined distractions relating to coital opportunity, the erection usually is dissipated without accompanying ejaculatory response. No man is considered primarily impotent if he has been successful in any attempt at intromission in either heterosexual or homosexual opportunity.

During the 11 years of the investigative program in sexual inadequacy 32 primarily impotent males have been accepted for treatment. Of these, 21 were unmarried when seen in therapy; 4 of the 21 men have histories of prior marriage contracts with either an annulment or a divorce legally attesting to their failures in sexual performance. The remaining 11 primarily impotent men were married when referred to the Foundation with their wives in the hope of consummating their marriages. These unconsummated marriages have ranged from 7 months' to 18 years' duration.

Negation of the young male's potential for effective sexual functioning has been thought to originate almost entirely in derogatory influences of family background. Without denying the importance of familial investment, the natural social associations of the adolescent as he ventures from his security base are also statistically of major importance. The etiological factors that are in large measure responsible for individually intolerable levels of anxiety either prior to or during initial attempts at sexual connection are untoward maternal influences, psychosocial restrictions originating with religious orthodoxy, involvement in homosexual functioning, and personal devaluation from prostitute experience.

137

It always must be borne in mind that multiple etiological factors usually are influencing the primarily impotent male. Categorical assignment of a dominant etiological role is purely an arbitrary professional decision. Others might differ significantly were they to review the same material. Case histories have been kept at a didactic level for illustrative purposes.

Usually it is impossible to delineate, without reservation, untoward maternal influence as a primary etiological factor in primary impotence. However, there have been three specific instances of overt mother-son sexual encounters in the histories of the 32 primarily impotent males. In all three instances the father was either permanently removed from or rarely encountered in the home. In two of the three instances the young male was the only child in the home and in the third, he was the youngest of three children by 11 years.

In all three instances the young man slept in the mother's bedroom routinely before, during, and after puberty. Two slept in their mothers' beds until they were well into their teenage years. Attempted incestuous coition has not been reported in this series of primarily impotent men but there is a positive history from one of the three males of awakening on several occasions to maternally manipulated ejaculatory experiences during the early teenage years. The second man, though reporting no instance of overt sexual advance from his mother, described his mother's sleeping nude with him.

In the third instance the mother insisted upon washing the boy's genitals when he was bathing. The practice, apparently continued from the diaper stage, was established so early that the man cannot remember otherwise. Maternal demands for adherence to such a behavioral pattern continued into the teenage years with occasions of violent scrubbing until ejaculatory episodes interposed in the bath. The maternal reactions varied initially from presumed anger and administration of physical punishment to specifically conducted manipulative episodes when the young man was in his midteens. There was obvious maternal pleasure in her son's ejaculatory response to her manipulation. Ultimately she assured her son that "no other girl will be able to please you as Mother can."

There are six histories among the 32 primarily impotent men

relating the tribulations of virginal men restricted from any form of overt sexual activity during the teenage courting years by family adherence to demanding forms of religious orthodoxy. The six men grew up in households (two Jewish and four Catholic) where strict religious orthodoxy was a way of life. These men, struggling with the repressive weight of an incredible number of behavioral "thou-shalt-nots," were supported by a negligible number of "thou-shalts." They uniformly approached their wedding nights tragically handicapped by misinformation, misconception, and unresolved sexual taboos.

To prejudice further any opportunity for developing an immediately successful sexual relationship, the new wife in five of the six marriages was equally physically and mentally virginal, as would be expected of a product of similarly strict religious orthodoxy. The wives' inadequacies of sexual knowledge, their misconceptions and their inevitable postmarital psychosocial adherence to premarital theological sexual taboos only contributed additional performance tensions to those placed by our culture upon the anxious, frightened, virginal males during their first attempts to consummate their marriages.

When premarital sexual expression has been restricted to hand-holding, the first fumbling, bumbling, theologically and legally acceptable attempts at sexual connection are often unsuccessful. This psychosocial diversion of the natural biophysical process may evolve into the disastrous combination of a severely shredded male ego further traumatized by the unreasonable, but so understandable, female partner's virginally blind insistence that he *do something.*" This semihysterical supplication first whispered, then suggested, eventually demanded, and finally, screamed, *"Do something,"* renders the equally virginal and equally traumatized male incapable not only of effective sexual function but also of situational comprehension. His wife's emotional importuning creates such a concept of frustration, failure, and loss of masculine stature that the marital unit's frequently repeated, obviously frantic attempts at sexual connection usually are doomed to failure.

Severe religious orthodoxy may indoctrinate the teenager with the concept that any form of overt sexual activity prior to marriage not only is totally unacceptable but is personally destructive, demoralizing, degrading, dehumanizing, and injurious to one's physical and/or mental health. Perhaps even more unfortunate, the psychosocial expectations, if any, for the sexual relationship in marriage are given no honorable factual support. Varying combinations of these precepts have become an integral part of the sexual value systems of the six men for whom religious orthodoxy was defined as a major etiological factor in their primary impotence and have been recited in parrotlike style to the cotherapists during intake interviews. It is fortunate that more virginal males of similar background, failing in their tension-filled initial exposures to the physical verities of marital sexual functioning, do not succumb to the pressures of these frightening initial episodes of failure by developing the relevant symptoms of primary impotence.

Each of the five virginal wives with orthodox religious backgrounds similar to those of their new husbands also had to be treated for vaginismus (see Chapter 9) at the same time their husbands were faced with therapeutic concerns for clinical reversal of their primary impotence. There was no positive concept of effective sexual functioning or confidence in sexual performance expressed by any of the 10 individuals involved in these traumatized marriages.

One of the wives did not have a background of religious orthodoxy parallelling that of her husband, although she was of similar faith. Reflecting more freedom of sexual expression, which included four instances of coital experience with an earlier fiancé, she accepted her future husband's orthodox religious concepts during their engagement period. At marriage she was as psychologically virginal as any of the other five wives. Although she could have helped immeasurably during her husband's first fumbling attempts at coital connection, she dared not suggest alternatives to his unbelievably untutored sexual approaches for fear she would evidence a suspicious degree of sexual knowledge. She thought that she had to protect his concept of her physically virginal state at all costs. In this case the cost was high. It amounted to 11 years of unconsummated marriage.

Commitment to an overt pattern of homosexual response in the early to middle teenage years also emerged as a major etiological factor in failed coital connection during initial and all subsequent heterosexual exposures for another 6 of the 32 primarily impotent men seen in therapy. For four of these men, homosexual relationships were established in the 13–16-year age bracket and were specifically meaningful to the involved teenagers. One relationship was with a peer and three others with older men (early twenties to midthirties). The fifth in this group of six primarily impotent men voluntarily established a semipermanent association at age 20 with a man in his early thirties. These five histories reflected homosexual relationships ranging in duration from nine months to more than three years. Although all relationships were discontinued before there was serious thought of establishing permanent heterosexual alliances, it is of interest that they were terminated by the partners of the young men. When initially seen in therapy all five of these heterosexually dysfunctional men considered themselves basically homophile in orientation and felt that a lifetime commitment had been made through their initial indoctrination into homosexual functioning.

None of these five men provided a history of attempted rectal intromission, although three of the five had submitted to rectal penetration. Since there was no mounting attempt on their part, the clinical diagnosis of primary impotence has not been challenged. Had they been successful in anal intromission, they would not have been classified as primarily impotent.

The remaining instance of homosexual identification as a plausible etiological agent in primary impotence was that of a virginal man of 21 years referred to psychotherapy for nervous tension, intermittent periods of depression, and compulsive lack of effective academic progress. The therapist convinced the young man that his unresolved tensions were derived from the natural frustrations of a latent homosexual and introduced him to the physical aspects of mouth-genital functioning in a patient-therapist relationship. This homosexual relationship lasted for 18 months, only to be terminated abruptly when the patient's family no longer could afford the cost of the twice-weekly sessions. Anal intromission was not attempted.

In three of these six instances of homophile identification, the totally dominant mother was in full control of family decisions— social, behavioral, and financial. The father was living in the home but was allowed no other role except provider. The remaining three young men described a relatively well-balanced family life.

The religious aspects of the six backgrounds ranged from atheism to family demand for regularity of church attendance. There was no strict orthodoxy.

Two of these six young men had married but neither was successful in consummating the union; nor had psychotherapeutic procedures, instituted some months after failed consummation, provided the men with confidence to think and feel sexually in their newly established heterosexual relationship. One marriage was dissolved legally; the other was ongoing at therapy. When first seen, each of these six men stated unequivocally their basic interest in and desire for facility of heterosexual functioning. In only two instances, however, was there also the collaterally expressed desire to withdraw permanently from any form of homosexual functioning.

There are four recorded histories (from the series of 32 primarily impotent males) of men with basically stable family, religious, and personal backgrounds whose initial failure at coital connection was specifically associated with a traumatic experience developing from prostitute involvement with their first experience at coition. Three of these virginal young men (two late teenage and one 22-year-old) each sought prostitute opportunity in the most debilitated sections of cities in which they were living and were so repulsed by their neophyte observations of the squalor of the prostitute's quarters, the dehumanizing quality of her approach, and the physically unappetizing, essentially repulsive quality of the woman involved that they could not achieve or maintain an erection. The fact that their own poor judgment had rendered them vulnerable to a level of social environment to which they were unaccustomed and for which they were unprepared never occurred to them. In two of these instances their frantic attempts to establish an erection amused the prostitutes and their obvious fears of performance were derided. The third young man was assured that "he would never be able to get the job done for any woman—if he couldn't get it done here and now with a pro."

In the fourth instance initial sexual attempt, also prostitute-oriented, took place during a multiple coital episode in which the same woman was being shared. The young man (age 19) was the last member of the group of five friends scheduled to perform sexually with the same prostitute. With no previous coital experience, his natural anxieties were markedly enhanced and quickly compounded into fears of performance by the enforced waiting period while his predecessors in line returned to describe in lurid detail their successes in the bedroom. Overwhelmed by the rapidly multiplying pressures inherent in these circumstances, the young man predictably had difficulty attaining an erection when his turn finally arrived. There were verbalized demands to hurry by his restless, satiated peers and from the impatient prostitute. Faced with a performance demand measured by a specific time span and a concept of personal inadequacy (he carried the usual virgin male's concern for comparative penile size into the bedroom), the young man was pressured beyond any ability to perform and unable to regard the pressured circumstances with objectivity. Inevitably, this initial failure at sexual functioning resulted in markedly magnified fears of performance. Subsequent attempts at coital connection both with members of the prostitute population and within his own social stratum also proved unsuccessful.

Not all instances of failed attempts at initial coital connection have an established etiological patterning that possibly predisposes to failure. In the histories of primarily impotent men seen in therapy, there is a wide variety of other factors associated with each man's ego-destructive episode of failure at his first coital opportunity. In fact, among the remaining 13 men from the 32 males referred with the complaint of primary impotence, there are (with one exception) no duplicates in the patterns of their initial traumatic sexual episodes.

There is the recorded history of one man whose failed attempt at initial coitus developed while he was partially under the influence of drugs; two men (the exception mentioned above) failed in their first attempts at vaginal penetration under the influence of excessive alcohol consumption. In none of the 12 individual patterns among these 13 men is there specific evidence to support psychodynamic concepts of the dominant mother and the meek and docile father or the inadequate mother and the supremely dominant father. The one factor the men had in common was restrictive input from an immature or even negatively disposed sexual value system. The psychosocial system certainly exerted overwhelmingly dominant influence on the biophysical component (see Chapter 2).

The interesting observation remains that, although there obviously are instances when primary impotence almost seems preordained by prior environmental influence, there frequently is a psychosexually traumatic episode directly associated with the first coital experience that establishes a negative psychosocial influence pattern or even a life-style of sexual dysfunction for the traumatized man.

The male with a meaningful, well-established homosexual orientation in his teenage years may be expected to experience varying strengths of conditioning against active heterosexual involvement. Similarly, a negative sexual value system can be anticipated from blind adherence to any form of religious orthodoxy. Particularly does orthodox orientation develop as a psychosexual handicap when the wife-to-be has matured in similar religious environment. Aside from prescribed religious orthodoxy, there is little evidence that familial influence, so frequently held the primary suspect in the multiple etiologies of sexual dysfunctions, carries much statistical weight. Certainly in the histories of primarily impotent males there are recorded instances of compulsively neurotic maternal influence, including forms of direct mother-son sexual encounter. But little is known of unopposed maternal dominance or direct mother-son sexual encounter relative to the anticipated percentage of resultant primary impotence.

What is known of the individual psychosocial characteristics of young men who are bent and occasionally broken almost beyond repair by the oppressive conditioning of unopposed maternal dominance, orthodox theological control, or homosexual orientation that another youth in similar circumstances might consider serious, but not of lasting moment? Most men so traumatized in their teens or early twenties survive the stresses of their initial opportunity for heterosexual coition, whether or not successful, and move into a continuum of effective sexual functioning with facility and pleasure. As time passes they at least partially neutralize the negative psychosocial influences that have accrued as a combination of their environmental backgrounds and the trauma of their initial coital failures.

One cannot propose that environmental influence inflicts upon young males such a depth of psychosocial insecurity that statistically they must find themselves inadequate to react to the tension-filled demand of the initial coital occasion. For to make such an assumption would be to negate the influence of their biophysical system. As an auxiliary to the Foundation's basic research concepts of evaluating sexual functioning in our culture, investigators continually record histories of young men sexually traumatized beyond any reasonably acceptable measure, indeed well beyond the scope of the acute episodes described in this chapter. These men may have failed to perform successfully during their initial coital exposure and for a considerable period of time thereafter may have continued sexually inadequate. Yet they have recovered from their experiences with sexual dysfunction without specific psychotherapeutic support and, as far as can be ascertained from corroborative histories of husband and wife, have led effectively functional heterosexual lives.

Regardless of the depth of the specific trauma resultant from a prejudicial sexual value system, ultimately it is the interdigital response patterns of the psychosocial and the biophysical systems and the individual characteristics of the men directly involved that predicate sexual survival or failure. Of these characteristics we know so little. It is relatively easy for the cotherapist retrospectively to identify etiological influence in states of sexual dysfunction, but to generalize from such specific retroflection is statistically unsupportable and psychodynamically unacceptable.

In brief, the etiology of primary impotence has a multiplicity of factors. In most of these instances, the unexplained sensitivity of the particular male to psychosocial influence adjudicates the specific failures of the virginal experience with sexual function into subsequently high levels of concern for performance. Most of his peers would not perform inadequately under similarly combined pressures of prior environmental handicapping or the immediacy of sexual trauma. At present it not only is statistically inadequate but also psychotherapeutically inappropriate to attempt definitive correlation of etiological factors for primary impotence. From an investigative point of view, it is infinitely healthier to admit that we really have no concept of the specific psychodynamic factors that render the young man failing in his first coital connection susceptible to continuing failure at sexual performance.

The approaches to reconstitution of male sexual function from secondary impotence are essentially similar to therapeutic considerations of primary impotence. Therefore, the treatment techniques and program statistics for both primary and secondary impotence will be presented in a separate discussion considering the subject from a composite point of view (See Chapter 7).

Since there have been more unmarried men referred for primary impotence than for any of the other three distresses in the continuum of male sexual dysfunction (premature ejaculation, incompetent ejaculation, and secondary impotence), a discussion of use of replacement partners, or partner surrogates, in cooperation with authority will be presented as an integral part of this chapter.

REPLACEMENT PARTNERS AND PARTNER SURROGATES

While developing therapy concepts and procedural patterns at onset of the clinical investigative approach to sexual dysfunction in 1959, there were many severe problems to be faced. One of the most prominent concerns was the demand to develop a psychosocial rationale for therapeutic control of unmarried men and women that might be referred for treatment. During the past 11 years, 54 men and 3 women were unmarried when referred by their local authority with complaints of sexual dysfunction. In a statistical breakdown relative to intake diagnosis, 16 men were premature ejaculators, one was an incompetent ejaculator, 21 were primarily impotent, and 16 were secondarily impotent. The three women were orgasmically dysfunctional, one primarily and two situationally (coital orgasmic inadequacy).

The immediate problem to be faced was the obvious clinical demand for a female partner—a partner to share the patient's concerns for successful treatment, to cooperate in developing physically the suggestions presented during sessions in therapy, and most important, to exemplify for the male various levels of female responsivity. All of these factors are essential, if effective sexual functioning is to be returned to the sexually inadequate man. In brief, someone to hold on to, talk to, work with, learn from, be a part of, and above all else, *give to* and *get from* during the sexually dysfunctional male's two weeks in the acute phase of therapy.

The term *replacement partner* is used to describe the partner of his or her choice brought by a sexually inadequate unmarried man or woman to share the experiences and the education of the clinical therapy program. *Partner surrogate* has been reserved to indicate the partner provided by the cotherapists for an unmarried man referred for treatment who has no one to provide psychological and physiological support during the acute phase of the therapy. The final listing, that of marital partners, includes not only husband and wife units, but also former husbands and wives, divorced or legally separated, who choose to join each other in mutual hope of a reversal of the sexual dysfunction that was a major contributor to the legal dissolution of the marriage. Nine such units legally separated at intake have been seen in therapy in the last 11 years. Statistically, these units have not been treated separately from the legally married units referred for therapy.

Thirteen of the 54 nonmarried men brought replacement partners of choice who were most willing to cooperate with the therapists to enable their sexually dysfunctional men to establish effective sexual performance. The three nonmarried women also brought replacement partners of their choice to participate in therapy. These replacement partners were men with whom they had established relationships of significant duration, as well as the personal warmth and security that develops from free exchange of vulnerability and affection.

Partner surrogates have been made available for 41 men during the last 11 years. This situation has involved basic administrative and procedural decisions. Should the best possible climate for full return of therapeutic effort be created for the incredibly vulnerable unmarried males referred for constitution or reconstitution of sexual functioning; or should there be professional concession to the mores of society, with full knowledge that if a decision to dodge the issue was made, a significant increase in percentage of therapeutic failure must be anticipated? Unmarried impotent men whose dysfunctional status could be reversed to allow assumption of effective roles in society would continue sexually incompetent. From a clinical point of view there really was only one alternative. Either the best possible individual return from therapeutic effort must be guaranteed the patient, or the Foundation must refuse to treat unmarried men or women for the symptoms of sexual inadequacy. Either every effort must be made to meet the professional responsibility of accepting referrals of severely dysfunctional men and women from authority everywhere in or out of the country, or admission to clinical procedure must be denied. It would have been inexcusable to accept referral of unmarried men and women and then give them statistically less than 25 percent chance of reversal of their dysfunctional status by treating them as individuals without partners. This figure has been reached by culling the literature for material published from other centers, since it is against Foundation policy to treat the sexually dysfunctional individual as a single entity. If the concept that therapy of both partners for sexual inadequacy has great advantage over prior clinical limitations to treatment of the sexually dysfunctional individual without support of marital partner, then partners must be available. Statistically there no longer is any question about the advantage of educating and treating men and women together when attacking the clinical concerns of male or female sexual inadequacy. For these reasons the therapeutic technique of replacement partners and partner surrogates will continue as Foundation policy.

It should be emphasized that no thought was ever given to employing the prostitute population. For reasons that will become obvious as the contributions of the replacement-partner and partner-surrogate populations are described, so much more is needed and demanded from a substitute partner than effectiveness of purely physical sexual performance that to use prostitutes would have been at best clinically unsuccessful and at worst psychologically disastrous.

Women volunteered for this assignment of partner surrogate. Over the last 11 years, 13 women have been accepted from a total of 31 volunteers for assignment as partner surrogates. Their ages ranged from 24 to 43 years when they joined the research program. Although all but two of the women had been previously married, none of the volunteers were married when living their role as a partner surrogate.

The levels of formal education for the partner surrogates were high-school graduate (3), additional formal secretarial training (2), college matriculation (2), college graduates (4), and post-graduate degrees in biological and behavioral sciences (2). Nine of the 13 women had a child or children before joining the program. Ten of these women also were committed to full-time employment outside of their role as partner surrogate; one did part-time volunteer work and the remaining two were caring for very young children.

Every effort has been made to screen from this section of the total research population women with whom the cotherapist did not feel totally secure attitudinally or socially, and approximately 60 percent of those women volunteering for roles as partner surrogate were not accepted. Of the 13 women accepted, 6 had previously served as members of the study-subject population during the physiological investigative phase of the research program, and 7 volunteered their services for this specific clinical function.

The reasons expressed for such voluntary cooperation were varied but of real significance. During the screening process, each woman was interrogated in depth while the interviewers were acquiring medical, social, and sexual histories from which to evaluate the individual's potential as a partner surrogate. The investigation was conducted by male and female interrogators both singly and in teams. If interrogation indicated potential as a substitute partner, the three involved individuals (volunteer and interrogators) discussed this concept in detail, examining both the positive and the negative aspects of such a service. No attempt ever was made to persuade any woman to serve as a partner surrogate. Volunteers who showed hesitancy or evidence of personal concern were eliminated from this potential role in the research program.

Of major interest was the fact that 9 of the 13 volunteers were interested in contributing their services on the basis of personal knowledge of sexual dysfunction or sex-oriented distress within their immediate family. Three women previously had contended with sexually inadequate husbands. One man committed suicide, one died in the armed services, and the third, unable to face the psychosocial pressures of his sexual dysfunction, became an alcoholic. This man's loss of security in his male role led to divorce, following which the woman volunteered as a partner surrogate.

In five instances there was positive history of sexually oriented trauma within the immediate family. The traumatic episodes varied from teenage gang rape of a younger sister to failure of a brother's marriage due to his overt homosexual orientation.

Of the remaining four volunteers, three women had more prosaic reasons for essaying the role of a partner surrogate. The expressed needs were unresolved sexual tensions, a need for opportunity of social exchange, and an honest interest in helping dysfunctional men repair their ego strengths as sexually adequate males. Finally, a physician, frankly quite curious about the partner-surrogate role, offered her services to evaluate the potentials (if any) of the role. When convinced of the desperate need for such a partner in the treatment of sexual dysfunction in the unmarried male, she continued as a partner surrogate, contributing both personal and professional experiences to develop the role to a peak of effectiveness.

The therapists are indeed more than indebted to this intelligent woman. Many of her suggestions as to personal approaches and psychosocially supportive techniques are original contributions to therapeutic process. They are solidly incorporated in the total investigative effort directed toward relief of male sexual inadequacy. Her contributions to the treatment program range far beyond substantiating the basic contribution inherent in the role of partner surrogate.

THE ROLE OF PARTNER SURROGATE

The specific function of the partner surrogate is to approximate insofar as possible the role of a supportive, interested, cooperative wife. Her contributions are infinitely more valuable as a means of psychological support than as a measure of physiological initiation, although obviously both roles are vitally necessary if a male's inadequacies of sexual performance are to be reversed successfully. As stated, partner surrogates have had a significant degree of sexual experience before joining the program. They are fully sexually responsive as women, and, as is true with most confidently responsive women, understandingly and compassionately concerned for the frustrations of a sexually inadequate male.

It would have been a tragic mistake to assign to the role of partner surrogate any woman with the slightest question as to her own facility for sexual responsivity, or a woman who could not convey pride and confidence in her own innate femaleness. It is only from a baseline of psychosocial confidence that effective therapeutic support can be projected by sexually secure women.

When a partner surrogate joins the therapy program she is subjected to exhaustive description of male sexual functioning with explanations oriented to both the physiology and psychology of male sexual response. The male fears of performance, his spectator role in sexual inadequacy, the inevitable sense of failure as an individual developed in the bedroom and then applied to daily living, his sense of personal inadequacy as a man—are all discussed in detail. Questions of sexual responsivity based on the woman's experience with adequate male sexual functioning are raised and answers are interpolated into examples of simple variations that develop into sexual dysfunctions. In short, as thorough an indoctrination as possible is always the procedure of choice.

In the orientation of a woman as a potential partner surrogate, specific attention is devoted to techniques that will tend to place the anxious, tension-filled male at ease socially as well as physically. The therapists begin by relying on the specifics of the woman's basic experience with interpersonal relationships as elicited from detailed history-taking during her interviews. Each woman's security in her own role as a human female is a vitally important departure point in the area of social exchange.

When assuming an active role in the clinical therapy of any sexually incompetent man, the partner surrogate is given detailed information of the individual male's psychosexual background and the cause for and specifics of his sexual dysfunction, and is kept thoroughly informed on a day-to-day basis as to the professional team's concept of therapeutic progress. No other identifiable personal details of the involved male other than name are ever provided. Even this is masked if the name is well-known. The patient is cautioned against providing relevant personal information. In the same vein, the partner surrogate never exchanges any personal information that might lead to her identification in the future.

Shortly after the roundtable discussion (see Chapter 2), the first meeting between the patient and his partner surrogate is arranged. The first meeting is always limited to a social commitment. Usually the couple go to dinner and spend a casual evening in order to develop communication and comfort in each other's company. It is at this first meeting that the partner surrogate makes one of her most important contributions. Before any attempt can be made toward reversal of existent sexual dysfunction, the anxious male must first be placed at ease socially. He develops this ease from firsthand knowledge of the partner surrogate through observing her personal appearance, preference in food or drink, manner of dress and of social conduct, and the way she verbally communicates with him. During the evening the man also has an opportunity to define the general level of her formal education. She may discuss at some length such relatively noncontroversial subjects as sports, the arts, current events, but discussions of such explosive subjects as comparative religions or partisan politics are left to the patient.

Every effort is made by cotherapists to match the dysfunctional man and his partner surrogate as to age, personality, and educational and social background. It has been infrequent that a partner surrogate has contributed in this clinical role more than once a year in view of the number of volunteers (13) available for the partnerless men (41), over the 11 years' existence of the research program. Some partner surrogates have not been utilized by the therapy teams with even this frequency. The psychosocial strain involved in making such an immeasurable personal contribution under the difficult circumstances prohibits frequent use of a particular partner surrogate.

Once social exchange has been established, the partner surrogate moves into a wife's role as the treatment phase is expanded. She joins the sexually inadequate male in both social and physical release of the tensions that accrue during the therapy. With the exception of attending the individual therapy sessions, every step that a wife would take as a participant with her husband in the therapeutic program is taken with the dysfunctional nonmarried male by his partner surrogate. The partner surrogate is briefed on a daily basis (as described above) but under separate circumstances so that her identity is never connected with the program.

The use of a partner surrogate (who is far better oriented to problems of male sexual dysfunction than most wives), although lacking the established pattern of communication possibilities and the mutual opportunity at full exchange of vulnerabilities potentially present in any established marriage, has achieved excellent results. Levels of success have been far better than originally anticipated.

One would expect that if the concept of the partner surrogate had real clinical value, the statistics of symptom reversal would have to approach those attained by the marital units referred to the Foundation for relief of sexual dysfunction. In fact, the values in reported reversals of male sexual dysfunctions returned by the admixture of partner surrogates and sexually inadequate males were approximately equal to those achieved by cooperative wives and husbands in marital-unit referrals (see Chapter 14).

The 41 unmarried men that worked with a partner surrogate included 12 premature ejaculators, 1 incompetent ejaculator, and 19 primarily impotent, and 9 secondarily impotent men. It should be emphasized that 8 of the 12 premature ejaculators, 7 of the 9 secondarily impotent, and 4 of the 19 primarily impotent men had previously been married. Three of these men had been married twice previously. In all cases the marriage had been terminated, reportedly due to the marital-unit distress occasioned by the basic sexual inadequacy. Each of these formerly married men had been previously exposed to psychotherapy to relieve their dysfunctional symptoms without success.

With direct support of the partner surrogate all 12 of the premature ejaculators and the 1 incompetent ejaculator were relieved of their dysfunctional symptoms. There were 7 failures to establish effective coital function among the 19 primarily impotent unmarried men treated with the support of partner surrogates. There were 2 failures to reverse symptoms among the 9 instances of secondarily impotent unmarried men.

Thus of the 41 unmarried men referred to the Foundation by

a source acceptable to the Foundation (see Chapter 1) for treatment of sexual dysfunctions, 32 had their symptoms reversed with the support of partner surrogates and 24 of these 32 have subsequently married. All 24 have described an on-going, successful marriage. There has been one reported reversal of sexually functional status (a secondarily impotent man) in the newly contracted 24 marriages.

In view of the statistics there is no question that the decision to provide partner surrogates for sexually incompetent unmarried men has been one of the more effective clinical decisions made during the past eleven years devoted to the development of treatment for sexual inadequacy.

THE ROLE OF THE REPLACEMENT PARTNER

Thirteen women have accompanied unmarried men to the Foundation, agreeing to serve as replacement partners to support these men during treatment for sexual dysfunction. In all instances both individuals were accepted in therapy with full knowledge of the referring authority. Since the women were selected by the men involved, they were accepted as if they were wives. They were interrogated in depth and attended all therapy sessions. They lived with the unmarried males as marital partners, in contrast to the partner surrogate, who spent only specific hours during each day with the sexually dysfunctional male. Details of treatment for the various forms of male sexual dysfunction need not be repeated; clinical situations with replacement partners are managed in the same way as with wives.

Of the 13 men, 4 were premature ejaculators who with the aid of their replacement partners had this particular symptom brought under control. Of the 2 men who were primarily impotent, 1 achieved success in coital function and the other finished the course of therapy without resolving his sexual dysfunction. Of 7 secondarily impotent men who brought replacement partners to therapy, 5 experienced successful reversal of their symptoms during the two-week clinical program.

Three unmarried women referred to the Foundation brought with them replacement partners of their choice. In each instance the current relationship was one of significant duration. The shortest span of mutual commitment was reported as six months. Two of the three women had previously been married. The replacement partners were treated as husbands of sexually inadequate wives. They attended all sessions and went through in-depth history-taking to provide information sufficient to define their roles in providing relief for their distressed women companions.

Two women provided histories of situational orgasmic dysfunction with occasional orgasmic return with manipulative or mouth-genital approaches, but they had never been orgasmic during coition. In one instance coital orgasmic return was accomplished; in the second it was not. In both circumstances the male replacement partners were totally cooperative with therapists and patients. In the third instance, a woman reporting that she had never been orgasmic was indeed fully orgasmic both with manipulative and coital opportunities during the acute phase of the therapeutic program. Again, full cooperation from the replacement partner was both expected and received.

No unmarried woman has been referred for therapy without being accompanied by a replacement partner of her choice, nor has there been any professional concept that a male partner surrogate would be provided if an unmarried woman had been unable to establish a meaningful relationship with a cooperative man before referral to the program. Refusing to make a male partner surrogate available to a sexually inadequate woman, yet providing a female partner surrogate for a dysfunctional man, seems to imply application of a double standard for clinical treatment; such is not the case. As repeatedly described, psychosocial factors encouraged in this method of psychotherapy are developed from the individual's *existing* value system (see Chapters 2 and 8).

A man places primary valuation on his capacity for effective sexual function. This is both valid and realistic. His sexual effectiveness fulfills the requirement of procreation and is honored with society's approval, thereby providing support for the cultural idiosyncrasy of equating sexual function with masculinity. Even prior exposure to a "sex is sin" environment does not preempt this primary valuation. As a result, a man usually regards the contribution made by a partner surrogate as he would a prescription for other physical incapacities. Further, he is able to value a woman who makes such a contribution. For him, the restoration of sexual function justifies putting aside temporarily any other value requirements which might exist.

Woman, on the other hand, does not have a similar sexual heritage. As far as is known, her effectiveness of sexual function is not necessary to procreation. In addition, prevailing attitudes through much of history have not encouraged valuation of female sexuality as a means of human expression. Therefore, partner surrogate selection for the sexually incompetent woman would require quite different psychosocial considerations than would a similar selection for a sexually inadequate man. Socioculturally induced requirements are usually reflected by woman's need for a relatively meaningful relationship which can provide her with "permission" to value her own sexual function. It is the extreme difficulty of meeting this requirement in a brief, two-week period which influenced Foundation policy to deny the incorporation of the male partner surrogate into treatment concepts, yet to accept male replacement partners selected by the unmarried women themselves to join them in the program. In all cases, the length and security of the relationship had been firmly established before the patient was referred. This key area of therapeutic concern was, of course, carefully checked with referring authority before accepting the unmarried woman for treatment.

For the sexually dysfunctional woman, security of an established man-woman relationship, real identification with the male partner, and warmth and expression of mutual emotional responsivity are all of vital concern—first, in securing a positively oriented sexual value system and, second, in promoting effective sexual functioning. These social and sexual securities cannot be established in the brief period of time available during the acute phase of the therapeutic program. For these reasons, the use of a male partner surrogate in the treatment of sexually dysfunctional unmarried women was felt contraindicated.

6

SECONDARY IMPOTENCE

Definition of secondary impotence depends upon acceptance of the concept of primary impotence as expressed and discussed in Chapter 5. Primary impotence arbitrarily has been defined as the inability to achieve and/or maintain an erection quality sufficient to accomplish coital connection. If erection is established and then lost from real or imagined distractions related to the coital opportunity, the erection usually is dissipated without an accompanying ejaculatory response. If diagnosed as primarily impotent, a man not only evidences erective inadequacy during his initial coital encounter but the dysfunction also is present with every subsequent opportunity.

If a man is to be judged secondarily impotent, there must be the clinical landmark of at least one instance of successful intromission, either during the initial coital opportunity or in a later episode. The usual pattern of the secondarily impotent male is success with the initial coital opportunity and continued effective performance with the first fifty, hundred, or even thousand or more coital encounters. Finally, an episode of failure at effective coital connection is recorded.

When the first erective failure occurs, the involved man certainly should not immediately be judged secondarily impotent. Many men have occasional episodes of erective failure, particularly when fatigued or distracted. However, an initial failure at coital connection may become a harbinger, and, as apprehension increases during episodes of erection, a pattern of erective failure subsequently may be established. Finally, erective inadequacy may become a relatively constant companion to opportunities for sexual connection. When an individual male's rate of failure at successful coital connection approaches 25 percent of his opportunities, the clinical diagnosis of secondary impotence must be accepted.

The sexual dysfunction termed *premature ejaculation* (see Chapter 3) has been labeled by various textbooks as a form of sexual impotence. It is difficult to accept this dilution of the clinical picture of both primary and secondary impotence, because the dysfunctions of impotence have in common the specter of male conceptive inadequacy as well as those of erective inadequacy. The physiological and psychological limitations of conceptive inadequacy do not apply to the premature ejaculator, nor, for that matter, is there any difficulty in attaining an erection. There is difficulty, of course, in maintaining an erection for significant lengths of time, but in opposition to the concerns of impotence, when the premature ejaculator loses his erection he does so as part of the male's total orgasmic process. If the impotent male succeeds in attaining erection and then loses it shortly before or shortly after penetration, he usually does so without ejaculating. The premature ejaculator characteristically functions with a high degree of reproductive efficiency and, unfortunately for the female partner, with little waste of time.

Previously, the man with ejaculatory incompetence (see Chapter 4) has not been separated from clinical concepts of impotence, and such separation is indeed long overdue. From a clinical point of view, ejaculatory incompetence is diametrically opposed to premature ejaculation in the kaleidoscope of male sexual dysfunctions. While the male with ejaculatory incompetence parallels the impotent male in reflecting clinical concerns for conceptive inadequacy, such a man could never be accused of the erective inadequacy so frustrating for both primarily and secondarily impotent men. There is essentially no time limitation to maintenance of erection for the man with ejaculatory incompetence. He simply cannot ejaculate intravaginally.

The premature ejaculator arbitrarily is excluded from the categorical diagnosis of impotence, even if on occasion he may not be able to achieve penetration with success. Frequently the sexual stimulation of coital opportunity, or of any form of precoital sex play, will cause him to ejaculate either before he can accomplish vaginal intromission or immediately after coital connection has been established. The clinical difference between the two types of inadequate coital function (premature ejaculation and secondary impotence) lies in the fact that acquiring ejaculatory control is more a matter of physiological than psychological orientation, while reconstituting the ability to attain or maintain an erection quality sufficient for effective coital connection requires psychological rather than physiological reorientation.

The man with incompetent ejaculation arbitrarily is excluded from a categorical diagnosis of impotence, even though both types of inadequate coital function have a multiplicity of etiologies almost entirely psychological rather than physiological in character. Their basic variation is that the incompetent ejaculator functions most effectively from a purely physiological point of view as a coital entity, while the impotent man does not.

Secondary impotence has such a varied etiology that a formalized frequency table for professional consideration is contraindicated at this time. Yet significant consideration must be devoted to dominant sources from which the fears of performance common to all forms of male sexual dysfunction can and do develop. Every man is influenced to a major degree by his sexual value system, which reflects directly the input from his psychosocial background (see Chapter 2).

Over the centuries the single constant etiological source of all forms of male sexual dysfunction has been the level of cultural demand for effectiveness of male sexual performance. The cultural concept that the male partner must accept full responsibility for establishing successful coital connection has placed upon every man the psychological burden for the coital process and has released every woman from any suggestion of similar responsibility for its success.

If anatomical anomalies such as vaginal agenesis or an imperforate hymen are exempted and the psychological dysfunction of vaginismus is discounted, it could be said provocatively that there has never been an impotent woman. Woman need only make herself physically available to accomplish coital connection or even to propagate the race. Legions of women conceive and raise families without ever experiencing orgasm and carry coition to the point of male ejaculation with little physical effort and no personal, reactive involvement. During coition woman has only to lie still to be physically potent. While this role of total passivity is no longer an acceptable psychological approach to sexual encounter in view of current cultural demand for active female participation, it is still an irrevocable physiological fact that woman need only lie still to be potent.

Any biophysical or psychosocial influence that can interfere with the male partner's ability to achieve and to maintain an erection can cast a shadow of conscious doubt upon the effectiveness of his coital performance, and, in due course, upon his concept of the state of his masculinity. Once a shadow of doubt has been cast, even though based only on a single unsatisfactory sexual performance after years of effective functioning, a man may become anxious about his theoretical potential for future coital connection. With the first doubt raised by any failed attempt at sexual connection in the past comes the first tinge of fear for the effectiveness of any sexual performance in the future. There are a number of theoretical factors and a combination of psychological, circumstantial, environmental, physiological, or even iatrogenic factors that can raise the specter of the fear of performance in the always susceptible mind of the male in our culture, be he 14 or 84 years of age.

It should come as no surprise that in the referred population of sexually dysfunctional men, by far the most frequent potentiator of secondary impotence is the existence of a prior state of premature ejaculation, and that the second most frequent factor in onset of secondary impotence can be directly related to a specific incident of acute ingestion of alcohol or to a pattern of excessive alcohol intake per se. Of course, both the factors of premature ejaculation and alcoholism accomplish their unfortunate purpose in the onset of impotence through engendering fears of performance. In premature ejaculation the fears of performance usually develop as the result of a slow but steady process of attrition spanning a period of years and are purely psychosocial in origin. In alcoholism the fears of performance usually develop rapidly, almost without warning, as the immediate result of untoward psychic trauma on circumstantial bases. By reason of the diverse patterns of clinical onset as well as the marked variation in their rapidity of development, these two major etiological factors will be considered in some detail, with the discussion amplified by representative case histories.

ETIOLOGICAL FACTORS

SECONDARY IMPOTENCE WITH PREMATURE EJACULATION AS AN ETIOLOGICAL FACTOR: COMPOSITE HISTORY

An established pattern of premature ejaculation prior to the onset of the symptoms of secondary impotence has been recorded in 63 of the total 213 men evaluated and treated for secondary impotence in the last 11 years. The premature ejaculation tendencies usually have been established for a significant period of time (generally a matter of years) before the symptoms of secondary impotence develop. The fact that the prior existence of a pattern of premature ejaculation often leads to secondary impotence is yet another reason for clinical confusion in the textual listing of the premature ejaculator as an impotent male. There is no established percentage of premature ejaculators who progress to secondary impotence. While the number is of considerable moment, this by no means suggests that a majority of premature ejaculators become secondarily impotent. A composite history typical of the sequential pattern of secondary impotence developing in a man distressed by prior symptoms of premature ejaculation is presented in detail.

Typically, the man is married, with some college education. Married in his mid-twenties, he usually is well into his thirties or even mid-forties before onset of the symptoms of secondary impotence forces him to seek professional support. Sexual dysfunction (premature ejaculation) has existed throughout the marriage. This man has had a moderate degree of sexual experience before marriage with, perhaps, three to five other partners, and has the typical premature ejaculator's history of having been conditioned in a rapid ejaculatory pattern during his first coital opportunities.

If authority has been approached in the interest of learning ejaculatory control, the results of such consultation have been essentially negligible in terms of improved sexual function. Professional relief of the psychosexual tensions created for the marital union by the continued existence of this form of sexual dysfunction rarely is sought until the youngest of any children of the marriage is at least of school age. By this time the female partner has little tolerance for the situation. She no longer can contend with the frustrations inherent in a relatively constant state of sexual excitation, occasional, if ever, release of her sexual tensions, and rare, if ever, male consideration of her unresolved sexual demands. Over the years of the marriage (ten to twenty), the issue of the husband's rapid ejaculatory termination of their coital encounters has been raised repetitively. Initially, the wife's complaint was registered quietly, even questioningly; in time, complainingly or accusingly; and finally, demandingly, shrewishly, or contemptuously, as her personality and the immediate levels of her sexual frustration dictated.

The male partner, rarely made aware of the inadequacy of his sexual performances during premarital sexual experience, and frequently totally insensitive to his wife's levels of sexual frustration during the early years of marriage, finally accepts the repetitively hammered concept that the dysfunctional state of their marital sexual status is "his fault" and, consequently, that he must "do something."

And so he tries. As described in Chapter 3, he bites his lips; thinks of work at the office; plans tomorrow's activities; constricts the rectal sphincter; counts backwards from one hundred; in short, does everything to distract himself from his partner's obvious demands for sexual fulfillment during coital connection. Insofar as possible, he consciously turns off both the functional and the subjective projections of his wife's sexual demands in order to reduce the input of his sexual stimuli.

For example, whenever his wife reaches that level of sexual tension that finds her responding to sexually oriented stimuli almost involuntarily (a high-plateau tension level), the physically obvious state of her sexual demand drives her husband rapidly toward ejaculation. The beleaguered premature ejaculator, trying for control, employs any or all of the subjectively distracting tactics described above. Thus, as much as possible, he not only denies the objective demand for his ejaculatory response inherent in his wife's pelvic thrusting, but also attempts to deny generally the subjective feeling of vaginal containment and specifically the constrictive containment of the penis by her engorged orgasmic platform. Insofar as possible, he compulsively negates the obvious commitment of her entire body to the elevated levels of her sexual demand. Whether or not this man ever acquires nominal physiological control of his premature ejaculatory tendencies by employing his diversionary tactics, one half of the mutually stimulative cycle that exists between sexually responsive men and women certainly has been dulled or even totally obviated (see Chapter 2). This conscious dulling or even negating of input from his wife's physical expressions of sexual demand is his first unintentional step toward secondary impotence.

There is marked individual variation in the particular moment at which the wife's repetitively verbalized complaints of inadequacy of ejaculatory control were extrapolated by the husband into a conscious concern for "inadequacy of sexual performance." Once the premature ejaculator develops any in-depth concept that he is sexually inadequate, he is ripe for psychosocial distraction during any sexual encounter.

While his wife continues to berate his premature ejaculatory tendencies as "his sexual failure," as "not getting the job done," as "being totally uninterested in her sexual release," or as "evidence of his purely selfish interests," the reasonably intelligent male frequently develops a protean concern for the total of his sexual prowess. Once a premature ejaculator questions the adequacy of his sexual performance, not only does he worry about ejaculatory control, but he also moves toward overconcentration on the problem of satisfying his wife. While overconcentrating in an attempt to force effective sexual control, he subjectively blocks full sensate input of the stimulative effect of his wife's sexual demand.

Frequently, the pressured male resorts to a time-honored female dodge: that of developing excuses for avoiding sexual activity. He claims he is tired—not feeling well—or has important work to do the next day. He displays little interest in sexual encounter simply because he knows the result of any attempted sexual connection will probably be traumatic—at best physical release for him but not satisfaction for his wife, and at worst a disaster of argument or vituperation. In brief, there is further blocking of the inherent biophysical stimulation derived from the consistent level of mutual sexual awareness that prevails between sexually adjusted marital partners (see Chapter 2) and a depreciation of the importance of mutual communication within the security of the marital bed.

Finally, the turning point. The wife pushes for sexual encounter on an occasion when the husband is emotionally distracted, physically tired, and certainly frustrated with his sexual failures. In a naturally self-protective sequence, he is totally uninterested in sexual encounter. When the husband is approached sexually by his demanding partner, there is little in the way of an erective response. For the first time the man fears that he is dealing with a sexual dysfunction of infinitely more gravity than the performance inadequacy of his premature ejaculatory pattern. Once this man, previously sensitized to fears of sexual performance by his wife's repetitively verbalized rejection of his rapid ejaculatory tendencies, fails at erection, fears of performance multiply almost geometrically, and his effectiveness as a sexually functional male diminishes with parallel rapidity.

SECONDARY IMPOTENCE WITH ACUTE ALCOHOLIC EPISODE AS ETIOLOGICAL FACTOR: COMPOSITE HISTORY

A typical history of an acute episode of alcohol consumption as an etiological factor in the onset of secondary impotence is classic in its structural content. The clinical picture is one of acute psychic trauma on a circumstantial basis, rather than the chronic psychosocial strain of years of steady attrition to the male ego as described in the case history for the premature ejaculator. There has been a specific history of onset of symptoms of secondary impotence as a direct result of episodes of acute alcoholic intake in 35 men from a total of 213 men referred with a complaint of secondary impotence.

The onset of secondary impotence in an acute alcoholic episode is so well known that it almost beggars description. A composite example is that of a relatively "successful" male aged 35–55, college graduate, working in an area which gears productive demand more to mental than physical effort. The perfect environmental situation for onset of secondary impotence is any occupational hazard where demands for high levels of psychosocial performance are irrevocably a part of the nine-to-five day and frequently carry over into an evening of professional socializing.

Mr. A is a man with an established pattern of cocktails before dinner, frequently wine with his meals, and possibly a brandy or its equivalent afterward. From a business point of view he has moved progressively up the ladder to the point at which alcohol intake at lunch is an integral part of the business picture. In short, consumption of alcohol has become a way of life.

This man and his wife leave home on a Saturday night for a party where alcohol is available in large quantity. Somewhere in the course of the late evening or the early morning hours, the party comes to an end. Mr. A has had entirely too much to drink, so his wife drives them home for safety's sake.

At home, a nightcap seems to be in order for Mr. A. His wife retires to the bedroom, and with a sense of vague irritation, a combination of a sense of personal rejection and a residual of her social embarrassment, prepares for bed. Mr. A has some trouble with the stairs, but with the aid of a strong banister and even stronger nightcap, manages to arrive at the bedroom door. Suddenly he decides that his wife is indeed fortunate tonight, for he is prepared to see that she is sexually satisfied. It never occurs to him that all she wants to do is go to bed, hoping to sleep, and avoid a quarrel at all costs.

He approaches the bed, moves to meet his imagined commitment, and *nothing happens.* He has simply had too much to drink. Dismayed and confused both by the fact that no erection develops and that his wife obviously has little or no interest in his gratuitous sexual contribution, he pauses to resolve this complex problem and immediately falls into deep, anesthetized slumber. Sunday, he is further traumatized by the symptoms of an acute hangover. He surfaces later in the day with the concept that things are not as they should be. The climate seems rather cool around the house. He can remember little of the prior evening's festivities except his deeply imbedded conviction that things did not go well in the bedroom. He is not sure that all was bad but he also is quite convinced that all was not good.

Obviously he cannot discuss his predicament with his wife—she probably would not speak to him at this time. So he putters and mutters throughout the evening and goes to bed early to escape. He sleeps restlessly only to face the new day with a vague sense of alarm, a passing sense of frustration, and a sure sense that all is not well in the household this Monday morning.

He thinks about this over a drink or two at lunch and another one during the afternoon, and, while contending with traffic on the way home from work, decides to check out this evening the little matter of sexual dysfunction, which he may or may not have imagined.

If the history of this reaction sequence is taken accurately, it will be established that Mr. A does not check out the problem of sexual dysfunction within 48 hours of onset, as he had decided to do on his way home from work. He arrives home, finds the atmosphere still markedly frigid, makes more than his usual show of affection to the children, retires to the security of the cocktail hour, and goes to supper and to bed totally lacking in any communicative approach to his frustrated, irritated marital partner.

Tuesday morning, while brushing his teeth, Mr. A has a flash of concern about what may have gone wrong with his sexual functioning on Saturday night. He decides unequivocally to check the situation out tonight. Instead of thinking of the problem occasionally as he did on Monday, his concern for "checking this out" becomes of paramount importance. On the way to work and during the day, he does not think about what really did go wrong sexually because he does not know. Rather he worries constantly about what could have gone wrong. Needless to say, there is resurgence of concern for sexual performance during the afternoon hours, regardless of how busy his schedule is.

Mr. A leaves the office in relatively good spirits, but thoroughly aware that "tonight's the night." He does have vague levels of concern, which suggest that a little relaxation is in order; so he stops at his favorite tavern for a couple of drinks and arrives home with a rosy glow to find not only a forgiving, but an anticipatory, wife, ready for the reestablishment of both verbal and sexual communication that a drink or two together before dinner can bring.

Probably for the first time in his life, he approaches his bedroom on Tuesday night in a self-conscious "I'll show her" attitude. Again there has been a little too much to drink—not as much as on Saturday night, but still a little too much.

And, of course, he does show her. He is so consumed with his conscious concern for effective sexual function (the onset of his fears of performance) that, aided by the depressant effect of a modest level of alcoholic intake (modest by his standards), he simply cannot "get the job done." When there is little or no immediate erective reaction during the usual sexual preliminaries, he tries desperately to force the situation—in turn, anticipating an erection, then wildly conscious of its abscence, and finally demanding that it occur. He is consciously trying to will sexual success, while subjectively watching for tumescence. So, of course, *no erection.*

While in an immediate state of panic, as he sweats and strains for the weaponry of male sexual functioning, he simultaneously must contend with the added distraction of a frightened wife trying to console him in his failure and to assure him that the next night will be better for both of them. Both approaches are equally traumatic from his point of view. He hates both her sympathy and blind support which only serve to underscore his "failure," and reads into his wife's assurances that probably he can do better "tomorrow" a suggestion that no longer can he be counted on to get the job done sexually when it matters "today."

A horrible thought occurs to Mr. A. He may be developing some form of sexual incompetence. He has been faced with two examples of sexual dysfunction. He is not sure what happened the first time, but he is only too aware this night that nothing has happened. He has failed, miserably and completely, to conduct himself as a man. He cannot attain or maintain an erection.

Further, Mr. A knows that his wife is equally distressed because she is frantically striving to gloss over this marital catastrophe. She has immediately cast herself in the role of the soothing, considerate partner who says, "Don't worry dear, it could happen to anyone," or "You've never done this before, so don't worry about it, dear." In the small hours of the morning, physically exhausted and emotionally spent from contending with the emotional bath her husband's sexual failure has occasioned, she changes her tune to "You've certainly been working too hard, you need a vacation," or "How long has it been since you have had a physical checkup?" (Any of a hundred similar wifely remarks supposed to soothe, maintain, or support are interpreted by the panicked man as tacit admission of the tragedy they must face together: the progressive loss of his sexual functioning.)

From the moment of second erective failure (72 hours after the first such episode), this man may be impotent. In no sense does this mean that in the future he will never achieve an erection quality sufficient for intromission. Occasionally he may do so—most men do. It does mean, however, that any suggestion of wifely sexual demand either immediate in its specific physical intensity or pointing coyly to future sexual expectations may produce pressures of performances quite sufficient to reduce Mr. A to and maintain him in a totally non-erective state. In brief, fears of sexual performance have assumed full control of his psychosocial system.

Mr. A thinks about the situation constantly. He occasionally asks friends of similar age group how things are going, because, of course, any male so beleaguered with fears of sexual failure is infinitely desirous of blaming his lack of effective function on anything other than himself, and the aging process is a constantly available cultural scapegoat.

He finds himself in the position of the woman with a lifetime history of nonorgasmic return who contends openly with concerns for the effectiveness of her own sexual performance and secretly faces the fear that in truth she is not a woman (see Chapter 8). In proper sequence he does as she has done so many times. He develops ways and means to avoid sexual encounter. He sits fascinated by a third-rate movie on television in order to avoid going to bed at the usual time with a wife who might possibly be interested in sexual expression. He fends off her sexual approaches, real or imagined, with "I don't feel well," or "it's been a terrible day at the office," or "I'm so tired." He jumps at anything that avoids confrontation as a drowning man would at a straw.

His wife immediately notices his disinclination to meet the frequency of their semiestablished routine of sexual exposure. In due course she begins to wonder whether he has lost interest in her, if there is anyone else, or whether there is truth in his most recent assertion that he couldn't care less about sex. For reassurance that she is still physically attractive, the concerned wife begins to push for more frequent sexual encounters, the one approach that the self-pressured male dreads above all else. Obviously, neither marital partner ever communicates his or her fears of performance nor the depth of their concerns for the sexual dysfunction that has become of paramount importance in their lives. The subject either is not discussed, or, if mentioned even obliquely, is hastily buried in an avalanche of words or chilled by painfully obvious avoidance.

Within the next two or three months, Mr. A has to fail at erective attainment only another time or two before both husband and wife begin to panic. She decides independently to avoid any continuity of sexual functioning, eliminate any expression of her sexual needs, and be available only should he express demand, because she also has developed fears of performance. Her fears are not for herself, but for the effectiveness of her husband's sexual functioning. She goes to great lengths to negate anything that might be considered sexually stimulating, such as too-long kisses, handholding, body contact, caressing in any way. In so doing she makes each sexual encounter much more of a pressured performance and therefore, much less of a continuation of living sexually, but the thought never occurs to her.

All communication ceases. Each individual keeps his own counsel or goes his own way. The mutual sexual stimulation in the continuity of physical exposure, in the simple physical touching, holding, or even verbalizing of affection, is almost totally withdrawn.

The lack of communication that starts in the bedroom rapidly spreads through all facets of marital exchange: children, finances, social orientation, mothers-in-law, whatever. In short, sexual dysfunction in the marital bed, created initially by an acute stage of alcoholic ingestion, supplemented at the next outing by an "I'll show her" attitude and possibly a little too much to drink can destroy the very foundation of a marriage of 10 to 30 years' duration. As the male panics, the wife only adds to his insecurity by her inappropriate verbalization, intended to support and comfort but interpreted by her emotionally unstable husband as immeasurably destructive in subjective content.

The dramatic onset of secondary impotence following an instance of excessive alcohol intake is only another example of the human male's extreme sensitivity to fears of sexual performance. In this particular situation, of course, the onset of fears of performance was of brief but dynamic duration as opposed to those in the preceding example of the premature ejaculator whose fears of performance developed slowly, stimulated by continued exposure to his wife's verbal denunciation of his sexual functioning.

Discussed above are examples of combinations of psychological and circumstantial factors that contribute the highest percentage of etiological input to the development of secondary impotence. Continuing through the listing of major influences there remain environmental, physiological, and iatrogenic factors. In the final analysis, regardless of listing category, secondary impotence is triggered by combinations of these etiological factors rather than by any single category with the obvious exception of psychosocial influence. Once onset of erective failure has been recorded, regardless of trigger mechanism involved, the individual male's interpretation of or reaction to functional failure must be dealt with on a psychogenic basis. The etiological factors recorded above are little more than categorical conveniences. From his initial heterosexual performance through the continuum of his sexual expression, every man constantly assumes a cultural challenge to his potency.

How he reacts to these challenges may be influenced directly by his psychosocial system, but of particular import is the individual susceptibility of the man involved to the specific pressures of the sexual challenge and to the influences of his background. When considering etiological influences that may predispose toward impotence, it always should be borne in mind that most men exposed to parallel psychosexual pressures and similar environmental damage shrug off these handicaps and live as sexually functional males. It is the factor of susceptibility to negative psychosocial input that determines the onset of impotence. These concepts apply to primarily as well as secondarily impotent men (see Chapter 5).

When considering environmental background as an etiological factor in secondary impotence, the home, the church, and the formative years are at center focus. What factors in or out of the home during the formative years tend to initiate insecurity in male sexual functioning? The preeminent factor in environmental background reflecting sexual insecurity is a dominant imbalance in parental relationships—dominant, that is, as opposed to happenstance, farcical, or even fantasied battles for family control. For discussion, parental imbalances can be described as maternal dominance, paternal dominance, and one-parent family.

Secondary, but still of major import is the factor of homosexuality, which is to be considered in the environmental category. In no sense does this placement connote professional opinion that homophile orientation is considered purely environmental in origin. Since homosexual activity may have derogatory influence upon the effectiveness of heterosexual functioning, the subject must be presented in the etiological discussion. The disassociations developing from homophile orientation are considered in the environmental category only for listing convenience.

SECONDARY IMPOTENCE WITH MATERNAL DOMINANCE AS CONTRIBUTING ETIOLOGICAL FACTOR: COMPOSITE HISTORY

There are innumerable classic examples in the literature of maternal dominance contributing to secondary impotence. Thirteen such instances reflecting maternal dominance have been referred to the Foundation for therapy. Since the picture is so classic, a composite history can be provided to protect anonymity without destroying categorical effectiveness.

Maternal dominance primarily depreciates the young male's security in his masculinity and destroys confidence in his socio-cultural role-playing by eliminating or at least delimiting the possibility of a strong male image. When the father is relegated to the role of second-class citizen within family structuring, the teen-age boy has no male example with which to identify other than that of a devalued, shadowy, sometimes even ludicrous male al-lowed access to the home but obviously subject to control of the dominant maternal figure.

Mr. B, a 34-year-old man, was referred with his wife for treatment of secondary impotence. He could remember little in family structur-ing other than a totally dominant mother making all decisions, large or small, controlling family pursestrings, and dictating, directing, and destroying his father with harsh sarcasm. He remembered the paternal role only as that of an insufficient paycheck, and of a man sitting quietly in the corner of the living room reading the evening news-paper. When he reached midteens, the parental representative at school functions was always the maternal figure, for both the young male and his younger sister (two siblings only). The same situation applied to church attendance and, eventually, to all social functions. The family matured with the concept that only three people mattered.

Masturbatory onset was in the early teens with a frequency of two or three times a week during the teenage years. As would be expected in a maternally dominated environment, dating opportunity for the boy was delayed, in this case until the senior year in high school. Through college there were rare commitments to female interchange, all of them of a purely social vein. The young man was insecure in most social relationships, particularly those having orientation to the male sex. He had been forbidden participation in athletics by his mother for fear of injury. He rarely pursued male companionship, feeling himself alternatively totally insecure in, or intellectually supe-rior to, the male peer group.

Finishing college, the young man, particularly interested in actuarial work, joined an insurance firm. Although mainly withdrawn from social relationships, at age 28 he met and within three months married a 27-year-old divorcee with a 2-year-old daughter. The divorcee, a dominant personality in her own right, was the mirror image of his mother. The two women were, of course, instant, bitter, and irrevocable enemies. The marriage, accomplished in spite of his mother's vehement objections, was a weekend justice-of-the-peace affair.

The sexual experience of the courtship had been overwhelming to the physiologically and psychologically virginal male. The uninitiated man literally was seduced by the experienced woman, who manipulated, fellated, and coitally ejaculated him within three weeks of their initial meeting. The hectic pace of the premarital sexual experience continued for the first 18 months of the marriage, with Mr. B awed by and made increasingly anxious by his wife's sexual demands. Coitus occurred at least once a day. Following the pattern established during the courtship, opportunities, techniques, positions, procedures, durations, and recurrences, in fact, all sexual expression in the marriage, was at his wife's able direction.

For the first year of the marriage the wife thoroughly enjoyed overwhelming her fully cooperative but naïve and insecure husband with the force and frequency of her sexual demands. As the marriage continued unwavering in the intensity of her insistence upon sexual and social dominance, his confidence in his facility for sexual functioning began to wane. He sought excuses to avoid coital connection, yet when cornered tried valiantly to respond to her demands. Finally, there were three occasions when sudden demand for coital connection forced failure of erection for the satiated male. Her comments were harsh and destructive, and the sarcasm struck a familiar chord.

The fourth time he failed to satisfy her immediate sexual needs, his wife's denunciations reminded him specifically of his mother and of her verbal attacks on his father. For the first time in his life he identified with the man sitting in a corner of the living room reading the newspaper, and within a month's time he had withdrawn to a similarly recessive behavioral patterning within his own home.

There is only one subsequent recorded episode of erection sufficiently successful for intromission with his wife. Aside from this, the man was totally impotent and had been so for three years when seen in therapy.

On an occasion when his wife was out of town, he followed the time-honored response pattern of the secondarily impotent man. There was attempted coition with a prostitute to see whether he could function effectively with any other woman. For the first time in several months there was a full erection, but when he attempted to mount, the concept of his mother's disapproval of his behavior disturbed his fantasy of female conquest. He immediately lost and could not recover the erection. This was his only attempt at extramarital sexual functioning.

SECONDARY IMPOTENCE WITH PATERNAL DOMINANCE AS CONTRIBUTING ETIOLOGICAL FACTOR: COMPOSITE HISTORY

Exactly the opposite type of history has been recorded in five cases of men referred for treatment of secondary impotence when there has been paternal dominance to the exclusion, almost complete obliteration, of the female figure other than in the role of nurse, cook, or housekeeper. Again a composite history covers more territory than a strictly factual account and provides more patient security.

Mr. C was 39 years old when seen with his 37-year-old wife in therapy. He had been married for 13 years. There were three children, the youngest of whom was 5 years old. The environment of his formative years as one of three children was dominated by a demanding, selfish, insensitive, but brilliant father, who brought into the home from a successful business career his executive impatience, impersonal demands for efficiency, and stringent standards of performance. The mother, an attractive woman, created an impression of always being overwhelmed—by the demands of the home, by the demands of the children, and above all else overwhelmed by her husband whom she alternately obviously adored and passionately hated. The father made little effort to hide his interest in other women outside the marriage, a particularly disturbing element to the son.

Mr. C does not remember any family social commitments, entertainment, or vacation times conducted other than under the direction of and in the interests of his father. Since the father was a devotee of classical music, this was the only type of music permitted in the home.

When seen in therapy, he had no concept of his mother's preferences in music. He presumed them to be classical also. His personal taste in music was more of the popular variety; rarely had he the courage to indulge his listening pleasure even with the father absent from the home.

His father's demand for adherence to excellence of performance was directed toward grades in school, social functions, and athletics. Since the boy was not well coordinated, there were countless hours of physical torture as he tried and failed to make several of the school teams, always at his father's direction.

Bitterness and resentment but, at the same time, pride and awe were constantly conflicting emotions concerning his father during his teenage years.

Starting at 13 years, he masturbated regularly two or three times a week during the teenage years. His dating pattern (suggested by his father) was fully acceptable socially, and he first had intercourse when a junior in high school. He continued with occasional coital experiences through college but gave no evidence of in-depth identification with any female partner. There was no evidence of any functional sexual distress. At the age of 26, he married after a six-months' engagement.

The courtship was current standard American, with initial petting moving into coital activity during the last few months before marriage.

In the first six years of the marriage there were three children and an established regularity of coital expression. A multiplicity of job opportunities became available, and an equal number of job changes occurred. His ventures into the business world were without specific identification or direction. In several of his professional opportunities he failed to perform satisfactorily; in others he lost interest. Mr. C found it hard to maintain any long-continued level of productivity.

As his fears for performance in the business world increased, he became less secure at home. Frequency of sexual functioning fell off when tensions created by less than effective work production left him tired and irritable during the evening hours. He spent less and less time with the children and drank progressively more than had been his previous pattern.

Finally he went to work in his father's business. After more than a year on the job, he still worried about his effectiveness of performance, panicked at the thought of losing his position, resented his father's demands, and in general was made grossly insecure in interpersonal relationships by his fears for performance. An error in judgment caused distress to a valued customer. This was reported to his father, who reprimanded him severely. His session with his father left him with a feeling of total inadequacy. He could not eat supper, paced angrily about the house, finally going to bed but not to sleep. Seeking to lose his tensions and reestablish some ego strength in sexual release, he turned to his wife and during routine precoital play achieved a strong erection. As he moved to position, the image of his bungled business performance and the scene of his father's denunciation flooded his consciousness. As he was attempting intromission he lost and was not able to regain the effective erection.

To this disturbed man, it seemed the end of the world. His sexual failure was only further evidence of the fact that he was not and never would be as good a man as his father, whose success both in business and in bed appeared legendary. With this concrete evidence of sexual failure, his frustrations were overwhelming. His fears for performance in business only amplified his fears for performance in bed and his erective incapacity continued essentially without relief.

Three months after the initial episode of erective failure, he awoke with an erection, quickly mounted and ejaculated. His unprepared wife became pregnant. Once the diagnosis of pregnancy was established, he had a reliable excuse to avoid the recently developed pressures of sexual performance, and intercourse was voluntarily contraindicated for the duration of the pregnancy, much to his wife's chagrin. When his wife demanded coital opportunity after birth of the child, Mr. C was totally impotent and continued so until referred for therapy. His fears for sexual performance and, for that matter, almost any measure of performance were overwhelming. His discussions in therapy were mixtures of praise and damnation for his father. His consistently hopeless personal comparisons with presumed levels of paternal performance were indeed sad to behold.

There have been five examples of one-parent family imbalance (permanent absence of either father or mother from the home). Retrospectively, the histories essentially join those of the composite reports of maternal or paternal dominance. Therefore, there seems little relevance in further illustration. It really matters little whether parental dominance is achieved by force of personality, with the opposite partner continuing in the home as a second-class citizen, or is irrevocably established by absence of one partner from the home on a permanent or semipermanent basis (professional demands, divorce, death, etc.).

Unopposed maternal or paternal dominance, regardless of how created, can destroy any susceptible young man's confidence in his masculinity. With maternal dominance, the paternal role can be painted so gray and meaningless that there is little positive male adult patterning available for an impressionable teenager. Unopposed paternal dominance may create such a concept of overwhelming masculinity for an impressionable teenager that it is impossible for him to match his ego strength with the paternal image enshrined by his fantasy.

With too little or too much masculinity as a pattern, he becomes increasingly sensitive to any suggestion of personal inadequacy. Failure of performance, any performance, may be overwhelming in its implications. The beleaguered male frequently extrapolates real or presumed social and professional pressures into demands for performance. As his anxieties increase, he becomes progressively more unstable emotionally, is quite easily distracted, and complains of feeling chronically tired in a well-recognized behavior pattern.

Finally, some occasion of sexual demand finds him unable to respond effectively. For any sexually oriented, personally secure man there is always tomorrow, but for the insecure, pressured male, it is the end of the line. All else fades into the background as he focuses on this new failure. Is this the final evidence of loss of his masculinity? Fears of performance, regardless of original psychosocial focus, are rapidly transferred to sexual concern because it is so easy to remove sexual functioning from its natural physiological context (see Chapter 1). From a single experience in erective failure may come permanent loss of erective capacity.

The real tragedy of unopposed parental dominance is that it leaves the susceptible male sibling vulnerable when his insecure masculinity must face the sexual challenge of our culture. Regardless of how innocuous the level of that challenge may seem to others, to the concerned man every bedding is indeed a demand for performance.

Religious orthodoxy provided the same handicap to the secondarily impotent male as that emphasized in the discussion of the primarily impotent man. Twenty-six instances of secondary impotence directly related to religious orthodoxy have been identified among 213 men referred for secondary impotence.

To a significant degree, the histories of primarily and secondarily impotent men are almost parallel when religious orthodoxy has major etiological influence. Six of 32 cases of primary impotence were at least sensitized to sexual dysfunction by their religious backgrounds (see Chapter 5). The histories of the 6 men with primary impotence and the 26 referred for treatment of secondary impotence show remarkable parallels with the exception that there must be at least one instance of successful coitus in the history of the secondarily impotent men.

The 26 cases of religious orthodoxy divide into 6 Jewish; 11 Catholic; 4 fundamentalist Protestant; and 5 mixed marriages in which both husband and wife, although professing different religious beliefs, were gravely influenced by rigid controls of religious orthodoxy during their formative years.

The symptoms of secondary impotence frequently do not appear for the first hundred or even thousand exposures to sexual function. A significant exception is established when reviewing the histories of these 26 men. Severity of religious orthodoxy places pathological stress on any initial coital process. For the relatively nonsusceptible male, regardless of the sexual handicap of theological rigidity, this tension-filled opportunity usually is met without failure at sexual functioning, or if there is failure, repetitive sexual exposure during the honeymoon provides ample opportunity for successful completion. There are, however, a number of susceptible men who do not follow the usual male pattern of successful consummation of marriage. These are the individuals who may develop symptoms of primary or secondary impotence.

Influenced by religious orthodoxy, the symptoms of secondary impotence develop through two well-identified response patterns. The first pattern divides into two specific forms: (1) Infrequent—success in the first coital opportunity usually followed, despite this initial success, by failure in the first few weeks or months of the marriage; (2) most frequent—erective failure usually underscored during the first sexual opportunity provided by the honeymoon and continuing despite virginally frantic efforts to accomplish consummation. For some ill-defined reason a successful vaginal penetration is recorded in the first month or six weeks of marriage; occasionally this is followed by a few more uneventful sexual experiences, but soon fears of performance assume unopposed dominance and, thereafter, the male is essentially impotent.

In the second pattern, at least six months and frequently many years will pass without consummation of the marriage. Then in some unexplained manner, vaginal penetration finally is accomplished and there is wild celebration, but the future is indeed dark. There usually is a brief period of time (a week to a year at the most) in which sexual function continues alternatively encouraged by a success and depressed by a failure. Fears of performance fight for dominance, but so does the sexually stimulative warmth of a partner. Effective sexual functioning assumes an off-again, on-again cyclic pattern. This cycling of sexual dysfunction is castrating in itself. The untoward effects are essentially as damaging as if the marriage had continued unconsummated. The pattern of occasionally successful sexual functioning followed by inexplicable erective failure produces a loss of masculine security and abject humiliation for the untutored, apprehensive, sexually immature male, and creates a high level of frustration and loss of both social and personal security for the female partner.

SECONDARY IMPOTENCE WITH ROLE OF RELIGIOUS ORTHODOXY AS CONTRIBUTING ETIOLOGICAL FACTOR

An illustration of the repressive influence of religious orthodoxy upon the potential effectiveness of sexual functioning can be provided by relating the history of one of the five marital units with both husband and wife products of different religious orthodoxies.

Mr. and Mrs. D were married in their early twenties. He was the product of a fundamendalist Protestant background, she of equally strict Roman Catholic orientation. The man had the additional disadvantage of being an only child, while the wife was one of three siblings. The marriage was established over the firm and often expressed objections of both families.

Prior to marriage the wife had no previous heterosexual, masturbatory, or homosexual history, and knew nothing of male or female sexual expression. She had been taught that the only reason for sexual functioning was for conceptive purposes.

Similarly, the husband had no exposure to sex information other than the vague directions of the peer group. He had never seen a woman undressed either in fact or in pictures. Dressing and toilet privacy had been the ironclad rule of the home. He also had been taught that sexual functioning could be condoned only if conception was desired. His sexual history consisted of masturbation during his teenage years with only occasional frequency, and two prostitute exposures. He was totally unsuccessful in each exposure because he was presumed a sexually experienced man by both women.

During the first episode the prostitute took the unsuspecting virginal male to a vacant field and suggested they have intercourse while she leaned against a stone fence. Since he had no concept of female anatomy, of where to insert the penis, he failed miserably in this sexually demanding opportunity. His graphic memory of the incident is of running away from a laughing woman.

The second prostitute provided a condom and demanded its use. He had no concept of how to use the condom. While the prostitute was demonstrating the technique, he ejaculated. He dressed and again fled the scene in confusion. These two sexual episodes provided only anxiety-filled examples of sexual failure. Since he had no background from which to develop objectivity when considering his "sexual disasters," inevitably the cultural misconception of lack of masculinity was the unfortunate residual of his experiences.

There was failure to consummate the marriage on the wedding night and for nine months thereafter. After consummation sexual function continued on a sporadic basis with no continuity. The wife refused contraception until after advent of the third child.

Sexual success was never of quality or quantity sufficient to relieve the husband of his fears of performance or to free the wife from the belief that either there was something wrong with her physically or that she was totally inadequate as a woman in attracting any man. They rarely discussed their sexual difficulties, as both husband and wife were afraid of hurting one another, and each was certain that their unsatisfactory pattern of sexual dysfunction was all that could be expected from indulgence in sexual expression at times when conception was not the prime motivation. With no appreciation of the naturalness of sexual functioning and with no concept of an honorable role for sexual response, the psychosocial pressures engendered from their negatively oriented sexual value systems left them with no positive means of mutual communication (see Chapters 2, 8).

The failure of this marriage started with the wedding ceremony. There was no means of communication available for these two young people. Trained by theological demand to uninformed immaturity in matters of sexual connotation, both marital partners had no concept of how to cope when their sexual dysfunction was manifest. Their first approach to professional support was to agree to seek pastoral counseling.

Here their individual counselors were as handicapped by orthodoxy as were their supplicants. There were no suggestions made that possibly could have alleviated the sexual dysfunction. When sexual matters were raised, either no discussion was allowed, or every effort was made to belittle the importance of the sexual problem.

Without professional support, the marital partners were again released to their own devices. Each partner was intimidated, frustrated, and embarrassed for lack of sexual knowledge. The sexual dysfunction dominated the entire marriage. The husband was never as effective professionally as he might have been otherwise. He withdrew from social functioning as much as possible. The wife was in a constant state of emotional turmoil, which had the usual rebound effect upon the children. By the time this marital unit arrived at the Foundation, she was well on the way to earning the title of "shrew."

The unit was first seen after a decade of marriage. As expected from individuals so handicapped in communication, each partner had established an extramarital coital connection while individually searching for some security of personal identity and effectiveness of sexual performance. The wife had been successful in establishing her own security of psychosexual performance; the husband, as would be anticipated in this instance, had not. After ten years of traumatic marriage, both individuals gravely questioned their religious beliefs. Although no longer channel-visioned, the wife continued church attendance, the husband rejected all church affiliations.

There can be no feeling for naturalness of sexual expression when there is no background of sexual comprehension. There can be no appreciation that sexual functioning is indeed a natural physical phenomenon, when material of sexual content is considered overwhelmingly embarrassing, personally degrading, and often is theologically prohibited.

In essence, when an individual's sexual value system has no positive connotation, how little the chance for truly effective sexual expression. The fact that most men and woman survive the handicap of strict religious orthodoxy to function with some semblance of sexual effectiveness does not mean that these men and women are truly equipped to enjoy the uninhibited freedom of sexual exchange. Their physical response patterns, developing in spite of their orthodox religious negation of an honorable role for sexual function, are immature, constrained, and, at times, even furtive. Sexual function is stylized, unimaginative, depersonalized, and indeed productive only of biological reproduction. A derogatory affect upon the total personality is the tragic residual of conditioned inability to accept or handle objectively meaningful material of sexual content.

SECONDARY IMPOTENCE WITH HOMOSEXUALITY AS CONTRIBUTING ETIOLOGICAL FACTOR

Homosexual influence in the formative years is an important etiological factor in the onset of secondary impotence for men in the 30- to 40-year age group. However, the age group in which homophile orientation has greatest influence on the development of symptoms of secondary impotence appears to be the twenties. Of a total number of 213 men referred to therapy for secondary impotence, 21 individuals found heterosexual functioning objectionable, repulsive, or impossible after making a marital commitment; 12 of these men were in their twenties, 7 in their thirties, and 2 in their forties.

In most instances, homophile interests developed in the early to midteens in similar pattern to those reported for the primarily im-

potent male (see Chapter 5). There was no history of overt heterosexual experience prior to homophile orientation. Recruitment
usually was accomplished by an older male, frequently in his
twenties, but occasionally men in their thirties were the initiators.
When the homosexual commitment was terminated, in most
instances, the relationship was broken by the elder partner. With
termination, the teenager was left with the concept that whether
or not he continued as an active homosexual, he always would be
homophile-oriented.

When positive homophile identification developed during the
early teenage years, heterosexual dating in the mid or late teens
was practically nil. Aside from required attendance at school functions or episodes of group partying, any consistency in heterosexual
dating patterns was rare.

Masturbatory patterns usually have been established by the
early to midteens. In several instances, however, a history of masturbatory activity predated puberty. Fantasy patterns for these
teenagers, usually male-oriented, revolve around high school heroes
and/or athletics in shower rooms. As the boys grow older, they
frequently develop some real or imagined identification with college athletic heroes.

The occasional heterosexual social relationship is classically that
of the "big brother." In the late teens to early twenties these men
are the understanding, friendly, sexually nondemanding, gentle-
manly individuals whom mothers of eligible girls dote on. In
college, dating patterns are established with more frequency than
in secondary school, but usually are not of individual commitment
as much as group function. Dating patterns are conceived by these
men primarily as a diversionary measure to avoid peer group
suspicion of homophile orientation, or as a personally protective
mechanism designed to alleviate response to homosexual stimulation.

At college level, homosexual activity varies tremendously. When
active, it usually is confined to an occasional pick-up in bar-society
atmosphere, but the majority of the men in the population ultimately to be referred to the Foundation did not have ongoing homosexual relationships after their teenage experiences. In fact, only
25 percent of those men reporting homosexual activity during

their teenage years describe any incidence of active homosexual function during college attendance.

Professed reasons for marrying have varied tremendously. In a few cases there has been the expression of a desire to reverse what they considered to be an established homophile orientation, even though active homosexual experience had been confined to the early teens or midteenage years. In most instances marriages were contracted purely as a matter of financial, social, or professional gain with no real identification with, interest in, or for that matter, attitudinal concern for the girls they married.

Once homosexual performance has been recorded and enjoyed before significant heterosexual exposure has been experienced, a pattern of heterosexual dysfunction may develop and generally follows one of two separate pathways. In the usual pattern, heterosexual performance fears are well defined during the courtship or in the immediacy of the marriage. However, a well-established second pattern reports relatively little if any difficulty in heterosexual functioning during courtship or in initial years of the marriage. The husband's basic homosexual orientation surfaces at a later date.

The first pattern reflects difficulty in achieving or maintaining an erection during premarital sexual encounter. If direct premarital sexual expression is obviated, as it frequently is under the guise of protecting the wife-to-be until marriage, sexual inadequacy can and usually does arise immediately subsequent to marriage. This situation has been described in the chapter on primary impotence (see Chapter 5).

The second pattern rarely reports difficulty with erective function in the initial months or even years of courtship and marriage. Typical histories report that somewhere in the course of from five to twenty years of marriage an overwhelming drive develops to return to homosexual functioning. This reorientation usually is occasioned by exposure to a specific male (usually a young male) who attracts sexually. Not infrequently the sexual object is a teen-age boy and, as occasionally happens, may be the man's own son. The revived demand for homosexual functioning, once acknowledged, is consuming. Usually the drive is released initially by turning to the gay-bar society. However, many of these men, after years of repressed homosexual demand, are much more interested in relating to teenage boys than to the occasional pickups of the bar society.

Temporarily, the homosexually reoriented men attempt to lead both homosexual and heterosexual lives. Difficulties develop in several different ways: the individuals may be apprehended by the law, caught in or suspected of homosexual activity by their wives, or (most frequently) betrayed socially by their male friends or relatives.

If overt social labeling as a homosexual does not develop, these men frequently focus attention on themselves by being unable to meet the physical demands of bisexual functioning. When actively oriented to homosexuality, they usually lose what little interest they may have developed in sexual connection with their wives. This loss of interest is evidenced to the wife by obviously increased intervals between sexual commitments, a multiplicity of excuses to dodge her sexual approaches, and by a coldly impersonal, coital performance when inescapably trapped.

Finally, pressured by the concerned wife, they fail to attain erection primarily because they have little or no psychosocial interest in and receive little or no biophysical stimulation from heterosexual functioning. The initial erective failure usually is passed off as a result of not feeling well, pressures of work, or any other excuse that immediately comes to mind. However, once an episode of erective failure has occurred, the homosexually oriented male usually cannot consistently attain and/or maintain an erection quality sufficient for effective coitus. His sexual value system is no longer attuned to heterosexual influence.

When referred to therapy these men occasionally may but usually do not deny their homosexual orientation in order to protect the psychosocial demands of their marriage. With denial of homophile orientation, therapy for secondary impotence may not progress successfully. When their recommitment to homosexuality has been pinpointed, any sense of guilt or at least of overcaution is removed. Usually they are quite free to discuss with their wives the concerns of their sexual reorientation. In most instances the wives are equally free to exchange their own vulnerabilities. Rarely does the wife assume other than a supportive role when faced with the competition of her husband's revived homosexual orientation. Two of the wives have sought sexual release outside the marriage, not so much from a revenge as from a personal need standpoint. One woman moved toward lesbianism, both intrigued by her responsivity and determined to maintain the marriage in any way possible. Most of the wives, however, play a restrained, conservative waiting game in the hope of reconstituting the heterosexual component in their marriage.

Men moving into secondary impotence subsequent to failed bisexual functioning are primarily interested in maintaining some semblance of heterosexual connection to protect their professional situation, their social position, and their financial commitments. For this reason, they visit the Foundation as a member of a distressed marital unit. Although they may bring to therapy little or no current interest in their female partner from a physical point of view, there is a real demand for socioeconomic protection and usually warmth and affection for their wives. This in itself is frequently motivation sufficient to stimulate their full cooperation with attempts to reconstitute effective heterosexual functioning.

PHYSIOLOGICAL CAUSES OF SECONDARY IMPOTENCE

The subject of physiological influence on sexual inadequacy will be considered in this chapter because at least 95 percent of the time when physical disability affects male sexual response, the symptoms are those of secondary impotence. It is almost impossible to list the diversity of physical defects, metabolic dysfunctions, or medications that may influence onset of secondary impotence.

Below is a list of some of the physical influences that have been reported to have resulted in secondary impotence on at least one occasion. This listing does not imply that these physical influences have been demonstrated in male patients referred to the Foundation for sexual dysfunction. The list has been culled from the literature and is presented only as a reminder that almost any physical dysfunction that reduces body economy below acceptable levels of metabolic efficiency can result in the onset of the symptoms of erective incompetence.

CLASSIFICATION OF PHYSICAL CAUSES OF SECONDARY IMPOTENCE

Anatomic
Congenital deformities
Testicular fibrosis
Hydrocele

Cardiorespiratory
Angina pectoris
Myocardial infarction
Emphysema
Rheumatic fever
Coronary insufficiency
Pulmonary insufficiency

Drug Ingestion
Addictive drugs
Alcohol
Alpha-methyl-dopa
Amphetamines
Atropine
Chlordiazepoxide
Chlorprothixene
Guanethidine
Imipramine
Methantheline bromide
Monoamine oxidase inhibitors
Phenothiazines
Reserpine
Thioridazine
Nicotine (rare)
Digitalis (rare)

Endocrine
Acromegaly
Addison's disease
Adrenal neoplasms (with or without Cushing's syndrome)

Castration
Chromophobe adenoma
Craniopharyngioma
Diabetes mellitus
Eunuchoidism (including Klinefelter's syndrome)
Feminizing interstitial-cell testicular tumors
Infantilism
Ingestion of female hormones (estrogen)
Myxedema
Obesity
Thyrotoxicosis

Genitourinary
Perineal prostatectomy (frequently)
Prostatitis
Phimosis
Priapism
Suprapubic and transurethral prostatectomy (occasionally)
Urethritis

Hematologic
Hodgkin's disease
Leukemia, acute and chronic
Pernicious anemia

Infectious
Genital tuberculosis
Gonorrhea
Mumps

Neurologic
Amyotrophic lateral sclerosis
Cord tumors or transection
Electric shock therapy
Multiple sclerosis
Nutritional deficiencies
Parkinsonism
Peripheral neuropathies
Spina bifida
Sympathectomy

Tabes dorsalis
Temporal lobe lesions

Vascular
Aneurysm
Arteritis
Sclerosis
Thrombotic obstruction of aortic bifurcation

While the above listing is of import, it must be emphasized in context that many of these conditions have been identified in individual case reports that are in many instances unsubstantiated by adequate patient evaluation. True biophysical dominance in the etiology of impotence is not a frequent occurrence. In any reasonably representative clinical series, the incidence of primary physiological influence upon onset of secondary impotence is indeed of minor consideration.

Among the 213 men referred to the Foundation for treatment of secondary impotence, there have only been 7 cases in which physiological dysfunction overtly influenced the onset of the sexual inadequacy. In the neurological group there has been one case of spinal-cord compression at the level of the eleventh and twelfth thoracic vertebrae subsequent to an automobile accident; this particular man did not accomplish erective success with therapy. In the drug-ingestion category, the influence of alcohol has been previously mentioned and is not included in this listing. There has been one case of the use of Reserpine for relief of hypertension that was referred without consideration of the possible influence this product might have had in the onset of secondary impotence. Reversal of the impotence was possible after alteration of the patient's medication. Eunuchoidism (Klinefelter's syndrome) has been recorded in one instance of referral to the Foundation for treatment that was not successful. There also has been a case of acromegaly and one of advanced myxedema, both referred without prior authoritative association of onset of symptoms of secondary impotence with exacerbation of the disease. In the first instance failure and in the second success marked therapeutic effort.

In two instances genitourinary surgical procedures have been responsible for onset of symptoms of secondary impotence. In one case a perineal prostatectomy was performed for carcinoma of the prostrate. Technically, the prostatic capsule was necessarily removed during surgery, damaging the innervation that controls the erective process. This is the usual result of such surgery. As expected, treatment was unsuccessful. In the second case, a suprapubic prostatectomy, there was sufficient postsurgical symptomatology to stimulate onset of symptoms of secondary impotence. In this situation the untoward surgical result was unfortunate. The distress in both instances was that the men had not been forewarned of the possible side effects of the surgery. The case of secondary impotence developing after the suprapubic prostatectomy was brought under control during therapy.

Patients facing surgery for prostatic cancer should be made aware by the operating surgeon that the loss of erective function can and does accompany such surgery. The psychosexual trauma forced upon the postoperative patient and his wife because they were not informed before surgery of the resultant sexual dysfunction is unforgivable.

The physiological influence of diabetes on secondary impotence is in a special category. In 6 of the total of 9 cases the onset of secondary impotence had been associated with the diabetes by consultative authority prior to referral for therapy, while in the remaining 3 instances no correlation between the established clinical condition of diabetes and the onset of impotence had been suggested by referring professionals.

Additionally, in 11 cases of referral for secondary impotence without concept of etiological influence clinical diabetes (3 cases) and preclinical diabetes (8 cases) were diagnosed during metabolic work-ups that are part of the routine physical and laboratory evaluations of the secondarily impotent male referred for diagnosis and treatment.

As described in Chapter 2, a routine five-hour glucose-tolerance test is conducted for men referred for secondary impotence. This evaluation technique has been in effect for five years but has not reached the stage of statistical significance. This work will be reported as a separate entity in monograph form at a later date. Current statistical evaluation suggests that there is a 200–300 percent higher incidence of a diabetic or prediabetic curve reported for men with the clinical symptoms of secondary impotence, when returns are compared to the incidence of diabetic or prediabetic curves in similar glucose-tolerance testing of a representative cross-section of the population. There is no supportable concept at this time that diabetes is an associate of equality with other etiological influences on secondary impotence. Nor does this work imply that the diabetic male has an established predisposition toward impotence. The amount of information available currently does not allow a firm clinical position. Of course, there frequently are other etiological foci to combine with a diabetic or prediabetic state to influence the onset of secondary impotence. However, if a man is referred for secondary impotence, evaluation of his diabetic status should be a routine part of the total physical and laboratory work-up.

It should be emphasized in context that even if symptoms of secondary impotence represent an end-point of etiological influence from a diabetic or prediabetic state, adequate institution and careful maintenance of medical control of the diabetes will *not* reverse the symptoms of impotence, once developed. Difficulty lies, of course, in the fact that regardless of etiology, once lack of erective security has been established, fears of performance unalterably become an integral part of the psychosocial influences of the man's daily life. Adequate medical control of the diabetes will provide no relief for his fears for sexual performance. If diabetes or a prediabetic state can influence the onset of secondary impotence in other than advanced states of diabetic neuropathy, this fact is but another example of the multiple etiological aspects of secondary impotence.

Understandably, for many years the pattern of the human male has been to blame sexual dysfunction on specific physical distresses. Every sexually inadequate male lunges toward any potential physical excuse for sexual malfunction. From point of ego support, would that it could be true. A cast for a leg or a sling for an arm provides socially acceptable evidence of physical dysfunction of these extremities. Unfortunately the *psychosocial* causes of perpetual penile flaccidity cannot be explained or excused by devices for mechanical support.

<h3 style="text-align:center">EFFECT OF INADEQUATE COUNSELING AS
ETIOLOGICAL FACTOR IN
SECONDARY IMPOTENCE</h3>

The most distressing etiological influence upon any dysfunction in the cycle of male sexual inadequacy is a derogatory effect of consulted therapeutic opinion. Careless or incompetent professionals inadvertently may either initiate the symptoms of sexual dysfunction or, as is more frequently the case, amplify and perpetuate the clinical distress brought to professional attention.

There have been 27 cases in the total 213 units referred for treatment of secondary impotence that have been told at first consultation with selected authority for relief of symptoms that nothing could be done about their problem. These cases are represented in all categories of etiological influence described previously in the chapter as prime initiators of the symptoms of secondary impotence.

When the sexually incompetent male finally gathers his courage and reaches for the presumed security of authoritative consultation only to be told that nothing can be done about his problem, the psychogenic effect of this denial of salvation is devastating. Of the 27 men denied hope of symptomatic relief by consultative authority, 21 individuals were so informed on their first and only visit to their local physician. Among these 21 men, 11 were told that the onset of symptoms of secondary impotence was concrete evidence of clinical progression of the aging process and that they and their wives would have to learn to adjust to the natural distress occasioned by the sexual dysfunction. Among these 11 men the eldest was 68, the youngest 42, and the average age was 53 years. These 11 men and their wives experienced an average of 28 months of sexual inadequacy before seeking further consultation.

In the 10 remaining instances of authoritative denial of hope of reprieve from symptoms of impotence, there were 4 instances of negation of clinical support by the consulted theologian; in 2 of these instances the men were informed that symptoms of impotence were in retribution for admitted adulterous behavior. One of the marital units was informed by a clergyman that the symptoms of secondary impotence developed as a form of penance because this particular unit had mutually agreed that a pregnancy conceived prior to marriage should be terminated by an abortion. Finally, one unit was assured that the symptoms of impotence would disappear if there were regularity in church attendance for at least one year. Two years later, despite fanatical attendance at all church functions, the symptoms of impotence continued unabated.

In each of the 6 remaining marital units there were individual patterns of authoritative denial of hope of symptomatic relief. They ranged from the statement that "once a grown man has a homosexual experience, he always ends up impotent," to the authoritative comment that "any man masturbating after he reaches the age of thirty can expect to become impotent." The authorities consulted were psychologists (4), marriage counselor (1), and lay analyst (1).

The incidence of erective failure progressed rapidly after authoritative denial of support. Male fears of performance were magnified and marriages were shaken and even disrupted by projection by the professional sources of a black future with full sexual disability. This mutually traumatic experience for husband and wife could easily have been avoided had the consulted authority figure accepted the fundamental responsibility either by admitting lack of specific knowledge in this area or by acquiring some basic understanding of human sexual response, or at least by not confusing personal prejudice with professional medical or behavioral opinion.

In addition to the 27 cases in which the presenting symptoms of sexual dysfunction were amplified or perpetuated by consultative authority, there were 6 instances in which consultative authority was directly responsible for the onset of symptoms of secondary impotence. The susceptibility of the human male to the power of suggestion with reference to his sexual prowess is almost unbelievable. Two classic histories defining iatrogenic influence as an etiological agent in onset of symptoms of secondary impotence provide adequate illustration of the concept.

A man in his early thirties married a girl in her midtwenties. Both had rather extensive premarital sexual experience. His was intercourse with multiple partners, hers was mutual manipulation to orgasm with multiple partners, but never vaginal penetration. She had retained her hymen for wedding-night sacrifice. However, the honeymoon was spent in repetitively unsuccessful attempts to consummate the marriage. The husband and wife felt that the difficulty was the intact hymen, so she consulted her physician for direction. She was told that it was simply a matter of relaxation, to take a drink or two before bedroom encounters. By relieving her tensions with alcohol she should be able to respond effectively. The drinks were taken as ordered, but the result was not as anticipated. The marriage continued in an unconsummated state for three years, with the wife's basic distress (in retrospect) a well-established state of vaginismus (see Chapter 9). Throughout the three-year period, the husband continued penetration attempts with effective erections at a frequency of at least two to three times a week. There usually was mutual manipulation to orgasm, when coitus could not be accomplished.

As a second consultant, her religious adviser assured the marital unit that consummation would occur if the husband could accept the wife's (and the adviser's) religious commitment. The husband balked at this form of pressure.

Finally, a gynecologist, third in the line of consultants, suggested that the difficulty was an impervious hymen. The wife immediately agreed to undergo minor surgery for removal of the hymen. (It is not only the human male that is delighted to find some concept of physical explanation for sexual dysfunction.) When the physician spoke with the husba:.d after surgery, the husband was assured that all went well with the simple surgical procedure and that his wife was fine. The physician terminated his remarks to the husband with the statement, "Well, if you can't have intercourse now, the fault is certainly yours."

Obviously, surgical removal of the hymen will provide no relief from a state of vaginismus, so three weeks after surgery, when coital connection was initiated, penetration was still impossible. For two weeks thereafter, attempts were made to consummate the marriage almost on a daily basis, but still without success. By the end of the second week both husband and wife noted that the penile erections were no longer full nor well-sustained.

The symptoms of impotence increased rapidly over the next few weeks. Three months after the hymenectomy, the husband was completely impotent. Both partners were now fully aware that the inability to consummate the marriage was certainly the husband's fault alone, for so he had been told by authority. The problem presented in therapy two-and-a-half years later by this marital unit was not only the concern for the wife's clinically established vaginismus but additionally the symptoms of secondary impotence that were totally consuming for the husband.

In another instance, the husband and wife in a three-year marriage had been having intercourse approximately once a day. They were somewhat concerned about the frequency of coital exposure, since they had been assured by friends that this was a higher frequency than usual. Personally delighted with the pleasures involved in this frequency of exposure, yet faced with the theoretical concerns raised by their friends, they did consult a professional. They were told that an ejaculatory frequency at the rate described would certainly wear out the male in very short order. The professional further stated that he was quite surprised that the husband hadn't already experienced difficulty with maintaining an erection. He suggested that they had better reduce their coital exposures to, at the most, twice a week in order to protect the husband against developing such a distress. Finally, the psychologist expressed the hope that the marital unit had sought consultation while there still was time for his suggested protective measures to work.

The husband worried for 48 hours about this authoritative disclosure. When intercourse was attempted two nights after consultation, he did accomplish an erection, but erective attainment was quite slowed as compared to any previous sexual response pattern. One night later there was even further difficulty in achieving an erection, and three days later the man was totally impotent to his wife's sexual demands with the exception of six to eight times a year when coitus was accomplished with a partial erection. He continued impotent for seven years before seeking further consultation.

When duly constituted authority is consulted in any matter of sexual dysfunction, be the patient man or woman, the supplicant is hanging on his every word. Extreme care must be taken to avoid untoward suggestion, chance remark, or direct misstatement. If the chosen consultant feels inadequate or too uninformed to respond objectively, there should be no hesitancy in denying the role of authority. There is no excuse for allowing personal prejudice, inadequate biophysical orientation, or psychosocial discomfort with sexual material to color therapeutic direction from duly constituted authority.

There are innumerable combinations of etiological influences that can and do initiate male sexual dysfunction, particularly that of secondary impotence. It is hoped that the survey of these agents in this chapter will serve not only as a categorical statement but also render information of value to duly constituted authority.

Secondary impotence is inevitably a debilitating syndrome. No man, or, for that matter, no marital unit emerges unscathed after battle with the ego-destructive mechanisms so intimately associated with this basic form of sexual dysfunction.

There must be support, there must be relief, and there must be release for those embattled marital units condemned by varieties of circumstance to contend with male sexual dysfunction.

As emphasized earlier in this chapter, most men are influenced toward secondary impotence by manifold etiological factors. Although case histories have been held didactically open and brief for teaching purposes, it must be understood that frequently there was a multiple choice of determining agents. Other professionals well might make a different assignment if given an opportunity to review the material. For example, there remain 12 cases referred for treatment that could not be categorized from an etiological point of view. No dominant factor could be established among a multiplicity of influences despite in-depth questioning by Foundation personnel.

It must be emphasized that, regardless of the multiplicity of etiological influences which can contribute to incidence of secondary impotence, it is the untoward susceptibility of a specific man to these influences that ultimately leads to sexual inadequacy. It is this clinical state of susceptibility to etiologic influence about which so little is known.

A statistical evaluation of the returns from therapy of secondary impotence will be considered as an integral part of the chapter on treatment of impotence (see Chapter 7).

Present concepts of treatment for secondary impotence have been joined with those of the current clinical approaches to primary impotence in a separate discussion devoted to these therapeutic considerations (see Chapter 7).

7

THE TREATMENT OF IMPOTENCE

Impotence is not a naturally occurring phenomenon. Yet there are men who never experience intromission regardless of available coital opportunity; they have been identified as primarily impotent. There are men, having succeeded in coital opportunity on single or multiple occasions, who develop erective inadequacy and ultimately cannot achieve or maintain an erection quality sufficient for intromission regardless of opportunity; they have been termed secondarily impotent. But are there naturally impotent men, men born without the slightest facility for effective sexual function? The answer must be a hesitant yes, but they are encountered so rarely as to be of no statistical significance.

There is a rare male never able to have intercourse for anatomical or physiological reasons. For example, men born with an endocrine dysfunction, such as Klinefelter's syndrome, may never be able to achieve sufficient steroid balance to develop an effective erection. These genetic misfortunes do occur, but with adequate knowledge and control some of their untoward clinical sequelae, such as impotence, may be reversed.

Erective incompetence occasionally develops from physical causes at various stages in the life cycle. Anything from extremely low thyroid function in the third decade to a perineal prostatectomy in the sixth decade can and does result in secondary impotence. But these obviously are pathological, not "natural," causes. "Natural" is used in terms of usual or routine or to be expected from birth.

Impotence may not be a naturally occurring phenomenon, but susceptibility to combinations of etiological factors can push any man so far from his natural cycle of sexual response that he develops fears for effective functioning. In turn, these fears can distract from or even obviate the possibility of full erective response to any form of sexual stimulation.

Concepts of treatment for symptoms of primary and secondary impotence are so basically identical that the following discussion can be applied without reservation to either syndrome. The focus of discussion, then, is the plight of any man currently unable to achieve an erection quality sufficient for intromission and maintenance of coital connection.

Whenever an impotent man commits himself to therapy for sexual dysfunction, he does so with far more personal insecurity than the usual degree of trepidation seen in most new patients. He approaches constituted authority with full conviction that nothing can be done to reverse his distress, yet he fantasies himself as a sexually effective male. The impotent man is certain that he stands alone in his sexual inadequacy, that there rarely, if ever, has been a situation so involved, so frustrating, and so hopeless.

Frequently, he has begun to view his marital partner as a major liability. He is all too aware that she is fully knowledgeable of the dimensions of his sexual inadequacy and therefore of the degree of his presumed loss of masculinity. Knowledge of his sexual inadequacy by anyone else is indeed threatening to sexual assurance for many men.

For some men this knowledge on the part of the wife also constitutes a threat to social confidence. Husbands are gravely concerned that wives will discuss the sexual inadequacy at the bridge table or the coffee klatch and, sadly enough, some wives do just that. Unable to contend with their own severe levels of personal and sexual frustration, they find release in suggesting subtly or pointing out graphically that the men they have married are sexually incompetent. Wives traumatize their sexually dysfunctional husbands just as husbands slight their sexually dysfunctional wives for a variety of reasons in addition to those of frustration or revenge. Wives must find explanation for their own lack of effective sexual functioning, but, above all, they seek reassurance that the state of sexual inadequacy in the marriage exists despite their every effort to resolve the difficulty, and that it is not their fault.

The fact that the psychosocial aspects of the marriage are not progressing satisfactorily usually is painfully obvious to all reasonably close observers. But to take the humiliating step of public accusation is indeed almost unforgivable. Inevitably this adds to the level of psychosocial trauma the man must bear. It further separates the marital partners from any hope of mutual support and certainly closes any remaining lines of communication. The difficulties in therapeutic reversal of the sexual dysfunction are thereby increased and, as a consequence, the percentage of positive return from any therapeutic procedure is reduced. For all these reasons, either partner's discussion of marital-unit sexual dysfunction other than with selected authority is potentially destructive.

Of course, most wives would not consider public discussion of the sexual inadequacy in their marriages. For a variety of reasons they choose to keep their own counsel. They may feel that their husband's dysfunction has origin in, or at least is magnified by, their own lack of physical appeal, or that they forced this inadequacy by their lack of competence of sexual functioning. Most women identify completely with, and suffer for, their husbands in the sexual inadequacy. They feel warmth and sympathy and understand the psychosocial trauma created by his obvious failure in the marriage bed. For a variety of reasons then, most women would not consider discussing their husband's sexual dysfunction even with their closest friend. But most women, whether they accuse publicly or support privately, do not comprehend the degree to which they have directly influenced their husband's sexual inadequacy.

There is no such entity as an uninvolved partner in a marriage contending with any form of sexual inadequacy. Sexual dysfunction is a marital-unit problem, not a husband's or wife's problem (see Chapter 1). Therefore, husband and wife should be treated simultaneously when symptoms of impotence distress the marital unit. The Foundation will not treat a husband for impotence or a wife for nonorgasmic return as single entities. If not accompanied by his wife, the impotent husband is not accepted in therapy. Both marital partners have not only contributed to, but are totally immersed in, the clinical distress by the time any unit is seen in therapy.

How best to treat clinical impotence? The first tenet in therapy

is to avoid the expected, direct clinical approach to the symptoms
of erective inadequacy. The secret of successful therapy for this dysfunction is not to treat the symptoms of impotence at all, for to
do so means attempting to train or educate the male to attain a satisfactory erection, and places the therapist at exactly
the same psychological disadvantage as that of the impotent male
trying to will an erection. Therapists cannot supplant or improve
on a natural process, and achievement and maintenance of penile
erection is a natural process.

The major therapeutic contribution involves convincing the
emotionally distraught male that he does not have to be taught to
establish an erection. He cannot be taught to achieve an erection
any more than he can be taught to breathe. Erections develop just
as involuntarily and with just as little effort as breathing. This is
the salient therapeutic fact the disturbed man must learn. No
man can will an erection.

Every impotent man has to negate or neutralize a number of
psychosocial influences (see Chapter 2) which have helped to
create his sexual dysfunction if he is to achieve erective effectiveness. However, the prevalent roadblock is one of fear. Fear can
prevent erections just as fear can increase the respiratory rate or
lead to diarrhea or vomiting.

At onset of therapy, the impotent man's fears of performance
and his resultant spectator's role are described specifically by the
cotherapists and must be accepted in totality by the distressed male
if reversal of the sexual dysfunction is to be accomplished. Every
impotent male is only too cognizant of his fears of performance,
and, once the point is emphasized, he also is completely aware
of the involuntary spectator role he plays during the coital attempt.

The three primary goals in treating impotence are: first, to
remove the husband's fears for sexual performance; second, to reorient his involuntary behavioral patterning so that he becomes an
active participant, far removed from his accustomed spectator's
role; and third, to relieve the wife's fears for her husband's sexual
performance.

Whenever any individual evaluates his sexual performance or
that of his partner during an active sexual encounter, he is removing
sex from its natural context (see Chapter 1). And this, of course,

is the all-important factor in both onset of and reversal of sexual inadequacy. With any form of sexual dysfunction, sex is removed from its natural context. The man watching carefully to see whether he is to achieve an erection sweats and strains to will that erection. The more the male strains the more distracted he becomes and the less input of sensual pleasures he receives from his partner; therefore, the more entrenched the continued state of penile flaccidity.

In a natural cycle of sexual response there is input to any sexually involved individual from two sources. As an example, presume an interested husband approaching his receptive wife. There are two principal sources of his sexual excitation. The first is developed as the husband approaches his wife sexually, stimulating her to high levels of sexual tension. Her biophysical response to his stimulative approach (her pleasure factor), usually expressed by means of nonverbal communication, is highly exciting to the male partner. While pleasing his wife and noting the signs of her physical excitation (increased muscle tone, rapid breathing, flushed face, abundance of vaginal lubrication), he usually develops an erection and does so without any direct physical approach from his wife. In this situation he is giving of himself to his wife and getting a high level of sexual excitation from her in return.

The second source of male stimulation develops as the wife approaches her husband with direct physical contact. Regardless of the technique employed, his wife's direct approach to his body generally, and the pelvic area specifically, is sexually exciting and usually productive of an erection. When stimuli from both sources are combined by mutuality of sexual play, the natural effect is rapid elevation of sexual tension resulting in a full, demanding erection.

Often men move into a pattern of erective failure because they do not experience sensate input from both sides of the give-to-get cycle. Loss of supportive sexual excitation frequently develops not because wives are unavailable or uninterested but because one or both of the basic modes of input of sexual stimuli is blocked. Sexual input can be blocked by any negative influence in the psychosocial system that distracts the male. If there has been a recent quarrel and his antagonistic wife plays a passive role in their next sexual encounter, evincing no pleasure from her husband's sexual approach, he receives no projection of her sensual interest and therefore half his input of sexual stimuli will be blocked. There is little sexual return for the husband or wife who feels as if he or she were approaching a wooden indian when attempting to excite a partner sexually.

The impotent male also denies himself potential biophysical input if, as his wife approaches him with manually or orally stimulative activity, he casts himself in the spectator role. As he mentally stands in the corner observing her activity, impersonally watching and waiting to see if full erection can be attained, he obviously is blocking a major degree of the sensate input created by her direct stimulative approaches. The same principle applies, of course, if he assumes the spectator role while approaching his wife in a stimulative manner. If he "pleasures" his wife with physical skill while remaining aloof and uninvolved as an impersonal spectator, waiting to approve of any degree of erective response resulting from her obvious sensual pleasure, he again blocks the psychosocial input created by her pleasure state.

It is important to emphasize, however, that an impotent man should never attempt to give pleasure to his wife with only the concept of receiving pleasurable stimuli from her in return. He must give of himself to his wife primarily for her pleasure, and then must allow himself to be lost in the warmth and depth of her response, and in so doing divest himself of his impersonal spectator's role. In brief, if a man is to get the essence of a woman's sensual warmth, he must give of himself to her. This concept has been dubbed the "give-to-get" principle. When the male loses himself in the giving, the female's sensate return will be reflected by positive interdigitation of his biophysical and psychosocial influences, and the erection he has tried time and again to force will develop freely when least expected.

The marital unit is assured that no attempt ever will be made to teach a husband to achieve an erection. Emphasis is placed on the fact that erective attainment is a natural physiological process and that every man is born with the facility to erect when responding to a definitive set of biophysical and psychosocial influences. A descriptive parallel is employed for members of the marital unit by suggesting to the husband that the wife's facility for vaginal lubrication follows the same natural initiative mechanism as does erective attainment. She cannot will, wish, or demand the production of vaginal lubrication. However, she can relax, approach her husband and be approached by him, allowing input of sensate focus from both sources while she concentrates only on the sensual pleasure arising from the mutuality of their sexual expression. When any woman achieves this state of involvement, lubrication develops spontaneously.

In many instances it helps to point out to the husband that exactly the same anatomical tissues, the same blood supply, and the same nerve supply that are involved in penile erection for the male produce vaginal lubrication for the female. Full penile erection is, for the male, obvious physiological evidence of a psychological demand for intromission. In exact parallel, full vaginal lubrication for the female is obvious physiological evidence of a psychological invitation for penetration. In a comparison of male and female sexual function, it always should be emphasized that in sexual response it is the similarities of, not the differences between, the sexes that therapists find remarkable.

The Foundation has taken the position that the secret of successful therapy is not to treat the symptoms of impotence at all. Instead, methodology consists of a direct therapeutic approach to causation. The marital unit combines to contribute the necessary ingredients, for when approaching problems of impotence, whether primary or secondary, symptoms are not treated—they are obviated by successfully treating the marital relationship.

The marital state is under therapy at the Foundation. Never are the impotent husband or the directly involved and frequently nonorgasmic wife considered separately as patients, and never as nonresponsive, pathological entities separate from the marital union.

The basic means of treating the sexually distraught marital relationship is, of course, to reestablish communication. The most effective means of encouraging communication is through a detailed presentation of information. There must be a point of departure— a common meeting ground—for the traumatized members of any sexually dysfunctional marriage. How better to provide for mutuality of interest and understanding than to educate the distressed marital unit to effective sexual functioning by dispelling their sexual misconceptions, misinformation, and taboos?

Marital-unit progress in the educational program is by encouraging verbal communication. The details of the techniques necessary for the unit to reverse the sexual inadequacy are spelled out in finite detail during the approximately 10 days remaining for therapy after the roundtable discussion (see Chapter 2). As sexual function improves, these techniques for biophysical release are held out as rewards to direct attention toward mutuality of interest and expression, while marital disharmony is attacked directly. When there is obvious improvement in physical responsivity, the distressed unit members are only too eager to reestablish a firm, secure marital state. They are most attentive to the educational process, for they shortly come to realize that permanent reversal of the dysfunctional symptomatology relates directly to the health of the marriage. When husband and wife visualize the results of their biophysical progression on a daily basis, they are intent upon providing the best possible psychosocial climate for continuing improvement once separated from direct professional control. Obviously, the more stable the marriage the better the climate for effective sexual function. Again, the marital relationship per se is under treatment at the Foundation, not its principals.

Discussions of the distractions of fears of performance and the spectator role, plus the necessity for duality of biophysical and psychosocial input from sexually stimulative activity, are conducted with both marital partners during the three days subsequent to the roundtable discussion. The acceptance of the "performance" and "spectator" concepts moves the marital unit well along the road to full appreciation of the mutuality of their involvement with the impotent state. From a psychotherapeutic point of view, the next step is to suggest to both members of the marital unit ways and means of avoiding the basic distractions of the spectator role and the fears of performance.

An effective way to prevent fears of performance is to state unequivocally to both husband and wife that as they attempt to follow therapeutic suggestion in the privacy of their bedroom there is no demand for good marks in their daily report on their degree of success in following the functional directions. Authority is infinitely more interested in the distressed marital unit making its mistakes, describing them in joint sessions with the cotherapists, and absorbing information to correct them in the immediacy of a 24-hour period, than in providing a cheering section. We tend to learn more from our mistakes than from our successes. The first step toward relief from fears of performance is to define the Foundation's position that failures of function not only are expected but are anticipated as an integral part of the process of reorienting the sexually dysfunctional male (see Chapter 1).

Once the marital unit fully accepts the concept that perfect report cards are not the order of the day, a major facet of concern for performance has been removed. The impotent male's first reaction to functional suggestions is to attempt to force responsivity in order to satisfy presumed authoritative demand. When it is made exquisitely clear that there is no authoritative interest in a perfect performance, his sense of relief is indeed obvious.

Remaining fears for sexual function can be neutralized by the direction that there be no attempt at coital connection during the first few days of therapy. Cotherapists should emphasize that there is concern whether or not the husband achieves an erection, for, even if he does, there should be no attempt by either husband or wife to take advantage of the erective state and move to ejaculation by either manipulative or coital opportunity. When any possibility of coital connection is obviated by authoritative direction, fears of performance disappear.

At the termination of the roundtable discussion, the marital unit contending with erective insecurity moves directly into discussion of and application of sensate-focus material (see Chapter 2). At this stage of treatment any direct approach to the male pelvis, female breast, and female pelvis is contraindicated. The marital unit relaxes from their prior anxious concepts of specific or demanding sexual functioning and, possibly for the first time, devotes total concentration through sensate focus toward pleasuring one another. Quiet, nondemanding stroking of the back, the face, the arms, the legs, provides opportunity to give and to receive sensate pleasure, but, of far greater importance, *opportunity to think and to feel sexually without orientation to performance.* Previously, the incompetent male, frozen into his demand for erective security, has blocked sensate input either primarily, from his wife's direct physical approach or secondarily, from his effective elevation of her sexual tensions. With sexual performance not only contraindicated but denied, the husband is quite free to receive sensate input from both direct and indirect sources, since his block to sensate pleasure (fear of performance) has been removed by authoritative interdiction of coital opportunity.

At this time the cotherapists describe in detail the concept of the dual systems of influence operant at all times in perception and interpretation of sexual stimuli. It is explained that the two systems of influence, the biophysical and the psychosocial structures, produce varying degrees of positive or negative input during opportunities for sexual expression. It is emphasized that these two systems operate in an interdigital manner, although without compulsion for mutual support. Once the marital unit accepts this working formula, sensate input can be comprehended (see Chapters 2 and 8). With comprehension comes attitudinal receptivity and the potential for sensate pleasure.

Often both husband and wife find that partial or complete penile erection develops when they are merely following directions to pursue alternative sensate patterns of "pleasuring" one another without direct physical approach to the pelvic areas. Whether a full erection develops during the first days of concentration on sensate focus is of little moment. What is important, erection or not, is for cotherapists to take advantage of the marital-unit's newfound means of physical communication, that of providing mutually for each other's sensate pleasure, in order to describe in detail the concept of erection as a natural physiological reaction. Again and again therapists should hammer at the basic principle that erective attainment, like breathing or bowel or bladder function, is a capacity men are born with, not a function they must be trained to accomplish. Husband and wife are assured and reassured that no man can will an erection and that the only thing accomplished by such attempts is blocking of sensate input from his sexual partner. The concept of the biophysical and psychosocial systems of influence aids immeasurably in marital-unit comprehension of the previously inexplicable results accrued from blocking of sensate input.

There are other advantages to the members of the sexually dysfunctional marital unit than absorption of the pleasures of sensate focus during the first two or three days after the roundtable discussion. This is a necessary period of mental and physical relaxation from the high tension levels inherent in the strain of cooperating with the detailed personal evaluations scheduled during the first three days of participation in the program. This respite also provides for release of nervous tensions accumulated during the last few days or weeks before marital units move to meet scheduled appearance dates at the Foundation. Finally, there is mutual opportunity to reestablish lines of communication of both verbal and nonverbal variety. These lines of communication have been markedly inhibited or essentially destroyed by the physical tensions and the psychic trauma developing directly from and/or secondary to their sexually dysfunctional status.

On the second day, after the roundtable discussion, the program moves toward coordinating the theoretical discussions between cotherapists and the marital unit, described above, and the specific functional directions to be followed by husband and wife in the privacy of their bedroom. Instructions are given to return to sensate focus procedures during the subsequent 24 hours. This time, direct approach to the male and female external genitalia, including the female breast, is encouraged. Underscored positively is the instruction that there is no concern for the amount of vaginal lubrication nor the effectiveness of the penile erection or, for that matter, whether or not there is any lubrication or an erection. The essence of the directions is that each individual take advantage of this nondemanding opportunity to show what most pleases him or her in any overt sexual approach to the pelvic organs.

When the husband is to excite his wife, it is suggested that they, rather than he, participate in her pleasuring and at her direction. After a comfortable period of sensate stroking of her total body area, the approach to the pelvic area should be under her control. The wife's hand should be placed on her husband's to guide and to show him what really pleases her in terms of manual positioning, pressure, direction, or rapidity of stroking. There is positive reenforcement for any man learning what really pleases the woman of his choice by having her quietly show him the specifics of her sensual interest (see Fig. 9, Chapter 11).

Then the husband must, in return, provide educative opportunity for his wife. When his wife, after tracing his face, rubbing his back, or playing with his fingers, approaches his pelvic area, his hand should be on hers. In this most effective form of nonverbal communication, he must indicate which of the multiple varieties of pelvic approach provides the most pleasure for him. The particular areas of the penis that are the most sensitive, the comfortable degree of manual constriction of the penile shaft, and the desired rapidity and tension of penile stroking are basic information that a wife wants to learn from her husband (see Fig. 3, Chapter 3).

Anything that husband or wife might have learned from prior masturbatory experience that would tend to increase the levels of sensate pleasure should be shared freely with the marital partner. Often this material can only be elicited at the direction of the cotherapist. At this time, authority should strongly emphasize in joint session that acquiring mechanical or technical skill is not a major focus of therapy. For example, it is important for a husband to know how to approach the clitoral area when stimulating his wife, but therapists should point out that a physical approach that is exciting for the wife today may be relatively nonstimulative or even irritating tomorrow. Attaining skill at physical stimulation is of minor moment compared to the comprehension that this is but another, most effective means of marital-unit communication.

It should be underscored constantly that what really is happening in their private sessions of physical expression is that a man and a woman committed to each other are learning to communicate their physical pleasures and their physical irritations in an area that heretofore in our culture has been denied the dignity of freedom of communication. What better level of nonverbal communication can be attained between the impotent man and his wife than, when placing his hand on hers, he teaches her what really pleases him in penile stimulation. With cotherapists constantly emphasizing the demand to open the lines of communication within the sexually traumatized marital unit, and husband and wife establishing their nonverbal communication at the most important of all communicative levels—that of the marriage bed—the marital unit is really doing its own therapy. They are teaching each other specifically what pleases. Although they frequently do not realize it at this stage in their therapy, husband and wife are focusing their attention on each other rather than involuntarily assuming roles as spectators to physical response and thus perpetuating their mutual fears for his performance.

Demand for male sexual performance is never made by authority. Historically, years of failure in treatment for sexual dysfunction has pinpointed the fact that, regardless of length, depth, concept, or technique of therapy, at some point in time the therapist has turned to his patient and suggested, permitted, or even directed that he "have intercourse tonight." Instantaneously with that fatal suggestion, all the fears of performance came flooding back and, regardless of the effectiveness of prior therapeutic commitment, the husband was placed under authoritative direction to "do something." Current therapeutic concept is that no dysfunctional man should ever be under any form of suggestion or direction to accomplish anything specifically of a sexual nature. When there is need to communicate specific functional direction, such suggestion always is made to the wife, not to the husband. For sexual functioning is a naturally occurring phenomenon and cannot be controlled, directed, or even initiated unless it is in some manner related to the natural cycle of sexual response. *No man can will an erection*, but he can relax and enjoy it.

Understandably, all therapy flows toward a concept of a mutual pleasure return for both members of the marital unit. Instead of being suggested, directed, or given permission, as in prior therapeutic concept, to go all the way from A to Z sexually on any specific occasion, it is suggested that marital units go from A to B one day, possibly from A to C or D the next, and even from A to E or F the third day. Although physical evidence of improvement of sexual functioning may come haltingly, it is definitive. Every step in the therapeutic program is explained in detail in advance of any opportunity for sexual expression. Both positive and negative reactions of the tentatively experimenting partners to sexual material and to overt sexual stimulation are anticipated, explained, supported, or dismissed. It is hoped that both authoritative suggestion and basic sexual information are understood and appreciated. With this low-key, nongoal-oriented technique, erection appears without fanfare, comfortably, and certainly without the husband's forcing or the wife's demanding its attainment. When erection does develop in these nonpressured circumstances, the marital unit, previously following the therapeutic tenet of maintaining "healthy skepticism" (see Chapter 2), soon becomes confident that the end of their sexual dysfunction is within sight.

Once erective return is reestablished, the most effective step in the physical aspect of the therapeutic program can be taken. The day after full erection is developed and maintained, it is suggested that the marital unit enjoy this return to erective prowess by experimenting with the erective reaction. A pattern for unit response is suggested that includes manipulative play to erective return, cessation of play to allow a period of distraction for the male with consequent loss of erection, then return to play and resurgence of erective attainment. This "teasing" technique is continued for a full half-hour in a slow, nondemanding fashion.

The man's immediate reaction to this suggestion may be fear-oriented—"How can I be sure that if I have an erection and lose it, I can get it back?" Cotherapists quickly underscore this specific evidence of the husband's indulgence in fears of performance and his return to the past patterning of anticipation of failure so firmly rooted before referral for therapy. It is pointed out that when he has relaxed, he and his wife have enjoyed the return of his erections during the sensate-focus period. It is further suggested that his wife also will enjoy the "teasing" technique. She will be sexually stimulated by the opportunity for developing, losing, and developing again the penile erections. This thought rarely if ever has occurred to the husband. He usually takes the next step in the natural progression of sexual functioning without much performance tension, for again it is emphasized that if he has an erection, fine, if not, there's another day.

With this attitude, the "teasing" technique usually works well. During the conference period on the day following some degree of success with this technique, the improved levels of male confidence are indeed obvious. What is even more important is that both members of the marital unit be made to realize that they are helping each other immeasurably with their mutual problem of sexual dysfunction. Cotherapists constantly must reemphasize the fact that authority is not capable of teaching a physical reaction. The marital units are given an opportunity to convince themselves that there is nothing wrong with their ability to respond to effective sexual stimulation. As partial or complete erective security returns in these first few days, the marital unit proves to itself that there is no suggestion of physical permanency to their established sexual dysfunction. As their confidence increases, the partners move toward the next step in sexual functioning.

Within a week after the roundtable discussion, the impotent male generally has evidenced partial or complete erection. When erections recur spontaneously, the wife is encouraged to place herself in the superior coital position, with her knees at or below his nipple line, before her sex play is directed toward penile manipulation (see Fig. 5, Chapter 3).

When the wife is comfortable in this position, penile play should be initiated. This position also allows the husband full access to the breasts. When or if a full erection is obtained, the wife may mount, but intromission should be attempted in a non-demanding manner. No hurry to mount—no rush to obtain sexual tension release—should be permitted. When she is attempting penile insertion, the penis should be angled at approximately 45 degrees from the perpendicular and directed cephalad (toward the head). When mounting, the wife is encouraged to move back on the shaft of the penis rather than to sit down on it (see Fig. 5, Chapter 3).

There should never be any question as to the mechanics of penile insertion. The woman always should control the insertive process. Many men have been distracted from a partial or even a full erection by bumbling, fumbling, vain attempts to describe the vaginal orifice in the process of penile insertion. The male usually is not sure anatomically where the penis goes and, during frantic moments of searching and finding, his opportunity for distraction is patently obvious. Every woman knows exactly where the penis goes; additionally, she is indeed sexually stimulated by the opportunity to assist actively in the act of intromission. Just quietly relieving the impotent male of the responsibility for penile insertion removes yet another distractive roadblock from his vitally necessary level of sensate input. Anything that can or does distract him will dull, dilute, or destroy his levels of sexual tension.

With the wife already posed in the proper position during the preliminary sex play, she can accomplish intravaginal containment with facility and grace. Even during the insertive process, she should continue active manual manipulation of the penile shaft. Positioning herself correctly ahead of time again avoids a distraction. Many males attain an erection with sex play but lose security of penile rigidity when attempting intromission. The actual mounting process is distracting to the impotent male. Both his wife's stimulation of the penis and his stimulation of her pelvic organs usually cease. He then moves to assume a male-superior position, hunts for the vaginal outlet, and finally attempts intromission. Since all this takes time, and mutual sexual stimulation stops, the husband loses his sense of continuity. Consequently, any man following this reactive pattern may lose the fullness if not the total of his erection in the process. The concerned male has only to notice the slightest loss of erective fullness and he panics, distracting himself completely in a spectator role and, of course, immediately loses the rest of his erective security.

Obviously, the concept underlying the use of this mounting technique is to remove inherent male distractions and to let the sensual pleasure developed from mutual sexual stimulation take control so that the tense male will not react in his usual pattern of performance fears or spectator role. This experience is repeated several times until erective security develops. This coital teasing technique is comparable to that of attaining, losing, and then returning to full penile erection with manual manipulation. Any male must have a series of obviously successful intromissions if he ever is to lose permanently his concerns for performance.

Once the marital unit can mount with security, another specific male fear of performance will surface. Impotent men having achieved intromission successfully still have not satisfied their performance fears. They immediately question whether the penis will retain sufficient rigidity for continuation of effective coital connection. These specific fears are easily obviated by once again contraindicating performance. It is authoritatively suggested first that the female move slowly up and down on the shaft of the penis, which she can do with facility in the described positioning. She is to move backward and forward rather than sit down on the penis. Regardless of her high levels of sexual demand, the wife should concentrate only on the concept of penile containment, without moving into the demanding type of pelvic thrusting that may have been her pattern in the past whenever opportunity presented. Understandably, in past patterning, she has tried to take advantage of whatever degree of erection was available in attempting to satisfy her own sexual needs.

The cotherapists must explain before exposure to any coital opportunity that a demanding pattern of female pelvic thrusting is indeed threatening to any man with erective insecurity. Demanding female participation in coital connection is immediately distracting to the impotent male, for his performance fears come flooding back. Obvious female demand demonstrated at this time is devastating to maintenance of erection. The husband fears that he will not be able to sustain an erection quality sufficient to satisfy his sexual partner. He worries about his response instead of enjoying the sensual pleasures of the moment. His distraction leads to some loss of erective security. Once conscious of loss of any degree of the erection, the impotent man panics, forgetting immediately that by his own actions as a phantom spectator, he distracts himself from sensate input. When he succumbs to this response pattern, the penis becomes flaccid in seconds, to the utter frustration of both sexual partners.

Both partners must learn that there is no time demand inherent in this female mounting technique. If the erection is satisfactory, intromission proceeds; if not, play is continued without pressure until a satisfactory erection does develop. If erection does not develop during a comfortable period of time with mutual play, there is never to be an attempt to force the issue. When by authoritative edict there is to be no forcing of the issue, erection usually is secured without difficulty.

After the wife has taken her turn at the sensate pleasure of feeling and thinking sexually while moving pelvically in a slow, nondemanding manner on the penile shaft, it is suggested that she in turn remain quiet, and the husband is encouraged to thrust slowly, concentrating on the sensate pleasures to be derived from the feelings of vaginal constriction and warmth of containment, and the sensations engendered by his wife's lubrication.

His concept in participating in the slow pelvic thrusting should be one of giving and receiving sensate pleasure just as though he were stroking his wife's back, rubbing her neck, or running his fingers through her hair. In this warm way he is distracted from concerns of performance, and the biophysical and psychosocial stimulative input of sensate pleasure is encouraged. The sensual stimuli from his vaginal containment get through to him in a non-demanding manner. His observation of his wife's free, nondemanding, coital cooperation frees him from any concept of pressuring from her and allows him to avail himself of the pleasure of her sensual response to his slow thrusting pattern. With her specific coital positioning, he simultaneously can enjoy breast play and vaginal containment. Once he indulges himself in his sexual opportunities, the overwhelming sensual input tends to distract from any previous patterning of performance concern or spectator role. Again, he is not performing; he is consciously pleasuring and being pleasured by intravaginal containment in a totally nondemanding, yet warmly pleasant and sexually satisfying fashion.

On subsequent days both partners are encouraged to move to simultaneous "pelvic pleasuring," feeling, thinking, and concentrating only on the sensations involved in this mutuality of their sexual stimulation. There must not be concern for satisfying the wife or forcing ejaculation by the husband. When these end-points of sexual functioning occur during coition, they should be by happenstance, involuntarily, naturally, and mutually rewarding, but *never* by direction.

A word must be said for the cooperative wives of sexually inadequate husbands. They may arrive in therapy frustrated, resentful, bitter, revengeful, or still devoted to this man of their choice. Regardless of the manner in which they approach therapy, once they have assured themselves that every effort is being made to treat the marital relationship, not just the sexually inadequate male, the full cooperation of more than 90 percent of the wives seen by Foundation personnel has made the vital difference between success and failure in therapy.

The wives' depth of cooperation with therapeutic suggestions is engendered primarily by the participation of the female member of the therapy team. When wives realize they always have available as a cotherapist not only a friend but also an interpreter, their willingness to cooperate usually is excellent. They realize they are working with their husbands for their marriage. Specific directions as to handling the psyche of her husband, her place in the scheme of therapy, and, above all, her role in a sexually functional marriage come from the female cotherapist, usually in individual sessions.

The overall results obtained from attempting symptom reversal of primarily and secondarily impotent men referred to the Foundation are far from satisfactory. The best statistical measure of the clinical results is the rate of failures. Although the results obtained represent significant improvement over previously published material, the failure rates are still far too high. There has been improvement as work has progressed, but there is still a long way to go before there can be professional satisfaction with clinical progress.

For the convenience of the reader, Tables 1 and 2 reflect the gross etiological categories to which the cases of impotence arbitrarily have been assigned. It should be emphasized once more that etiological influence usually was multiple in origin, and that category assignment has been merely on the basis of professional decision as to the major influence among the multiple etiological forces. For example, the preclinical diabetes category in Table 2 is but one of several etiological factors influencing the 11 men so listed.

TABLE 1

Primary Impotence
32 Units

Basic Etiology	No. Cases	No. Failures
Mother-son encounter	3	1
Religious orthodoxy	6	4
Homosexual influence	6	2
Prostitute trauma	4	1
Alcoholism	2	1
Varied pathogenesis	11	4
TOTAL	32	13

Failure rate 40.6%

TABLE 2
Secondary Impotence
213 Units

Basic Etiology	No. Cases	No. Failures
Premature ejaculation	63	7
Alcoholism	35	8
Maternal dominance	13	4
Paternal dominance	5	1
One-parent family	5	1
Religious orthodoxy	26	13
Homosexual influence	21	7
Physiological dysfunction	7	4
Diagnosed diabetes	9	3
Preclinical (undiagnosed) diabetes	11	2
Iatrogenic influence	6	1
Noncategorized cases	12	5
TOTAL	213	56

Failure Rate 26.2%

Brief survey of the tables indicates a 40.6 percent failure rate in the treatment of primary impotence during two weeks of intensive educational process. There is hope for continuing improvement if we state additionally that there were 9 failures in the treatment of the first 16 cases and 4 failures in treating the last 16 cases of primary impotence over the last 11 years. The downward trend certainly should continue in this failure rate.

There was a 26.2 percent failure rate recorded in the two weeks' attempt to reverse the symptoms of secondary impotence over the last 11 years. Unfortunately, there has been no significant reduction in the failure rate as experience has accrued.

Of course these statistics represent only the percentage failure of symptom removal during the acute phase of treatment. Any treatment termed successful by this measure has little clinical value unless the symptom reversal proves to be permanent. Therefore, while failure rates in the acute-treatment phase are of obvious import, consideration of any corresponding success rate must be held in abeyance until at least five years after termination of the acute phase of therapy. Chapter 14, Program Statistics, considers this follow-up information.

The influences of religious orthodoxy and homosexual orientation represent the two areas of ideological influence associated with the highest level of treatment failure in primary and secondary impotence. There was a 66.6 percent immediate failure to reverse symptoms of primarily impotent men, and a 50 percent failure to reverse symptoms of secondarily impotent men influenced by religious orthodoxy. No other category approaches this in treatment failure. The nearest approach is provided by those men with an etiological background of homosexuality, usually adolescent in onset. Here 33.3 percent of the primarily impotent men and exactly the same figure of secondarily impotent men failed to respond positively to the two weeks' intensive-treatment program. It is in these two areas that so much more work needs to be done. Currently there is an inexcusably high level of failure rate in therapeutic return for patients handicapped by either of these two specific etiological influences.

It must always be borne in mind that it is the individual man's susceptibility to etiological influences that determines whether he is to survive as a sexually functional male or is to fall into a pattern of inadequate sexual responsivity. Of the factors initiating or controlling this innate susceptibility we know so little.

8

ORGASMIC DYSFUNCTION

SECTION A

CONCEPT

In the past, the sociocultural requisite that the female dissemble her sexual feelings did not lessen general interest in female sexuality. The nature of female sexual response has been interpreted innumerable times, with each interpretation proposing a different concept or variation on a concept. Interestingly, more than 95 percent of these interpretive efforts have been initiated by men, either from the defensive point of view of personal masculine bias or from a well-intentioned and often significant scientific position, but, because of cultural bias, without opportunity to obtain unprejudiced material. Even the small number of women combining research expertise with their own firsthand awareness of female sexual behavior have been disadvantaged by cultural limitations on scientific investigation of human sexual response. Conceptually these women also have shared cultural bias with their male professional peers.

Even though definitive research findings have emerged in the field of sexual behavior, the handicap of cultural bias has so constrained progress that there has been little professional concurrence in a final definition of female sexual function. There are three apparent reasons for this stalemate in definition of female psychosexual expression: (1) Until recently there was failure to develop a directly related body of biophysical information. (2) There has been little interest in duplication of physiological investigative procedures to validate research findings. (3) There has been little or no effort to incorporate established laboratory findings into clinical treatment of female sexual dysfunction.

A psychophysiological interpretation of female sexual response must be established and accepted, for it is impossible to consider sexual dysfunction with objectivity unless there is a base for comparison afforded by an acceptable concept of woman's sexually functional state. In an effort to establish such a baseline interpretation, female sexual response will be contemplated as an entity separate from male sexual response—not, as might be presumed, because of any vast difference in their natural systems of expression (for beyond the influence of fortunate variations in reproductive anatomy and their individual patterns of physiological function the sexes are basically similar, not different) but because of sex-linked differences that are largely psychosocially induced.

A separate discussion of female sexuality is necessary primarily because the role assigned to the functional component of woman's sexual identity rarely has been accorded the socially enforced value afforded male sexuality. While the parallel between sexes as to physiological function has gained general acceptance, the concept that the male and female also can share almost identical psychosocial requirements for effective sexual functioning brings expected protest. Only when a male requests treatment for symptoms of sexual dysfunction, and possible contributing factors are professionally scrutinized in the clinical interest of symptom reversal, are the psychosocial influences noted to be undeniably similar to those factors which affect female responsivity. Then such factors as selectivity, regard, affection, identity, and pride (to name a few of the heterogeneous variables) are revealed as part of the missing positive or present negative influence or circumstances surrounding the sexual dysfunction.

It is obvious that man has had society's blessing to build his sexual value system (see Chapter 2) in an appropriate, naturally occurring context and woman has not. Until unexpected and usually little understood situations influence the onset of male sexual dysfunction, his sexual value system remains essentially subliminal and its influence more presumed than real. During her formative years the female dissembles much of her developing functional sexuality in response to societal requirements for a "good girl" facade. Instead of being taught or allowed to value her sexual feelings in anticipation of appropriate and meaningful opportunity for expression, thereby developing a realistic sexual value system, she must attempt to repress or remove them from their natural context of environmental stimulation under the implication that they are bad, dirty, etc. She is allowed to retain the symbolic romanticism which usually accompanies these sexual feelings, but the concomitant sensory development with the symbolism that endows the sexual value system with meaning is arrested or labeled—for the wrong reasons—objectionable.

The reality of female sexual function today, aside from its vital role in reproduction, still carries an implication of shame, although such a dishonorable role has been rather difficult to sustain with objectivity. The arbitrary social assignment of the role of sin to female sexuality has not contributed a desirably consistent level of marital harmony. Nor has society always found it easy to eliminate recognition of female sexuality while still supporting and maintaining the male's role of tacit permission to be sexual with honor, or even praise. Especially is this true of a society that continues to celebrate events before and after the fact of sexual expression (marriage, birth, etc.), and mourns the female menopause because it is presumed to signify demise of sexual interest.

Since, as far as is known, elevated levels of female sexual tension are not technically necessary to conception, the natural function of woman's sexuality has been repressed in the service of false propriety and restricted by other unnecessary psychosocial controls for equally unsupportable reasons. In short, negation of female sexuality, which discourages the development of an effectively useful sexual value system, has been an exercise of the so-called double standard and its sociocultural precursors.

Residual societal patterns of female sexual repression continue to affect many young women today. They mature acutely aware of repercussions from sexual discord between their parents and among other valued adults, so they grope for new roles of sexual functioning. Since discomfort in the communication of sexual material still prevails between parents and their children, the young frequently are condemned, by lack of information about what is sexually meaningful, to live with decisions equally as unrewarding sexually as those made by their parents. In other words, because of cultural restraints the members of younger generations must continue to make their own sexual mistakes, since they, like previous generations, rarely have been given benefit of the results of their parents' past sexual experience—good, bad, or indifferent as that experience may have been. The necessary freedom of sexual communication between parents and sons and daughters cannot be achieved until the basic component of sexuality itself is given a socially comfortable role by all active generations simultaneously.

In the face of rapidly increasing complaints of inadequacy of human sexual function, it would seem that the potpourri of cultures that influence the behavior of so many might designate some area less vital to the quality of living than sexual expression to receive and to bear the burden of the social ills of human existence.

As recently as the turn of the century, after marriage rites and advent of offspring were celebrated as evidence of perpetuation of family and race, woman was considered to have done her duty, fulfilled herself, or both, depending of course upon the individual frame of reference. In reality society honored her contribution as a sexual entity only in relation to her capacity for breeding, never relative to the enhancement of the marital relationship by her sexual expression.

In contradistinction to the recognition accorded her as a breeding animal, the psychological importance of her physical presence during the act of conception was considered nonexistent. It must be acknowledged, however, that there always have been men and women in every culture who identified their need for one another as complete human entities, each denying nothing to the other including the vital component of sexual exchange. Unfortunately, whether from sexual fear or deprivation (both usually the result of too little knowledge), those who socially could not make peace with their sexuality were the ones to dictate and record concepts of female sexual identity. The code of the Puritan and similar ethics permitted only communication in the negative vein of rejection. There was no acceptable discussion of what was sexually supportive of marital relationships.

So far the discussion has focused on an account of past influences from which female sexual function has inherited its baseline for functional inadequacy. Because this influence still permeates the current "cultural" assignment of the female sexual role, its existence must be recognized before the psychophysiological components of dysfunction can be dealt with comprehensively. Sociocultural influence more often than not places woman in a position in which she must adapt, sublimate, inhibit or even distort her natural capacity to function sexually in order to fulfill her genetically assigned role. *Herein lies a major source of woman's sexual dysfunction.*

The adaptation of sexual function to meet socially desirable conditions represents a system operant in most successfully interactive behavior, which in turn is the essence of a mutually enhancing sexual relationship. However, to adapt sexual function to a philosophy of rejection is to risk impairment of the capacity for effective social interaction. To sublimate sexual function can enhance both self and that state to which the repression is committed, if the practice of sublimation lies within the coping capacity of the particular individual who adopts it. To inhibit sexual function beyond that realistic degree which equally serves social and sexual value systems in a positive way, or to distort or maladapt sexual function until the capacity or will to function is extinguished, is to diminish the quality of the individual and of any marital relationship to which he or she is committed.

When it is realized that this psychosocial backdrop is prevalent in histories developed from marital units with complaints of female sexual inadequacy, the psychophysiological and situational aspects of female orgasmic dysfunction can be contemplated realistically.

SYSTEMS OF PSYCHOPHYSIOLOGICAL INFLUENCE

The human female's facility of physiological response to sexual tensions and her capacity for orgasmic release never have been fully appreciated. Lack of comprehension may have resulted from the fact that functional evaluation was filtered through the encompassing influence of sociocultural formulations previously described in this chapter. There also has been failure to conceptualize the whole of sexual experience for both the human male and female as constituted in two totally separate systems of influence that coexist naturally, both contributing positively or negatively to any state of sexual responsivity, but having no biological demand to function in a complementary manner.

With the reminder that finite analysis of male sexual capacity and physiological response also has attracted little scientific interest in the past, it should be reemphasized that similarities rather than differences are frequently more significant in comparing male and female sexual response. By intent, the focus of this chapter is directed toward the human female, but much of what is to be said can and does apply to the human male.

The biophysically and psychosocially based systems of influence that naturally coexist in any woman have the capacity if not the biological demand to function in mutual support. Obviously, there is interdigitation of systems that reinforces the natural facility of each to function effectively. However, there is no factor of human survival or internal biological need defined for the female that is totally dependent upon a complementary interaction of these two systems. Unfortunately they frequently compete for dominance in problems of sexual dysfunction. As a result, when the human female is exposed to negative influences under circumstances of individual susceptibility, she is vulnerable to any form of psychosocial or biophysical conditioning, i.e., the formation of man's individually unique sexual value systems (see Chapter 2). Based upon the manner in which an individual woman internalizes the prevailing psychosocial influence, her sexual value system may or may not reinforce her natural capacity to function sexually.

One need only remember that sexual function can be displaced from its natural context temporarily or even for a lifetime in order to realize the concept's import. Women cannot erase their psychosocial sexuality (sexual identity—being female), but they can deny their biophysical capacity for natural sexual functioning by conditioned or deliberately controlled physical or psychological withdrawal from sexual exposure.

Yet woman's conscious denial of biophysical capacity rarely is a completely successful venture, for her physiological capacity for sexual response infinitely surpasses that of man. Indeed, her significantly greater susceptibility to negatively based psychosocial influences may imply the existence of a natural state of psychosexual-social balance between the sexes that has been culturally established to neutralize woman's biophysical superiority.

The specifics of the human female's physiological reactions to effective levels of sexual tension have been described in detail, but brief clinical consideration of these reactive principles is in order. For woman, as for man, the two specific total-body responses to elevated levels of sexual tension are increased myotonia (muscle tension) and generalized vasocongestion (pooling of blood in tissues), both superficial (sex flush) and deep (breast enlargement).

When clinical attention is directed toward female orgasmic dysfunction, one particular biological area—the pelvic structures—is of moment. Specific evidence has been accumulated of the incidence of both myotonia and vasocongestion in the female's pelvis as she responds physiologically to sex-tension elevation. The four phases of the female cycle of sexual response established in 1966 will be employed to identify clinically important vasocongestive and myotonic reactions developing in the pelvic viscera of any woman responding to sexual stimulation.

During woman's *excitement phase* of sex-tension increment, the first physical evidence of her response to sexual stimulation is vaginal lubrication. This lubrication is produced by a deep vasocongestive reaction in the tissues surrounding the vaginal barrel. There also is evidence of increasing muscle tension as the vaginal barrel expands and distends involuntarily in anticipation of penetration.

When sex tensions reach *plateau phase* levels of responsivity, a local concentration of venous blood develops in the outer third of the vaginal barrel, creating partial constriction of the central lumen. This vaginal evidence of a deep vasocongestive reaction has been termed the *orgasmic platform*. The uterus increases in size as venous blood is retained within the organ tissues, and the clitoris evidences increasing smooth-muscle tension by elevating from its natural, pudendal-overhang positioning and flattening on the anterior border of the symphysis.

With *orgasm*, reached at an increment peak of pelvic-tissue vasocongestion and myotonia, the orgasmic platform in the outer third of the vagina and the uterus contract within a regularly recurring rhythmicity as evidence of high levels of muscle tension.

Finally, with the *resolution phase*, both vasocongestion and myotonia disappear from the body generally, and the pelvic structures specifically. If orgasmic release has been obtained, there is rapid detumescence from these naturally accumulative physiological processes. The loss of muscle tension and venous blood accumulation is much slower if orgasm has not been experienced and there is obvious residual of sexual tension.

It is the presence of involuntary-muscle irritability and superficial and deep venous congestion that woman cannot deny, for these reactions develop as physiological evidence of both conscious and subconscious levels of sexual tension. With accumulation of myotonia and pelvic vasocongestion, the biophysical system signals the total structure with stimulative input of a positive nature.

Regardless of whether women voluntarily deny their biological capacity for sexual function, they cannot deny the pelvic, irritative evidence of inherent sexual tension for any length of time. Once a month with some degree of regularity women are reminded of their biological capacity. Interestingly, even the reminder develops in part as the result of local venous congestion and increased muscle tension in the reproductive organs. On occasion, the menstrual condition, through the suggestive sensation created by pelvic congestion, stimulates elevated sexual tensions.

The presence or absence of patterns of sexual desire or facility for sexual response within the continuum of the human female's menstrual cycle also has defied reliable identification. Possibly, confusion has resulted from the usual failure to consider the fact that two separate systems of influence may be competing for dominance in any sexual exposure. Necessity for such individual consideration can best be explained by example: It is possible for a sexually functional woman to feel sexual need and to respond to high levels of sexual excitation even to orgasmic release in response to a predominantly biophysical influence in the absence of a specific psychosocial requirement. This freedom to respond to direct biophysical-system demand requires only from its psychosocial counterpart that the female's sexual value system not transmit signals that inhibit or defer the manner in which erotic arousal is generated. In any situation of biophysical dominance, effective sexual response requires only a reasonable level of interdigital contribution by the psychosocial system.

Conversely, it also is possible for a human female to respond to erotic signals initiated by the predominant psychosocial factors of the sexual value system, regardless of conditions of biophysical imbalance such as hormonal deficiency or obvious pathology of the pelvic organs. A woman may respond sexually to the psychosocial system of influence to orgasmic response in the face of surgical castration and in spite of a general state of chronic fatigue or physical disability. In any situation of psychosocial dominance, effective sexual response requires only a reasonable level of inter-digital contribution by the biophysical system.

BACKGROUND OF ORGASMIC DYSFUNCTION

The potential for orgasmic dysfunction highlighted in the psychosocial-sexual histories of those women in marital units referred to the Foundation can be described in composite profile.

A baseline of dysfunctional distress was provided by specific material recalled not only from sexually developmental years but further encompassing all opportunities of potential sexual imprint-ing, conditioning, and experience storage. Within this body of material, described in many settings, the dissimulation of sexual feeling consistently was reported as a manifest requirement or as a residual of earlier learning, operant as a requirement. (Imprint-ing is that process which helps define the behavioral patterns of sexual expression and signal their arousal; see Chapter 11.)

Origin of the negative conditioning varied widely. At one pole it represented the influence of deliberate parental omission of reference to or discussion of sexual function as a component of the pattern of living. This informationally underprivileged background also failed to provide any example of female sexuality, recognizably secure in expression, which could be emulated. In both situations, the sexually and socially maturing young woman was left to draw formative conclusions by negative implication, or, in the absence of this form of direction, she was forced to react to any influence available from her sociocultural environment.

The other extreme of rejective conditioning was reported as rigidly explicit but consistently negative admonition by parental and/or religious authority against personal admission or overt expression of sexual feeling.

Between these negative variants, there were many levels of uninformed guidance for the young girl or woman as she struggled with psychosocial enigmas, cultural restrictions, and her own physical sexual awareness. Usually such guidance, though often well intentioned, was more a hindrance than a help as she developed her sexual value system and ultimately her natural sexual function.

In direct parallel to the degree to which the young girl developing a sexual value system seemed to have dissimulated her sexual interests during phases of imprinting, conditioning, and information storing, older women, now sexually dysfunctional, reported consistent precoital evidence of repression of sexual identity in mature sexual encounters.

Residual repression of sexual responsivity in the adult usually went well beyond any earlier theoretical requirements for a social adaptation necessary to maintain virginity, to restrain a partner's sexual demand, or even to conduct interpersonal relationships in a manner considered appropriate by representative social authority. Not infrequently the residual repression of sexual responsivity was so acute as to be emphasized clinically with the time-worn cry of "I don't feel anything."

Thus, for most primarily nonorgasmic women, repressed expression of sexual identity through ignorance, fear, or authoritative direction was the initial inhibiting influence in failure of sexual function. Not infrequently this source of repression was identified as a crucial factor of influence for situationally nonorgasmic women as well, although these individuals had the facility to overcome or circumnavigate its control under certain circumstances.

When requirements of the sexual value system prevailing during initial opportunities at sexual function could not be fulfilled because of the component of repression, each woman attempted without success to compensate in her desire for sexual expression by developing unrealistic partner identification, concept of social secureness, or pleasure in environmental circumstance. In the failure of her own sexual values to serve, there was almost a blind seeking for value substitutes. When a workable substitution was not identified and the void of psychosexual insecurity remained unfilled, sexual dysfunction became an ongoing way of life.

An interesting variation on this classification of repression should be mentioned. There were several primarily nonorgasmic women whose receptivity to the repressive conditioning was slightly different. Their own particular personality characteristics or their relationship to negatively directive authority was such that they fully accepted the concept of sexual rejection. They developed pride in their ability to comply with sexual repression and did so with apparent social grace.

Their selection of a mate in most cases represented a choice of similar background. The difficulty arose with marriage. On the wedding night a completely unrealistic, negative sexual value system usually was revealed during their attempt to establish an effective sexual interaction. These women reported either total pelvic anesthesia ("I don't feel anything") or isolation of sexual feelings from the context of psychosocial support.

Women entering therapy in a state of nonorgasmic return reflected complete failure of any effective alignment of their biophysical and their psychosocial systems of influence. They had never been able to merge either their points of maximum biophysical demand or their occasions of maximum psychosocial need with optimum environmental circumstances of time, place, or partner response in order to fulfill the requirements of their sexual value systems.

Primary orgasmic dysfunction describes a condition whereby neither the biophysical nor the psychosocial systems of influence that are required for effective sexual function is sufficiently dominant to respond to the psychosexually stimulative opportunities provided by self-manipulation, partner manipulation, or coital interchange.

If the concept of two interdigital systems influencing female sexual responsivity can be accepted, what can be considered the weaknesses and the strengths of each? Input required by either system for development of peak response is, of course, subject to marked variation. There may be some value in drawing upon the previously described psychophysiological findings returned from preclinical studies. As a human female responds to subjectively identifiable sexual stimuli, reliable patterns of accommodation by one system to the other can be defined, and tend to follow basic requirements set by earlier imprinting. Patterns of imprinting can be either reinforced or redirected by controlled experimental influence. They can also be diverted in their signaling potential by reorientation of a previously unrealistic sexual value system. The sexual value system, in turn, responds to reprogramming by new, positive experience (see Chapter 11).

Variations in the human female's biophysical system are, of course, relative to basic body economy. Is the woman in good health? Is there a cyclic hormonal ebb and flow to which she is particularly susceptible? Are the reproductive viscera anatomically and physiologically within "normal" limits, or is there evidence of pelvic pathology? Is there evidence of broad-ligament laceration, endometriosis, or residual from pelvic infection (see Chapter 10)? Certainly most forms of pelvic pathology would weigh against effective functioning of the biophysical system.

On the other hand, are there those biophysical patterns that tend to improve the basic facility of her sexual responsivity? Is there well-established metabolic balance, good nutrition, sufficient rest, regularity of sexual outlet? Each of these factors inevitably improves biophysical responsivity. There must be professional consideration of multiple variables when evaluating the influence of the biophysical system upon female sexual responsivity.

However, the system with the infinitely greater number of variables is that reflecting psychosocial influence. Most dysfunctional women's fundamental difficulty is that the requirements of their sexual value systems have never been met. Consequently, the resultant limitations of the psychosocial system have never been overcome.

There are many women who specifically resist the experience of orgasmic response, as they reject their sexual identity and the facility for its active expression. Often these women were exposed during their formative years to such timeworn concepts as "sex is dirty," "nice girls don't involve themselves," "sex is the man's privilege," or "sex is for reproduction only." There are also those whose resistance is established and sustained by a stored experience of mental or physical trauma (rape, dyspareunia, etc.), which is signaled by every sexual encounter.

Again from a negative point of view there may be extreme fear or apprehension of sexual functioning instilled in any woman by inadequate sex education. Any situation leading to sexual trauma, real or imagined, during her adolescent or teenage years or her sexual partner's crude demonstration of his own sexual desires without knowledge of how to protect her sexually would be quite sufficient to create a negative psychosocial concept of woman's role in sexual functioning. The woman living with residual of specific sexual trauma (mental or physical) frequently is encountered in this category.

Finally, there is the woman whose background forces her into automatic sublimation of psychosexual response. This individual simply has no expectations for sexual expression that are built upon a basis of reality. She has presumed that sexual response in some form simply would happen, but has little idea of its source of expression. In these instances sexual sublimation is allowed to become a way of life for many reasons. Particularly is this reaction encountered in the woman who has failed to enjoy the privilege of working at being a woman.

On the positive side, the psychosocial value system can overcome physical disability with dominant identification that may be personal and/or situational in nature. In states of advanced physical disability, the strength of a loved-partner identification can provide orgasmic impetus to a woman physically consigned to be sexually unresponsive. When there has been a pattern of little biophysical sexual demand, as in a postpartum period, sexual tension may be rapidly restored by the psychosocial stimulation of a vacation, anniversary, or other experience of special significance.

Again the biophysical and psychosocial systems of influence are interdigital in orientation, but there is no biological demand for their mutual complementary responsivity.

It is in the areas of involuntary sublimation that the psychosocial system is gravely handicapped and would tend to exert a negatively dominant influence in contradistinction to any possible biophysical stimulative function.

SECTION B

PRIMARY ORGASMIC DYSFUNCTION

In order to be diagnosed as having primary orgasmic dysfunction, a woman must report lack of orgasmic attainment during her entire lifespan. There is no definition of male sexual dysfunction that parallels in this severity of exclusion. If a male is judged primarily impotent, the definition means simply that he has never been able to achieve intromission in either homosexual or heterosexual opportunity. However, he might, and usually does, masturbate with some regularity or enjoy occasions of partner manipulation to ejaculation. For the primarily nonorgasmic woman, however, the definition demands a standard of total inorgasmic responsivity.

The edict of lifetime nonorgasmic return in the Foundation's definition of primary orgasmic dysfunction includes a history of consistent nonorgasmic response to all attempts at physical stimulation, such as masturbation or partner (male or female) manipulation, oral-genital contact, and vaginal or rectal intercourse. In short, every possible physical approach to sexual stimulation initiated by self or received from any partner has been totally unsuccessful in developing an orgasmic experience for the particular woman diagnosed as primarily nonorgasmic.

If a woman is orgasmic in dreams or in fantasy alone, she still would be considered primarily nonorgasmic. Foundation personnel have encountered two women who provided a positive history of an occasional dream sequence with orgasmic return and a negative history of physically initiated orgasmic release. However, no woman has been encountered to date that described the ability to fantasy to orgasm without providing a concomitant history of successful orgasmic return from a variety of physically stimulative measures.

There are salient truths about male and female sexual interaction that place the female in a relatively untenable position from the point of view of equality of sexual response. Of primary consideration is the fact of woman's physical necessity for an effectively functioning male sexual partner if she is to achieve coitally experienced orgasmic return. During coition the nonorgasmic human female is immediately more disadvantaged than her sexually inadequate partner in that her fears for performance are dual in character. Her primary fear is, of course, for her own inability to respond as a woman, but she frequently must contend with the secondary fear for inadequacy of male sexual performance.

The outstanding example of such a situation is, of course, that of the woman married to a premature ejaculator. From the point of view of mutual responsibility for sexual performance, the woman has only to make herself physically available in order to provide the male with ejaculatory satisfaction. When the premature ejaculator in turn makes himself available, there usually is little correlation between intromission, rapid ejaculation, and female orgasmic return during the episode.

When married to a premature ejaculator, the biophysically disadvantaged female usually is additionally disadvantaged from a psychosocial point of view. Not only is there insufficient biophysical opportunity to accomplish orgasmic return, but in short order the wife develops the concept of being sexually used in the marriage. She feels that her husband has no real interest in her personally nor any concept of responsibility to her as a sexual entity. As pointed out in Chapter 3, many times the wife might be at a peak of sexual excitation with intromission. Without fear for her husband's sexual performance she could be orgasmically responsive shortly after coital connection, displaying full biophysical capacity for sexual response, but as she sees and feels the male thrusting frantically for ejaculatory release, she immediately fears loss of sexual opportunity, is distracted from input of biophysical stimuli by that fear, and rapidly loses sexual interest. With the negative psychosocial-system influence from the concept of being used more than counterbalancing the high level of biophysically oriented sexual tension she brought to the coital act, orgasmic opportunity is lost.

A brief attempt should be made to highlight the direct association of male and female sexual dysfunction in marriage, for there were 223 marital units referred to the Foundation for treatment with bilateral partner complaints of sexual inadequacy (see Chapter 14). By far the greatest instance of a combined diagnosis was that of a nonorgasmic woman married to a premature ejaculator.

Of the total 186 premature ejaculators treated in the 11-year program, 68 were married to women reported as primarily nonorgasmic and an additional 39 wives were diagnosed as situationally nonorgasmic. Thus, in 107 of the 223 marriages with bilateral partner complaint of sexual dysfunction, the specific male sexual inadequacy was premature ejaculation.

Since the in-depth descriptions of the premature ejaculator presented in Chapters 3 and 6 include full descriptions of the problems of female sexual functioning in this situation, there is no need for a detailed history representative of the 68 women primarily nonorgasmic in marriages to prematurely ejaculating men.

Another salient feature in the human female's disadvantaged role in coital connection is the centuries-old concept that it is woman's duty to satisfy her sexual partner. When the age-old demand for accommodation during coital connection dominates any woman's responsivity, her own opportunities for orgasmic expression are lessened proportionately. If woman is to express her biophysical drive effectively, she must have the single-standard opportunity to think and feel sexually during coital connection that previous cultures have accorded the man.

The male partner must consider the marital bed as not only his privilege but also a shared responsibility if his wife is to respond fully with him in coital expression. The heedless male driving for orgasm can carry along the woman already lost in high levels of sexual demand, but his chances of elevating to orgasm the woman who is trying to accommodate to the rhythm, depth, and power of his demanding pelvic thrusting are indeed poor.

It is extremely difficult to categorize female sexual dysfunction on a relatively secure etiological basis. There is such a multiplicity of influences within the biophysical and psychosocial systems that to isolate and underscore a single, major etiological factor in any particular situation is to invite later confrontation with pitfalls in therapeutic progression.

RELIGIOUS ORTHODOXY

While the multiplicity of etiological influences is acknowledged, the factor of religious orthodoxy still remains of major import in primary orgasmic dysfunction as in almost every form of human sexual inadequacy. In the total of 193 women who have never achieved orgasmic return before referral to the Foundation for treatment, 41 were products of rigidly channelized religious control. Eighteen were from Catholic, 16 from Jewish, and 7 from fundamentalist Protestant backgrounds. It may also be recalled that 9 of these 41 primarily nonorgasmic women reflecting orthodox religious backgrounds also were identified as having the clinical complaint of vaginismus, while 3 more women with orthodox religious backgrounds had to contend with situational orgasmic dysfunction and vaginismus simultaneously (see Chapter 9). A history reflecting the control of orthodox religious demands upon the orgasmically dysfunctional woman and her husband is presented to underscore the Foundation's professional concern for any orthodoxy-influenced imprinting and environmental input that can and does impose severely negative influences upon the susceptible woman's psychosocial structure relative to her facility for sexual functioning.

After 9 years of a marriage that had not been consummated, Mr. and Mrs. A were referred to the Foundation for treatment. He was 26 and she 24 years old at marriage. Mrs. A's family background was one of unquestioned obedience to parents and to disciplinary religious tenets. She was one of three siblings, the middle child to an elder brother by three years and a younger sister by two years. Other than her father, religion was the overwhelming influence in her life. The specific religious orientation, that of Protestant fundamentalism, encompassed total dedication to the concept that sex and sin were synonymous words.

Mrs. A remembers her father, who died when she was 19, as a Godlike figure whose opinion in all matters was absolute law in the home. Control of dress, social commitment, educational direction, and in fact, school selection through college were his responsibility. There were long daily sessions of family prayer interspersed with paternal pronouncements, never family discussions. On Sunday the entire day was devoted to the church, with activities running the gamut of Sunday school, formal service, and young people's groups.

The young woman described a cold, formal, controlled family environment in which there was complete demand for dress as well as toilet privacy. Not only were the elder brother and sisters socially isolated, but the sisters also were given separate rooms and encouraged to protect individual privacy. She never remembers having seen her mother, father, brother, or sister in an undressed state. The subject of sex was never mentioned, and all literature, including newspapers, available to the family group was evaluated by her father for possibly suggestive or controversial material. There was a restricted list of radio programs to which the children could listen.

Mrs. A had no concept of her mother except as a woman living a life of rigid emotional control, essentially without a described personality, fully dedicated to the concept that woman's role was one of service. She considered it her duty and her privilege to clean, cook, and care for children, and to wait upon her husband. There is no recall of pleasant moments of quiet exchange between mother and daughter, or, for that matter, of any freedom to discuss matters of moment with either her brother or her sister.

As a young girl she was totally unprepared for the onset of menstruation. The first menstrual period occurred while she was in school; she was terrified, ran home, and was received by a thoroughly embarrassed mother who coldly explained to the young girl that this was woman's lot. She was told that as a woman she must expect to suffer this "curse" every month. Her mother warned her that once a month she would be quite ill with "bad pains" in her stomach and closed the discussion with the admonition that she was never to discuss the subject with anyone, particularly not with her younger sister. The admonition was obeyed to the letter. The mother provided the protective materials necessary and left the girl to her own devices. There was no discussion of when or how to use the menstrual protection provided.

Menstrual cramping had its onset with the second menstrual period and continued to be a serious psychosocial handicap until Mrs. A was seen in therapy. She also described the fact that her younger sister was confined to bed with monthly frequency while maturing.

During the teenage years, dating in groups was permitted by her father for church-social activities and occasionally, well-chaperoned school events. College, selected by her father, was a coeducational institution which was described by her as living by the "18-inch rule," i.e., handholding was forbidden and 18 inches were required between male and female students at all times. Her dating was rare and well chaperoned. After graduation she worked as a secretary in a publishing house specializing in religious tracts. Here she met and married a man of almost identical religious background.

The courtship was completely circumspect from a physical point of view. The couple arrived at their wedding night with a history of having exchanged three chaste kisses, which not only was the total of their physical courtship but also represented the only times she remembered ever being kissed by a man. Her father had felt such a display of emotion unseemly.

The only time her mother ever discussed a sexual matter was the day of her wedding. Mrs. A was carefully instructed to remember that she now was committed to serve her husband. It would be her duty as a wife to allow her husband "privileges." The privileges were never spelled out. She also was assured that she would be hurt by her husband, but that "it" would go away in time. Finally and most important, she was told that "good women" never expressed interest in the "thing." Her reward for serving her husband would be, hopefully, in having children.

She remembers her wedding night as a long struggle devoted to divergent purposes. Her husband frantically sought to find the proper place to insert his penis, while she fought an equally determined battle with nightclothes and bedclothes to provide as completely a modest covering as possible for the awful experience. The pain her mother had forecast developed as her husband valiantly strove for intromission.

Although initially there were almost nightly attempts to consummate the marriage, there was total lack of success. It never occurred to Mrs. A that she might cooperate in any way with the insertive attempts—since this was to be her husband's pleasure, it therefore was his responsibility. She evidenced such a consistently painful response whenever penetration was attempted that frequency of coital attempt dwindled rapidly. The last three years before referral, attempts at consummation occurred approximately once every three to four months.

For nine years this woman only knew that she was physically distressed whenever her husband approached her sexually, and that for some reason the distress did not abate. Her husband occasionally ejaculated while attempting to penetrate, so she thought that he must be "satisfied." Whenever Mr. A renewed the struggle to consummate, she was convinced that he had little physical consideration for her. Her tense, frustrated, negative attitude, initially stimulated by both the pain and the "good woman" concept described by her mother, became in due course one of complete physical rejection of sexual functioning in general and of the man involved in particular.

When seen in therapy, Mrs. A had no concept of what the word masturbation meant. Her husband's sexual release before marriage had been confined to occasional nocturnal emissions, but he did learn to masturbate after marriage and accomplished ejaculatory release approximately once a week, without his wife's knowledge. There was no history of extramarital exposure.

Of interest is the fact that Mrs. A's brother has been twice divorced, reportedly because he cannot function sexually, and her younger sister has never married.

As would be expected, at physical examination Mrs. A demonstrated a severe degree of vaginismus in addition to the intact hymen. In the process of explaining the syndrome of involuntary vaginal spasm to both husband and wife, the procedures described in Chapter 9 were followed in detail.

When vaginismus was described and then directly demonstrated to both husband and wife, it was the first time Mr. A had ever seen his wife unclothed and also the first time she had submitted to a medical examination.

There obviously were multiple etiological influences combining to create this orgasmic dysfunction, but the repression of all sexual material inherent in the described form of religious orthodoxy certainly was the major factor. Under Foundation direction, the process of education had to include reorientation of both the sexual and social value systems. The influence of the psychosocial system was turned from a dominant negative factor to a relatively neutral one during the acute phase of treatment. This alteration in repressive quality allowed Mrs. A's natural biophysical demand to function without determined opposition, and orgasmic expression was obtained. Obviously, the husband needed a definitive psychosexual evaluation as much as did his wife.

ABSENCE OF DOMINANT INFLUENCE

Professionals many times look for a specific influence or conditioning that predetermines sexual failure, and in most instances it can be identified if the delving goes deep enough. There are, however, instances of neither positive nor negative dominance by either biophysical or psychosocial influence structures.

If a woman has never established a close juxtaposition between the biophysical and psychosocial systems of influence because she has lived in a protective vacuum, she will not have been stimulated to develop her own sexual value system and therefore will tend to neutralize most input material of sexual implication.

The case history below is presented to emphasize the fact that there need be no dominant influence (either positive or negative) in the development of primary orgasmic dysfunction.

Mrs. B was an only child of parents in their thirties when she was born. Both parents, teachers in a small, church-oriented college, were more restrained by habit of life-style and their own relationship than by religious influence. The child did not develop as an extension of their presumed intellectual interests but became the "doll" whom they dressed exquisitely, handled little, and disregarded emotionally (as she perceived her upbringing). There was no real source of female identification, no opportunity to establish a sexual value system.

All decisions in her behalf included the theoretically objective presentation of two alternatives, but parental, primarily mother's, preference was emphasized. Mrs. B had no recollection of making a definitive decision of her own until her sophomore year at college, when she chose for a husband a relatively older man (he was in graduate school and seven years her senior). With this one decision she again relinquished all opportunity for self-determination.

They married upon his graduation at the end of her junior year in college. His assumption of total authority in marriage appeared more by default than demand and continued through 11 years of marriage, during which two children were born.

During the first years of the marriage, Mrs. B maintained a complacent attitude toward her sexual role within the marriage. However, in the last six years of the marriage she developed an intense desire to realize full sexual expression for herself and greater sexual pleasure for her husband. During this latter period her husband's behavior, though warm and protective, was highly restrained in sexual as well as other facets of the marital relationship. He participated in the Foundation's program with complete willingness, although with little concept of what or how anything in the marriage could be changed. Reared by an older aunt and uncle he had learned little, by direction or observation, of the potential for human interaction on a personal level. However, he fortunately had not been given any primarily negative indoctrination.

Mrs. B's enthusiasm for an effective sexual relationship within the marriage was and still is defined as real, but she has been unable to overcome anesthesia to any sensory perception that she can relate to erotic arousal. She has been unable to establish sensory reference within which to develop and relate her well-defined affection and regard for her husband. The two contributing systems of influence on sexual function have remained in displaced positioning one from the other. To date she has demonstrated insufficient emotional and/or intellectual capacity to establish a symbiotic state between her two systems of influence.

It is with mixed clinical reaction that the cotherapists regard the positive reaction of Mr. B to therapy. His response was one of delighted enthusiasm to the concept of interaction marked by both physical and verbal communication. His feeling for his wife was intensified and he has become completely comfortable in a demonstrative marital role. While both partners feel that the alteration in the quality of the marital relationship is of significant proportion, the therapy has in fact failed to achieve the aim of reversal of the presenting distress. This case represents a strikingly intense degree of negative conditioning, yet there was little of content in the history that could be termed specifically negative in its rejection of sexual expression.

This case also represents an example of the possible clinical warning system revealed by a negative reaction to the use of a moisturizing lotion as a medium of physical exchange. Mrs. B found its use "distracting" and of little meaning to the exchange with her partner, while Mr. B found it to be the crucial contribution to establishing his initial ability to touch and feel with comfort and receptivity (see Chapter 2).

NEGATIVE PSYCHOSOCIAL DOMINANCE

For many women one of the most frequent causes for orgasmic dysfunction, either primary or situational, is lack of complete identification with the marital partner. The husband may not meet her expectations as a provider. He may have physical or behavioral patterns that antagonize. Most important, he may stand in the place of the man who had been much preferred as a marital partner but was not available or did not choose to marry the distressed woman. For myriad reasons, if the husband is considered inadequate according to his wife's expectations, a negative dominance will be created in the psychosocial structure of many women. Such a situation is exemplified by the following case history.

Mr. and Mrs. C were 46 and 42 years of age, respectively, when referred to the Foundation. The wife complained of lack of orgasmic return. The unit had been married 19 years when seen in treatment. The marriage was the only one for either partner. There were three children, the eldest of whom was 17, the youngest 12. There were barely adequate financial circumstances.

Mrs. C's adolescent background had been somewhat restrictive. Her mother was a dominant woman with whom she developed little rapport. Her father died when she was 9 years old. There was one other sibling, a sister 8 years younger. Mrs. C went through the usual high-school preparation, had two years of college, and then withdrew to take secretarial training and go to work in a large manufacturing company.

During her formative years there was a number of friends, none of them particularly close with the exception of one girl with whom she shared all her confidences. Mrs. C as a girl was fairly popular with boys, dated with regularity, and went through the usual petting experiences, but decided to avoid coital connection until marriage. She had no masturbatory history but described pleasure in the petting experiences, although she was not orgasmic.

Shortly after her twenty-second birthday she fell in love with a young salesman for the company in which she worked. Theirs was a very happy relationship with every evidence of real mutuality of interest. She came to know and thoroughly enjoy his family, and they made plans to marry. Three weeks before the marriage, her fiancé, on a business trip, met and a week later married another woman, a divorcée with two children.

The jilted girl was crushed by the turn of events. This had been her only serious romantic attachment, and it had been a total commitment on her part. Their sexual expression had been one of mutual petting and she had manipulated her fiancé to ejaculation regularly. Although she had been highly stimulated by his approaches she had not been orgasmic. Coital connection had not been attempted.

Six months later she married Mr. C, whom she thought "kind and considerate." Their sexual experiences together were pleasant, but she achieved nothing comparable to the high levels of excitation provided by the first man in her life. She described life with her husband as originally a "good marriage." The children arrived as planned and the husband continued to progress satisfactorily in his business ventures, but husband and wife had very few mutual interests.

As the years passed Mrs. C became obsessed with the fact that she had never been orgasmic. She began to masturbate and reached high levels of excitation. Straining and willing orgasmic return without being able to fully accept the unrealistic nature of her imagery and fantasying, she failed, of course, in accomplishment. Her husband, with very little personal sexual experience other than in his marriage, had no real concept of effective sexual approach. She repeatedly tried to tell him of her need, but his cooperative effort, maintained for only brief periods of time, was essentially unsuccessful.

After 12 years of marriage, Mrs. C sought sexual release outside the marriage with a man sexually much more experienced than her husband. He did excite her to high plateau levels of sexual demand, but she always failed to achieve orgasmic release. This connection lasted off and on for a year and was only the first of several such extramarital commitments, always with the same disappointment in sexual return. She was never able to avoid fantasy of her former fiancé whenever she approached orgasmic return, but her fantasy included a primarily negative impetus. Her frustration at "marrying the wrong man" was a constant factor in her coital encounters, as it was in most other aspects of her life.

As time passed she blamed her husband increasingly for her lack of orgasmic facility and became progressively more discontented with her lot in the marriage. She began to find fault with his financial return and social connections. In short, Mrs. C felt that her husband was not providing satisfactorily for her needs and inevitably compared him with the man "she almost married." This man had become a relatively well-known figure in the local area, had done extremely well financially, and apparently had a happy, functioning marriage. Although Mrs. C never saw her former fiancé, she constantly dwelt on what might have been, to the detriment of the ongoing relationship.

Mrs. C sought psychiatric support for her nonorgasmic status but was unable to achieve the only real goal in her life, orgasmic release. Finally, the marital unit was referred to the Foundation.

How does one overcome professionally the conditioning of an adult lifetime? How many men could have met and/or continued to cope with the requirements of her sexual value system, impaired by the trauma it sustained when she was jilted by a man with whom she identified totally? Can necessary adjustment to both her social and her sexual value systems be made in the hope of reversing or at least neutralizing the negative input of her psychosocial structure? What possibility is there for positive stimulation of the biophysical structure? These are the questions cotherapists should ask themselves when facing a problem such as that exemplified by the marital unit reported above.

There is no possible means of restructuring the negative input from "I married the wrong man" unless the problem is attacked directly. First, in private sessions the immature deification of her former fiancé must be underscored. Second, Mr. C must be presented to his wife in a different light, not in a platitudinal manner, but as the female cotherapist objectively views him. A man's positive attributes as he appears in another woman's eyes carry value to the dysfunctional woman.

Then there must be stimulation of the biophysical structure to levels of positive input. This, of course, is initiated by sensate-focus procedures (see Chapter 2). Finally, the contrived somatic stimulation must be interpreted to Mrs. C's sexual value system both by the cotherapists and by her husband (see Chapter 11). If these treatment concepts are followed successfully there is every good chance to reach the goal of orgasmic attainment.

MALE PRIMARY OR SECONDARY IMPOTENCE

Although emphasis has been placed upon the role of premature ejaculation in the etiology of primary orgasmic dysfunction, primary or secondary impotence also contributes. Again the basic theme of man-woman coital interaction must be emphasized. If there is not a sexually effective male partner, the female partner has the dual handicap of fear for her husband's sexual performance as well as for her own. If there is no penile erection there will be no effective coital connection.

Frequently women married to impotent men cannot accept the idea of developing masturbatory facility or being manipulated to orgasm as a substitute for tension release. However, if there has been a masturbatory pattern established before coital inadequacy assumes dominance, most women can return to this sexual outlet. In this situation there is sufficient dominance of the previously conditioned biophysical structure to overcome negative input from a psychosocial system distressed by sexual performance fears. But if there have been no previous substitute measures established, many women cannot turn to this mode of relief once impotence halts effective coital connection. In this situation the psychosocial structure, unopposed by prior biophysical conditioning, assumes the dominant influence in the woman's sexual response pattern. Such a situation is illustrated by the following case history.

Mr. and Mrs. D were referred to the Foundation for treatment of orgasmic inadequacy after four years of marriage. When seen in therapy she was 27 and her husband 43 years old. He had been married twice previously. There were children of both marriages and none in the current marriage. The husband also was sexually dysfunctional in that he was secondarily impotent.

His second marriage had been terminated due to his inability to continue effective coital connection. Although, when the unit was seen in consultation the marriage had been consummated, coitus occurred only once or twice a year.

Mrs. D's background reflected somewhat limited financial means. Her father had died when the three siblings were young, and the family had been raised by their mother, who worked while the grandmother took care of the children. Clothes were hand-me-downs, food the bare essentials. Her education had of necessity terminated with high school, and she worked as a receptionist in several different offices before her marriage. She continued to live at home while working and contributed what salary she made to help with the family's limited income.

Mrs. D met her future husband when he visited the office where she worked. He invited the young woman to lunch. She accepted and married him four months later without knowledge of his sexual inadequacy, although she had been somewhat puzzled by his lack of forceful sexual approach during the brief courtship.

Mrs. D's own sexual history had been one of a few unsuccessful attempts at masturbation, numerous petting episodes with boys in and out of high school, but no attempted coital connection. She had never been orgasmic.

Her husband had inherited a large estate and his financial situation certainly was the determining factor in his wife's marital commitment. Since the girl had been distressed by a family background of genteel poverty, she felt the offer of marriage to be her real opportunity both to escape her environment and to help her two younger siblings.

The wedding trip was an unfortunate experience for Mrs. D when she realized for the first time that her husband had major functional difficulties. She knew little of male sexual response beyond the petting experiences but did try to help him achieve an erection by a multiplicity of stimulative approaches at his direction. There was no success in erective attainment.

The marriage was not consummated until six months after the ceremony. In the middle of the night Mr. D awoke with an erection, moved to his wife, and inserted the penis. She experienced mild pain but reacted with pleasure, feeling that progress had been made. However, following the usual pattern of a secondarily impotent male, progress was fleeting. As stated, there were only a few other coital episodes in the course of the four-year marriage. In these instances she always was awakened from sleep by her husband when he awoke to find himself with an erection. Then there was rapid intromission and quick ejaculation. There was no history of a successful sexual approach by her husband under her conscious direction, insistence, or stimulation.

Mr. D tried repetitively during long-continued manipulative and oral-genital sessions to bring his wife to orgasm, without result. When they were referred for treatment, neither husband nor wife described sexual activity outside the marriage.

There have been 193 women treated for primary orgasmic dysfunction during the past 11 years. Basically, in this method of therapy the sexually dysfunctional woman is approached through her sexual value system. If its requirements are nonserving—limited, unrealistic, or inadequate to the marital relationship—by suggestion she is given an opportunity, with her husband's help, to manipulate her biophysical and psychosocial structures of influence until an effective sexual value system is formed (see Chapter 11).

SITUATIONAL ORGASMIC DYSFUNCTION

In order to be considered situationally nonorgasmic, a woman must have experienced at least one instance of orgasmic expression, regardless of whether it was induced by self or by partner manipulation, developed during vaginal or rectal coital connection, or stimulated by oral-genital exchange. For instance, orgasmic experience during homosexual encounter would rule out any possibility of a diagnosis of primary orgasmic dysfunction. Three arbitrary categories of situational sexual dysfunction have been defined—masturbatory, coital, and random orgasmic inadequacy.

A woman with masturbatory orgasmic inadequacy has not achieved orgasmic release by partner or self-manipulation in either homosexual or heterosexual experience. She can and does reach orgasmic expression during coital connection.

Coital orgasmic inadequacy applies to the great number of women who have never been able to achieve orgasmic return during coition. The category includes women able to masturbate or to be manipulated to orgasmic return and those who can respond to orgasmic release from oral-genital or other stimulative techniques.

The random orgasmic-inadequacy grouping includes those women with histories of orgasmic return at least once during both manipulative and coital opportunities. These women are rarely orgasmic and usually are aware of little or no physical need for sexual expression. For example, they might achieve orgasmic return with coital activity on a vacation, but never while at home. Occasionally these women might masturbate to orgasm if separated from a sexual partner for long periods of time. Usually when they obtain orgasmic release, the experience is as much of a surprise to them as it is to their established sexual partner.

The situational nonorgasmic state may best be described by again pointing out the varying levels of dominance created by the biophysical and the psychosocial structures of influence. If the woman's sexual value system reflects sufficiently negative input from prior conditioning (psychosocial influence), she may not be able to adapt sexual expression to the positive stimulus of the particular time, place, or circumstance of her choosing nor develop a responsive reaction to the partner of her choice.

If that part of any woman's sexual value system susceptible to the influence of the biophysical structure is overwhelmed by a negative input from pain with any attempted coital connection, there rarely will be effective sexual response.

Thus there is a multiplicity of influences thrown onto the balance wheel of female sexual responsivity. It is fortunate that the two major systems of influence accommodate these variables through involuntary interdigitation. If there were not the probability of admixture of influence, there might be relatively few occasions of female orgasmic experience.

ORIENTATION TO PARTNER

A major source of orgasmic influence for both primarily and situationally dysfunctional women, is partner orientation. What value has the male partner in the woman's eyes? Does the chosen male maintain his image of masculinity? Regardless of his acknowledged faults, does he meet the woman's requirements of character, intelligence, ego strength, drive, physical characteristics, etc.? Obviously every woman's partner requirements vary with her age, personal experience and confidence, and the requisites of her sexual value system.

The two case histories below underscore the variables of woman's orientation to her male sexual partner. The histories of Mr. and Mrs. E and Mr. and Mrs. F are presented to emphasize that a potential exists for radical change in attitudinal concepts during the course of any marriage.

Mr. and Mrs. E were referred for treatment of orgasmic dysfunction after 23 years of marriage; they had two children, a girl 20 and a boy 19. The history of sexual dysfunction dated back to the twelfth year of the marriage.

Both had relatively unremarkable backgrounds with relation to family, education, and religious influences. Both had masturbated as teenagers and had intercourse with other partners and with each other before marriage. Mrs. E usually had been orgasmic during these coital opportunities with her husband-to-be and with two other partners.

During the first twelve years of the marriage the couple prospered financially and socially, and had many common interests. Their sexual expression resolved into an established pattern of sexual release two or three times a week. There was regularity of orgasmic return (frequently multiorgasmic return) during intercourse.

During the twelfth year of the marriage, the unit experienced a severe financial reversal. Mr. E was discharged from his position with the company that had employed him since the start of the marriage. In the following 18 months he was unsuccessful in obtaining any permanent type of employment. He became chronically depressed and drank too much. The established pattern of marital-unit sexual encounter was either quite reduced or, on occasions, demandingly increased.

Then Mrs. E found that her husband was involved in an extramarital relationship and confronted him in the matter. A bitter argument followed, and she refused him the privilege of the marital bed. This sexual isolation lasted for approximately six months, during which time Mr. E began working again, regained control of his alcohol intake, and terminated his extramarital interest.

For the duration of this isolation period Mrs. E had no coital opportunity and did not masturbate. When the privilege of the bedroom was restored, to her surprise she was distracted rather than stimulated by her husband's sexual approaches and was not orgasmic. She had lost confidence in her husband not only as an individual but also as a masculine figure. Mrs. E found herself "going through the motions" sexually. From the time the bedroom door was reopened until the unit was seen in therapy, she was nonorgasmic regardless of the mode of sexual approach. Coital connection had dwindled to a ten-day to two-week frequency of "wifely duty."

When a major element in any woman's sexual value system (partner identification in this instance) is negated or neutralized by a combination of circumstances, many women find no immediate replacement factor. Until they do, their facility for sexual responsivity frequently remains jeopardized.

When Mr. E combined loss of his masculine image as provider with excessive alcohol intake and, in addition, acquired another sexual partner, he destroyed his wife's concept of his sexual image, and, in doing so, removed from availability a vital stimulative component of her sexual value system. The negative input of psychosocial influence created by Mr. E's loss of masculinity and impairment of her sense of sexual desirability was sufficient to inhibit her natural sexual responsivity.

Mr. and Mrs. F were referred for treatment six years after they married when he was 29 and she was 24 years old. They had one child, a girl, during their third year together. Mrs. F was from a family of seven children and remembers a warm community experience in growing up with harried but happy parents.

Her husband had exactly the opposite background. He was an only child in a family where both father and mother devoted themselves to his every interest—in short, the typical overindulged single child. He had masturbated from early teens, had a number of sexual experiences, and one brief engagement with coital connection maintained regularly for six months before he terminated the commitment.

Mrs. F, although she dated regularly as a girl, was fundamentally oriented to group-type social commitments. She rarely had experienced single dating.

The school years were uneventful for both individuals. They met and married almost by accident. When they first began dating, each was interested in someone else. However, their mutual interest increased rapidly and developed into a courtship that included regularity of coital connection for three months before marriage. Every social decision was made by Mr. F during the courtship. The same pattern of total control continued into marriage. He insisted on making all decisions and was consistently concerned with his own demands, paying little or no attention to his wife's interests. A constant friction developed, as is so frequently the case with marital partners whose backgrounds are diametrically opposed.

Mrs. F had not been orgasmic before marriage. In marriage she was orgasmic on several occasions with manipulation but not during coition. As the personal friction between the marital partners increased, she found herself less and less responsive during active coital connection. There was occasional orgasmic success with manipulation. Pregnancy intervened at this time, distracting her for a year, but thereafter her lack of coital return was distressing to her and most embarrassing to her husband. He worried as much about his image as a sexually effective male as he did about his wife's levels of sexual frustration. Mrs. F's lack of effective sexual response was considered a personal affront by her uninformed husband.

They consulted several authorities on the matter of "her" sexual inadequacy. The husband always sent his wife to authority to have something done to or for her. The thought that the situation might have been in any measure his responsibility was utterly foreign to him.

When the unit was referred for therapy he at first refused to join her in treatment on the basis that it was "her problem." When faced with Foundation demand that both partners cooperate or the problem would not be accepted for treatment, Mr. F grudgingly consented to participate.

Little comment is needed. This intentionally brief history is typical of the woman who cannot identify with her partner because he will not allow such communication. There is no world as closed to the vital ingredient of marital expression (vulnerability exchange) as that of the world of the indulged only child. Particularly is this attitudinal background incomprehensible to a woman with a typical large family orientation. When Mr. F failed to accord his wife the representation of her own requirements, she had no opportunity to think or feel sexually. The catalytic ingredient of mutual partner involvement was missing.

HOMOSEXUAL INFLUENCE

For many women, a basic homophile orientation is a major etiological factor in heterosexual orgasmic dysfunction. For those women committed to homosexual expression, lack of orgasmic return from heterosexual opportunity is of no consequence. But there are a large number of women with significant homosexual experience during their early teenage years that, in time, have withdrawn from active homophile orientation to live socially heterosexual lives. When they marry, many are committed to orgasmic dysfunction by the prior imprinting of homosexual influence upon their sexual responsivity. Prior homosexual conditioning acts to create a negatively dominant psychosocial influence. Their biophysical capacity, freely evidenced in homosexual opportunity, continues operant in their electively chosen heterosexual environment, but it may not be of sufficient quality to overcome the negative input from their psychosocial system.

It is difficult to evaluate homosexual influence upon heterosexual function. There can be no question that both means of sexual expression will always be an integral part of every culture. So it has been for recorded time.

The problems of sexual adjustment do not rest with those committed unreservedly to a specific pattern of response. Rather, it is the gray-area dweller that creates for him or herself a sexually dysfunctional status. When moving from one means of sexual expression to the other for the first time, the sexual value system must be reoriented if the desired transfer of sexual identification is to be completed. Such was the problem of Mrs. G who had not been able to adapt her sexual value system to her elected heterosexual world when seen in therapy.

When Mr. and Mrs. G were referred for treatment after seven years of marriage, she was 33, her husband 38 years old. The current marriage was his second, the first ending in divorce. The presenting complaint was that Mrs. G had never been orgasmic in the marriage.

Her childhood and adolescence were spent in a small midwestern town as an only child of elderly parents. Her mother was 41 when she was born. Introverted as a teenager, the girl did well in school but had few friends and was not popular with male classmates. When she was 15 years old she formed a major psychosexual attachment to a high-school teacher, who seduced the girl into a homosexual relationship. The courtship continued for six months before physical seduction was accomplished. Once fully committed to the homosexual relationship, the girl matured rapidly in personality and took a great deal more care with her dress and person. She vested total psychosexual commitment in her "teacher" throughout her high-school years.

Full responsivity in the sexual component of the relationship developed slowly for the teenager, although she was occasionally orgasmic with manipulation within a few months of her first physical experience. Initially, hers was primarily a receptive role, but as she matured in the relationship psychologically, mutual manipulation and oral-genital stimulation in natural sequence became part of the unit's pattern of sexual expression. During the girl's last year in high school, mutual sexual tensions were maintained at a high level, and physical release was sought by either or both women at a minimum frequency level of three to four times a week. Both women were multiorgasmic. Mrs. G has no history of heterosexual dating in high school.

There was physical separation when Mrs. G went to college, but since the separation represented a distance of only fifty miles, she and the teacher spent many weekends together. However, toward the end of Mrs. G's sophomore year in college, the high-school teacher was apprehended approaching other girls, was discharged, and left the geographical area.

This was a major blow to the girl. She had lost her love and at the same time was made aware that the teacher had sought other outlets. Her grades suffered and she became severely depressed and totally antisocial. She dropped out of school for a semester, during which time she did very little but write long forgiving letters to her mentor, and even visited her for a ten-day period under the pretext of going to see friends.

It was not until Mrs. G graduated from college that the homosexual relationship was finally terminated. During the four college years she had only two dates, both involving attendance at school events and of no sexual portent.

After graduation Mrs. G took secretarial training and began working in a larger city in the Midwest. She still suffered from recurrent bouts of depression and finally sought psychiatric support. Helped by this counseling, she gradually enlarged her social circle, began heterosexual dating, and once more showed an interest in her dress and person.

While in college she had developed masturbatory patterns for tension release. The frequency throughout college and during her early years working as a secretary was several times per week. She usually was multiorgasmic, as she had been during her continuing homosexual relationship.

At age 25 Mrs. G deliberately took advantage of an available partner to attempt intercourse. This experience was sought purely from curiosity demand. There were several coital exposures with this eager but relatively inexperienced young man. She found herself repulsed by the man's untutored, harsh approaches as opposed to those of her high-school teacher. She was not physically responsive and found the seminal fluid objectionable. Added to this general rejection of heterosexual interest was the fact that shortly after establishing the sexual relationship there was a 10-day delay in the onset of a menstrual period. Her fear of pregnancy only contributed to her rejection of any psychosocial concept of heterosexual functioning.

Shortly thereafter Mrs. G met her husband. He had been divorced six months previously for the stated reason that his wife had wanted to marry another man. There were two children of the marriage, both living with their mother. They were both lonely people and gravitated to each other. There was warmth and affection between them and a number of mutual interests, so they married. Mr. G was sexually well versed, kind, considerate, and gentle with his wife. She felt warmly toward him and enjoyed providing him with sexual release. In doing so she lost her incipient phobia for the seminal fluid. However, she was unstimulated by his sexual approaches beyond that degree necessary to produce adequate vaginal lubrication. Both partners agreed they did not want children, so contraceptive medication was taken by the wife.

The marriage, though warm and comfortable, for several years was essentially one of convenience. However, as time passed, the two partners grew closer together, learned to communicate and to exchange vulnerabilities. Yet there was no improvement in the wife's sexual responsivity, and this became an increasingly important factor in their lives. Mrs. G had never told her husband of her homosexual experience and was guilt-ridden by the concept that her past sexual orientation might have precluded any possibility of effective response in her now-desired heterosexual state. The marital unit was referred for treatment at her insistence.

LOW SEXUAL TENSION AS A POTENTIAL CLINICAL ENTITY

Random orgasmic inadequacy is illustrated in the history below. With but two episodes of orgasmic attainment in her life, Mrs. H provides a history of one manipulative and one coital effort to orgasmic release. Her two highlighted sexual experiences were as much of a surprise to her when they occurred as they were to her husband.

There seems to be a clinical entity of low sexual tension which by history does not represent specific trauma to a sexual or any other value system. If so, it is rare both in occurrence and in professional identification. Perhaps the case history reported below is representative of such a situation.

Mr. and Mrs. H were referred to the Foundation after 11 years of marriage with the wife's stated complaint that "she was just not interested in sex." She was 47 and her husband 44 years old.

Her childhood and adolescent years had been spent in comfortable surroundings. She was the eldest by three years of two sisters and reported a relatively uneventful, nontraumatic background for growth and development. Mrs. H was a relatively attractive woman with a reasonable number of dating opportunities during high-school and college years. Despite thoroughly enjoying the social aspects of the dating opportunities, there was little sexual stimulation from the few petting experiences she accepted. She never masturbated and recalled no awareness of pleasant pelvic sensation during her childhood.

Her mother was a relatively self-sufficient woman with multiple sociocultural interests. She never discussed material of sexual content with her daughter. When Mrs. H. was 15, her father was killed in an automobile accident.

After college Mrs. H sought opportunity for a professional career in the business world. She continued working throughout her twenties, doing exceptionally well professionally. There was established social opportunity, but she found herself resistant to both male and female (one occasion) approaches to shared sexual experience. Her resistance was not described as aversion. It was just that she was essentially unstimulated by any sexual approach and saw no point in a commitment without interest.

She had a number of women and men friends and many interests.

She worked hard, enjoyed her vacations, traveled extensively, but simply avoided sexual approach.

At age 36 she met and married a man three years her junior who was working in the same professional field. They formed their own business venture. From Mrs. H's point of view the marriage was simply a form of business merger. The same could not be said for her husband. He was very much interested in sexual functioning. He had been married for less than two years in his midtwenties and listed a large number of sexual opportunities with a wide variety of experiences before this marriage.

Mrs. H was totally cooperative in sexual functioning, but was basically unmoved. She lubricated well with coital connection, found pleasure in providing release for her husband, but was totally uninvolved personally. She had never masturbated, and her husband's attempts to stimulate her not only were unsuccessful but at times she even found them amusing when "nothing happened." Neither repulsed nor frustrated, she simply wasn't involved in sexual expression.

This was not her husband's reaction to their mutual sexual experiences. He found her lack of responsiveness utterly frustrating. Together they prospered from a financial point of view, but her obvious lack of sexual interest was depressing to him as an individual.

Eighteen months before referral to the Foundation, Mrs. H was highly stimulated on one occasion during coital connection and was orgasmic. The marital unit thought success had been attained, but subsequent coital episodes found her essentially unstimulated. There was one other such episode of orgasmic attainment. On this occasion, the business had gained an important new source of financial return and the unit had celebrated their success with dinner and the theater. She was orgasmic that night by manipulation only. Thereafter, there was no significant level of response regardless of the mode of stimulation. It was a high level of male frustration that brought the unit to the Foundation for treatment.

MASTURBATORY ORGASMIC INADEQUACY

There were only 11 cases of masturbatory orgasmic inadequacy. The classification represents a stage of woman's sexual responsivity and, other than for categorizing purposes, has no assigned value and will not be illustrated in depth. There are two types of history that dominate this classification. The first is the story so often obtained from women guilt-ridden from masturbatory experimentation. They try to masturbate as young women, and after failing a time or two, simply withdraw from experimentation with the concept that they have fallen from grace. Later in their mature sexual experience, genital-area manipulation as a means of sexual excitation is at best moderately successful, but they are not orgasmic except during coition.

The secondary history is that of the female "don't touch" syndrome. When taught that masturbation is evil they react by avoiding any approach to self-stimulation during adolescence and their maturing years. They may be orgasmic during socially acceptable coital opportunity but cannot be manually or orally elevated to orgasmic return.

The sexually dysfunctional woman has been discussed in depth. There are so many variations on the theme of orgasmic inadequacy that several chapters could have been written, and the subject still would not have been covered adequately. The concepts of a duality of psychosocial and biophysical structuring which influence woman's sexual response patterns has been advanced. If any woman's sexual value system is either undeveloped or damaged by an imbalance of either of these two theoretical systems of influence, the return may be varying degrees of orgasmic inadequacy. When faced with the clinical responsibility of treatment demand for primary or situational orgasmic dysfunction, the cotherapist must have established theoretical concepts of sexual dysfunction if he is to treat effectively. This chapter has been a discussion of concept and background; the treatment of orgasmic dysfunction is the subject of Chapter 11.

9

VAGINISMUS

Vaginismus is a psychophysiological syndrome affecting woman's freedom of sexual response by severely, if not totally, impeding coital function. Anatomically this clinical entity involves all components of the pelvic musculature investing the perineum and outer third of the vagina (Fig. 6B, page 262). Physiologically, these muscle groups contract spastically as opposed to their rhythmic contractural response to orgasmic experience. This spastic contraction of the vaginal outlet is a completely involuntary reflex stimulated by imagined, anticipated, or real attempts at vaginal penetration. Thus, vaginismus is a classic example of a psychosomatic illness.

Vaginismus is one of the few elements in the wide pattern of female sexual dysfunctions that cannot be unreservedly diagnosed by any established interrogative technique. Regardless of the psychotherapist's high level of clinical suspicion, a secure diagnosis of vaginismus cannot be established without the specific clinical support that only direct pelvic examination can provide. Without confirmatory pelvic examination, women have been treated for vaginismus when the syndrome has not been present. Conversely, there have been cases of vaginismus diagnosed by pelvic examination when the clinical existence of the syndrome had not been anticipated by therapists.

The clinical existence of vaginismus is delineated when vaginal examination constitutes a routine part of the required complete physical examination (see Chapter 2). The presence of involuntary muscular spasm in the outer third of the vaginal barrel, with the resultant severe constriction of the vaginal orifice, is obvious. The literature has remarked on an unusual physical response pattern of a woman afflicted with vaginismus. She reacts in an established pattern to psychological stress during a routine pelvic examination that includes observation of the external genitalia and manual vaginal exploration. The patient usually attempts to escape the examiner's approach by withdrawing toward the head of the table, even raising her legs from the stirrups, and/or constricting her thighs in the midline to avoid the implied threat of the impending vaginal examination. Frequently this reaction pattern can be elicited by the woman's mere anticipation of the examiner's physical approach to pelvic examination rather than the actual act of manual pelvic investigation.

When vaginismus is a fully developed clinical entity, constriction of the vaginal outlet is so severe that penile penetration is impossible. Frequently, manual examination can be accomplished only by employing severe force, an approach to be decried, for little is accomplished from such a forced pelvic investigation, and the resultant psychosexual trauma can make the therapeutic reversal of the syndrome more difficult. The diagnosis of vaginismus can easily be established by a one-finger pelvic examination. If a nontraumatic pelvic exploration is conducted, and a markedly apprehensive woman somewhat reassured in the process, the first step has been taken in therapeutic reversal of the involuntary spasm of the vaginal outlet.

Vaginismus may be of such severity that a marriage cannot be consummated. Medical consultants frequently have mistaken unrecognized involuntary vaginal spasm for the presence of a pressure-resistant hymen. As the result of this clinical confusion, surgical excision of the presumed resistant hymen has been recommended and conducted on many occasions without providing the patient and her husband with the expected relief from physical obstruction to effective coital connection. The possibility of coexistent vaginismus should be explored in depth by means of an accurate psychosexual-social history as well as a definitive, but not forced, pelvic examination before surgical excision of a presumed all-resistant hymen is conducted.

Vaginismus has been encountered frequently in marriages with rarely occurring coitus as well as in nonconsummated marriages. Interestingly, the syndrome has a high percentage of association with primary impotence in the male partner, providing still further clinical evidence to support procedural demand for simultaneous evaluation and treatment of both marital partners when sexual dysfunction within a marital unit is the presenting complaint.

In retrospect, when primary impotence and vaginismus exist in a marriage, it is difficult to be sure whether there was involuntary spasm of the vaginal outlet prior to the unsuccessful attempts at coital connection or whether the vaginismus emerged from the wife's high levels of sexual frustration developing secondary to the male partner's lack of erective security. Primary impotence and vaginismus probably antedate one another with equal frequency, but when either exists a marriage cannot be consummated, and sexual dysfunction is likely to appear in the other partner.

If severe vaginismus exists prior to attempted consummation of a marriage, primary or secondary impotence can result from repetitive failures at intromission. Of course, within many marital units involuntary vaginal spasm has existed for years without resulting in any symptoms of male sexual dysfunction. In such cases either the husband is satisfied with ejaculatory release with minimal or partial penetration or the degree of involuntary spasm is sufficient only to delay and not to deny vaginal penetration.

Twenty-nine cases of vaginismus have been diagnosed and treated in the past 11 years. While etiological factors are multiple, the syndrome is frequently identified in association with male sexual dysfunction. Equaling male dysfunction as an etiological agent is the psychosexually inhibiting influence of excessively severe control of social conduct inherent in religious orthodoxy. Third in etiological frequency are the symptoms of involuntary vaginal spasm which have been identified as related to specific episodes of prior sexual trauma. Fourth in order of occurrence is the stimulus toward vaginismus derived from attempted heterosexual function by a woman with prior homosexual identification.

There are in the clinical files 12 examples of religious orthodoxy as a major etiological factor in the onset of vaginismus. The presence of this syndrome contributed to 9 nonconsummated marriages and 3 in which coitus was infrequent. Of the female partners with vaginismus 4 were oriented to a restrictive orthodox Jewish background, 6 were products of a psychosexually repressive Catholic background, and 2 had the religious orientation of stringent Protestant fundamentalism.

In these 12 cases in which religious orthodoxy was a factor in vaginismus, 5 male partners were primarily impotent and also had similar orthodox religious backgrounds (see Chapter 5); 2 husbands who had been successful in coital connection with other women before meeting their wives-to-be became secondarily impotent after repetitively unsuccessful attempts at vaginal penetration. Another 2 husbands had not been able to penetrate their wives more than three times during marriages of five and eight years although they were potent prior to and after marriage and additionally potent during marriage with other partners; in the two years before referral to the Foundation, these husbands reported increasing frequency of erective failure and, although not completely impotent, were well on their way toward that status when seen in therapy. There were 2 husbands who continued potent despite marriages of fourteen and two years without successful vaginal penetration. Neither described sexual activity outside of the marriage. Male-partner tension relief usually was obtained from manipulation by the wife. The wives were not responsive to similar approaches.

In one marriage, the male partner was a severe premature ejaculator. Intromission rarely occurred during the first four years because the husband could not control his ejaculatory process sufficiently to accomplish vaginal penetration. It must be pointed out, however, that a heavy burden had been placed upon this premature ejaculator by the extremely difficult vaginal penetration. The excessive stimulation returned to the male by difficult penetrative efforts contributed to the husband's acknowledged rapid ejaculatory tendencies. When seen in therapy, the wife, denying coital experience before marriage, had involuntary vaginal spasm. Whether spasm was present at marriage is debatable, but the marital combination of premature ejaculation and vaginismus was insuperable sexually for both husband and wife.

Of specific interest is the fact that 6 primarily impotent males with religious orthodoxy as the major etiological factor influencing their sexual dysfunction have been treated at the Foundation (see Chapter 5). Five of these men married women who have been categorized as evidencing vaginismus. For the wives as well as the husbands, the indisputable etiological factor in both partners' sexual inadequacy was the overwhelming influence of religious orthodoxy. Clinical histories illustrative of the potential sexual difficulties inherent in marriages between orthodox partners have been presented in the discussion on primary impotence and primary orgasmic dysfunction (Chapters 5 and 8) and will not be repeated. Histories describing direct association of vaginismus with male sexual inadequacy are made available to underscore the fact that sexual dysfunction, regardless of whether originally invested in the male or the female partner, is a marital-unit rather than an individual problem.

RELIGIOUS ORTHODOXY AND VAGINISMUS

Marital Unit A is illustrative of an etiological factor frequently encountered in vaginismus, that of the influence of channel-visioned religious orthodoxy upon the immature and/or adolescent girl.

When the unit was first seen in consultation, Mr. and Mrs. A's marriage had existed unconsummated for 4½ years. The wife, from a sibling group of four females and one male, was the only one not to take the vows of a religious order. Her environmental and educational backgrounds were of strictest parental, physical, and mental control enforced in a stringent disciplinary format and founded in religious orthodoxy.

She was taught that almost any form of physical expression might be suspect of objectionable sexual connotation. For example, she was prohibited when bathing from looking at her own breasts either directly or from reflection in the mirror for fear that unhealthy sexual thoughts might be stimulated by visual examination of her own body. Discussion with a sibling of such subjects as menstruation, conception, contraception, or sexual functioning were taboo. Pronouncements on the subject were made by the father with the mother's full agreement. Her engagement period was restricted to a few chaste, well-chaperoned kisses, for at any sign of sexual interest from her fiancé, the girl withdrew in confusion.

Mrs. A entered marriage without a single word of advice, warning, or even good cheer from her family relative to marital sexual expression. The only direction offered by her religious adviser relative to sexual behavior was that coital connection was only to be endured if conception was desired.

Mrs. A's only concept of woman's role in sexual functioning was that it was dirty and depraved without marriage and that the sanctity of marriage really only provided the male partner with an opportunity for sexual expression. For the woman, the only salvation to be gained from sexual congress was pregnancy.

With the emotional trauma associated with wedding activities, and an injudicious, blundering, sexual approach from the uninformed but eager husband, the wedding night was a fiasco quite sufficient to develop or to enhance any preexisting involuntary obstruction of the vaginal outlet to a degree sufficient to deny penetration.

The husband, of the same orthodox background, had survived these traumatic years without developing secondary impotence. His premarital experience had been two occasions of prostitute exposure, and there was no reported extramarital experience. He masturbated occasionally and was relieved manually by his wife once or twice a week. His wife had no such outlet. Her only source of effective relief was well-controlled psychotherapy.

With an incredible number of thou-shalt-nots dominating Mrs. A's environmental background, it is little wonder that she was never able to develop a healthy frame of reference for the human male in general and her husband in particular as a sexual entity. Her sexual value system reflected severe negative conditioning.

The presenting complaint for Marital Unit B upon referral to the Foundation was that of secondary impotence. The husband's history was one of successful response to coital opportunities with three women over a period of 18 months before meeting his wife. An eight-month courtship followed without attempted coital connection or, for that matter, any physical approach, as the man was overwhelmed by the multitude of restrictions placed upon courtship procedure by the girl's religious control. The husband-to-be was of the same faith, but his background was not orthodox.

Following a chaste engagement period, failure to consummate the marriage occurred on the wedding night. Religious orthodoxy, although of major import, was not the only factor involved in this traumatized marriage. With both husband and wife tired and tense, he unfortunately hurried the procedure. All too cognizant of prior coital success and totally frustrated by lack of sexual exposure to his wife, he attempted penetration as soon as erection developed. While attempting rapid consummation, his wife, unprepared for the physical onslaught, was hurt. She screamed; he lost his erection and could not regain function. By mutual agreement, further attempts at consummation were reserved for the seclusion of the wedding trip.

Attempts at coition were repeated during the honeymoon and thereafter almost daily for the first five to six months of the marriage and two to three times per week for the next year, but there was no success in vaginal penetration. Eighteen months after the wedding the husband developed marked loss of erective security. He rarely could achieve or maintain an erection quality sufficient for intromission. When there was erective success, frantic attempts at vaginal penetration stimulated pain, fear, and physical withdrawal from his female partner.

During the remaining two years before consultation, attempts at coition gradually became less frequent. The husband's history included a report of eight months of psychotherapeutic support without relief of the symptoms of secondary impotence. No consideration had been given to the possibility of coexistent female pathology.

The involuntary vaginal spasm certainly could have been present before marriage, invalidating the initial attempt at intromission. Also, it is possible that over a 3½-year period, the severe degrees of frustration resultant from multiple unsuccessful attempts to penetrate could initiate involuntary vaginal spasm. If a moderate degree of spasm were present at marriage, the sexual ineptitude of the husband and the episodes of pain with attempted penetration would tend to magnify the severity of the syndrome well beyond any initially existent level. Secondary impotence resulting from long-denied intromission is not at all uncommon.

VAGINISMUS FOLLOWING PSYCHOSEXUAL TRAUMA

The following history exemplifies onset of vaginismus subsequent to episodes of psychosexual trauma. There have been three women referred to therapy so physically and emotionally traumatized by unwelcome sexual attack that vaginismus developed subsequent to their traumatic experiences.

When first seen, Unit C had been married for 18 months, with repeated attempts to consummate the marriage reported as unsuccessful. The husband, age 31, reported effective sexual function with several other women prior to marriage. The wife, age 28, described successful sexual connection with four men over a five-year period before the specific episode of sexual trauma. One of these relationships included coitus two or three times a week over a 10-month time span. She had been readily orgasmic in this association.

The traumatic episode in her history was a well-authenticated episode of gang rape with resultant physical trauma to the victim requiring two weeks' hospitalization. Extensive surgical reconstruction of the vaginal canal was necessary for basic physical rehabilitation. No psychotherapeutic support was sought by or suggested for the girl following this experience.

Mr. and Mrs. C met one year after the rape episode and were married a year after their introduction. Prior to the marriage the husband-to-be was in full possession of the factual history of the gang raping and of the resultant physical distress.

During the latter stages of their engagement period, several attempts at intercourse proved unsuccessful in that despite full erection, penetration could not be accomplished. It was mutually agreed that in all probability the security of the marital state would release her presumed hysterical inhibitions. This did not happen. After the marriage ceremony, attempts at consummation continued unsuccessful despite an unusually high degree of finesse, kindness, and discretion in the husband's sexual approaches to his traumatized partner. Severe vaginismus was demonstrated during physical examination of the wife after referral to the Foundation.

The remaining two rape experiences were family-oriented and almost identical in history. In both instances young girls were physically forced by male members of their immediate family to provide sexual release, on numerous occasions, for men they did not know. In one instance, a father, and in another, an older brother, forced sexual partners upon teenage girls (15 and 17 years of age) and repeatedly stood by to insure the girls' physical cooperation. Sexually exploited, emotionally traumatized, and occasionally physically punished, these girls became conditioned to the concept that "all men were like that." When released from family sexual servitude each girl avoided any possibility of sexual contact during the late teens and well into the twenties, until married at 25 and 29 years of age. Even then, they could not make themselves physically available to consummate their marriages, regardless of how strongly they willed sexual cooperation. Severe vaginismus was present in both cases.

The husbands' physical and psychosexual examinations were within expected limits of normal variability. Neither husband had been made aware of the family-oriented episodes of controlled rape that had occurred years before their association with their wives-to-be. Once apprised of the etiology of their wives' psychosomatic illness, both men offered limitless cooperation in the therapeutic program.

There are various etiological orientations to vaginismus. As evidenced previously, trauma initiating involuntary vaginal spasm can be either physiological or psychological, or both, in origin. Of course there are factors of psychosomatic influence that predispose to vaginismus other than those frequently noted categories of channelized religious orthodoxy, male sexual dysfunction, and episodes of sexual trauma.

VAGINISMUS SECONDARY TO DYSPAREUNIA

Vaginismus occasionally develops in women with clinical symptoms of severe dyspareunia (painful intercourse). When dyspareunia has firm basis in pelvic pathology, the existence of which escapes examining physicians, and over the months or years coition becomes increasing painful, vaginismus may result. The patient is not reassured by the statement that "it's all in your head" or equally unsupportive pronouncements, when she knows that it is always severely painful for her when her husband thrusts deeply into the vagina during coital connection.

As examples of this situation, vaginismus has been demonstrated as a secondary complication in two cases of severe laceration of the broad ligaments (see Chapter 10). Also recorded are two classic examples of onset of vaginismus, the first in a young woman with pelvic endometriosis, the second in a 62-year-old postmenopausal widow (without sex-steriod-replacement therapy) who through remarriage sought return to sexual functioning after seven years of abstinence.

The two women developing a syndrome of vaginismus subsequent to childbirth laceration of the broad ligaments supporting the uterus (universal-joint syndrome) have similar histories. A composite history will suffice to demonstrate the pathology involved.

Marital Unit D was seen with the complaint of increasing difficulty in accomplishing vaginal penetration developing after 6 years of marriage. There were two children in the marriage, with onset of severe dyspareunia oriented specifically to the delivery of the second child. The second child, a postmature baby of 8 pounds 14 ounces, had a precipitous delivery. There is a positive history of nurses' holding the patient's legs together to postpone delivery while waiting for the obstetrician. As soon as sexual activity was reconstituted after the delivery the patient experienced severe pain with deep penile thrusting. During the next year the pain became so acute that the wife sought subterfuge to avoid sexual exposure. The coital frequency decreased from two to three times a week to the same level per month. On numerous occasions the patient was assured, during medical consultation, that there was nothing anatomically disoriented in the pelvis and that pain with intercourse was "purely her imagination."

Supported by these authoritative statements, the husband demanded increased frequency of sexual function. When the wife refused, the unit separated for 10 months. During this 10-month period, the woman assayed intercourse on two separate occasions with two different men, but with each experience the pelvic pain with deep penile thrusting was so severe that her obvious physical distress terminated sexual experimentation.

The marital unit was reunited with the help of their religious adviser, but with attempted intercourse vaginal penetration was impossible. After 8 months of repeatedly unsuccessful attempts to reestablish coital function, the unit was referred for therapy.

Family Unit E had been married 8 years when seen in the Clinic. They mutually agreed that coital connection had not been possible more than once or twice a month in the first two years of marriage. Each time, the wife had moaned or screamed in pain as her husband was thrusting deeply into her pelvis. After the first two years of marriage, every attempt at vaginal penetration had been unsuccessful.

Both Mr. and Mrs. E had been under intensive psychotherapy, the husband for three and the wife for four years, when referred to the Foundation. During the routine physical examinations (see Chapter 2), advanced endometriosis was discovered (see Chapter 10), and severe vaginismus was demonstrated. In due course the wife underwent surgery for correction of the pelvic pathology. After recovery from the surgery she returned with her husband for therapeutic relief of the vaginismus which, as would be expected, still existed despite successful surgical correction of the endometriosis.

Marital Unit F, a 66-year-old husband and his 62-year-old wife, were seen in consultation. When the wife was 54 years old, her first husband died after a three-year illness during which sexual activity was discontinued. She remarried at 61 years of age, having had no overt sexual activity in the interim period. She had never been given hormone-replacement therapy to counteract the natural involution of pelvic structures. First attempts at coital connection in the present marriage produced a great deal of pain and only partial vaginal penetration. With reluctance the wife sought medical consultation. Her physician instituted hormone-replacement techniques. After a 6-week respite, further episodes of coital activity also resulted in pain and distress. Despite the fact that by this time the vaginal walls were well stimulated by effective steroid replacement, the new husband found it impossible to attain vaginal intromission.

The wife had developed obvious psychosocial resistance to the concept of sexual activity in the 60-plus age group based on (1) the pain that had been experienced attempting to consummate her new marriage, and (2) a real sense of embarrassment created by the need for medical consultation and the necessity of admitting that she had been indulging in coital activity at her age. As a result of the trauma that developed with attempts to renew sexual function subsequent to almost ten years of continence, she developed involuntary spastic contraction of the vaginal outlet. Judicious use of Hegar dilators and a detailed, thorough, and authoritative refutation of the taboo of aging sexual function (based on the belief that sexual activity in the 60-, 70-, or even 80-year age groups represents some form of perversion) were quite sufficient to relax and relieve the vaginal spasm (see Chapter 13).

ROLE OF HOMOSEXUAL ORIENTATION

Two case histories illustrate the occasional effect of homosexual orientation upon the female partner.

Marital Unit G was composed of a 26-year-old woman married to a man 37 years old. The wife had been actively homosexual since seduction by an elder sister when she was 12 years old. There had been no history of heterosexual function before meeting her husband. He was a successful professional man and offered the woman much in the form of social status and financial security. He had been previously married and divorced.

Sexual exposure during the short engagement had been restricted, by female edict, to multiple manipulative approaches. There was total inability to penetrate on the wedding night or to consummate the marriage thereafter. When the unit was seen after 18 months of marriage, the wife's hymen was not intact but there was evidence of severe vaginismus.

Once all of her pertinent history was obtained and shared with her marital partner, there was little further resistance to penile penetration. She was orgasmic with intercourse within two weeks after termination of the acute phase of therapy.

Marital Unit H had been married for 7 years. There were two children. The husband became an alcoholic, lost his job, and left his family without warning. He was out of the home for 3 years before he could be persuaded to seek professional help. There was another year spent in treatment before he could return to family and social position. Fortunately, there was sufficient financial resource, so no great financial hardship was suffered by his family.

The wife, distraught at first, sought support from her best friend, also married and living in the neighborhood. Within a year an overt homosexual relationship developed. Mrs. H had no prior history of homophile orientation.

Two years after her husband left the home, Mrs. H attempted sexual intercourse on several different occasions with two different men, but neither man could penetrate. There was no further heterosexual exposure after these failures until her husband was released from institutional control to return to normal activity.

When attempting intercourse, Mr. H could not penetrate, nor was he able to during the subsequent two years before the marital unit was seen in therapy.

The vaginismus was obvious at physical examination. The probable cause of her involuntary rejection of coitus was explained and accepted by both partners. Dilators were used effectively and coital functioning was reestablished quickly.

One marriage had existed in a sexual successful state for almost 10 years when the husband was detected in an extramarital affair. There was a 4-month period of continence while marital fences were mended with help from clergy. Although verbally forgiving his transgressions, the wife evidenced vaginal spasm during subsequent attempts at coital connection. The marital unit's inability to reestablish a successful coital pattern continued for almost 18 months until, consumed with fears for performance, feelings of guilt, and finally of personal rejection, the husband became secondarily impotent. When seen in therapy, both vaginismus and impotence were presenting systems.

There have been 7 more instances of vaginismus treated by Foundation personnel. Onset of symptoms has ranged from evidence of involuntary vaginal spasm with a first coital opportunity to dysfunction secondary to physiological or psychologic trauma. There seems little need for further illustration of the onset of the syndrome.

Regardless of onset, an effective therapeutic approach is to establish the etiological influences by careful history-taking (see Chapter 2), and then to approach treatment confidently. With adequate dissemination of information so that full appreciation of onset of the sexual dysfunction is acquired by marital unit involved, and the sexual partners' mutual cooperation in therapy, reversal of the syndrome of vaginismus is accomplished with relative ease.

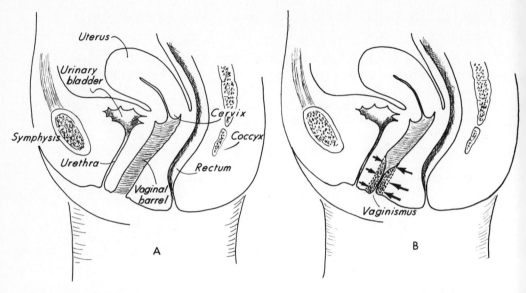

FIGURE 6

A: Normal female pelvic anatomy (lateral view). B: Involuntary constriction (outer third of vagina).

TREATMENT OF VAGINISMUS

The initial and most important step in the treatment of vaginismus is physical demonstration of the existence of the involuntary vaginal spasm conducted to the clinical satisfaction of both marital partners. First, anatomical illustrations (Fig. 6A and B) of the involuntary constriction in the outer third of the vagina are made available to the marital partners and the specific anatomical involvement explained in detail. Then the basic aspect of clinical therapy is accomplished in a medical treatment room with the female partner draped and placed in the gynecological examining position. The obvious presence of involuntary vaginal spasm, demonstrated by any attempt at vaginal insertion of an examining finger, frequently is more of a surprise to the female partner than it is to her husband. She may be completely unaware of the existence, much less the severity, of the involuntary spastic constriction of her vaginal outlet. The chaperoned pelvic examination is not terminated before the husband also has been gloved and encouraged to demonstrate to his and to his wife's satisfaction the severity of the involuntary constriction ring in the outer third of the vagina.

Once the clinical existence of vaginismus has been demonstrated to the satisfaction of both marital partners, resolution of this form of sexual inadequacy becomes relatively easy. Hegar dilators in graduated sizes are employed in the privacy of the marital bedroom. The actual dilatation of the vaginal outlet is initiated and conducted by the husband with the wife's physical cooperation, at first with her manual control and then verbal direction. Again, the rationale behind the Foundation's demand for availability and cooperation of both marital partners, when attempting to alleviate varying forms of human sexual inadequacy, is underscored.

After the larger-sized dilators can be introduced successfully, it is good policy to encourage intravaginal retention of the larger dilators for a matter of several hours each night. Usually a major degree of the involuntary spasm can be eliminated in a matter of 3 to 5 days, presuming daily renewal of dilating procedures.

To date there has not been a failed attempt to relieve the involuntary spasm of vaginismus, once the clinical existence of the outlet contraction has been demonstrated to both husband and wife and the cooperation of both partners in the dilatation therapy has been elicited. When coitus is attempted during the first month or six weeks after initial relief of the involuntary vaginal spasm, preliminary dilatation of the vaginal outlet occasionally may be indicated. In many instances, however, the simple clinical demonstration of the existence of the vaginal constriction and the subsequent controlled usage of the dilators for a few days is quite sufficient to remove permanently this involuntary obstruction to vaginal penetration.

While physical relief of the spastic constriction of the vaginal outlet is usually accomplished without incident, the psychosocial trauma that contributed to the involuntary constriction must not be ignored. When physical symptoms of sexual dysfunction are relieved or removed, the tensions that have led to onset of the symptoms usually become much more vulnerable to treatment.

For a marital unit contending with vaginismus, an explanation of the psychophysiology of the distress, what it is, how it developed, and assurance that relief is possible are all important factors in the therapeutic program. As stated previously, the first and most important step in symptomatic relief is to demonstrate to both husband and wife the clinical existence of the dysfunction. Thereafter, the therapist is dealing with a receptive, if somewhat surprised, audience.

The easiest way to relieve the sexual tensions, the sexual misconceptions, even the established sexual taboos, is through direct dissemination of information. Women handicapped sexually by the influence of religious orthodoxy, married to men with sexual dysfunction, victimized by rape, contending with unexplained dyspareunia, frustrated by aging constriction of the vaginal barrel, or confused by homosexual and heterosexual conflict all have one thing in common. They all exhibit almost complete lack of authoritative information from which to gain some degree of objectivity when facing the psychosocial problem evidenced by the symptoms of their sexual dysfunction.

With no knowledge of what to expect sexually, no concept of natural levels of sexual responsivity, and even real distrust for authority, theirs is a desperate need for definitive information. Education to understand the psychophysiological aspects of the problem is a point of departure for these traumatized women. Confidence comes slowly from a gradually increasing degree of objectivity that develops from their psychosocial acceptance of the basic concepts of the naturalness of human sexual functioning.

With pertinent sexual information absorbed, with the physical dysfunction illustrated, explained, and relieved, women with resolution of involuntary vaginal spasm have been reoriented to lives of effective sexual functioning. Of the 29 women referred for relief of their sexual dysfunction, all have recovered from the vaginismus, and 16 were orgasmic for the first time in their lives during the two-weeks attendance at the Foundation. Four more women have reported orgasmic return during the follow-up period after termination of the acute phase of their treatment. Six women were previously orgasmic before onset of the secondarily acquired symptoms of vaginismus. Their orgasmic responsivity returned spontaneously after treatment. Three women remained nonorgasmic, despite clinical relief from their involuntary vaginal spasm.

Vaginismus, once diagnosed, can be treated effectively from both psychological and physiological points of view, presuming full cooperation from both members of the sexually dysfunctional marital unit.

IO

DYSPAREUNIA

The term *dyspareunia*, difficult or painful coitus, has always been presumed to refer to coital distress in women. The word stems from the Greek, and somewhat freely translates into "badly mated." Since no comparable word reflecting or suggesting coital distress for men has been established, poetic license will be begged. The chapter is comprised of two separate sections devoted to consideration of individual complaints of female and male sexual dysfunction identified by the individuals involved as difficult or painful coitus. Men can be "badly mated" too!

That factor in the total of male and female sexual dysfunction perhaps most difficult for the therapist to define involves the psychophysiological complaint of dyspareunia. Diagnostic insecurity relates directly to the fact that dyspareunia has a varied number of both subjective and objective origins that frequently give rise to combinations of psychophysiological distress rather than complaints that can be categorized individually.

FEMALE DYSPAREUNIA

For years, woman's complaint "it hurts when I have intercourse" has been an anathema to the therapist. Even after an adequate pelvic examination, the therapist frequently cannot be sure whether the patient is complaining of definitive but undiagnosed pelvic pathology or whether, as has been true countless thousands of times, a sexually dysfunctional woman is using the symptomatology of pain as a means of escaping completely or at least reducing markedly the number of unwelcome sexual encounters in her marriage. For it is true that once convinced that there is no recourse for reversal of his or her dysfunctional status, the sexually inadequate partner in any marriage manufactures excuse after excuse to avoid sexual confrontation. As women have long since learned, a persistent, aggressive male partner can overwhelm, neutralize, or even negate the most original of excuses to avoid sexual exposure. However, presuming any degree of residual concern for or interest in his partner as an individual, the husband is rendered powerless to support his insistence upon continuity of sexual contact when the wife complains of severe distress during or after sexual connection.

If the female partner complains and flinches with penile insertion, moans and contracts her abdominal and pelvic musculature during the continuum of male thrusting, cries out or screams with deep vaginal penetration, sheds bitter tears after termination of every sexual connection, or complains angrily of aching in the pelvis or burning in the vagina during or even hours after a specific coital episode, the male partner's sexual approach must be accepted as the probable potentiator of a physiological basis for his female partner's evidenced sexual dysfunction. Thereafter, the husband has minimal recourse. There is little he can do other than to avoid or at least reduce marital-unit sexual exposure on his own cognizance, and/or to insist that his wife seek professional consultation.

Once consulted, the twofold problem that constantly baffles authority is first whether a specific physiological basis can be defined for the objective existence of pain. Second, if not, whether the existence of pelvic pathology should arbitrarily be ruled out, thereby defining the registered complaint of dyspareunia as subjective in origin. When a woman complains of pain during or after intercourse, there are very few diagnostic landmarks to follow for treatment, so that consideration of the etiology of the painful response seems appropriate.

As in vaginismus (see Chapter 9), a differential diagnosis cannot be established for a complaint of dyspareunia unless careful pelvic and rectal examinations are conducted. Even then there can be no sure diagnosis if the existence of pelvic pathology is denied purely on the basis of negative examinations by competent authority. Yet, in a positive vein, there are obvious pelvic or rectal findings that can and do support objectively a woman's subjective complaint of coital discomfort. The female partner's persistent complaint of pain with any form of coital connection must not be authoritatively denied or, for that matter supported, purely on the basis of interrogation, regardless of how carefully or in what depth the questioning has been conducted.

There are many varieties of dyspareunia, varying from postcoital vaginal irritation to severe immobilizing pain with penile thrusting. Symptomatic definition relating not only to the anatomy of the vaginal barrel but also to the total of the reproductive viscera is in order.

In no sense will the discussion include all possible forms of pelvic distress. Considered, however, will be the major sources of pelvic pathology engendering painful response from the female partner during or after coital connection. The dyspareunia will be considered in relation to specific areas of the vaginal barrel, the reproductive viscera, and the soft-tissue components of the pelvis, and to painful stimuli developing in a time-related sequence during or after coital connection.

THE VAGINAL OUTLET

The complaint of pain with penile intromission should demand clinical inspection of the vaginal outlet and the labial (major and minor) area. Direct observation can easily delineate any of the following minor areas of concern—minor only in the sense of easy reversibility of physical distress by adequate clinical measures.

An intact hymen or the irritated or bruised remnants of the hymenal ring can and do cause outlet pain during attempted coital connection. Less obvious is an unprotected scar area just at the mucocutaneous juncture of the vaginal mucosa and the perineal body. These scars, primarily residuals of episiotomies sustained during childbirth, occasionally have been observed to result from criminal abortion techniques or gang-rape episodes. The Bartholin-gland area in the minor labia should be carefully palpated for enlargement in the gland base, which can contribute to a locally painful reaction as the vaginal outlet is dilated by the penile glans at onset of intromission. Finally, in postmenopausal women the labia and vaginal outlet may have so lost elasticity and become so shrunken in size that any penile insertive attempt will return a painful response (see Chapters 9 and 13).

THE CLITORIS

With any complaint of outlet pain, the clitoral area also should be inspected carefully. Many women simply cannot define anatomically or are too embarrassed to discuss objectively the exact location of the outlet distress occasioned by attempts at coital connection. Smegma beneath the clitoral foreskin can cause chronic irritation and burning that becomes severe as the penis is introduced into the vaginal orifice. Rarely adhesions beneath the minor labial foreskin anchoring the foreskin to the clitoral glans can cause distress when the foreskin is moved or pulled from its specific pudendal-overhang position by manipulative approaches to the mons area or by intromissive attempts.

When the minor labial hood of the clitoris is pulled down toward the perineum by the act of penile intromission, an intense pain response from the presensitized clitoral glans or even the clitoral shaft may become of major clinical moment.

The same type of reaction can be elicited if foreplay in the clitoral area has been irritative rather than stimulative in character, as so often happens when the sexually uneducated male tries to follow "authoritative" directions in attempts to stimulate his partner sexually. Heavyhanded manipulation or frequent masturbatory irritation can elicit painful responses from the clitoral-glans area. This irritative reaction may develop rapidly to a full-fledged painful response subsequent to dilation of the vaginal outlet by penile intromission.

THE VAGINAL BARREL

INFECTION

Among the most distressing of the many factors in dyspareunia are the complaints of burning, itching, or aching in the vagina during or after intercourse. The existence of chronic vaginal irritation frequently robs women of their full freedom of sexual expression, for they are well aware that any specific coital connection may be severely irritative rather than highly stimulative. Presuming adequate production of vaginal lubrication, rarely, if ever, does a woman complain of burning, itching, or aching during coition or describe these symptoms immediately after or even in a delayed postcoital time sequence without concomitant evidence of established pathology in the vaginal barrel.

This form of dyspareunia registered as a complaint by the female partner should have an important connotation to the cotherapist. This specific response pattern is not described by women who are subjectively impelled to register an excuse to avoid impending or threatened coital connection. When women use the complaint of pain to avoid or delay the necessity for submitting to psychogenically unappealing coital experience, their most frequent complaint is one of severe pain with penile thrusting, "a hurting" deep in the pelvis.

When considering the complaints of burning, itching, or aching in the vagina, initially clinical concern is focused on infectious vaginal invaders. The primary sources of vaginal infection are coition and rectal contamination; secondary sources are manual contact, clothing material, insertion of foreign material, and functional disuse.

Support of and control of the acidity of the vaginal environment is the fundamental means of protection against the bacterial pathogens that can create symptoms of burning, itching or aching. The vagina naturally maintains a strongly acid environment as a protective mechanism against all forms of infectious invasion. With an experimentally controlled environment, vaginal acidity has been established as varying clinically from pH 3.5 to pH 4.0.

Thus, there is a rather wide margin for error in vaginal protection against concurrent infectious agents, for acidity must be sufficiently neutralized to raise the pH level to five or above, before bacterial invaders can flourish freely in the vaginal environment.

The one time that natural vaginal protection against infection breaks down is during the period of established menstrual flow. For many women vaginal acidity consistently registers in the neighborhood of pH 5 or above during menstrual flow, particularly if vaginal tampons are employed. The neutralizing effect of blood serum constrained to the vaginal tract by retentive tampons directs vaginal acidity into pH 5 levels routinely. It is not surprising, then, that most vaginal infections either have clinical onset or flourish during menstrual flow.

Bacteria are the infective organisms most constantly encountered in vaginal infections, yet trichomonal and fungal forms of infection are seen frequently enough to provide additional causes for clinical concern. Probably the most persistent vaginal-tract invader in any woman's lifespan are the coliform organisms (*Streptococcus faecalis, Escherichia coli,* and the type of *Streptococcus viridans*), which are the basic contaminants of bowel environment.

From the point of view of patterns of sexual functioning alone, a persistent vaginitis, from which pathogenic organisms repeatedly are cultured in the adult, sexually functioning woman, should always make the therapist question the possibility of occasions of rectal intercourse. A popular technique employed during rectal intercourse includes the expected format of initial rectal penetration during the excitement phase and repetitive thrusting during the plateau phase of the male sexual response cycle. But many men withdraw from the rectum and plunge the bacterially contaminated penis into the vaginal barrel just before or during the stage of ejaculatory inevitability, terminating the orgasmic phase of their sexual cycle by ejaculating intravaginally. Recurrent coliform vaginal infections that are resistant to treatment may have origin in this coital technique.

When rectal intercourse is practiced, the ejaculatory episode should be confined to the lumen of the bowel. There should never be penetration of both rectal and vaginal orifices during any single coital episode, if the woman wishes protection against the probability of recurrent vaginal infections.

If coliform vaginitis persists despite both adequate treatment and patient denial of rectal intercourse, a direct rectal examination frequently will solve the therapist's diagnostic dilemma. If a woman is experiencing rectal intercourse with some regularity, there may be a specific involuntary reaction of the sphincter to the rectal examination. When the examining finger is inserted, the response of the rectal sphincter at first will be one of slight to moderate spasm, following the expected reactive pattern of most men or women undergoing routine rectal examinations. But if the examining finger is retained rectally for a few seconds, the sphincter may relax quite rapidly in a completely involuntary manner, as opposed to the routine response pattern of continuing in spastic contraction for the duration of the examination. If involuntary sphincter relaxation develops, this response pattern, while certainly not reliably diagnostic, should make the cotherapist skeptical of the patient's denial of rectal coital episodes. The involuntary sphincter relaxation develops because the retained examining finger stimulates a pleasurable response for those women enjoying regularity of rectal coital exposure as opposed to those finding rectal examinations subjectively objectionable and objectively painful.

(As a clinical note, the same type of involuntary sphincter relaxation may develop in male homosexuals whose preferred pattern of sexual expression includes interest in regularity of rectal penetration. Again, the involuntary sphincter response pattern has been used by the Foundation's professional staff as a clinical diagnostic aid when dealing with homosexual male patients employing the rectum as the means of providing ejaculatory release for sexual partner or partners.)

When the cotherapist can be reasonably certain by both history and examination of some regularity of rectal intercourse, techniques to avoid vaginal contamination with fecal material should be discussed at length with the women involved. Although the basic premise of the clinical advice is to avoid recurrent episodes of coliform vaginitis if possible, there is an accrued secondary effect of reducing dyspareunia during occasions of intravaginal coitus.

When trichomonal vaginitis is suggested by direct inspection of the vaginal barrel and confirmed by adequately stained vaginal smear or hanging-drop preparation of the vaginal discharge, which may be profuse and irritating, the husband also should be suspected of harboring the trichomonads, possibly beneath the foreskin if he is uncircumcised, but more frequently in the prostate gland, the seminal vesicles, or the urinary bladder. If both husband and wife are not treated simultaneously for this particular distress, the infection may become a source of chronic dyspareunia, as it may be exchanged frequently between marital partners during repeated opportunity at coital connection. It does little good to treat the wife for trichomonal vaginitis and then have her reinfected by her husband. And it obviously does little good to treat the husband individually and have him reinfected by his wife. With chronic trichomonal vaginitis there may be recurrent bouts of dyspareunia, particularly with coital connection of any significant duration.

Fungal vaginitis is seen clinically more and more frequently. Incidence of this particular infectious entity used to be primarily confined to the late spring, summer, and early fall months, but now such pathogens as *Monilia* and *Candida albicans* are encountered regularly throughout the year. Chronic fungal infection creates a debilitating situation for the recipient woman. Burning and itching is intense, and swelling and weeping of soft tissues are frequent complications. Coital connection is virtually impossible due to the pain involved when a fungal infection dominates in the vaginal environment.

Chronic fungal infection is seen with increasing frequency, since women may develop this type of vaginitis subsequent to treatment of an illness requiring antibiotic medication; suppression of an infection by an antibiotic often results in overgrowth of organisms not susceptible to the particular medication. Attention to restoring or maintaining vaginal acidity by the use of pH-controlled vaginal jellies or douches during indicated treatment of infections with antibiotics frequently will protect women from the complications of fungal vaginitis.

SENSITIVITY REACTIONS

Aside from direct infective agents, there are many other sources of burning, itching, or aching in the vaginal barrel that can produce chronic dyspareunia. Among those most frequently encountered are the sensitivity reactions associated with intravaginal chemical contraceptive materials. Many women develop vaginal sensitivity to chemical factors included in contraceptive creams, jellies, suppositories, foams, or foam tablets. When persistent itching or burning is intense enough to engender the symptoms of dyspareunia during or shortly after intercourse, and when any of these above-mentioned intravaginal chemical contraceptive agents are employed routinely during coital connection, the possibility of sensitivity to the chemical agents should always be kept in mind.

There also are occasional irritations created by the rubber used in manufacturing both diaphragms and condoms. In a few women the response of the vaginal mucosa to latex products is quite irritative in character. When these contraceptive techniques are employed with regularity and a chronic noninfectious irritation in the vagina causes obviously increasing dyspareunia, sensitivity to rubber products should be suspected. The sensitivity to rubber is quite infrequent but must be kept in mind in the differential diagnosis of noninfectious, irritative, vaginal dyspareunia.

Agents frequently most often responsible for making the vaginal mucosa sensitive to infective processes and emphasizing the potential irritation of maintained penile thrusting are the various douching preparations. Many women feel they must douche after every coital exposure to maintain cleanliness. This is one of the most persistent and widespread misconceptions in the folklore of human sexual functioning. From a cleanliness point of view, there is not the slightest need for douching after intercourse. The vagina returns to its natural protective pH value within 6 to 8 hours after seminal-fluid deposition. Repeated douching usually accomplishes only the untoward result of washing protective levels of residual acidity from the vagina. Thereafter, secondary infection frequently develops from the elevated levels of pH usually found in the post-douching vaginal environment. Additionally, proprietary products used in douching can create a reactive, chemical-type vaginitis of the same pattern as that stimulated by intravaginal chemical contraceptives. Esthetically concerned women should be reassured by authority that the simple expedient of external washing with soap and water is all that is necessary to maintain security from post-ejaculatory drainage and to avoid any suggestion of postcoital odor.

SENILE AND RADIATION VAGINITIS

There is another type of chronic vaginal irritation that should be highlighted. It frequently is seen associated with clinical complaints of dyspareunia and is described as senile vaginitis (see Chapter 13). Older women not supported by steroid protection techniques develop thin, atrophic mucosal surfaces in the vagina. These tissue-paper-thin areas crack and bleed easily under duress of forceful or maintained penile thrusting. Many women in the 50- to 70-year age group complain of vaginal burning and irritation not only during but even for hours and occasionally days after coital exposure due to the atrophic condition of the mucosal lining of the vagina. Aging women can be fully protected from these distressing symptoms by initiation of adequate sex steroid support.

Although seen infrequently, yet in the same physiological category as senile vaginitis, is radiation reaction in the vagina. After local radiation for carcinoma, the vaginal barrel shrinks, the mucosa becomes atrophic, and dyspareunia usually develops not only from the atrophic mucosa but also on the basis of loss of vaginal-wall elasticity and marked reduction of lubrication production.

INSUFFICIENT VAGINAL LUBRICATION

Probably the most frequent cause for dyspareunia originating with symptoms of burning, itching, or aching is lack of adequate production of vaginal lubrication with sexual functioning. During attempted penile intromission or with long-maintained coital connection, there must be adequate lubrication or there will be irritative distress for either or both coital partners. Adequate production of vaginal lubrication is for women the physiological equivalent of erective attainment for men—her representation to her male partner of a psychological readiness for vaginal penetration. A consistent lack of functional levels of vaginal lubrication is as near as any woman can come to paralleling a man's lack of effective erection.

Inadequate development of vaginal lubrication has many causes, but by far the most common is lack of interest in the particular opportunity or identification with the involved sexual partner. Women must experience positive input from their sexual value systems if they are to respond repetitively and effectively to their mate's sexual approaches. Women who cannot think or feel sexually, those reflecting fears of sexual performance, and even those acting out a spectator's role in sexual functioning, either do not develop sufficient vaginal lubrication to support a painless coital episode or, if penetrated successfully, they cease production of the necessary lubricative material shortly after intravaginal penile thrusting is initiated.

Additionally, women fearful of pain with deep vaginal penetration, fearful of pregnancy with any coital connection, fearful of exposure to social compromise, and fearful of sexual inadequacy are frequently poor producers of vaginal lubrication. Any component of fear present in sexual experiences reduces the receptivity to sensate input, thereby blunting biophysical responsivity.

If there is insufficient vaginal lubrication, there may or may not be acute pain with full penile intromission, depending primarily upon the parity of the woman, but there usually will be vaginal burning, irritation, or aching both during and after coital connection. There are tens of thousands of women who become markedly apprehensive at onset of any definitive sexual approach, simply because they know severe vaginal irritation will be experienced not only during but frequently for hours after any significantly maintained coital connection.

Not to be forgotten as a specific segment among the legions of women afflicted by inadequate production of vaginal lubrication are those in their postmenopausal years. If they are not supported by adequate sex-steroid-replacement techniques, production of vaginal lubrication usually drops off markedly as the vaginal mucosa routinely turns atrophic. There well may be aching and irritation in the vagina for a day or two after coital connection for women contending with this evidence of sex-steroid starvation.

A major category of women tending to be poor lubrication producers during coital connection is that significant segment of the female population with overt lesbian orientation. Many women psychosexually committed to an homophile orientation attempt regularity of coital connection for socioeconomic reasons. Frequently, they may not lubricate well during heterosexual activity, although there usually is ample lubrication when they are directly involved in homosexual expression.

In most instances, inadequate production of vaginal lubrication can be reversed with definite therapeutic approach. Certainly women burdened by a multiplicity of sex-oriented fears can be provided psychotherapeutic relief of their phobias and subsequently reversed with relative ease from their particular pattern of sexual inadequacy. Those women with chronic vaginal itching and irritation can be protected from continuing dyspareunia, because both infectious and chemical vaginitis are reversible under proper clinical control. Senile vaginitis responds in short order to adequate sex-steroid-replacement techniques.

There are only two major categories of women for whom the cotherapists have little to offer in an effort to constitute effective production of vaginal lubrication: first, women mated to men for whom they have little or no personal identification, understanding, affection, or even sexual respect; and second, homosexually oriented women practicing coition for socioeconomic reasons with no interest in their male companions as sexual partners.

SOMATIC SOURCES OF PAIN IN THE PELVIC STRUCTURES

As opposed to the symptoms of aching, irritation, or burning in the vagina, complaints of severe pain developed during penile thrusting provide the most difficulty in delineating between subjective and objective etiology. Although many women register this type of complaint when seeking to avoid undesired sexual approaches, there are some basic pathological conditions in the female pelvis that can and do engender severe pain in response to active coital connection. One of the difficulties in delineating the severity of the complaint of dyspareunia is to identify pelvic pathology of quality sufficient to support the female partner's significant complaints of painful coition. Pelvic residual from severe infection or pelvic implants of endometriosis usually are easily identified by adequate pelvic and rectal examinations. These clinical entities will be discussed briefly in context later in the chapter. Current attention is drawn to probably the most frequently overlooked of the major physiological syndromes creating intense pelvic pain during coital connection.

TRAUMATIC LACERATION OF UTERINE SUPPORT

One of the most obscure of pelvic pathological syndromes, yet one of the most psychosexually crippling, is traumatic laceration of the ligaments supporting the uterus. This syndrome was first described clinically by Willard Allen. Five women have been referred to the Foundation for relief of subjective symptoms of dyspareunia after referral sources had assured the husbands that there was no plausible physical reason for the constant complaint of severe pain with deep penile thrust. These 5 postpartum women had severe broad-ligament lacerations and were relieved of their distress by definitive surgical approaches, not by psychotherapy. Therefore, they do not represent a component of the statistical analysis of treatment for sexual dysfunction.

Three women reflecting onset of dyspareunia subsequent to criminal abortion techniques also have been seen in consultation and are not reflected in the statistics of the sexual-inadequacy study.

Three more women have been seen in gynecological consultation for acquired dyspareunia subsequent to gang-rape experiences. They also have not been an integral part of the sexual-dysfunction study. These clinical problems will be mentioned in context.

When first seen clinically, women with traumatic lacerations of the uterine supports, acquired with delivery or by specific criminal-abortion techniques, present complaints that commonly accrue from pelvic vasocongestion—dyspareunia, dysmenorrhea, and a feeling of being excessively tired. These complaints are secondary or acquired in nature. The traumatized women consistently can relate onset of their acquired dyspareunia to one particular obstetrical experience even from among three or four such episodes. The basic coital distress arises with deep penetration of the penis. Women describe the pain associated with intercourse to be as if their husbands had "hit something" with the penis during deep vaginal penetration.

These involved women may note other physical irritations frequently seen with chronic pelvic vasocongestion—a constantly nagging backache, throbbing or generalized pelvic aching, and occasionally, a sense that "everything is falling out." These symptoms are made worse in any situation requiring a woman to be on her feet for an exceptional length of time, as a full day spent doing heavy housecleaning or working as saleswoman in a department store.

Most women lose interest in any regularity of sexual expression when distressed by acquired dyspareunia. Handicapped by con-

stant anticipation of painful pelvic stimuli created by penile thrusting, they also may lose any previously established facility for orgasmic return.

The basic pathology of the syndrome of broad-ligament laceration is confined to the soft tissues of the female pelvis. The striking
features of the pelvic examination are the position of the uterus
(almost always in severe third-degree retroversion) and the particularly unique feeling that develops for the examiner with manipulation of the cervix. This portion of the uterus feels just as if it
were being rotated as a universal joint. It may be moved in any
direction, up, down, laterally, or on an anterior-posterior plane
with minimal, if any, correspondingly responsive movement of the
corpus (body of the uterus). Even the juncture of the cervix to
the lower uterine segment is ill-defined. The feeling is one of an
exaggerated Hegar's sign of early pregnancy, in which the cervix
appears to move in a manner completely independent of the attached corpus. In addition to the "universal joint" feeling returned
to the examiner when moving the cervix, a severe pain response
usually is elicited by any type of cervical movement. However, pain
is primarily occasioned by pushing the cervix in an upward plane.
In the more severe cases (either in advanced bilateral broad-ligament laceration or in a presenting complaint of five years or more
in duration) even mild lateral motion of the cervix will occasion
a painful response.

During examination the retroverted uterus appears to be perhaps
twice increased in size. Pressing against the corpus in the cul-
de-sac in an effort to reduce the third-degree retroversion (which
usually is readily accomplished) also will produce a marked pain
response. When the examiner applies upward pressure on the
cervix or pressure in the cul-de-sac against the corpus, the patient
frequently responds to the painful stimulus by stating, "It's just
like the pain I have with intercourse." A detailed obstetrical history
is the salient feature in establishing the diagnosis of the broad-
ligament-laceration syndrome. The untoward obstetrical event
creating the lacerations may be classified as surgical obstetrics, as
an obstetrical accident, or even as poor obstetrical technique.

Occasionally, women with both the positive pelvic findings and
the subjective symptoms of this syndrome cannot provide a posi-

tive history of obstetrical trauma, but this situation does not rule out the existence of the syndrome. Many women are unaware of an unusual obstetrical event because they were under advanced degrees of sedation or even full anesthesia at the time. Precipitate deliveries, difficult forceps deliveries, complicated breech deliveries, and postmature-infant deliveries are all suspect as obstetrical events that occasionally contribute to tears in the maternal soft parts. If these tears are established in the supports of the uterus (broad ligaments), the immediate postpartum onset of severe dyspareunia can be explained anatomically and physiologically.

It is important to emphasize clinically that although a woman may not be able to describe a specific obstetrical misfortune in her past history, she well may be able to date the onset of her acquired dyspareunia to one particular obstetrical event.

Three cases have been seen in which a criminal abortion was performed by extensively packing the vaginal barrel, leading ultimately to dilation of the cervix and expulsion of uterine content. These extensive vaginal-packing episodes created tears of the broad ligaments, completely parallel to those occasioned by actual obstetrical trauma. Each woman, although unaware of the etiological significance, dated the onset of the symptoms of acquired dyspareunia to the specific experience with the vaginal-packing type of abortive technique.

There have been three cases referred as problems of dyspareunia in which individual women were involved in gang-rape experiences. In all three instances there were multiple coital connections, episodes of simultaneous rectal and vaginal mountings, and finally traumatic tearing of soft tissues of the pelvis associated with forceful introduction of foreign objects into the vagina.

Superficial and deep lacerations were sustained throughout the vaginal barrel and by other soft tissues of the pelvis. Included in the soft-tissue lacerations were those of the broad ligaments (in each case only one side was lacerated), but these lacerations were quite sufficient to produce severe symptoms of secondary dyspareunia.

For some years after the rape episodes each of the three women was presumed to be complaining of the subsequently acquired pain with intercourse as a residual of the psychological trauma associated with their raping. The immediately necessary surgical repair to pelvic tissues had been conducted, but beyond the clinically obvious lacerations of vaginal barrel, bladder, and bowel, the remainder of the pelvic pathology understandably had not been described at the time of surgery. Before gaining symptomatic relief by a second surgical procedure, these three women underwent a combined total of 21 years of markedly crippling dyspareunia, involving a total of five marriages.

The only way that broad-ligament lacerations can be handled effectively is by surgery. Operative findings are relatively constant: (1) The uterus usually is in third-degree retroversion and enlarged from chronic vasocongestion; (2) A significant amount of serous fluid (ranging from 20 to 60 ml. in volume) arising from serous weeping developing in the broad-ligament tears is consistently found in the pelvis; (3) There may be unilateral or bilateral broad-ligament and/or sacrouterine-ligament lacerations. Figure 7 defines the laceration of the broad ligament, and Figure 8 pictures a combination of broad-ligament and sacrouterine-ligament lacerations. It is the inevitable increase in pelvic vasocongestion associated with sexual stimulation added to the already advanced state of chronic pelvic congestion in these traumatized women that can elicit a painful pelvic response. Particularly does such a response arise when the chronically congested pelvic viscera are jostled by the vaginally encased thrusting penis.

It is not within the range of this textbook to describe the surgical procedures for repair of the traumatic tears of the uterine supports. The reader is referred to the bibliography for more definitive consideration.

Subsequent to the definitive surgery, the symptoms of acquired dyspareunia, dysmenorrhea, and the sensations of extreme fatigue usually show marked improvement or may be completely alleviated.

These pelvic findings have been described in far more than usual detail for this type of text, primarily to alert examining physicians to the possibility of the broad-ligament-laceration syndrome. When these pelvic findings have been overlooked, the complaining woman frequently has been told by authority that the pain described with intercourse is due to her imagination. The intelligent

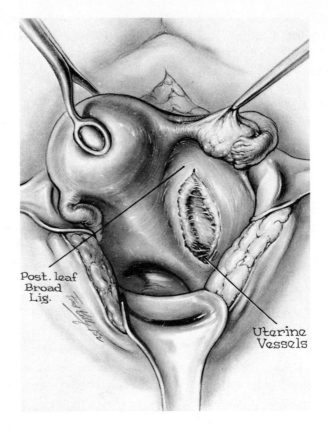

FIGURE 7

Broad-ligament laceration (reproduced from W. M. Allen and W. H. Masters, *Amer. J. Obstet. Gynec.* 70:507, 1955).

woman has grave difficulty accepting this suggestion. She knows unequivocally that coital activity, particularly that of deep vaginal penetration, is severely painful. Actually, she finds that with vaginal acceptance of the full penile shaft, pain is almost inevitable. Even if she has been orgasmic previously, it is rare that she accomplishes orgasmic release of her sexual tensions during intercourse after incurring broad-ligament lacerations, simply because she is always anxiously anticipating the onset of pain.

Any woman with acquired pelvic disability restraining her from the possibility of full sexual responsivity is frustrated. Without orgasmic release with coital connection there will be a marked

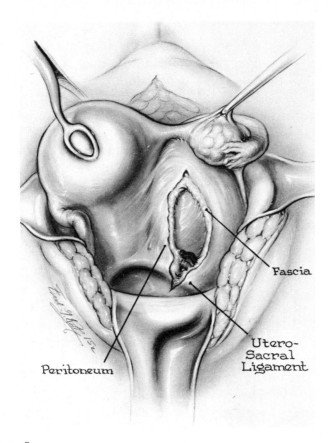

Fascia

Utero-
Sacral
Ligament

Peritoneum

FIGURE 8

Broad- and sacrouterine-ligament lacerations (reproduced from W. M. Allen and W. H. Masters, *Amer. J. Obstet. Gynec.* 70:507, 1955).

residual of acute vasocongestion to provide further pelvic discomfort during a long, irritating resolution phase.

Probably the most frustrating factor of all is to have the acquired dyspareunia disbelieved by authority when the pain with penile thrusting is totally real to the woman involved. The vital question for the therapist to ask should be, "Did this pain with deep penile thrusting develop after a specific delivery?" If the woman can identify a particular pregnancy subsequent to which the dyspareunia became a constant factor in her attempts at sexual expression, the concept of the broad-ligament-laceration syndrome should come to mind.

PELVIC INFECTION AND ENDOMETRIOSIS

When considering intense pain elicited during coital functioning as opposed to vaginal aching or irritation, the therapist generally should look beyond the confines of the vaginal barrel for existent pathology involving the reproductive viscera. Infection (acute or chronic) and endometriosis are pathological conditions involving the reproductive viscera (uterus, tubes, and ovaries) that consistently may return a painful response as the female partner is sharing coital experience. Although these two entities will be discussed separately, they do have in common similar physiological creation of painful response patterns during intercourse. In both instances the response arises from peritoneal irritation resulting in local adhesions not only between folds of peritoneum but also involving tubes, ovaries, bowels, bladder, and omentum. The combination of involuntary distention of the vaginal barrel created by female sex-tension increment and active male thrusting during coital connection places tension on relatively inelastic pelvic tissues stabilized by minor or even major degrees of fibrosis resulting from the infection or the endometriosis. In short, any clinical condition that creates an untoward degree of rigidity of the soft tissues of the female pelvis, so that they do not move freely during sexual connection can return a painful response to the female partner involved.

Infections in the reproductive viscera start with chronic involvement of the cervix (endocervicitis). By drainage through lymphatic channels, long-maintained endocervicitis can involve the basic supports of the uterus (Mackenrodt's ligament) in a chronic inflammatory process. The resultant low-grade peritoneal irritation initiates painful stimuli when the cervix is moved in any direction, particularly by a thrusting penis.

The uterus itself can be involved with infection in the uterine cavity (endometritis) or with a residual of infection throughout the muscular walls (myometritis) to such an extent that any pressure upon the organ is responded to with pain. Retrograde involvement of the peritoneal covering of the uterus and its supports is quite sufficient to cause distress if the uterus is moved, either with involuntary elevation into the false pelvis with female sex-tension increment or during a male thrusting phase in coital connection.

Obviously there are many sources of infection of the oviducts (tubes). Any infections that originate in the cervix have opportunity to spread through the uterine cavity and into the tubal lumina. The major infective agents are the gonococcus, streptococcus, staphylococcus, and coliform organisms. First infections in the tubal lumina frequently spill into the abdominal cavity, causing at least localized pelvic inflammation and at most generalized abdominal peritonitis. Subsequently, as the acute stage of the infection subsides those areas involved in the infectious process remain open to the development of adhesions between loops of bowel, the omentum, and the pelvic viscera. There even may be abscess formation involving the tubes and ovaries. In all these situations there is tension on and tightening of the peritoneum and rigid fixation of the pelvic soft-tissue structures to such an extent that vaginal distention and coital thrusting create a markedly painful response for the woman.

In no sense does this brief clinical description of pelvic inflammatory processes imply that whenever any woman acquires infection in the pelvic viscera she is committed thereafter to pain during coital connection. With early and adequate medical care most pelvic infections do not create a residual of continuing pain with coital exposure.

The degree of residual pelvic pain depends upon the severity of the occasional sequelae of the infectious process. Where are the adhesions and how extensive are they? To what extent is natural expansion of the vaginal barrel restricted by filling of the cul-de-sac with an enlarged tube, by an ovary firmly adhered to the posterior wall of the broad ligament, or by a uterus held in severe third-degree retroversion by adhesions? Any of these situations may create painful stimuli with penile thrusting.

Endometriosis is a disease in which implants of endometrial tissue spread throughout the pelvic viscera and their protective covering, the peritoneum. When examined microscopically, this ectopic tissue resembles the lining of the inner cavity of the uterus. The tubes, ovaries, broad ligaments, omentum, and the posterior wall of the uterus may be involved by firm fibrous adhesions. There are even many instances of tying together omentum and bowel with the reproductive viscera into large pelvic masses. The etiology of endometriosis has not been fully established. It would not serve the purposes of this text to enter into a detailed discussion of the subject. Although endometrial implants appear in many anatomical areas other than the pelvic viscera, consideration will be focused alone on local pelvic implants.

Even if there are no major adhesions in the pelvis, there are at least minor elements of continuous local peritoneal irritation. Endometrial nodules usually can be felt most effectively with simultaneous manual pelvic-rectal examination. Again, the pain created by intercourse is due to the constriction and immobilization of the peritoneum and the firming up of the soft tissues of the pelvis by adhesions. The pelvic structures have progressively less facility to distend, expand, and move freely as the endometriosis progresses. There is consequently more local tissue resistance to involuntary vaginal expansion, uterine elevation, and male pelvic thrusting.

In all situations that create chronic irritation of the pelvic peritoneum, fixation of the uterus, or constriction of the vaginal barrel, pain with intercourse is a relatively constant finding. Treatment for endometriosis is either medical or surgical depending upon the degree of soft-tissue and pelvic visceral involvement. But once endometriosis has developed to a point at which there is significantly severe pain in response to coital activity, there must be definitive treatment of the condition, or the individual woman will have little hope of relief from the symptoms of progressively increasing dyspareunia.

POSTSURGICAL DYSPAREUNIA

There are three important sources for acquired dyspareunia following removal of the uterus for specific organ pathology.

First, dyspareunia results from thoughtless surgical technique. Physicians, when performing a hysterectomy, may overlook the fact that the cervix enters the vagina through the superior wall of that organ. When the wound in the vaginal barrel is repaired after removal of the cervix, if care is not taken to retain a superior position for the vaginal cuff, the scarred area, instead of being retained in the superior vaginal wall, may be pulled into the depth of the barrel by tissue constriction or by excessive folding or removal of vaginal tissue. Postoperatively when the husband thrusts deeply into the vagina, the penis can come into contact with the resistant scarred area. There is little residual facility for involuntary vaginal distention in the area of the surgical scar. Therefore, dyspareunia of significant proportion develops occasionally as a post-surgical complication. Since this unfortunate result usually does not develop for months or even a year after surgery, the operating surgeon may never be made aware of the acquired dyspareunia.

The second opportunity to acquire dyspareunia is occasioned by the surgical indications for removal of the ovaries at the time the uterus is removed, or for that matter, at any time. If post-operative sex-steroid-replacement is not initiated, many women will develop senile changes in the vagina and, in time, secondary dyspareunia.

The third incidence of dyspareunia after hysterectomy rarely comes to the attention of the operating surgeon. The etiology of the acquired dyspareunia may be subjective in origin. If the woman facing hysterectomy and/or removal of the ovaries is not reassured with her husband that there need not be reduction of sexual drive or orgasmic facility after surgery, her fantasy and her friends' "old wives' tales" may, by power of suggestion, create fears of sexual performance for the anxious woman. If she feels that she is going to be castrated, and sex-steroid-replacement therapy is not explained and offered as indicated, she well may believe that after surgery there will be loss of ability to respond in a sexually effective manner in the future. What is worse, an uninformed husband may have similar concepts.

If anything, sexual responsivity should be higher shortly after than immediately before surgery. The pelvic pathology for which the hysterectomy or oophorectomy is indicated usually detracts from sexual effectiveness by creating a state of ill health which, in turn, reduces innate sexual tension. When the offending condition is removed and the general state of health consequently improved, there usually is a reawakening of sexual interest.

If women are not reassured before surgery, many presume that, in the future, intercourse will provide no return for them or for their husbands, or that intercourse will even be painful. Any woman has only to be sure that she will be distressed by future coital connection to take a long step toward acquired dyspareunia.

There are, of course, many factors other than the major ones of infection, endometriosis, postsurgical objective and subjective complications, and the syndrome of broad-ligament laceration that create painful stimuli from irritated peritoneal and pelvic soft tissues in response to coital connection. These include tumors of the uterus, such as myomas (fibroids), ovarian cysts and solid tumors, and, carcinoma of the female reproductive tract. Any of these tumor growths occasionally incite onset of the complaint of acquired dyspareunia. Those interested can find more definitive evaluations of this physiological source of dyspareunia in current gynecology textbooks.

Thus, the basic premise with which the Foundation approaches the problem of dyspareunia is one of elimination of possible pathological reasons for the complaint. If a woman complains of pain with intercourse, her complaint is accepted at face value, and steps are taken to identify the biophysical source of the coital distress.

The diagnosis of psychosomatic dyspareunia, unquestionably of moment in the sexual-response field, must be made by exclusion. To assign subjective origins to pelvic pain, regardless of the patient's personality structure, without definitive physical evaluation of the pelvis, can result in clinical mismanagement of patients. Certainly there are times when, after every effort has been made to establish physical source of the pelvic pain, subjective etiology for the complaint will be considered strongly. But the initial biophysical investigative effort must be made by competent authority.

MALE DYSPAREUNIA

Painful coition is not limited to women. Many men are distracted from and even denied effective sexual functioning by painful stimuli occasioned during or after sexual functioning. The symptoms will be described in relation to the anatomical site of pain—the external anatomy, such as the surface of the penis and the scrotal sac, or the internal anatomy, such as the penile urethra, the prostate, or the bladder. No attempt will be made to provide definitive discussion for the varieties of male-oriented dyspareunia. Situations are mentioned only to emphasize their existence and to provide the therapist with an awareness of the fact that, in truth, there are "badly mated" men.

EXTERNAL ANATOMY

Many men complain of severe sensitivity of the glans penis, not only to touch but to any form of containment (including intravaginal retention) immediately after ejaculation. This severity of glans pain recalls the intensely painful response that may be elicited from the clitoral glans when it is approached during forceful male manipulative attempts to incite sex-tension increment for his female partner. Once a man is fully aware that immediately after his ejaculatory episode there may be exquisite tenderness of the glans, he realizes that he must immediately withdraw from intravaginal containment. Generally there is marked variation in the severity of the individual response pattern. Men noting variation in the severity of glans pain have no preejaculatory warning of the intensity of the particular response pattern, which may range from minor irritation with containment to crippling pain with the slightest touch.

The glans occasionally is irritated rather than protected, as might be presumed, by a retained foreskin. Two men have been referred to the Foundation complaining that relief from painful stimuli immediately after ejaculation can be obtained only by retracting the foreskin well back over the glans and in this fashion relieving the irritation of glans confinement.

There are occasional irritative responses created by the retained foreskin of uncircumcised men. In almost all instances these irritative responses have to do with lack of effective hygienic habits. Primarily, smegma and, secondarily, various bacterial, trichomonal, or fungal infections sometimes collect beneath the foreskin. If the foreskin is not retracted regularly and the area washed with soap and water, chronic irritation can easily develop. With chronic irritation or even frank infection present, there usually will be pain with coital thrusting or with any form of penile containment. In almost all instances the dyspareunia responds readily to adequate cleansing principles.

Phimosis (a tightness or constriction of the orifice of the prepuce) clinically is marked by a foreskin that cannot be retracted over the glans penis. With an excessively constrained foreskin, infection is almost always present to at least a minor degree, and penile irritation is a consistent factor for men so afflicted. Adhesions frequently develop between the foreskin and the glans proper so that there is no freedom of movement between the two structures. Engorgement of the penis with sex-tension increment may bring pressure to bear on the foreskin constraint of the glans. Without freedom of foreskin movement, this constriction frequently causes local pain with penile erective engorgement. When any male is diagnosed as having a degree of clinical phimosis sufficient for chronically recurrent infectious processes and/or pain or irritation with coital connection, circumcision certainly is in order.

There are also occasional men with a true hypersensitivity of the penile glans. These men are almost constantly irritated by underclothes or by body contact. They are continually aware of a multiplicity of irritants and are particularly susceptible to trauma to the glans. One man referred for consideration found glans constraint in the vaginal environment intolerable. There was a constant blistering and peeling of the superficial tissues of the glans' surface. Despite a history of numerous changes in sexual partners, the postcoital results were identical. This individual simply could not tolerate the natural pH levels of the vagina. Since the reaction was confined to the glans area and never involved the penile shaft, there is room for presumption that if he had not been circumcised routinely, he might not have been so handicapped. Protective coating of the glans area precoitally resolved his problem but was a nuisance factor for him and possibly for his sexual partners.

There are occasional instances of referred pain from the posterior urethra (usually occasioned by posterior urethritis) that produce pain in the glans penis. Very rarely, this type of glans pain is a factor in coition.

Peyronie's disease, produced by induration and fibrosis of the corpora cavernosa of the penis (see Fig. 1, Chapter 2) and evidenced as an upward bowing of the penis, plus a gradually increasing angulation to the right or left of the midline, makes coital connection somewhat difficult, and in advanced stages coition is virtually impossible. There also may be pain attached to attempts at coital connection due to the unusual angulation of the penis creating resultant penile shaft strain, both with inserting and with thrusting experience.

Penile chordee (downward bowing) is seen rarely in situations of penile trauma and only occasionally with neglected gonorrheal urethritis. Consultation has been requested by four men with severe penile chordee as a posttraumatic residual. In two instances the fully erect penis was struck sharply by an angry female partner. The remaining two men each described severe pain with a specific coital experience. During uninhibitedly responsive coital connection with the female partner in a superior position, the penis was lost to the vaginal barrel. In each case, the women tried to remount rapidly by sitting down firmly on the shaft of the penis. The vaginal orifice was missed in the hurried insertive attempt and the full weight of the woman's body sustained by the erect penis.

Each of the four men gave the remarkable verbal description that he felt or heard "something snap." Shortly thereafter an obvious hematoma appeared on the anterior or posterior wall or lateral walls of the penile shaft. Over a period of weeks, as the local hemorrhage was absorbed, fibrous adhesions developed and, with subsequent scar formation, there slowly developed a downward bowing and (in three cases) mild angulation of the penis. Urologists state that due to the type of tissue involved in the penile trauma, there is little to offer in the way of clinical reprieve for men afflicted with these embarrassing erective angulations (Peyronie's disease or chordee). Attempts at surgical correction currently are of relatively little value and not infrequently make the situation worse. Any of these situations create responses of pain and tenderness during both masturbation and coital connection.

It always should be borne in mind that the erect penis can be traumatized by a sudden blow, by rapidly shifting coital position, by applying sudden angulation strain to the shaft, or from violent coital activity that places sudden weight or sudden pressure on the fully erect penis. The unfortunate residuals of such trauma have been described above.

Direct trauma of the penis occasioned by major accidents, war injuries, or direct physical attack sometimes requires that treatment for sexual dysfunction be patterned to include marked variation in the anatomical structuring of the penis. In anatomical deformity of the penis, the complaint of dyspareunia can be raised by either the male or female sexual partner.

Testicular pain, usually of the dull, aching variety, develops for some men who spend a significant amount of time in sexual play or in reading pornographic literature, concurrently maintaining erections for lengthy periods of time without ejaculating within the immediate present. Frequent returns to excitement- or even plateau-phase levels of sexual stimulation without ejaculatory relief of the accompanying testicular vasocongestion can cause an aching in either or both testes, particularly in younger men. Relief is immediate with ejaculation, which disperses the superficial and deep vasocongestion and returns the testicles to their normal size. No permanent damage is occasioned by maintaining chronic testicular congestion for a period of days. Men with this syndrome of testicular pain occasioned by long-maintained sexual tension are in the minority. Usually, the syndrome of involuntary testicular pain is relieved somewhat as the man ages.

There are painful reactions that develop during or shortly after coital connection that particularly reflect the influence of the vaginal environment. These situations are mentioned only in passing, but the therapist should keep in mind the fact that the basic pathology involved rests within the vaginal environment. Many men complain of burning, itching, and irritation after coital connection with women contending with chronic or acute vaginal infections. Not infrequently small blisters appear on the glans penis, particularly around the urethral outlet. If there are any abrasions on either the glans or shaft of the penis, secondary infection can occur in these local sites. The same type of irritative penile reaction may develop from exposure to a noninfectious vaginal environment as a response to the chemicals in contraceptive creams, jellies, foams, etc. It may not be the female that responds in a sensitive manner to an intravaginal chemical contraceptive agent but rather her male partner. Sensitivity to intravaginal chemical contraceptives is seen quite frequently in the male and, if symptoms develop, contraceptive technique should be changed.

The same sort of irritative penile reaction can be elicited by a repetitive pattern of vaginal douching. There are some douche preparations to which not the female but the male partner becomes sensitive. Not infrequently, vesicles form on the glans penis. If these blisters rupture, the raw areas on the glans are quite painful, particularly during sexual connection.

In the actual process of ejaculation there are many situations that return painful stimuli to the involved male. If the individual has had gonorrhea there may be strictures (adhesions) throughout the length of the penile urethra, and attempts to urinate and/or to ejaculate may cause severe pain spreading throughout the penile urethra and radiating to the bladder and prostate. If there is infection in the bladder, the prostate, or the seminal vesicles, there may be the sensation of intense burning during and particularly in the first few minutes after ejaculation. Particularly if the offending agent has been the gonococcus, the pain with ejaculation sometimes is exquisite. Immediate medical attention should be given to any complaint of burning or itching during or immediately after the ejaculatory process.

There is a spastic reaction of the prostate gland seen in older men during the stage of ejaculatory inevitability (see Chapter 12). In this situation the prostate contracts spastically rather than in its regularly recurring contractile pattern, and the return can be one of very real pelvic pain and/or aching radiating to the inner aspects of the thighs or into the bladder and occasionally to the rectum. This pathologic spastic contraction pattern can be treated effectively by providing a minimal amount of testosterone replacement therapy.

Care should be taken to evaluate the possibility of concurrent infection in the prostate. Occasionally, chronic prostatitis has caused significant degrees of pain during an ejaculatory process. As a point in differential diagnosis, the painful response with prostatic infection is with the second, not the first, stage of the orgasmic experience, while that of prostatic spasm has just the reverse sequence. Careful questioning usually will establish specifically the timing in onset of the painful response and thus suggest a more definitive diagnosis.

Benign hypertrophy of the prostate gland primarily and carcinoma of the prostate rarely may be responsible for onset of pain with the ejaculatory process. The pain is secondary (acquired) in character and radiates to bladder and rectum. Usually confined to older age groups, onset of this type of dyspareunia should be investigated immediately by competent authority.

This review of the major causes of dyspareunia has been primarily directed toward the female partner, for from her come by far the greater number of complaints of painful coital connection. However, male dyspareunia no longer should be ignored by the medical and behavioral literature. The review of the etiology of male dyspareunia has not been exhaustive, nor is it within the province of this text to do so. In concept, the entire chapter has been designed to suggest to cotherapists, faced daily with a myriad of problems focusing upon both male and female sexual dysfunction, that there are physiological as well as psychological causes for sexual inadequacy. Combined pelvic and rectal examinations for the female and rectal examination for the male partner are a routine part of the total physical examination provided for both members of any marital unit referred to the Foundation for treatment of sexual dysfunction.

To attempt to define and to treat the basic elements of sexual dysfunction for either sex without including the opportunity for thorough physical examination and complete laboratory evaluations as an integral part of the patient's diagnostic and therapeutic program is to do the individual and the marital unit a clinical disservice.

I I

TREATMENT OF
ORGASMIC
DYSFUNCTION

Neither the biophysical nor the psychosocial systems which influence expression of the human sexual component have a biologically controlled demand to make specifically positive or negative contributions to sexual function (see Chapter 8). This fact does not alter the potential of the systems' interdigitational contribution to the formation of effective patterns of sexual response. When this potential is not realized by the natural development of psychophysiological sexual complements, the result is sexual dysfunction.

The initial psychosocial contributions toward realization of this potential may come through positive experience of early imprinting. As defined by John Money, imprinting is a process whereby a perceptual signal is matched to an innate releasing mechanism which elicits a behavioral pattern. Established at critical periods in development, imprints thereafter are considered more or less permanent.

Infantile imprinting of sexually undifferentiated sensory receptivity to the warmth and sensation of close body contact is considered a source of formative contribution to an individual's baseline of erotic inclinations and choices. This material essentially is unobtainable in specific form during history-taking. It becomes important to the rapid-treatment program only as it is reflected by statements of preference in physical communication or other recall pertinent to ongoing patterns of sexual responsivity.

In the treatment of orgasmic dysfunction, Foundation personnel make use of two primary sources of material. These sources reliably reflect the female's prevailing sexual attitudes, receptivity, and levels of responsivity. The first source, derived from the history, is identification by the nonorgasmic woman of erotically significant expectations or experiences (positive or negative) currently evoked during sexual interchange with her marital partner. The cotherapists must identify those things which the husband does or does not do that may not meet the requirements of his wife's sexual value system previously shaped by real or imagined experience or expectation.

Past experiences of positive content involving other partners, or unrealizable expectations perceived as ideal, may be over idealistically compared by her to the current opportunity; or negative experiences or negative expectation-related attitudes may intrude upon receptivity to her partner's sexual approach. Thus, a rejection or blocking of sexual input may be the end result.

A discussion of memories of perceptual and interpretive reactions associated with specific sexual activity may add further dimension to knowledge of the wife's currently constituted sexual value system, since these memories often have been noted to function as signals for subconscious introduction of stored experience, either positive or negative in nature.

The second source of reliable, directly applicable material upon which the rapid-treatment therapy relies for direction—indeed, it characterizes this particular mode of psychotherapy—is developed from the daily discussions that follow each sensate-focus exercise. As repeatedly stressed, defining the etiology of the presenting sexual inadequacy does not necessarily provide the basis for treatment. A reasonably reliable history is indispensable, but it is used primarily to provide interpretive direction and to amplify definition of that which is of individual significance. (It even is used from time to time to demonstrate negative patterns of sexual behavior.)

During the two-week rapid-treatment program, the daily report and ensuing discussions between the cotherapists and marital partners describing the nonorgasmic wife's reactions (as well as those of her interacting husband) provide an incisive measure of the degree to which the requirements of her functioning sexual value system are being met or negated, or the extent to which she progressively is able to adapt her requirements. These discussions provide simultaneous opportunity for a more *finite* evaluation of the levels of interactive contribution to sexual function by her biophysical and psychosocial systems (see Chapters 2, 8).

The treatment of both primary and situational orgasmic dysfunction requires a basic understanding by patients and cotherapists that the peak of sex-tension increment resulting in orgasmic release cannot be willed or forced. Instead, orgasmic experience evolves as a direct result of individually valued erotic stimuli accrued by the woman to the level necessary for psychophysiological release. Just as the trigger mechanism which stimulates the regularity of expulsive uterine contractions sending a woman into labor is still unknown, so is the mechanism that triggers orgasmic release from sex-tension increment. Probably they are inseparably entwined—to identify one may be to know the other.

It seems more accurate to consider female orgasmic response as an *acceptance* of naturally occurring stimuli that have been given erotic significance by an individual sexual value system than to depict it as a learned response. There are many case histories recorded in this and related studies reporting orgasmic incidence in the developing human female at ages that correspond with ages reported in histories of onset of male masturbation and nocturnal emission. These clearly described, objective accounts are considered accurate by reason of their correlation with subjective recall provided by several hundred women interrogated during previously reported laboratory studies.

The initial authoritative direction in therapy includes suggestions to the marital unit for developing a nondemanding, erotically stimulating climate in the privacy of their own quarters. At no time during the two-week therapy program is either of the marital partners under any form of observation, laboratory or otherwise. Only the phenomenon of vaginismus is directly demonstrated to the husband of the distressed wife, under conditions routinely employed by appropriate practitioners of clinical medicine (see Chapter 9).

The cotherapists' initial directions suggest ways of putting aside tension-provoking behavioral interaction for the duration of the rapid-treatment program and allow the woman to discover and share knowledge of those things which she personally finds to be sexually stimulating. Further professional contribution must suggest to the marital unit ways and means to create an opportunity for the woman to think and feel sexually with spontaneity. She must be made fully aware that she has permission to express her sexual feelings during this phase of the therapy program without focusing on her partner's sexual function except by enjoying a personal awareness of the direct stimulus to her sexual tensions that his obvious physical response provides.

Every nonorgasmic woman, whether distressed by primary or situational dysfunction, must develop adaptations within areas of perceptual, behavioral, and philosophic experience. She must learn or relearn to feel sexually (respond to sexual stimuli) within the context of and related directly to shared sexual activities with her partner as they correlate with the expression of her own sexual identity, mood, preferences, and expectations. The bridge between her sexual feeling (perception) and sexual thinking (philosophy) essentially is established through comfortable use of verbal and nonverbal (specifically physical) communication of shared experience with her marital partner. Her philosophic adaptation to the acceptance and appreciation of sexual stimuli is further dependent upon the establishment of "permission" to express herself sexually. Any alteration in the sexual value system must, of course, be consistent with her own personality and social value system if the adaptation is to be internalized. Keeping in mind the similarities between male and female sexual response, the crucial factors most often missing in the sexual value system of the nonorgasmic woman are the pleasure in, the honoring of, and the privilege to express need for the sexual experience. In essence, the restoration of sexual feeling to its appropriate psychosocial context (the primary focus of the therapy for the nonorgasmic woman) is the reversal of sexual dissembling. This, in turn, encourages a more supportive role for her sexuality. In the larger context of a sexual relationship, the freedom to express need is part of the "give-to-get" concept inherent in capacity and facility for effective sexual responsivity.

Professional direction must allow for woman's justifiable, socially enhancing need for personal commitment, because her capacity to respond sexually is influenced by psychosocial demand. The commitment functions as her "permission" to involve herself sexually, when prior opportunities available to formation of a sexual value system have not included an honorable concept of her sexuality as a basis upon which to accept and express her sexual identity (see Chapter 8). Commitment apparently means many things to as many different women; most frequently encountered are the commitments of marriage or the promise of marriage, the commitment of love (real or anticipated) according to the interpretation of "love" for the particular individual. Regardless of the form the commitment takes, after it is established the goal to be attained is enjoyment of sexual expression for its own positive return and for its enhancement of those involved.

During daily therapy sessions, interrogation of the sexually dysfunctional woman is designed to elicit material that expresses the emotions and thoughts that accompany the feelings (sexual or otherwise) developed by the sensate-focus exercise. Also continually explored are the feelings, thoughts, and emotions that are related to the behavior of her marital partner. Her reactions when discussing material of sexual connotation are evaluated carefully to determine those things which may be contributing to ongoing inhibition or distortion being revealed by the regular episodes of psychophysiological interaction with her husband.

When a nonorgasmic female involves herself with her partner in situations providing opportunities for effective sexual function, her ever-present need is to establish and maintain communication. Communication, both physical and verbal in nature, makes vital contributions, but it loses effectiveness in the rapid-treatment method if allowed to be colored by anger, frustration, or misunderstanding. While verbal communication is encouraged throughout the two-week period, physical communication is introduced in progressive steps following the initial authoritative suggestion to provide a nondemanding, warmly encompassing, shared experience for the woman, with optimal opportunity for feeling.

After the early return from sensate-focus opportunity as directed at the roundtable discussion has been judged fully effective by marital partners and cotherapists (see Chapter 2), the marital unit is encouraged to move to the next phase in sensate pleasure—

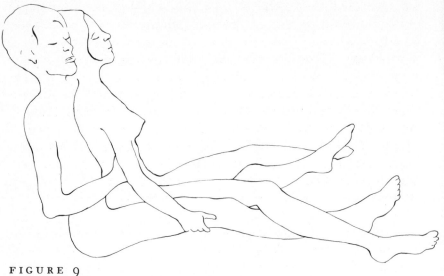

FIGURE 9

Nondemand position for female stimulation.

genital manipulation. The cotherapists should issue specific instructions to the marital partners as "permission" is granted to the female to enjoy genital play. Instructions should include details of positioning, approach, time span, and above all, a listing of ways and means to avoid the usual pitfalls of male failure to stimulate his partner in the manner she prefers rather than as she permits him the privilege to function.

The husband is directed to place himself in a sitting (slightly reclining, if desired) position, with his back against a comfortable placement of pillows at the headboard of the bed. With the husband's legs adequately separated to allow his wife to sit between them, she should recline with her back against his chest, pillowing her head on his shoulder. Length of torsos should determine the reclining angle that permits her head to rest comfortably. Her legs are then separated and extended across those of her husband (Fig. 9). This position provides a degree of warm security for the woman ("back-protected" phenomenon) and allows freedom of access for the man to encourage creative exploration of his wife's entire body in the sensate-focus concept.

The level of physical communication in the manipulative sessions is encouraged further by direction for the female partner to place her hand in a lightly riding position on that of her husband. By using slight increase in pressure or gentle directional movement, the "where and how" of her need of the moment may be immediately communicated to her receptive husband. This and other forms of nonverbal communication allow sharing of her particular desires as they occur as manifestations of her sexual value system, and constitute a secure way by which her marital partner can identify and fulfill these desires by meaningful interaction. This means of direct physical communication also provides the woman with freedom to request specifics of genital play without the distraction of forced verbal request or a detailed explanation.

Any spontaneous form of expression of a man's own sexual tensions is one of the most interactive contributions that he can make to his wife. It is a viable component of sexual "give to get" in any circumstance of physical sharing. This principle applies equally to the marital unit carrying out the simplest sensate-focus exercise in the therapy program as it does to a marital unit that has never known sexual dysfunction.

The husband must not presume his wife's desire for a particular stimulative approach, nor must he introduce his own choice of stimuli. The husband's assumption of expertise has no place in the initial learning phase of a marital unit seeking to reverse the wife's nonorgasmic condition. The trial-and-error hazard this poses is not worth the small possibility of accidental pleasure that might be achieved. In truth, error in some facet of this controlled manipulative form of physical communication has already been established, or the marital-unit members probably would not consider themselves in need of professional support. Only after both marital partners have established the fact of the wife's sexual effectiveness with controlled genital play and have developed dependable physical signal systems should trial-and-error stimulative techniques become a naturally occurring dimension of pleasure. It is well to mention that even those partners with an established, effective sexual relationship may find it both appropriate and advisable to check out their physical signal systems by verbal communication from time to time.

An additional value derived from the nondemand position (see

Fig. 9) and its accompanying sensate exercises is its contribution to removal of the potential spectator's role. This role can become as much a pitfall for the nonorgasmic woman as it is for the impotent male (see Chapters 5 and 6). Already considered in descriptions of female-oriented patterns of sexual dissimulation, the spectator role is dissipated when sexual involvement of husband and wife becomes mutually encompassing for both partners.

Educational direction for the husband is an integral part of the genital-play episodes. The cotherapists must be certain that the basics of effective pelvic play are clearly enunciated if the male partner is to provide effective measure of stimulative return for the woman involved. The husband is instructed both to allow and to encourage his wife to indicate specific preferences in stimulative approach either by the light touch of her hand on his or by moving slightly toward desired approach or away from excessive pressure.

Probably the greatest error that any man makes approaching a woman sexually is that of direct attack upon the clitoral glans (see Fig. 2, Chapter 2), unless this is the stated wish of his particular partner. The glans of the clitoris has the same embryonic developmental background as that of the penis, but usually is much more sensitive to touch. As female sex tensions elevate, sensations of irritation, or even pain, may result from direct clitoral manipulation.

Rarely do women, when masturbating, manipulate the clitoral glans directly. Therefore, the male approach to clitoral stimulation would do well to correspond to that employed by women when providing self-release. There is a further, perhaps more subtle, reason for relative care in the intensity of stimulative concentration directed to the clitoris. This originates from the fact that the clitoris, as a receptor and a transmitter of sexual stimuli, can rapidly react to create an overwhelming degree of sensation. When such a high level of biophysical tension is reached before the psychosocial concomitant has been subjectively appreciated, the woman experiences too much sensation too soon and finds it difficult to accept.

In the interest of a pleasurable, evolving sexual responsivity, the clitoris should not be approached directly. Specifically, manipulation should be conducted in the general mons area, particularly along either side of the clitoral shaft. It must be remembered that the inner aspects of the thighs and the labia also are erotically identified areas for most women. Pressure and direction of manual stimulation should be controlled initially by the female partner for two educative reasons. First, full freedom of manipulative control provides her with opportunity to feel and think sexually without having to adjust to a partner's assumption of what pleases her; and second, female control of manipulative activity also educates the male partner into the particular woman's basic preferences in stimulative approach to the clitoral area.

It must also be borne in mind by the male partner that there is no lubricating material available to the clitoris. As female sex tension increases there will be a sufficient amount of lubrication at the vaginal outlet. This should be maneuvered manually from the vagina to include the general area of the clitoris. Vaginal lubrication used in this manner will prevent the irritation of the clitoral area that always accompanies any significant degree of manipulation of a dry surface.

A further dimension of sexual excitation is derived from manipulation of the vaginal outlet when lubricating material is acquired for clitoral spread by superficial finger insertion. There is usually little value returned from deep vaginal insertion of the fingers, particularly early in the stimulative process. While some women have reported a mental translation of the ensuing intravaginal sensation to that of penile containment, few had any preference for the opportunity.

Probably the most effective technique is that of the teasing approach of light touch moving at random from the breasts to the abdomen to the thighs to the labia to the thighs and back to the abdomen and breasts without concentrating specifically on pelvic manipulation early in the stimulative episode. Particularly should direct approach to the clitoral area be avoided initially in this process. This "exercise" becomes even more effective as a means of female sex-tension increment, when interlaced with sensate-focus, stroking techniques introduced after roundtable discussion (see Chapter 2).

The male partner must be careful not to inject any personal demand for sexual performance into his female partner's pattern of response. The husband must not set goals for his wife. He must not try to force responsivity. His role is that of accommodation, warmth, understanding, and holding, but he should not be so pacific that his own sexual pleasure is negated for either himself or his partner. Through total cooperation he allows his wife to drift with sensate pleasure and provides her with sensual stimulation without forcing her to contend with an accompanying sense of goal-oriented demand to respond to a forcing form of manipulation.

The cotherapists must make it quite clear to the husband that orgasmic release is not the focus of this sexual interaction. Manipulation of breast, pelvis, and other body areas varying from the lightest touch to an increase in pressure only at partner direction, should provide the wife with the opportunity to express her sexual responsivity freely, but without any concept of demand for an end-point (orgasmic) goal. It must be emphasized that the effectiveness of a stimulative session is not lost to the woman simply because the session is terminated without orgasmic experience. There is a tremendous accrual of sexual facility and interest for any woman when she knows that there will be a repeat opportunity for further sexual expression in the immediate future. Thus, the husband's light, teasing, nondemanding approach to touch and manipulation allows the female partner full freedom to express her interests, her demands, her sexual tensions. This sequence of opportunities permits accumulation of stimulative effects which will provide the source of her ultimate release of maximum sex-tension increment at some future point.

All specific exercises aimed toward the wife's fulfillment of her orgasmic capacity always are introduced by direction of the cotherapists on the basis of marital-unit report. When husband and wife describe the fact that previous directions have produced a positive return of stimulative pleasure, their next level of sexual involvement is approached. This treatment concept means, of course, that a steady progression of exercises does not necessarily take place on daily schedule. For instance, marital partners who never have verbally shared sexual reactions or expressed sexual preferences to each other usually take longer to appreciate a positive level of sexual-tension return than less restrained, more communicative husbands and wives. Yet another example of delayed reactive potential centers upon marital units that have coped with functional distress for extended periods of time. These husbands and wives usually require longer to adapt to and become comfortable with their revised patterns of sexual behavior than those whose sexual dysfunction has been relatively brief. It has been further observed that successful marital-unit adaptation to a state of sexual dysfunction, in itself a possible indication of individual and marital-unit strengths, may present a higher level of inherent resistance to reversal of the stated inadequacy than more dissident, fragmented marital relationships.

Cotherapists must constantly bear in mind during the rapid-treatment program that the authoritative introduction of specific exercises represents a deliberate breakdown of woman's sexual responsivity into its natural components. Each exercise is introduced singly and continued until appreciated. All exercises are accrued one after another in a natural building process until they have been reassembled into the whole of an established sexual response pattern.

For descriptive purposes, the directive pattern might be likened to the song *Partridge in a Pear Tree*, in which each item is repeated as a new one is added in each successive verse until all items are assembled. Therefore, the marital unit must be reminded quietly each time a new direction for specific sexual activity is introduced that this introduction of new material is not an indication that previous exercises and their concomitant pleasures must be relinquished in order to enjoy the new experience. Rather, as each new psychophysiological concept is provided for marital partner assimilation, older exercises are constantly restated until the whole reactive process is assembled.

At this point, marital partners frequently may have acquired a gavotte-like approach to sexual expression when employing the directive suggestions rather than spontaneously incorporating each new physical approach or stimulative concept into their own style or pattern of behavior. The marital unit will need reminding that on a long-range basis there is little return from clocking each component of the therapeutic pattern for a specific length of time or introducing each new exercise into their sexual interaction in a purely mechanical manner, solely because it has been suggested by impersonal authority rather than mutually evolved.

Emphasis should be placed upon the fact that there is marked individual variation in the time span in which each area of sensory perception is appreciated. Mood, level of need, quality of partner involvement, etc., all vary widely, frequently on a day-to-day basis. There will be occasions when spontaneous nonspecific or even asexual social interaction will replace all the "touch and feeling" (foreplay) that have been so enjoyable and so necessary at other times. Whenever exercises in sensate focus (especially those using specifically positioned opportunities) have initiated newfound levels of stimulative appreciation for the nonorgasmic woman, the appropriately sequential step is suggested for unit exploration during their next phase of sexual interaction.

It is essential to successful therapy to emphasize again and again the concept that sexual response can neither be programmed nor made to happen. The marital unit also must be encouraged continually to create an environment that fulfills the stimulative (biophysical and psychosocial) requirements of each partner and in which sex-tension increment can occur without any concept of performance demand.

Each successive phase of physical approach is introduced subsequent to establishing some evidence of encompassing psychosensual pleasure as perceived by the nonorgasmic woman during a prior episode. These phases develop in sequence from the first day's sensory exploration which takes place following the roundtable discussion (see Chapter 2). If there is obvious female pleasure in the first sensate experience, the next phase includes specific manipulative approach to genital excitation, using, if possible, the positioning suggested by Figure 9 (this chapter). If the first day's exercise in sensate pleasure has not developed a positive experience for the nonorgasmic woman, the second day will again be devoted to these primary touch-and-feeling episodes, instead of moving into the genital manipulative episodes usually scheduled for Day 2. In turn, the genital manipulative episodes are continued until there is obvious evidence of elevated female sex tension, before moving on to the next phase in the psychosensory progression.

Subsequent to reported success in manual genital excitation, the marital partners are asked to try the female-superior coital position, by which means the wife may translate previously established levels of sensate pleasure into an experience which includes the sensation of penile containment. The specific techniques of this position have been discussed and illustrated in Chapter 3. Female-superior mounting is but another step in the gradual development of sexual awareness leading from simple, sensate focus to effective response in coital connection.

The husband is asked to assume a supine position in anticipation of his wife's superior mounting. Intromission is to take place when both partners have reached the level of sexual interchange (full erection for the man; well-established lubrication for the woman) that suggests the desire for further physical expression.

When the marital partners extend their psychosensory interchange to coition in the female-superior position, the wife once mounted is instructed to hold herself quite still and simply to absorb the awareness of penile containment. Interspersed with moments of sensate pleasure created by her proprioceptive awareness of vaginal dilatation should be the opportunity to feel and think sexually. The vaginal distention should be interpreted in relation to the sensual desire for further increment in sexual pleasure. This increasing demand for sexual stimulation can be further implemented by the female partner if she will institute a brief period of controlled, slowly exploring, pelvic thrusting. The husband's specific responsibility at this moment is to provide the needed erect penis without any concept of a demanding thrusting pattern on his part. In anticipation of her need, the cotherapists must encourage the wife to think of the encompassed penis as hers to play with, to feel, and to enjoy, until the urge for more severe pelvic thrusting involuntarily emerges into her levels of conscious demand.

It may take several episodes of female-superior coital positioning, as the woman plays pelvically with the contained penis, before full sensate focus develops vaginally. Once vaginal sensation develops in a pleasant or even a fully demanding vein, the next phase is to add to the sensate picture the male-initiated, nondemanding, slow pelvic thrusting. The nondemanding thrusting by the husband should be kept at a pace communicated by his wife. This constrained form of male pelvic thrusting is suggested for two reasons: (1) to create obvious opportunity for extension of the female's sensory potential and (2) to provide sufficient stimulative activity to maintain an effective erection.

At this time the question frequently asked by the male member of marital units whose concept of sexual interaction has been based primarily on the stock formula of perform, produce, and achieve is, "What if I feel like ejaculating?" It requires continuing effort by the cotherapists to convey the concept not only that acquiring ejaculatory control is possible but also that such facility usually is enhancing for the male as well as his female partner. The unit must be educated to understand that ejaculatory control enlarges the range of sensual pleasure in the sexual relationship for both marital partners. However, it is appropriate for cotherapists to emphasize the fact that ejaculation or spontaneously occurring orgasm is not cause for alarm, nor is this involuntary breakthrough considered a breach of direction. The marital unit must be reassured that if such a breakthrough from the original direction occurs, the experience should be enjoyed for itself. Within a reasonable length of time, the unit is encouraged to provide another opportunity in which to follow the originally described interactive concepts.

When the husband has developed security of erective maintenance, the episodes of vaginal containment with exploratory pelvic thrusting should continue for as long as both partners demonstrate pleasurable reactions. At appropriate intervals during the total coital episode, the partners should separate two or three times and lie together in each other's arms. Once rested, they should return to whatever manner of manual sensate pleasuring they previously enjoyed and continue without any concept of time demand. They should remount, again using the female-superior position, repeating earlier opportunity for the wife's stimulative proprioceptive awareness of vaginal containment of the penis to be emphasized by alternate periods of exploratory thrusting and lying quietly together in coital connection. The timing and duration of sexually stimulative activity should follow the directive formula as outlined in Chapter 2. Generally interpreted, any period of time is acceptable that emerges from mutual interest and continues to be enjoyable for both marital partners without incidence of either emotional or physical fatigue.

Once both partners have been successfully educated to employ experimental pelvic movement during their episodes of coital connection rather than following the usual prior pattern of demanding pelvic thrusting, a major step has been accomplished. Women have little opportunity to feel and think sexually while pursuing or receiving a pattern of forceful pelvic thrusting before their own encompassing levels of excitation are established. If a woman initiates the demanding thrusting, she usually is attempting to force or to will an orgasmic response. The wife repeatedly must be assured that this forceful approach will not contribute to facility of response. If the husband initiates the driving, thrusting coital pattern, the wife must devote conscious effort to accommodate to the rhythm of his thrusting, and her opportunity for quiet sensate pleasure in coital connection is lost.

Frequently, it is of help to assure the wife that once the marital unit is sexually joined, the penis belongs to her just as the vagina belongs to her husband. When vaginal penetration occurs, both partners have literally given of themselves as physical beings in order to derive pleasure, each from the other. When conceptually she has a penis to play with, usually the woman will do just that. If she will allow the vaginally contained penis to stimulate slowly and feelingly in the same manner she enjoyed sensate pleasure from manual body stroking or the manipulation of her genital organs under her controlled directions, she will find herself overwhelmed with sexual feeling.

As vaginal sensation increases for the woman and confidence in ejaculatory control develops for the man, penile-containment episodes progress in a more confident vein. The teasing technique of mounting, dismounting, and remounting is extremely valuable as a means of female sex-tension increment.

There are several clinical pitfalls to be avoided under careful cotherapist direction as the marital unit is moved from phase to phase of increasing sexual responsivity by day-by-day consideration and direction.

First, the cooperating male partner must be manipulated to ejaculation with a regularity at least approximating that described during the interrogation periods on Day 1 or 2 as his concept of ideal ejaculatory frequency. This concern for regularity of release of cooperative male partners' sexual tensions is but turn-about application of the principles of sex-tension relief, directed toward regularity of orgasmic release for the cooperative wife of the premature ejaculator (see Chapter 3).

Second, there must be regularly recurring vacations from physical expression of sexual functioning. At least every fourth day is declared a holiday from physical sexual expression. However, the daily conferences between marital partners and the cotherapists continue at a seven-day-a-week pace through the two-week period during which the distressed marital unit is following the Foundation program. There is so much material that must be presented, evaluated, and restated when the unit's marital relationship is explored in depth that daily conferences are a regular part of the treatment format. When the wife's physical progress is obvious, the partners are infinitely more willing to look at their particular contributions (or lack of them) to the marital relationship. As they improve the climate of the marriage, inevitably they are contributing a vital ingredient to the woman's psychosocial structuring. This structure, in turn, positively influences the accrual of her sexual tensions.

There is yet another factor of sex-tension increment derived from daily living with the subject by the marital partners. Presuming strategically placed vacations from overt sexual function, there is tremendous tension increment in continuity of sexual expression, if orgasmic or ejaculatory levels of tension are restricted by frequency control.

Once confidence in the female-superior coital position has been established, with the woman enjoying the sensate pleasure of pelvic play with the intravaginally contained penis, the marital unit is directed to convert the female-superior position to a lateral coital position (Fig. 10).

With husband and wife mounted in a female-superior position there may be some difficulty in converting to a lateral coital position without first practicing the maneuver. Initially practice should take place without intromission if the conversion is to be accomplished smoothly, but the functional return for both sexual partners certainly is well worth the effort expended in the learning process. The lateral coital position is reported as the most effective coital position available to man and woman, presuming there is an established marital-unit interest in mutual effectiveness of sexual performance.

As described in Chapter 3, when facility in lateral coital positioning has been obtained, there is no pinning of either the male or female partner. There is mutual freedom of pelvic movement in

FIGURE 10

Lateral coital position.

any direction, and there will be no cramping of muscles or necessity for tiring support of body weight.

The lateral coital position provides both sexes flexibility for free sexual expression. This position particularly is effective for the woman, as she can move with full freedom to enjoy either slow or rapid pelvic thrusting, depending upon current levels of sexual tensions. In this coital position the male can best establish and maintain ejaculatory control.

In order to convert from the female-superior (Fig 5, Chapt. 3) to a lateral coital position, there are several successive steps to be taken. The husband with his left hand should elevate his wife's right leg while moving his leg under hers so that his left leg (now outside of her right leg) is extended from his trunk at about a 45-degree angle. The wife simultaneously should extend her right leg (the one that is being elevated) so that positionally she is now supporting her weight on her left knee with the right leg extended, instead of being on her knees as in the female-superior position. As she makes these adjustments, she should lean forward to parallel her trunk to that of her husband. Then the male clasps his partner with his left arm under her shoulders, his hand placed in the middle of her back, and his right hand on her buttocks, holding the two pelves together. The two partners then should roll to his left (her right) while still maintaining intravaginal containment of the penis.

Once the partners have moved into the lateral positioning, the two trunks should be separated at roughly a 30-degree angle. The male rolls back from his left side to rest on his back. The female remains relatively on her stomach and chest with minimal elevation of her left side and her head turned toward her husband. Pillows should be placed beneath both heads for comfort and to provide support for the woman's slightly angled position. Occasionally there is value in a supportive pillow placed along her right side. The only weight that must be supported is that of the wife's right thigh, which rests upon the husband's left thigh. His left thigh is supported by the bed, so there is no problem of long-continued weight support.

The concern for arm placement is resolved if the woman's right arm is circled under her pillow and the husband's left arm (in the same fashion) moves under her pillow beneath her shoulders or underneath her neck. This leaves the woman's left arm and hand and the husband's right arm and hand for mutual play and body caressing.

The female accomplishes leverage for pelvic thrusting by pulling up her extended right leg slightly so that her knee comes to rest on the bed. Her left leg should be cast over her husband's right hip with the knee resting comfortably on the bed. The two knees provide her with all the traction she needs for pelvic thrusting whenever sex-tension demands for any form of thrusting develop.

In view of the physical complexity of changes in position, usually it is suggested that man and wife try converting the simulated female-superior mounting position to the lateral position at least two or three times before establishing coital connection and then attempting conversion from superior to lateral positions. The trial runs usually begin in a humorous vein; yet with functional seriousness husband and wife easily can work out the problems of comfortable arms and legs placement and rapidly accomplish facility with the position-conversion technique. Again, the lateral coital position is the most effective coital position from a mutuality of shared male and female freedom of sexual experimentation. The potential return is well worth the effort of the marital unit involved in learning to convert from the female-superior positioning.

One of the more realistic goals this form of therapy may suggest to the nonorgasmic woman relates to self-reorientation which tends to improve or helps to insure maximum interdigitation of the dual-system basis of effective sexual function theorized in Chapters 2 and 8. The goal seeks to create or encourage the best possible climate in which each system (biophysical and psychosocial) can function.

The attainment of this climate first is dependent upon self-knowledge. A sexually dysfunctional woman can be therapeutically assisted to identify and develop understanding of her own psychosocial needs (the psychosocial system of sexual function). She also can be educated to take advantage of her naturally occurring, maximum levels of sexual drive (the biophysical system of sexual function). Much can be derived from the exchange of information among the nonorgasmic woman, her husband, and the cotherapists, to help her define her actual physical awareness of sexual desire. This specific awareness of sexual need is relied upon by most sexually effective women, although not necessarily at an actively conscious level. The dysfunctional woman's husband has a definitive contributing role in helping to develop her sense of freedom and grace in the spontaneous expression of her sexual feelings.

The husband's role is vital to success in the treatment of orgasmic dysfunction. His attitudinal approach is the most important contributing factor (positively or negatively) to therapeutic procedure. If he is totally cooperative, interested, supportive, and identifies quietly and warmly with his wife as she lives through the strain of the interpretive look in the mirror provided by the cotherapists, her chances of orgasmic attainment are significantly increased.

If the husband's attitude is one of hostility, indifference, impatience, or even regimented cooperation, the chances of failure in treatment are correspondingly increased. It is not sufficient to be simply a cooperative partner. There must be the opportunity for the beleagured wife to identify with her husband. She must be able to feel the warmth of his interest in her as an individual and as a woman, to count on him for emotional support and, above all, to feel him as much a partner in concern and as vitally interested in reversing her dysfunction as she is in accomplishing full expression as a woman.

Under authoritative control many women can and do break through the shell created by a husband's indifference and ultimately develop a pattern of orgasmic release. Many more fail.

For discussion purposes, the immediate failure rates for both primary and situational orgasmic dysfunction are included in Table 3 (below). A detailed presentation of failure rates and five-year follow-up of treated patients is presented in Chapter 14.

TABLE 3

Orgasmic Dysfunction

Complaint	No. Patients	No. Failures	Immediate Failure Rate (%)
Primary orgasmic dysfunction	193	32	16.6
Situational orgasmic dysfunction	149	34	22.8
Masturbatory orgasmic inadequacy	11	1	9.1
Coital orgasmic inadequacy	106	21	19.8
Random orgasmic inadequacy	32	12	37.5
TOTAL	342	66	19.3

The failure rate in reversal of the presenting complaint of orgasmic dysfunction in the two-week rapid-treatment program is 19.3 percent.

There is little difference between the failure rates returned in treating the primarily or situationally nonorgasmic woman. The one category that obviously needs significant improvement of therapeutic approach is that of random orgasmic inadequacy (IFR 37.5 percent).

Infrequent or rare orgasmic return with both masturbatory and coital experience has defied the Foundation's current therapeutic approaches. In some cases there were detrimental interpersonal relationships that could not be altered successfully. In others there was no evidence of inherent levels of sexual tension either presently or historically described. In the majority of situations, however, the cotherapists did not find an answer to resolve the problem of random orgasmic inadequacy. Were the failure rate in this category improved to parallel that of other categories of orgasmic inadequacy, there would be no statistical significance in reported return between the failure rates in treatment of primary or situational orgasmic dysfunction.

The close approximation of failure rates in the two arbitrary clinical divisions of woman's nonorgasmic status supports the concept of uniformity of treatment approach, regardless of whether the woman has ever had previous orgasmic experience.

An overview of female sexual dysfunction commonly reveals a stalemate in the sociosexual adaptive process at the point at which a woman's desire for sexual expression crashes into a personal fear or conviction that her role as a sexual entity is without the unique contribution of herself as an individual. For some reason, her "permission" to function as a sexual being or her confidence in herself as a functional sexual entity has been impaired.

The stalemate may be derived from negation of her own sexual identity or from the attitudes and circumstances of marital interaction. The influence may emanate from her partner's unwitting or deliberate contribution to her loss of personal and sexual self-esteem; or it may emerge on signal from her earlier imprinted, conditioned, and experientially created sexual value system. The blocking of receptivity to sexual stimuli is an unfortunate result of factors which deprive her of the capacity to value the sexual component of her personality or prevent her from placing its value within the context of her life.

I 2

SEXUAL INADEQUACY
IN THE AGING MALE

The natural aging process creates a number of specific physiological changes in the male cycle of sexual response. Knowledge of these cycle variations has not been widely disseminated. There has been little concept of a physiological basis for differentiating between natural sexual involution and pathological dysfunction when considering the problems of male sexual dysfunction in the post-50 age group. If all too few professionals are conversant with anticipated alterations in male sexual functioning created by the aging process, how can the general public be expected to adjust to the internal alarms raised by these natural occurring phenomena?

Tragically, yet understandably, tens of thousands of men have moved from effective sexual functioning to varying levels of secondary impotence as they age, because they did not understand the natural variants that physiological aging imposes on previously established patterns of sexual functioning.

From a psychosexual point of view, the male over age 50 has to contend with one of the great fallacies of our culture. Every man in this age group is arbitrarily identified by both public and professional alike as sexually impaired. When the aging male is faced by unexplained yet natural involutional sexual changes, and deflated by widespread psychosocial acceptance of the fallacy of sexual incompetence as a natural component of the aging process, is it any wonder that he carries a constantly increasing burden of fear of performance?

Before discussing specifics of sexual dysfunction in the aging population, the natural variants that the aging process imposes on the established male cycle of sexual response should be considered. For sake of discussion, the four phases of the sexual response cycle

—excitement, plateau, orgasm, and resolution—will be employed to establish a descriptive framework. Also for descriptive purposes, the term *older man* will be used in reference to the male population from 50 to 70 years of age and the term *younger man* used to describe the 20–40-year age group. In recent years the younger man's sexual response cycle has been established with physiological validity and will serve as a baseline for comparison with the physiological variations of aging.

If an older man can be objective about his reactions to sexual stimuli during the excitement phase, he may note a significant delay in erective attainment compared to his facility of response as a younger man. Most older men do not establish erective response to effective sexual stimulation for a matter of minutes, as opposed to a matter of seconds as younger men, and the erection may not be as full or as demanding as that to which previously he has been accustomed. It simply takes the older man longer to be fully involved subjectively in acceptance and expression of any form of sensate stimulation.

If natural delays in reaction time are appreciated, there will be no panic on the part of either husband or wife. If, however, the aging male is uninformed and not anticipating delayed physiological reactions to sexual stimuli, he may indeed panic and—responding in the worst possible way—try to will or force an erection. The unfortunate results of this approach to erective security have been discussed at length in Chapter 7 on treatment of impotence.

As the aging male approaches the plateau phase, his erection usually has been established with fair security. There may be little if any testicular elevation, a negligible amount of scrotal-sac vasocongestion, and minimal deep vascular engorgement of the testes. Most older men who have had a preejaculatory fluid emission (Cowper's gland secretory activity) will notice either total absence of, or marked reduction in, the amount of this preejaculatory emission as they age.

From the aspect of time-span, the plateau phase usually lasts longer for an older man than for his younger counterpart. When an aging male reaches that level of elevated sexual tension identified as thoroughly enjoyable, he usually can and frequently does wish to maintain this plateau-phase level of sensual pleasure for an indefinite period of time without becoming enmeshed by ejaculatory demand. This response pattern is age-related; the younger man tends to drive for early ejaculatory release when plateau-phase levels of sexual tension have accrued. One of the advantages of the aging process with specific reference to sexual functioning is that, generally speaking, control of ejaculatory demand in the 50–70-year age group is far better than in the 20–40-year age group.

In the cycle of sexual response, the largest number of physiological changes to come within objective focus for older men occur during the orgasmic phase (ejaculatory process). The orgasmic phase is relatively standardized for younger men, varying minimally in duration and intensity of experience unless influenced by the psychosexual opposites of long-continued continence or high level of sexual satiation.

For younger men the entire ejaculatory process is divided into two well-recognized stages. The first stage, ejaculatory inevitability, is the brief period of time (2–4 seconds) during which the male feels the ejaculation coming and no longer can control it, before ejaculation actually occurs. These subjective symptoms of ejaculatory inevitability are created physiologically by regularly recurring contractions of the prostate gland and, questionably, the seminal vesicles. Contractions of the prostate begin at 0.8-second intervals and continue through both stages of the male orgasmic experience.

The second stage of the orgasmic phenomenon consists of expulsion of the seminal-fluid bolus accrued under pressure in the membranous and prostatic portions of the urethra, through the full length of the penile urethra. Again, there are regularly recurring 0.8-second intercontractile intervals. This specific interval lengthens after the first three or four contractions of the penile urethra in younger men. Subjectively, the sensation is one of flow of a volume of warm fluid under pressure and emission of the seminal fluid bolus in ejaculatory spurts with pressure sufficient to expel fluid content distances of 12 to 24 inches beyond the urethral meatus.

As the male ages he develops many individual variants on the basic theme of the two-stage orgasmic experience described for the younger man. Usually his orgasmic experience encompasses a shorter time span. There may not be even a recognizable first stage to the ejaculatory experience, so that an orgasmic experience without the stage of ejaculatory inevitability is quite a common occurrence.

Even with a recognizable first stage, there still may be marked variation in reaction pattern. Occasionally, the older man's phase of ejaculatory inevitability lasts but a second or two as opposed to the younger man's pattern ranging from 2 to 4 seconds. In an older man's first-stage experience, there may be only one or two contractions of the prostate before involuntary initiation of the second stage, seminal-fluid expulsion.

Alternatively, the first stage of orgasmic experience may be held for as long as 5 to 7 seconds. Occasionally the prostate, instead of contracting within the regularly described pattern of 0.8-second intervals, develops a spastic contraction, creating subjectively the sense of ejaculatory inevitability. The prostate may not relax from spasm into rhythmically expulsive contractions for several seconds, hence the 5–7-second duration of the first-stage experience.

In addition to objective variants in a first-stage orgasmic episode, there may be no possible objective or subjective definition of the first stage of orgasmic experience at all. The stage of ejaculatory inevitability may be totally missing from the aging male's sexual response cycle. A single-stage orgasmic episode develops clinically in two circumstances. The first circumstance is that of clinical dysfunction developing as the result of inadequate testosterone production. Actually the lack of a recognizable first stage in orgasmic experience can result from low sex-steroid level for the male just as steroid starvation in the female may produce an orgasmic experience of markedly brief duration (See Chapter 13). The second occasion of an absent first stage in the orgasmic experience develops after there has been prior denial of ejaculatory opportunity over a long period of intravaginal containment in order to satisfy the aging male's coital partner sexually.

There also are obvious physiological changes in the second stage of the orgasmic experience that develop with the aging process. The expulsive contractions of the penile urethra have onset at 0.8-second intervals but are maintained for only one or two contractions at this rate. The expulsive force delivering the seminal fluid bolus externally, so characteristic of second-stage penile contractions in the younger man, also is diminished, with the distance of unencumbered seminal-fluid expulsion ranging from 3 to 12 inches from the urethral meatus.

Seminal-fluid volume is gradually reduced during the aging process. In the younger man with 24–36 hours of prior ejaculatory continence, the total seminal-fluid volume averages 3–5 ml., while with a similar continence pattern, an output of 2–3 ml. is within normal limits for the post-50 male.

These definitive physiological changes seem not to detract from the aging male's orgasmic experience, subjective interpretation of which usually is one of extreme sensate pleasure. The orgasmic episode is fully enjoyed, regardless of whether the first stage is altered significantly or even totally missing from the experience. Obvious reductions in ejaculatory pressure and volume do not alter the male's basic focus upon the sensate pleasure of the experience.

The clinical concern that develops with advent of these physical changes in the cycle of sexual response occurs when aging males do not understand the physiological appropriateness of their altered sexual response patterning. If a man who experiences a brief one-stage orgasmic episode and ejaculates a reduced seminal-fluid volume under little or no pressure does not understand that these altered reaction patterns are naturally occurring phenomena subsequent to voluntarily prolonged excitement or plateau phases of sexual tension, he may become extremely concerned about his sexual functioning. He may be frightened by the fallacious concept that he is in the process of losing his ability to function in a sexually effective manner.

The fact that on the very next occasion for coital connection there may be very rapid progress from excitement through plateau to a two-stage orgasmic process, significant ejaculatory pressure and an adequate seminal-fluid volume does not appease the anxious male. He has noted specific physiological variants in aging sexual functioning on at least one occasion and is aware of no logical explanation for their development. It never occurs to him that during the first episode, when there was marked alteration of his usual response pattern, the marital partners were selectively directing themselves to the wife's pleasure, while during the second experience the sexual partners had turned the tables and obviously were intent upon deriving male release and sexual satiation. Following the usual dictates of our culture, when any alteration occurs in the structuring of man's sexual response pattern that he does not understand, he falls into the psychosocial trap of the cultural demand for constancy of male sexual performance and worries about possible loss of masculinity.

The resolution phase of the older man's sexual response cycle also evidences marked physiological alteration from his previously established response patterning. As the male ages, his refractory period—the period following ejaculation during which the male is biophysically unresponsive to sexual stimuli—extends in parallel fashion. The refractory period of the younger man usually continues for but a matter of minutes before he can return to full erection under the influence of effective sexual stimulation. For the aging male, the refractory period occasionally may continue for a matter of minutes, but usually it is a matter of hours before return to full erection is possible. Again, if this phenomenon is understood by women as well as by men, the older man will not worry about being unable to respond to a repetitive mounting opportunity as he could when in the 20–40-year age group. Neither he nor his wife will be creating fears for sexual performance if there is no attempt to force erective return when he is in a physiologically extended refractory period.

It also should be pointed out that, as opposed to the younger man, the aging male may lose his erection after ejaculation with extreme rapidity. There may not be a two-stage loss of erection as in the younger man's natural response pattern. Frequently, the older man's penis returns to its flaccid state in a matter of seconds after ejaculation, instead of the younger man's pattern of minutes or even hours.

The informed older man will not be concerned by his response variants if educated to understand that the variants are natural results of physiological involution. But should he not have this information, the penis's literally falling from the vagina immediately after ejaculation can stimulate real fears for adequacy of performance. When an uninformed older man endures the first experience of losing an erection so rapidly, he immediately may wonder whether he will be able to achieve a fully effective erection the next time there is coital opportunity. When he worries about erective capacity, he tends to try to force or will an effective erection with subsequent coital exposure. Then he is in difficulty (see Chapter 6).

A plea must be entered for wide dissemination of information on the natural physiological variants of the aging male's sexual response cycle, to support not only the men but also the women in our society. The wife of the 50–70-year-old man also must understand the natural involutionary changes inherent in her husband's aging process. Once she appreciates the continuing male facility for sexual expression regardless of changed response pattern, she will be infinitely more comfortable about importuning her husband sexually. She will not worry about his delayed erection time when fully aware that it does not mean that he no longer finds her attractive. The less than fully erect penis sometimes present in the plateau phase can be readily inserted by a perceptive woman with the sure knowledge after successful intromission that her husband's first few penile strokes will aid in full development of the erection.

An informed wife will not hesitate to be sexually demonstrative when she realizes that once coital connection has been established her husband has increased facility for ejaculatory control. Confident of her own and her husband's facility to respond successfully, even though the typical response patterns of their younger years have been altered, the concerned wife can meet her husband freely without the usual cultural reservations. This security of sexual performance for the aging man and woman comes only from wide dissemination of information from authoritative sources.

EFFECTS OF AGING ON MALE EJACULATORY DEMAND

Probably the most important psychophysiological alteration of sexual patterning to develop during the 50–70-year period is the human male's loss of high levels of ejaculatory demand. So many men in the older age groups consider themselves too old to function sexually, yet cannot explain how they have arrived at this conclusion.

As the male ages, he not only enjoys a fortuitous increase in ejaculatory control but also has a definite reduction in ejaculatory demand. For example, if a man 60 years of age has intercourse on an average of once or twice a week, his own specific drive to ejaculate might be of major moment every second or third time there is coital connection. This level of innate demand does not imply that the man cannot or does not ejaculate more frequently. He can force himself and/or be forced by female-partner insistence to ejaculate more frequently, but if left to resolve his own individual demand level he may find that an ejaculatory experience every second or third coital connection is completely satisfying personally. Explicitly his own subjective level of ejaculatory demand does not keep pace with the frequency of his physiological ability to achieve an erection or to maintain this erection with full pleasure on an indefinite basis.

This factor of reduced ejaculatory demand for the aging male is the entire basis for effective prolongation of sexual functioning in the aging population. If an aging man does not ejaculate, he can return to erection rapidly after prior loss of erective security through distraction or female satiation.

The older man can easily achieve and maintain an erection if there is no ejaculatory threat in the immediate offing. The uninformed woman poses an ejaculatory threat. She believes that she has not accomplished woman's purpose unless her coital partner ejaculates. How many women in our culture feel they have fulfilled the feminine role if their partner has not ejaculated? Whether he likes it or needs it, she must be a good sexual partner—"Everybody knows that a man needs to ejaculate every time he has intercourse"—so goes the refrain.

The message should reach both sexes that after members of the marital unit are somewhere in the early or middle fifties, demand for sexual release should be left to the individual partner. Then coital connection can be instituted regularly and individual male and female sexual interests satisfied. These interests for the woman can range from demand for multiorgasmic release to just desiring vaginal penetration and holding, without any effort at tension elevation. If the male is encouraged to ejaculate on his own demand schedule and to have intercourse as it fits both sexual partners' interest levels, the average marital unit will be capable of functioning sexually well into the 80-year age group, presuming for both man and woman a reasonably good state of general health and an interested and interesting sexual partner.

Effective sexual function for any man in the 50–70-year age group depends primarily upon his full understanding of the sexual involutional processes that he may encounter. Effective sexual function for most women also depends upon their knowledge of male sexual physiology in the declining years. Men and women must understand fully the alterations of sexual patterning that may develop if they are to cope effectively with their aging process.

MALE SEX-STEROID REPLACEMENT

Little is known of the male climacteric. When does it occur, if it develops? Is it a constant occurrence? What is the specific symptomatology? Should sex-steroid-replacement techniques be employed? What, if any, are the patterns of sexual responsivity engendered by these replacement techniques? So little is known of the male climacteric because until the last few years there has been no method of definitive evaluation of serum testosterone levels that had reasonably wide clinical application.

Now that these definitive laboratory studies can be done with some confidence, relative rapidity, and at not too staggering a cost, much more will be known of the male climacteric within the next few years. There will be more basic information of the effects of steroid replacement not only upon the aging male's sexual response cycle per se but also, and infinitely more important, upon the total metabolic function of the climacteric male.

Without the gross advantage of fully supportive laboratory data, tentative clinical conclusions have been drawn with reference to the influence of steroid-replacement techniques upon the aging male's sexual functioning. These conclusions may have to be restated or even possibly abandoned in the not-too-distant future as more definitive information is accrued from the healthy combination of clinical and laboratory evaluations.

When the male notices alteration of his orgasmic response pattern from the usual two-stage to a one-stage process, when he consistently responds during orgasmic experience with loss of seminal-fluid volume without significant ejaculatory pressure, when average ejaculatory volume is cut at least in half, and when none of these reactions develop under the extenuating circumstances of a long-continued plateau phase of voluntary ejaculatory control, he may be experiencing the physiological expression of reduced production of male sex-steroid to metabolically dysfunctional levels.

Occasionally prostatic pain develops from spastic contractions of the organ during the ejaculatory process. These spastic contractions create a continuing sense of ejaculatory urgency that may last through the entire orgasmic experience until full expulsion of the seminal-fluid bolus has occurred. With the subjectively painful evidence of physiological prostatic spasm recurring with most ejaculatory experiences and no obvious pathology of the prostate gland demonstrable to adequate urological examination, sex-steroid replacement also may be indicated.

Until there is a more reliable laboratory definition of a general metabolic need for testosterone replacement and until the clinical existence of the male climacteric can be defined with security during treatment of older men for sexual dysfunction, individual cases must be treated empirically. If the sexually dysfunctional male describes a physiological or psychological symptomatology that appears to indicate clinical need for sex-steroid replacement and if the general physical and laboratory evaluations are negative, there is no professional hesitancy to institute such replacement techniques. However, sex-steroid-replacement techniques are not employed routinely for the 50–70-year age group man referred for therapy. Steroid replacement concepts and specific techniques, together with indications and contraindications for the aging male, will be presented in more complete form by the Foundation in monograph format in the future.

ERECTIVE RESPONSE IN THE AGING MALE

The sexual myth most rampant in our culture today is the concept that the aging process per se will in time discourage or deny erective security to the older-age-group male. As has been described previously, the aging male may be slower to erect and may even reach the plateau phase without full erective return, but the facility and the ability to attain erection, presuming general good health and no psychogenic blocking, continues unopposed as a natural sequence well into the 80-year age group.

The aging male may note delayed erective time, a one-stage rather than a two-stage orgasmic experience, reduction in seminal-fluid volume, and decreased ejaculatory pressure, but *he does not lose his facility for erection at any time*. If this concept can be presented to and accepted by the general population, one of the great deterrents to sexual functioning of the aging male will have been eliminated. When conceptive ability is no longer important and reduction in seminal-fluid volume and total sperm production no longer is of consequence, the aging male is potentially a most effective sexual partner. He needs only to ejaculate at his own frequency and not on the basis of uninformed sociocultural demand.

There are even some sexual advantages that accrue as the male ages. He has increased ejaculatory control and can, if he wishes, serve his female partner deftly and with full erective security. His sexual effectiveness is based not only upon his prior sexual experience but also upon the specific element of increased physiological control of the ejaculatory process. If the aging male does not succeed in talking himself out of effective sexual functioning by worrying about the physiological factors in his sexual response patterns altered by the aging process, if his peers do not destroy his sexual confidence, if he and his partner maintain a reasonably good state of health, he certainly can and should continue unencumbered sexual functioning indefinitely.

SEXUAL DYSFUNCTION IN THE AGING MALE

Composite case studies have been selected to identify and illustrate the dysfunctional characteristics of the male aging process.

Mr. and Mrs. A were 66 and 62 years of age when referred to the Foundation for sexual inadequacy. They had been married 39 years and had three children, the youngest of which was 23 years of age. All children were married and living outside the home.

They had maintained reasonably effective sexual interchange during their marriage. Mr. A had no difficulty with erection, reasonable ejaculatory control, and, aside from two occasions of prostitute exposure, had been fully committed to the marriage. Mrs. A, occasionally orgasmic during intercourse and regularly orgasmic during her occasional masturbatory experiences, had continued regularity of coital exposure with her husband until five years prior to referral for therapy.

Mr. A had recently retired from a major manufacturing concern. He had been relatively successful in his work and there were no specific financial problems facing man and wife during their declining years. Both members of the marital unit had enjoyed good health throughout the marriage.

At age 61, he had taken his wife abroad on a vacation trip which entailed many sightseeing trips with a different city on the agenda almost every day. They were chronically tired during the exhausting trip, but because they were on vacation and away from home there was a definite increase over the established frequency of coital connections. Mr. A noted for the first time slowed erective attainment. Regardless of his level of sexual interest or the depth of his wife's commitment to the specific sexual experience, it took him progressively longer to attain full erection. With each sexual exposure his concern for the delay in erective security increased until finally, just before termination of the vacation trip, he failed for the first time to achieve an erection quality sufficient for vaginal penetration.

When coital opportunity first developed after return home, erection was attained, but again it was quite slow in development. The next two opportunities were only partially successful from an erective point of view, and thereafter he was secondarily impotent.

After several months they consulted their physician and were assured that this loss of erective power comes to all men as they age and that there was nothing to be done. Loath to accept the verdict, they tried on several occasions to force an erection with no success. Mr. A was seriously depressed for several months but recovered without apparent incident.

Approximately 18 months after the vacation trip, the marital unit had accepted their "fate." The impotence was acknowledged to be a natural result of the aging process. This resigned attitude lasted approximately four years.

Although initially the marital unit and their physician had fallen into the sociocultural trap of accepting the concept of sexual inadequacy as an aging phenomenon, the more Mr. and Mrs. A considered their dysfunction the less willing they were to accept the blanket concept that lack of erective security was purely the result of the aging process. They reasoned that they were in good health, had no basic concerns as a marital unit, and took good care of themselves physically. Therefore, why was this dysfunction to be expected simply because some of their friends reportedly had accepted loss of male erective prowess as a natural occurrence? Each partner underwent a thorough medical checkup and sought several authoritative opinions (none of them encouraging), refusing to accept the concept of the irreversibility of their sexual distress. Finally, approximately five years after the onset of a full degree of secondary impotence, they were referred for treatment.

Sexual functioning was reconstituted for this marital unit within the first week after their arrival at the Foundation—as soon as they could absorb and accept the basic material directed toward the variation in physiological functioning of the aging male. No longer were they concerned with delay in erective attainment; there were no more attempts to will, force, or strain to accomplish erection under assumed pressures of performance. In short, they needed only the security of knowledge that the response pattern which initially had raised the basic fear of dysfunction was a perfectly natural result of the involutional process. When they could accept the fact that it naturally took longer for an older man to achieve an erection, particularly if he were tired or distracted, the basis for their own sexual inadequacy disappeared. Some six years after termination of the acute phase of therapy, this couple, now in the early seventies and late sixties, continue coital connection once or twice a week. The husband has learned to ejaculate on his own demand schedule, and neither partner attempts rapid return to sexual function after a mutually satisfactory sexual episode.

Marital Unit B, the husband, age 62 and his wife, age 63, were referred to the Foundation. They had two children, both of whom were married and lived out of the home. Their sexual dysfunction had begun when the husband was 57 years old. He had noted some delay in attaining erection and marked reduction in ejaculatory volume and was particularly concerned with the fact that the ejaculatory experience was one of a mere dribbling of seminal fluid from the external urethral meatus, under obviously reduced pressure. All these involutional signs and symptoms developed within approximately a year after he had noticed some delay in onset of erection attainment. The more he worried about his symptoms the more frequent the occasions of impotence.

Mrs. B was completely convinced that this pattern of sexual involution was indeed to be expected as part of the aging process. Rather than distress her husband, she suggested that they use separate bedrooms. She changed from a pattern of free and easy exchange of sexual demand to one of availability for coital connection only at her husband's expression of interest. In order to resolve her own sexual tensions, she masturbated about once every ten days to two weeks without her husband's knowledge.

Finally, Mr. B developed severe prostatic spasm with ejaculation during approximately half the increasingly rare occasions when there was sufficient erective security to establish coital connection. It was persistence of this symptom of pain that first brought medical consultation and ultimately referral for treatment.

In evaluation of this man during the physical examination (see Chapter 2), there was marked muscular weakness noted, a history of easy fatigability, and increasing lassitude in physical expression. Mr. B also had been distressed in the last two to three years before referral to therapy with distinct memory loss for recent events. He described loss of work effectiveness for approximately the same length of time.

With these overt symptoms suggestive of steroid starvation, testosterone replacement was initiated empirically. Within 10 days there was partial return of ejaculatory pressure and a moderate shortening of the time span for the delayed erective reaction. The prostatic pain did not recur. Once Mrs. B could accept the explanation for the onset of her husband's sexual dysfunction, she was pleased to return to the role of an active sexual partner. Coital connection has continued regularly for the past three years with both members of the marital unit supported by steroid-replacement techniques.

In brief, for the sexually dysfunctional aging male the primary concern is one of education so that both the man and his wife can understand the natural involutional changes that can develop within their established pattern of sexual performance. Sex-steroid replacement should be employed only if definite physical evidence of the male climacteric exists. As the newer techniques for establishing testosterone levels in blood serum become more widely disseminated, it will be infinitely easier to define and describe the male climacteric and therefore to offer testosterone replacement to those who need it, on a more definitive basis than empirical diagnosis.

With effective dissemination of information by proper authority, the aging man can be expected to continue in a sexually effective manner into his ninth decade. Fears of performance are engendered by lack of knowledge of the natural involutional changes in male sexual responsivity that accompany the aging process. *Really, the only factor that the aging male must understand is that loss of erective prowess is not a natural component of aging.*

Statistical evaluation of the aging population and a consideration of treatment failure rates will constitute the following section.

This material arbitrarily has been placed in the male rather than the female chapter. First, it was felt important to keep the statistical consideration of the aging marital units together and second, because there were 56 males 50 years old or over in marital units accepted for treatment and only 37 wives 50 or older, it seemed appropriate to include the brief statistical discussion in the chapter reflecting the larger segment of the aging population.

THE AGING MALE AND FEMALE POPULATIONS: STATISTICAL CONSIDERATIONS

Arbitrarily, statistics reflecting the failure rates of treatment procedures for sexual dysfunction in the aging population will be considered in this section rather than dividing the material between the discussions of sexual inadequacy in the aging male and female (see Chapter 13). A brief single presentation seems in order, since only marital units are available for consideration in this age group. The male and female statistics are essentially inseparable from a therapeutic point of view, and the overall sample is entirely too small for definitive individual interpretation.

In 51 of the total of 56 aging marital units treated for sexual dysfunction, the husband was the instigating agent in bringing the marital unit to therapy. Among the remaining 5 units, the referral apparently was by mutual accord in 3 and only at the demand of the wife in 2 units. There also was a higher incidence of referred male sexual dysfunction than of female sexual inadequacy in the aging population. Therefore the discussion will focus on the male partner's age as a point of departure. Since the husband was the partner most often involved in dysfunctional pathology and was the member of the unit that usually took the necessary steps to accomplish referral to the Foundation, the aging male will be statistically highlighted.

An overall appraisal of the minimal clinical material available to statistical scrutiny in the older marital units is in order (Table 4).

The 56 marital units referred for treatment divide into 33 units with bilateral complaints of sexual dysfunction and 23 units with

TABLE 4
Age Distribution in 56 Marital Units

Husband Age Group (Years)	No. Marital Units	No. Wives in Age Group					
		70–79 Years	60–69 Years	50–59 Years	40–49 Years	30–39 Years	20–29 Years
70–79	4	2	2	—	—	—	—
60–69	18	—	6	7	4	1	—
50–59	34	—	—	20	9	3	2

unilateral complaints of sexual inadequacy. Thus, there were 89 individual cases of sexual dysfunction treated from the 56 units with husbands' age 50 years or over as a common baseline. This 33:23 ratio is a reversal of the overall statistics for dual-partner involvement of marital units as opposed to singly involved units (see Chapter 14). The fact that there was a dominance of bilateral sexual deficiency among the older marital units is in accord with previously expressed concepts of cultural influences (see Chapter 1). Certainly, the older the marital unit the better chance for the Victorian double standard of sexual functioning. With these pressures of performance, one could almost expect more male than female sexual pathology to be in identified unit partners over 50 years of age referred to the Foundation.

The clinical complaints registered by the aging population (male and female) in the 56 marital units referred for treatment are listed in Table 5.

TABLE 5
Clinical Complaints in 56 Marital-unit Referrals

Husbands' Complaint	No.	Wives' Complaint	No.
Primary impotence	1	Primary orgasmic dysfunction	23
Secondary impotence	28	Situational orgasmic dys-	
Premature ejaculation	19	function	18
Total complaints	48	Total complaints	41
(Sexually functional	8)	(Sexually functional	15)

The 8 sexually functional men and the 15 sexually functional women are partners in marital units describing specific sexual dysfunction for their individual mates. These 23 individuals will not be considered further in the brief statistical review of aging sexual dysfunction.

Since 19 of the 56 wives were under the age of 50 years when their marriage was treated for sexual dysfunction, a total of 37 women over age 50 were integral partners in marital units referred to the Foundation. The comparative tables reflecting the clinical status of the two age groups of women are seen in Table 6.

TABLE 6

Clinical Status of Women by Age Group in 56 Marital Units

Complaint	No. Wives 50–79 Years	No. Wives 28–49 Years	Total
Primary orgasmic dysfunction	15	8	23
Situational orgasmic dysfunction	12	6	18
TOTALS	27	14	41
Sexually functional	10	5	15

Finally, a statistical breakdown of the immediate clinical failures evident during the acute-treatment phase should be reviewed. The different-age-group wives are reviewed both separately and jointly as a statistical unit comparable to that of their husbands. A gross comparison will be drawn between the failure rates of treatment

TABLE 7

Male Dysfunction in Husbands 50–79 Years Old—48 Marital Units

Complaint	No. Units	No. Failures	Failure Rate (%)
Primary impotence	1	1	100.0
Secondary impotence	28	10	35.7
Premature ejaculation	19	1	5.3
TOTALS	48	12	25.0

TABLE 8
Female Dysfunction in 41 Marital Units

Complaint	No. Units	No. Failures	Failure Rate (%)
Wives 50–79 Years			
Primary orgasmic dysfunction	15	6	40.0
Situational orgasmic dysfunction	12	5	41.6
Totals	27	11	40.7
Wives 28–49 Years			
Primary orgasmic dysfunction	8	2	25.0
Situational orgasmic dysfunction	6	2	33.3
Totals	14	4	28.5
Total Female Aging Population			
Primary orgasmic dysfunction	23	8	34.8
Situational orgasmic dysfunction	18	7	38.8
Totals	41	15	36.6

TABLE 9
Treatment Failure in 89 Cases of Sexual Dysfunction in Aging Males and Females

	Number	No. Failures	Failure Rate (%)
Patients treated	89	27	30.3

for the older population and the overall treatment-failure rates of the research population (Tables 7–9).

The aging population represents too small a sample to warrant consideration of the statistics involved in other than the most general of terms.

It is obvious that the statistics of the aging population show a higher failure rate than the overall statistics of the total research population (see Chapter 14). It also should be recalled that the overall statistics are further compromised by inclusion of those of the aging population.

There was a 30.3 percent failure rate to reverse sexual dysfunction, regardless of whether both partners or a single partner is involved, in any marriage with the husband over 50 years of age. With gender separation, for the aging male (50–79) there was a 25 percent failure rate to reverse his basic complaint of sexual inadequacy as compared to a 40.7 percent failure rate for the aging female (50–79). These statistics simply support the well-established clinical concept that the longer the specific sexual inadequacy exists, the higher the failure rate for any form of therapeutic endeavor.

On the other hand, there was significantly less than 50 percent failure rate in treatment for any form of sexual dysfunction, regardless of age of the individuals involved. In short, even if the sexual distress has existed for 25 years or more, there is every reason to attempt clinical reversal of the symptomatology. There is so little to lose and so much to gain. Presuming generally good health for the sexual partners, and mutual interests in reversing their established sexual dysfunction, every marital unit, regardless of the ages of the partners involved, should consider the possibility of clinical therapy for sexual dysfunction in a positive vein. The old concept "I'm too old to change" does not apply to the symptoms of sexual dysfunction.

Treatment of male and female sexual inadequacy follows specifically the guidelines established in Chapters 3–8 and 11. There has been no alteration in concepts of treatment (see Chapter 1), regardless of the male or female applicant's age.

13

SEXUAL INADEQUACY
IN THE AGING FEMALE

The misconceptions, fallacies, and even taboos directed toward the sexual functioning of women in menopausal and postmenopausal years are legion. Knowledge of natural variations in the female sexual cycle developing with the aging process has been extremely limited. With little of psychological or physiological security established for sexual functioning of the aging woman, there have been few professional attempts at clinical approach to reverse female sexual inadequacy in the post-50 age groups.

Biologists and behaviorists must aid in dispelling the gross psychosocial misconception that postmenopausal women find little of personal interest in continuing opportunity for effective sexual functioning. We must, in fact, destroy the concept that women in the 50–70-year age group not only have no interest in but also have no facility for active sexual expression. Nothing could be further from the truth than the often-expressed concept that aging women do not maintain a high level of sexual orientation.

Before discussion of specifics of sexual dysfunction, there should be some understanding of the aging female's natural cycle of sexual response to effective stimulation. Possibly the best way to establish some concept of natural response cycling is to compare the physiological responsivity of the woman in the 50–70-year age group with that of a woman in the 20–40-year age group, using the four phases of the sexual response cycle (excitement, plateau, orgasm, and resolution) as a descriptive framework for discussion. The basic physiological responses to sexual stimulation of 20–40-year-old women have been recently established. To facilitate illustration, the composite physiological picture of the 20–40-year-old

335

female will be identified as the "younger woman" and that of the 50–70-year-old as the "older woman."

With the onset of any form of effective sexual stimulation, the first definitive physiological evidence of female responsivity is the production of vaginal lubrication. In the younger woman, lubrication is naturally evident within 15 to 30 seconds of initiation of the excitement phase of the sexual response cycle. As women age, particularly after termination of their climacteric era, there is obvious delay in development of lubrication when responding to sexual stimulation. In this pattern the aging female parallels exactly the physiological involution of the aging male (see Chapter 12), in whom delay in development of an erective response to sexual stimulation is the natural concomitant to the aging process.

It may take 1, 2, sometimes even 4 or 5 minutes of nondemanding sexual play before any significant degree of lubrication develops for older women. If pressured for rapid intromission, there may be little lubricative reaction to sexual approach.

There are two basic mechanisms involved in this physiological delay of lubricative response. First, most forms of physical responsivity are slowed as men and women age, and repressed production of vaginal lubrication is but one more example of this established reactive pattern. Second, with aging there is natural involution of ovarian function. When contending secondarily with the resultant reduction of sex-steroid levels, the older woman's vaginal barrel constricts in size and the vaginal walls become thin and atrophic. Instead of the younger woman's usual corrugated mucosal pattern, in older women the lining of the vaginal barrel is tissue-paper-thin, noncorrugated, and pink rather than purple in color. When the mucosal lining of the vagina is atrophic, there is not a well-developed tissue medium through which lubrication can develop effectively as a transudate-like reaction.

There also is significant reduction in the involuntary expansion potential of the vagina with aging. When responding to sex-tension increment, expansion of the vaginal barrel in length and in diameter at the transcervical depth is delayed in reactive efficiency and significantly reduced in extent.

The vagina is a potential rather than an actual space. The walls of the vaginal barrel are collapsed together in a sexually unstimulated state. From this basic state, the vagina of the younger woman has the expansion potential to accommodate a baby's head without detriment to that head or to the vaginal barrel itself. During the aging process this essentially limitless facility for clinical expansion is lost. A major degree of this organ's amazing elasticity disappears, yet the vagina retains a definitive potential for involuntary expansion in response to effective sexual stimulation even in the advanced age groups. This expansion can best be protected and/or reconstituted effectively with adequate sex-steroid-replacement techniques during the postmenopausal years.

When plateau-phase levels of sexual stimulation are attained by the older woman, involuntary uterine elevation is significantly reduced as compared to the younger woman, whose uterus (presuming anterior placement) is elevated well into the false pelvis during this phase of the sexual response cycle. This is but one more factor in the reduction of the expansion potential of the vaginal barrel, for when the uterus elevates from the pelvis a tenting effect is created at the transcervical diameter of the vagina as an additional dimension to the vagina's reaction of involuntary expansion in response to sexual stimulation.

The minor labia of older women frequently do not demonstrate the sex skin coloration change so pathognomonic of impending orgasm in younger women. Particularly is this true if postmenopausal women are not supported by sex-steroid-replacement techniques. The major labia, which at plateau phase in younger age groups usually have elevated and flattened against the perineum in an involuntary mounting invitation, hang in limp folds surrounding the vaginal outlet. There is some involuntary separation of the major labia from the midline in a tentative mounting invitation, but the elevation and flattening reactions of these major labia disappear in older women as further clinical evidence of progressive loss of tissue elasticity.

There may be modest reduction in clitoral size during the postmenopausal years, but it is a late (60–70 years) development. Frequently, no definite change in shaft or glans size occurs. The minor labial covering (hood) of the clitoris atrophies, as does the fat pad in the mons area (see Fig. 2, Chapter 2). However, there is no objective evidence to date to suggest that there is any appreciable loss in sensate focus. The clitoris continues to function in both its receptor and transformer roles for sexual stimuli. In the older woman the physiological response of the clitoris to advanced plateau-phase levels of sexual excitation is to elevate and flatten on the anterior border of the symphysis, exactly in the manner described for younger women. Subjective concerns of clitoral responsivity will be discussed later in the chapter.

Usually the orgasmic phase of 50–70-year-old women is significantly shortened when compared to that of younger women. Particularly is this true if the older women have not been protected by adequate sex-steroid-replacement techniques. The contractions of the orgasmic platform in the outer third of the vagina still are initiated with 0.8-second intervals, but the contractions usually recur four or five times at the most, as opposed to an average pattern of eight to twelve recurrent contractions for younger women.

The natural pattern of uterine contractility in orgasm may follow two different reaction pathways for older women. In the first reaction, uterine contractions may simply continue in the manner of younger women with the typical expulsive-type contraction starting in the fundus, continuing through the midzone, to terminate in the noncontractile lower uterine segment. One or two uterine contractions will develop in the postmenopausal woman as part of her orgasmic expression as opposed to the regularly recurring three to five identifiable expulsive contractions for her younger counterpart.

The second type of uterine reaction to the aging process is a spastic contraction rather than the usual rhythmic contractile response during orgasmic-phase expression. This spasm of the uterus frequently lasts a minute or more and is reflected subjectively to the postmenopausal woman as pain in the lower abdomen, occasionally radiating the length of the vaginal barrel and into the major labia or even to one or both legs. This painful response has been reported occasionally as quite severe in degree. Uterine spasm is one of the few but very real complaints of postmenopausal women elicited by orgasmic experience that has not been recorded in younger women unless a state of pregnancy exists. The symptom of uterine spasm rarely develops in older women until sex-steroid levels have been reduced by natural involution of ovarian-steroid productivity to levels of metabolic imbalance. Fortunately, this symptom of lower abdominal pain with spastic contraction of the uterus can be alleviated with proper sex-steroid-replacement techniques.

Resolution-phase return of the pelvic viscera to the unstimulated baseline after orgasmic experience is rapid. If there has been a minor labial color change, it is minimal in character and disappears even as the orgasmic phase is experienced. If the uterus has been elevated it returns to its true pelvic positioning during orgasm, and the moderately distended vaginal barrel collapses rapidly. In brief, the resolution-phase expression is more rapid for the menopausal and postmenopausal woman than for her younger counterpart. Resolution-phase involution follows closely the patterning of the aging male, in whom a very rapid resolution-phase response is a sign of sex-steroid imbalance.

CONCEPT OF STEROID REPLACEMENT IN THE POSTMENOPAUSAL WOMAN

The onset of the female climacteric may be traumatically indicated by such clinically obvious symptoms as termination of menses, hot flushes, emotional instability, occipital headaches and neckaches, and, ultimately, a feeling of chronic fatigue or exhaustion far beyond that naturally expected from the normal commitment of physical and mental energy to the day's activity. Physiological changes in the pelvis, such as constriction of the vaginal barrel, loss of thickness and corrugation of the mucosal lining of the vagina, reduced production of vaginal lubrication, shortened duration of orgasmic experience and spastic contraction of the uterus, are all secondary evidence of an aging woman's clinical state of sex-steroid starvation.

Many older women describe an irritative, painful, vaginal response during and after coital connection, particularly if the connection is of significant duration or repeated after brief respite. The cause of the dysfunction is the thin senile lining of the vagina. Postmenopausal women also complain of bladder and urethral irritability after coition and frequently have the urge to void immediately following coital connection. Particularly in this response of bladder and urethral irritation noted after any long-maintained coital connection or any repetition of coital experience without at least a day's interval. This "bride's cystitis" is the result of the thinned mucosal lining and a vaginal barrel constricted to such an extent that it no longer provides the anatomic cushion necessary to protect the urethra and bladder from the mechanical irritation of a thrusting, firm penis.

As described previously, there is loss of fatty tissue in the mons area and in the major labia with aging. The minor labial hood thins and provides a relatively nonprotective covering for the clitoral glans and shaft. For these reasons the clitoris is easily irritated by direct physical approach, and a painful response rather than one of sex-tension increment is elicited frequently from attempts at manual manipulation of the area. Degrees of pressure, rapidity of stroking, or even stroking direction that may usually have produced elevation in the sexual tensions of a younger woman may subjectively irritate or even initiate a painful response in an older woman.

This does not mean that subjectively the older woman is less reactive to stimulative approaches. There is no evidence that subjective levels of sexual tension initiated or amplified through clitoral influence are any less involving or demanding of older than of younger women. Subjectively, clitoral function in sex-tension increment is as effective in older as in younger age groups. What must be constantly borne in mind is that the clitoral area of older women is much more sensitive to irritation or trauma from uncontrolled or thoughtless male approach than is true for younger women. If a restrained approach to the clitoris is used, it continues to function most effectively in its specific role as the organ of sex-tension increment in the aging woman's body.

When adequate sex-steroid techniques are employed, the involutional changes in the mons, major labia, and minor labia do not develop to the extent they do in unprotected older women, so excessive clitoral irritability is rarely a problem.

There also may be marked reduction in subjective levels of sexual interest in addition to the obvious depletion in objective facility for sexual response as further clinical evidence of a state of sex-steroid starvation. These symptoms can be alleviated, if not removed, with adequate steroid replacement in the menopausal and postmenopausal years.

If the postmenopausal woman is denied sufficient steroid replacement to maintain some degree of mucosal stimulation in the vaginal barrel and a relatively normal-sized uterus, in advanced years she may well be condemned to sexual dysfunction by such interdiction.

Many articles have been written on the subject of the techniques of sex-steroid replacement. These techniques are now well established and are currently widely employed in medical practice in many parts of the world. It would be redundant to discuss the technical aspects of the problem of sex-steroid replacement in the aging women in this text.

It should be noted, however, that there are women that, despite lack of adequate sex-steroid replacement, continue to function effectively in terms of sexual responsivity during the 50–70-year age groups. There are many variations on this theme, but two distinct patterns are seen most frequently. The first response pattern is the well-established one of women who terminate menstrual flow in their late forties or early fifties, yet continue with reduced clinically apparent sex-steroid production for years thereafter. These women have few if any menopausal symptoms, and their vaginal smears evidence a 10–20% cornification well into the 60-year age group. Their high levels of strength and energy, in contrast to that of their peers, is obvious to the most casual observer. Effective sexual functioning continues unabated and the vaginal barrel retains some of its corrugated pattern, lubricates well with sexual excitation, and the labia, clitoris, and mons area retain a significant degree of the configuration of the younger woman.

The second pattern has been established by older women regularly having intercourse once or twice a week and having done so over a period of many years. There is tremendous physiological and, of course, psychological value in continuity of sexual exposure, as expressed by the physical efficiency of vaginal response to sexual stimulation. To a significant degree, regularity of sexual exposure will overcome the influence of sex-steroid inadequacy in the female pelvis. Such a woman, unsupported by sex-steroid-replacement techniques, develops all of the physiological stigmata of steroid starvation, but the pink, atrophic vaginal barrel still produces suffi-cient lubrication and, with regular usage, does not constrict sig-nificantly in size. The uterus shrinks to atrophic size, but if the woman is enjoying regularity of sexual expression with orgasmic release of her sexual tension, the orgasmic experience develops physiologically to a degree comparable to that of a younger woman; spastic contractions of the uterus in this type of older woman have not been observed or reported. However, most older women have not been exposed to this frequency of coital connection as a consistent pattern of sexual expression over the continuum of a long-maintained marriage.

Since the majority of women in the 50–70-year age group have not retained adequate ovarian function to stimulate the reproduc-tive viscera effectively and do not experience coital connection fre-quently enough to accomplish the same effect by regularity of usage, sex-steroid replacement frequently is indicated in order to enable most women to continue to function effectively as inter-ested and interesting sexual partners.

Mention should be made of the increased masturbatory rate of women in the 50–70-year age groups. The pattern of masturbatory release of sexual tensions reportedly increases in frequency after the menopause, at least into the 60-year age range, for many rea-sons. Unmarried women committed to regularity of manipulative relief as younger women continue their pattern into the older age group. In addition, there are women who are married to men failing in health, and who are widowed, divorced, or socially isolated for any reason in the declining years. They frequently find need for some regularity of the sexual tension release denied them by loss or unavailability of sexual partners. Since these forms of social isolation are particularly prevalent among women in the 50–70-year age group, a relative increase in frequency of masturbatory rate is understandable. Psychosocial freedom to enjoy masturbatory relief of unresolved sexual tensions has more and more become an acceptable behavioral pattern for those women so handicapped by limited partner availability in this age group.

For a variety of reasons women in the aging population are re-ferred to the Foundation with their husbands for treatment of sexual dysfunction. Only three women, however, have come at their own instigation because they were nonorgasmic and felt that they did not wish to continue sexually dysfunctional throughout the remaining portion of their lifespan. It is indeed rare that marital units in this age group are referred primarily at the instigation of a female partner wishing correction for her own basic sexual dysfunction. There have been quite a few women, however, referred with their husbands for correction of male symptoms of sexual dysfunction, such as secondary impotence or premature ejaculation, who have never been orgasmic even in their younger years. These women are, of course, treated just as if the primary concern in referral for treatment was focused upon their particular sexual dysfunction.

There have been three marital units referred basically at the instigation of the husbands because they were distressed by the change in their wives' attitudes toward sexual functioning after the menopausal years. In all three instances the wives (ages 57–64 years) felt that continuation of sexual function after menopause was psychosocially unacceptable.

Mr. and Mrs. A were 61 and 58 years of age when they were referred to the Foundation. They married when she was 30 years old, and produced four children during the decade of their thirties, three boys and a girl, born in that order. The eldest boy had just married and the younger children were still in college or graduate school.

The marital unit had requested referral to the Foundation from both their physician and clergyman, with the hope of establishing orgasmic return for Mrs. A, who had never achieved this experience in her lifetime and felt cheated of an important life experience. The marital partners formed a fully compatible unit, secure in their respect and admiration for each other, devoted to their children, well-established socially and financially in their community, yet without the slightest ability to communicate in the sexual area.

As young people, they had family backgrounds of warmth and security, but sexual material had never been discussed. Mr. A had gone through college and business school training, and his wife had two years of college. They each had a modest degree of sexual experience with other partners before their engagement, and established their own regular coital pattern during the three or four months before their marriage.

Mr. A had difficulty with ejaculatory control. This improved somewhat over the first ten years of the marriage, but he never achieved fully effective ejaculatory control. His wife frequently experienced plateau-phase levels of sexual excitation and thoroughly enjoyed her sexual experiences with her husband, but at times was quite frustrated by the inability to achieve orgasmic expression. The marital unit had consulted authority three different times during their marriage in attempts to provide the wife with orgasmic experience, but the consultations had not been fruitful.

They finally decided to live within the framework of their mutual sexual expression, confident that all possible effort had been made to improve their response patterns. Their minds were changed by observing the mutual excitation and physical attraction between their son and his fiancée. After the wedding both Mr. and Mrs. A felt that one last attempt should be made to achieve mutual sexual satisfaction. Again they consulted their personal physician and their clergyman who together referred them for treatment.

These two socially well-oriented people were determined to be in good physical condition. Mrs. A had been controlled with sex-steroid-replacement techniques, so the task of reconstituting effective sexual functioning between husband and wife was indeed an easy one. It was only in this area of sexual functioning that facility for basic communication had not been established.

She had never been able to bring herself to experiment in a masturbatory fashion or to encourage her husband to experiment in an effort to please her, either by manipulative or oral-genital approaches. Simply by following the established pattern of exposure to sensate focus and then moving to include pelvic exploration (see Chapter 2), while simultaneously improving the husband's ejaculatory control (see Chapter 5), the unit was mutually fully responsive within ten days' time. The response pattern was the usual one of first manipulatively and then coitally experienced orgasmic expression after establishing mutual confidence in the husband's ejaculatory control.

This brief history is presented not to indicate any depth of therapeutic concern but rather to emphasize the fact that with growing professional knowledge of the physiology of sexual functioning in advanced age groups, and with some mutual security of sexual communication established between members of the marital unit under authoritative direction, sexual interaction between older marital partners can be established easily, warmly, and with dignity.

The fact that innumerable men and women have not been sexually effective before reaching their late fifties or early sixties is no reason to condemn them to continuing sexual dysfunction as they live out the rest of their lifespan. The disinclination of the medical and behavioral professions to treat the aging population for sexual dysfunction has been a major disservice perpetrated by these professions upon the general public. Certainly, it is time the trend was reversed.

Mr. and Mrs. B's ages were 63 and 57, respectively. They had two children, both sons, who were grown, married, and with children of their own. The husband's basic complaint was that his wife refused coital opportunity after expressing the concept that "following change of life, women continuing to have intercourse must be perverted."

The marital unit's history of sexual connection in younger years was spotty at best, with granting or refusal of conjugal rights used by the wife in a reward-and-punishment pattern of control. Sexual exposure was always intiated at the husband's insistence, with the wife fulfilling her concept of the role of a dutiful wife who, nevertheless, used the weaponry of sex as noted. She had never been orgasmic either during coition or with manipulation, nor had she ever attempted masturbation. She had always been sure that sexual function was only of interest to men, that "good" women never responded sexually, and that her only reward from sexual activity was reproduction.

Mrs. B was the third of three daughters. Her mother and father separated shortly after her birth, and the frustrated, resentful mother educated her girls to be grossly suspicious of and to have as little exchange with the male sex as possible. She was so successful in her indoctrination of the concept of the evil male that the two elder sisters never married, instead worked and lived together in a totally feminine world. Mrs. B married the only man she ever dated socially, over violent maternal objection that changed over the years to grudging neutrality with the advent of the grandchildren. However, the mother exerted such a constant influence over this daughter that her control amounted to a basic supervision of the marriage. This total maternal dominance continued until the mother's death when Mrs. B was 46 years old. With the mother's death, the spinster sisters became Mrs. B's established source of consultation and advice on all problems relating to woman's role in marriage. Mr. B tolerated the influence of his wife's family with a combination of resignation and indifference. There were two short-term extramarital episodes that provided little of value.

Fortunately, the two children were both boys. Their father played an adequate role. The mother was relatively restricted in her own maternal role, evidencing real lack of security in contending with the young males. When the second son married and left the home free of maternal responsibility, Mrs. B was 53 years old.

Approximately a month after the son's wedding she refused her husband at a specific sexual opportunity and, while doing so, told him for the first time that she had never had the slightest interest in sex, that she had fulfilled her wifely duties fully, and that it was undignified for a woman of her years to be expected to continue sexual connection. She insisted upon separate bedrooms.

He complied with his wife's demands, thinking this to be a passing attitude, but after a period of two years with no reversal of her stand, the frustrated man sought mutual consultation with their clergyman under the guise of marriage counseling. This approach to the problem was accepted by his wife. To Mr. B's consternation, their minister firmly agreed that any woman in Mrs. B's age group should not be expected to live an active sexual life, for "no woman after the change of life should be expected to continue in a role that nature had reserved as the responsibility of younger women."

Thereafter, when consultation with alternative authority was requested, Mrs. B refused. Finally, Mr. B's physician was able to secure her cooperation for referral to the Foundation, this time under the guise that his physical and mental well-being were in jeopardy. His wife was quite belligerent about the imposed cooperative venture but accompanied her husband in her "good wife" role, secure in the knowledge that medical opinion would support her position in the matter.

When told at the roundtable discussion (see Chapter 2) that there was no reason that sexual functioning couldn't continue effectively not only into the 60-year but also the 70-year age groups, she was initially deeply disturbed, then quite angry, soon very distrustful and, at best, only minimally cooperative. If for no other reason than to prove once and for all the impossibility of authoritative contention that both pleasant and effective sexual function was possible, she most reluctantly joined her husband in active therapy. Subsequent to elective reorientation of both husband and wife to the concerns of mutual communication and to detailed psychosexual education, Mrs. B became intrigued with the new information at her disposal, lost her high level of suspicion, grew totally cooperative, and in short order became fully responsive sexually. She actually was orgasmic during the acute phase of the treatment.

The only area of residual concern during posttreatment follow-up was that of the continuing influence of the two elder sisters. They made major but unsuccessful attempts to salvage their younger sister from the state of moral debasement into which she had been unsuspectingly lured by her husband and his physician.

Mr. and Mrs. C were 62 and 57 years of age, respectively when referred to the Foundation. Their children were mature and had left the home. They were referred by their local physician because the husband was experiencing erective insecurity and developing fears for sexual performance. His was an increasing concern that his wife might be a "nymphomaniac."

She had terminated menstrual flow at age 49 and, although initially handicapped by symptoms of the menopausal syndrome, continued in excellent health. Her menopausal symptomatology was brought under control without difficulty with sex-steroid-replacement techniques. With adequate estrogen replacement she continued to show sexual interest following the coital frequency pattern established during her premenopausal years.

Mr. C, somewhat handicapped by arthritis, was a diet-controlled diabetic with obvious loss of physical strength and energy following a long series of recurrent infections. During the five-year period prior to consultation with authority, he had found his wife's basic demand for intercourse at a once-or-twice-a-week level somewhat overwhelming. Although in their younger years his wife's freedom of sexual expression had delighted him, real concern had developed in his early fifties that she was "oversexed" because he frequently found himself forced into ejaculation by a seemingly relentless partner. On occasion his wife would assure him that he needed tension release and would initiate sexual performance. Frequently intimidated into sexual connection and forced into ejaculation when he had felt no innate demand, he followed the usual pattern of any sexually threatened marital partner by seeking excuses to avoid sexual exposure. Finally, varying degrees of secondary impotence developed in perhaps half the coital opportunities during the year before the marital unit's referral to the Foundation. Mr. C was frequently depressed and moody during the six months prior to therapy.

Mrs. C had the usual but unfortunate misconception that every man must ejaculate with regularity to maintain his best physical and mental health and was certain that men needed and expected ejaculatory release at every sexual exposure. When any sexual approach was instituted, no matter how tentative the venture, she forced the issue of ejaculatory experience in such a positive manner that her mere physical approach eventually became a threat to her anxious husband's psychosexual security. Mr. C thought that in her positive approach she was evidencing a high level of unresolved sexual tension. So, knowing Mrs. C to be regularly orgasmic within the cycle of their sexual encounters, he finally determined that she must be "oversexed."

Once Mrs. C had been educated to accept the psychosexual concept that the older male need not ejaculate at every given opportunity and that man's physical need for regularity of ejaculation at every sexual encounter was only a sexual myth, she was totally responsive to authoritative suggestion that her husband be free to seek and express his own level of ejaculatory demand. He was then reoriented to full erective security, supported by the concept of ejaculating only at his own demand level.

The fears of performance and the spectator role were rapidly resolved once he was completely assured that a fully cooperative wife no longer posed a threat to his sexual functioning. Coital connection has continued on a once-or-twice-a-week level for the past two years, with the husband ejaculating every 10 days to 2 weeks and his wife fully satisfied sexually.

Mr. D was 56 and his wife 55 when referred for therapy. The basic complaint was of dyspareunia that had increased in severity since onset four years previously. At age 46 Mrs. D underwent a complete abdominal hysterectomy and bilateral salpingoophorectomy, the surgical indication being excessive vaginal bleeding from what was described as a myomatous uterus. There had been no medical consideration of postoperative sex-steroid support. For three years after surgery she was harassed with hot flushes, emotional instability, and a severe degree of physical lassitude. She lost all interest in sexual functioning, simply accommodating her husband's coital interest without the slightest concept of self-initiation or, for that matter, self-interest. Sexual patterning prior to surgery had been coital opportunity at one or two times a week during the decade of their forties until Mrs. D began having a heavy menstrual flow and increasing intermenstrual bleeding, ultimately leading to the hysterectomy. She estimated that before surgery she had been orgasmic in about 75 percent of coital opportunities. Neither partner described any extramarital sexual experience before her hysterectomy.

Some three to four years after the surgery, the menopausal symptoms of hot flushes and emotional instability had disappeared, leaving as residuals the extreme physical lassitude and expressed lack of interest in sexual functioning. Coital frequency dropped to every 10 days to two weeks, with Mrs. D occasionally finding new excuses to avoid coital exposure, but usually relying on the old refrain, "I'm too tired."

Approximately five years after the surgery, with coital frequency now estimated at twice-a-month level, Mrs. D became increasingly distressed by vaginal burning after coital connection, and experienced urinary urgency immediately after coition. She also noticed that there was little or no natural lubrication during sexual connection. Artificial lubricants were employed which partially relieved the vaginal irritation but did not resolve the additional pain that developed with deep vaginal penetration. If coital connection was maintained for any significant length of time, there was pelvic discomfort the following day.

By this time Mrs. D was deeply introspective, had lost interest in any activity outside the home, and assumed the attitude of a much older person afflicted with a chronic disability. She verbalized multiple complaints, evidenced obvious physical weakness and, in short, was rapidly losing contact with reality. Her husband became involved extramaritally with another woman and directed his sexual energies and his psychosocial interest outside the home. Soon he discontinued demand for coital release and the frequency schedule degenerated to less than once a month.

Mrs. D, aware that her husband had lost all interest in her as an individual and concerned with the probability of an interest outside the home, finally sought advice from medical authority.

When her symptoms of sexual dysfunctioning and complete loss of sexual interest were reported to her physician, she and her husband were referred to the Foundation. On the basis of the referring physician's description of the symptomatology, the initiation of adequate sex-steroid replacement was suggested before acceptance of the marital unit in therapy. Accordingly, Mrs. D was placed on effective levels of steroid support for approximately four months before she and her husband entered active therapy for sexual dysfunction.

During the four-month waiting period under sex-steroid influence, the symptoms of extreme physical lassitude, the burning and pain of the vagina with intercourse, and the urgent demand to void immediately after coital connection all disappeared. This wife's lack of confidence in herself both as a woman and as a sexual partner, her continued expression of total lack of sexual interest, and her husband's professed level of disinterest in the marriage were the concerns attacked in treatment.

The husband was provided a detailed explanation of the reasons behind his wife's extreme physical lassitude, lack of sexual interest, and multiple physical complaints before, during, and after intercourse. Subsequent to this exchange of information, communication was reestablished within the marital unit. Once Mrs. D understood that her blanket rejection of sexual interest was purely a defense mechanism, she returned to effective sexual functioning and approximated her presurgical levels of orgasmic attainment. Her husband was redirected and reoriented to his wife as an individual, and her confidence in herself improved significantly subsequent to his obvious renewed interest in her.

Adequate steroid replacement is only one phase of the total of preventive medicine directed toward clinical support of aging women. Aside from regularity of medical and laboratory evaluations, by far the most important aspect of this support is provided in the form of education. There are many misconceptions related to the aging process that are reflected by progressive lack of psychosocial confidence.

That phase of human activity most surrounded by misconception, fallacy, and taboo is sexual function. If some concept of the naturalness of sexual functioning in the 50–70-year age group can be accepted by the medical and behavioral professions, there will be no reason to confuse symptoms relating to sexual dysfunction with those of the natural, physiological involution of the aging process.

The Foundation's fundamental theme still applies. There are only two basic needs for regularity of sexual expression in 70–80-year-old women. These necessities are a reasonably good state of general health and an interested and interesting partner.

Treatment for orgasmic dysfunction has been conducted along patterns suggested in Chapter 11. The aging woman responds to the direct approaches to problems of sexual function originally designed for the younger woman. A brief statistical consideration of rapid-treatment failure rates for the older woman has been included in Chapter 12 together with similar consideration of rapid treatment failure rates for the aging male.

14

PROGRAM STATISTICS

Statistics mean little in biological or behavioral research if the statistician is attempting to establish subjective responsivity to objective stimuli. When the clinical interpreter cannot define points A, B, or C with exactitude, it is shaky business to claim statistical significance when evaluating a multipoint interaction. On the other hand, statistical failures always loom large on any clinical horizon. If the clinician errs on the side of conservatism, declares as unimproved or as treatment failures all units of clinical measurement about which the slightest question of therapeutic progress exists, failure statistics will become increasingly important. Therefore, statistical evaluation of therapeutic procedure in the 11 years of investigative treatment for sexual inadequacy will be considered only from the point of view of "failure rates."

The Foundation's position has been specifically established in this matter. Claims for statistical reliability in successful psychotherapeutic treatment cannot and should not be made without equivocation. For who is qualified to define with confidence the clinical success of any psychotherapeutic venture? The therapists? —inevitably prejudiced positively. The patient?—prejudiced negatively or positively. The statistician?—too many variables. But, if based upon a most conservative evaluation of clinical progress, a statistical failure rate may be reported that at least can be equaled and probably improved upon by any similar clinical program. For decades, reported successes in any new form of clinical treatment have had only one impeccable judgmental yardstick: are the reported successes reproducible in other geographical areas, by independent clinical treatment centers, following outlined techniques of therapy? With evaluation of subjective criteria reported in the most stringent of terms as failure rates, this clinical yardstick certainly can be applied without reservation to programs such as represented by the current report. If the reported failure rates from this clinical investigation cannot be lowered by other objectively controlled research programs in the future, then there will be little evidence of continued clinical progress in the treatment of human sexual inadequacy by medical and/or behavioral professions.

There is yet another factor. The Foundations' therapeutic program for relief of sexual dysfunction is fundamentally a process of marital-unit education with concomitant dissipation of misconception, misinformation, and taboo. The educational program is designed primarily to encourage the sexually dysfunctional individual not to attempt to improve upon, but hopefully to return to, the basic physiological patterns of natural sexual responsivity. How does one objectively grade success in such a venture?

Finally, in the evaluation of any psychotherapeutic procedure, clinical success in therapeutic venture dare not be claimed at termination of the acute stage of the therapy. Regardless of whether the marital unit or either of its partners is in therapy for two weeks or two years, how can therapists be sure that specific reconstitution of marital sexual functioning under authoritative control offers any assurance of permanency after termination of the immediate or acute phase of treatment?

Might not a reversal of the treatment-acquired positive behavioral interaction between marital-unit partners arise next week or next year? What significant value is there in two weeks or two years of intensive therapy in an attempt to reverse any form of sexual inadequacy, if the positive results of improved sexual functioning carry no real implication of permanency of performance? How can any professional rate initial treatment a success if there is no recorded evidence of continuing symptom reversal?

Far better, then, to consider statistical failure as a reproducibly positive element. Overall statistical failure in the rapid-treatment program has been determined from a coalescence of two different sources. A combination of initial treatment failures and of follow-up failures provides an effective means of clinical appraisal. Initial failure is defined as indication that the two-week rapid-treatment phase has failed to initiate reversal of the basic symptomatology of sexual dysfunction for which the unit was referred to the Foundation.

From onset, it has been Foundation policy to follow patients for five years subsequent to termination of the two-week acute phase of the program in order to evaluate therapeutic concept and to establish some indication of permanency of the reversal of the symptoms of sexual dysfunction. Aside from the initial failure rates in the rapid-treatment phase, the statistics of real value are those of percentage reversal to a sexually dysfunctional status from the state of effective sexual functioning achieved during the acute phase of the overall treatment program. If there is return to sexual inadequacy during the five-year period after termination of the acute-treatment phase, the overall clinical effort must be judged a failure and will be so reported in this chapter in the overall failure-rate statistics.

For the first time, five years of follow-up of a psychotherapeutic endeavor are reported for professional consideration. There are six years of individual five-year follow-up to report in view of the 11 years' duration of the statistical control period arbitrarily imposed at onset upon this specific clinical-research venture by Foundation policy.

A few elemental statistics should be highlighted before analytical consideration of immediate failure and long-range (overall) reversal rates is in order. The youngest member of the statistically controlled population was a woman of 23 years, the oldest a man of 76 years. A total of 510 marital units comprised the major portion of the clinical research population. In this controlled population were units both with unilateral partner sexual inadequacy and with bilateral partner sexual inadequacy.

There were 287 marital units in which a unilateral complaint of sexual dysfunction was isolated and applied to a specific marital partner. However, both partners in the marital unit (with or without demonstrable sexual pathology) participated in the marital unit's educational program, accepting Foundation concept that there is no uninvolved partner in any marriage describing symptoms of sexual dysfunction. Thus, a diagnosis of unilateral sexual dysfunction was made in 56.3 percent of the referred marital units. A total of 171 men and 116 women comprised the sexually dysfunctional members in the 287 marital units with unilateral sexual in-adequacy. This is approximately a 60:40/male:female ratio of in-cidence of sexual dysfunction in marital units with unilateral part-ner involvement.

The number of marital units with bilateral sexual inadequacy (i.e., each partner sexually dysfunctional) was 223. Thus, in 43.7 percent of all marital units referred to the Foundation for treat-ment, it was found necessary to treat each marital partner for a specific form of sexual inadequacy during the two-week rapid-treat-ment phase of the overall program.

Since each partner in the 223 marital units with bilateral sexual dysfunction was treated for a specific sexual inadequacy, the num-ber of individual cases was doubled. This figure (446) combined with that for single-partner sexual dysfunction in a marital unit (287) provides a total of 733 cases of sexual inadequacy treated in 510 marital units referred to the Foundation over a period of the last 11 years.

There were, in addition, 54 single men and 3 single women treated in an unmarried state, bringing the total to 57 individual units handicapped by sexual dysfunction. The advantages of part-ner surrogates and replacement partners in the therapy of these 57 individuals have been considered in Chapter 5.

After the 57 unmarried sexually inadequate men and women are added to the 733 sexually dysfunctional married men and women, the number of individual cases of human sexual inade-quacy treated by Foundation personnel totals 790 cases. This level of clinical research population provides a bare minimum of ma-terial sufficient for consideration of initial failure rates and for an accumulation of overall failure-rate statistics from five-year follow-up reviews of patient status.

In order to provide for continuity of clinical discussion, brief statistical reviews of failure rates have been presented for the multiplicity of sexual dysfunctions (see Chapters 3, 4, 7, 9, 11, and 12). Rather than consider in detail the failure rates for the various sexual dysfunctions, a brief statement of the initial failure rate in the acute-treatment approach to each sexual inadequacy will be presented. Thereafter, attention will be turned to two valuable areas of clinical consideration. First to be evaluated will be the returns from the rapid-treatment techniques of the research population as a whole, and second will be general consideration of the results evidenced from six years of five-year follow-up of sexually inadequate marital units after termination of the two-week rapid-treatment program for human sexual inadequacy.

There have been three therapy teams treating the problems of sexual dysfunction in this clinical series. As described, each team has been comprised of a male and a female cotherapist. However, teams have not been maintained in a static state. Over the past two years each male cotherapist has worked with each female co-therapist. When the problems of the training phase for professional additions to the Foundation's permanent staff are evaluated, in addition to the markedly increased pressures placed upon professional staff for clinical productivity during the last few years, it is evident that there has been approximately a 10 percent increase in the level of the immediate failure-rate statistics for the clinical program. This level should be lowered significantly in years to come as clinical control and teaching experience improve.

The clinical caseload at the Foundation has consistently increased and, particularly in the last two years, has expanded to a point difficult to control with objectivity. In the calendar year 1969, 114 marital and 9 single units experienced the routine two-week acute phase of the therapy program.

Prior to a restatement of failure rates for treatment of an individual sexual dysfunction, brief consideration of the character of the clinical research population as a whole is in order.

The total of 510 marital units and 57 single units that comprise the clinical research segment represents a highly selective population. The population is selective in several ways:

1. Geographic distribution: Of the total of 567 units, married or single, seen in therapy, only 67, or 11.8 percent, have been referred from the St. Louis area. Patient referral has been from throughout the United States and Canada. This involuntary restriction in marital units referred from the local area to an approximate incidence of 10 percent affords the advantage of marital-unit social isolation in treatment for the remaining 90 percent of the referred problems of sexual dysfunction. As stated in Chapter 1, an extra week in therapy is allocated (3 weeks) to patients re-

ferred from the local area to counterbalance home, social, and business distractions. It is always more difficult to deal with marital units referred from the immediate geographical area because of inherent problems in achieving social isolation.

2. Since referral of patients by authority is a Foundation requirement, there is generally a higher income distribution and, consequently, a higher educational level in this segment of the clinical population than in a general population. Of the 790 individuals treated in the 11 years' control period, 578 (72.7 percent) had matriculated in a college or university. Only 29 individuals of the total 790 men and women treated somehow escaped the referral screening process during the statistical control period. The specific exception to the Foundation's demand for authoritative screening has been the privilege of professional self-referral. This privilege has been accorded physicians and clinical psychologists.

3. The social structuring of the clinical research group has been middle-class or above, despite marked freedom from monetary restriction. From 1959 to 1964, the first five years of the program, no patients were charged for clinical treatment. The investigators felt it unreasonable to charge for services while stabilizing investigative techniques and developing a background of clinical experience with the newly conceived rapid-treatment methods. As experience accrued, and financial necessity intervened, charges for treatment were instituted. Yet, despite strict Foundation adherence during the last six years to a policy of 25 percent free care, 25 percent adjusted fee scale, and 50 percent full-fee payment, there has not been a socially representative population referred for treatment.

There are other sociological factors influencing the marked selectivity in patient referral. The specific complaint of sexual dysfunction appears infrequently at any treatment center available to low-income or low-social-stratum patients. Whether there is infinitely less sexual dysfunction at this level in the social scale, as has been suggested by others, or whether there remains at this social level a double standard-oriented male hesitancy or even rejection of opportunity to seek relief from sexual dysfunction or to allow his female partner such release, has not been established.

4. Yet another factor in patient selectivity is the incidence of advanced education among the clinical research population. As

stated, the gross exception to the rule for patient referral is that applied to physicians and clinical psychologists. These individuals, permitted the professional courtesy of self-referral, comprise a significant segment of the research population. Among the 510 total marital-unit population, there have been 89 marital units in which the husband, the wife, or both marital partners have had prior medical training. Frequently there has been the marital-unit combination of physician and behaviorist (clinical psychologist, sociologist, or social worker). Self-referral by a physician of his or her marital unit for treatment of sexual inadequacy provides an incidence of 17.5 percent of the total marital-unit population.

The self-referred physician group can be further subdivided with statistical security to emphasize the high degree of involuntary selectivity inherent in this clinical research population. Among the 89 physicians' marriages self-referred to the Foundation for treatment of sexual dysfunction, there have been 43 marital units (48.4 percent of the physician group) in which at least one marital partner has represented the specific medical discipline of psychiatry.

5. The most influential factor in group selectivity is that of self-motivation. Since approximately 90 percent of the caseload has been referred from outside the St. Louis area, there is every evidence of intense motivation for reversal of symptomatology among those making the effort to reach beyond their local environment for relief of sexual dysfunction. Patient motivation for reversal of symptomatology is of major import in any form of psychotherapeutic endeavor, but it is of vital concern in the treatment of marital-unit sexual dysfunction.

6. There was indeed a mixed blessing in the fact that 413 of the 790 individuals (52.3 percent) treated for sexual dysfunction had a history of prior or continuing exposure to psychotherapeutic procedure at the time of their two-week commitment to the acute phase of treatment at the Foundation. Thus approximately one-half the patients had experienced prior treatment for the specific sexual dysfunction for which they were referred to the Foundation. Prior patient experience with the psychotherapeutic process was of significant value during history-taking. Pertinent material was immediately forthcoming. Previously treated patients discussed

material of sexual content with obvious freedom, as compared to those unexposed to prior therapy.

However, there was marked tendency of previously treated sexually dysfunctional patients to dissect every concept in finite detail, and unfortunately to bend every group discussion or educational session to direct consideration of their own personal problems with little regard for marital-partner interests. It was infinitely more difficult for previously treated individuals to *feel and think* sexually, but usually much easier for them to *talk* about problems of sexual function or dysfunction without constraint.

With the multiple facets of involuntary selectivity in the clinical research population running entirely in support of the treatment program, failure rates should always be evaluated with the conscious realization that Foundation personnel have had every possible advantage in treatment opportunity during the last 11 years.

The initial-failure-rate statistics will be stated with brief clinical comment. N represents the total of those treated for a specific distress; F, the number of failed opportunities of symptom reversal with the rapid-treatment method; and IFR, the initial failure rate.

1. *Primary Impotence:* N = 32; F = 13; IFR = 40.6%.

Treatment approach to this dysfunction represents the Foundation's clinical disaster area. An initial failure rate of 40 percent can only be improved upon. Some manner of professional encouragement can be extracted from the fact that there were 9 failures in treatment of the first 16 primarily impotent men referred to the Foundation, and this number of initial treatment failures was reduced to 4 in the second series of 16 men referred for therapy. There remains an embarrassingly large margin for clinical improvement.

2. *Secondary Impotence:* N = 213; F = 56; IFR = 26.3%.

Again, the initial treatment failure rate is too high. The failure rates have varied from 22 to 30 percent each year for the last five years. This relative constancy of statistical return establishes the fact that there is much to be learned in the treatment of secondary impotence. Progress in description of newer clinical approaches to this problem of male sexual dysfunction, though initially most encouraging, has plateaued and has not been particularly impressive in recent years.

3. *Premature Ejaculation:* N $= 186$; F $= 4$; IFR $= 2.2\%$.
The low initial failure rate emphasizes the fact that premature ejaculation is the easiest of the male sexual dysfunctions to treat effectively. Premature ejaculation as a sexual dysfunction should and can be brought fully under control in our culture during the next decade. There remains only to establish an effective postgraduate training program to provide such a result.

4. *Ejaculatory Incompetence:* N $= 17$; F $= 3$; IFR $= 17.6\%$.
This is a relatively infrequent complication of male sexual function. Generally, difficulty in symptom reversal relates to a psychosocially traumatic episode. N is too small for objective discussion. The importance of considering this dysfunction as an entirely separate clinical entity from prior or current concepts of impotence is emphasized in the body of the discussion.

5. *Vaginismus:* N $= 29$; F $= 0$; IFR $= 0$.
A statistic of this order underscores the fact that if there is clinical difficulty, it is with diagnosis, not with treatment. This complication of female sexual function has not been included in the sexually inadequate population, since the women with vaginismus were also victims of primary or situational orgasmic dysfunction and are included statistically in these specific studies. Diagnosing and treating vaginismus successfully was but a first step in clinical attack on an orgasmically dysfunctional status. Once diagnosed, the dysfunction of vaginismus is clinically reversible.

6. *Primary Orgasmic Dysfunction:* N $= 193$; F $= 32$; IFR $= 16.6\%$.
As opposed to previous theoretical concept, initial failure rates incurred in treatment for primary and for situational orgasmic dysfunction have been essentially comparable when recorded in an overall review. Since clinical approaches to both dysfunctional classifications are identical, the minimal 6 percent difference be-

tween initial failure rates for the two types of orgasmic dysfunctions is not surprising to Foundation personnel.

7. *Situational Orgasmic Dysfunction:* $N = 149$; $F = 34$; IFR = 22.8%.

When this classification is divided into its three integral components, the Achilles' heel in the Foundation's treatment approach to the orgasmically inadequate woman becomes apparent.

Masturbatory orgasmic inadequacy:	$N = 11$; $F = 1$; IFR $= 9.1\%$
Coital orgasmic inadequacy:	$N = 106$; $F = 21$; IFR $= 19.8\%$
Random orgasmic inadequacy:	$N = 32$; $F = 12$; IFR $= 37.5\%$

Obviously, random orgasmic inadequacy has proved a stumbling block to clinical resolution and in turn has influenced the initial failure rate for situational orgasmic dysfunction. If this subclassification had responded satisfactorily to treatment approach, the initial failure rates in therapy for the two arbitrary divisions of orgasmic dysfunction would have proved essentially equal.

Thus, there is statistical support for the Foundation's clinical dissatisfaction with the initial treatment failures for men with primary impotence and for women with random orgasmic inadequacy. These indeed are areas in which clinical treatment approaches were established as inadequate, warranting major revision.

8. *Sexual Inadequacy—Men and Women 50 Years or Older:*

Aging male:	$N = 48$; $F = 12$; IFR $= 25.0\%$
Aging female:	$N = 27$; $F = 11$; IFR $= 40.7\%$
Totals	$N = 75$; $F = 23$; IFR $= 30.6\%$

The initial failure rates for treatment of sexual dysfunction in the aging population are above the average of the total population. Actually greater treatment difficulty for problems of the aging woman is apparent. Here the initial failure rate was at least 50 percent above that of younger women.

Yet the Foundation is encouraged by these figures. N is too small (particularly on the female side) to be of statistical import, but certainly the results, poor as they are, support the contention that sexual dysfunction in the aging population should be attacked with all the vigor mustered for the younger population. With more clinical experience, the failure rates in treatment of aging sexual dysfunction certainly will be lowered. Even if there are (as reported) only two chances out of three for reversal of any form of sexual dysfunction, regardless of the years of existence of the chief complaint in the aging population, every clinical effort should be expended to relieve this socially restrictive inadequacy without reference to the age of the distressed individual.

9. Finally, the overall totals of initial failure rates in treatment of sexual dysfunction, first separated by sexes and then recorded for the total research population, are as listed:

Total male: $N = 448$; $F = 76$; IFR $= 16.9\%$

Total female: $N = 342$; $F = 66$; IFR $= 19.3\%$

This accumulation of initial-failure-rate statistics supports the Foundation's contention that there is no significant clinical difference between initial failure rates returned from treating the sexually dysfunctional man and the sexually inadequate woman, when a dual-sex team is employed as the basic ingredient of the treatment program.

Total (male and female): $N = 790$; $F = 142$; IFR $= 18.9\%$.

In essence, there has been a one-in-five initial failure rate in treatment of the sexually dysfunctional man or woman accepted in referral by the Foundation regardless of his or her type of sexual inadequacy. It must be emphasized that this figure only represents the level of statistical failure to reverse symptoms of a specific sexual inadequacy during the two-week rapid-treatment phase of the program.

Of equal import is the composite or overall failure rate determined by five-year follow-up of patients. What percentage of men and women revert to prior patterns of sexual inadequacy in the five-year control period after exposure to the Foundation's treatment procedures? Do men revert more frequently than women? Is there a specific form of sexual dysfunction that has a greater tendency to retrogress subsequent to presumedly effective treatment than any other form of sexual inadequacy?

The statistics of six years of the five-year follow-up period are presented with pertinent comment.

In order to provide a full picture of the five-year follow-up concept, statistical control techniques will be described briefly. In this vein, it must be restated that patients determined to be clinical failures during the rapid-treatment phase of the program have not been included in the follow-up observations. The investigators, though fully cognizant of the specific values that would accrue from such a study, felt that continued attempts to follow cases of acknowledged treatment failure might prejudice the success of further attempts at symptom reversal sought from other clinical sources. Therefore, with reluctance, marital units or single individuals acknowledged to be clinical-therapy failures were not followed after termination of the rapid-treatment phase.

The years 1959 through 1964 will be reviewed (Tables 10, 11, 12) to provide the rapid-treatment failure rates, statistical distribution both by sex and by complaint category, treatment reversal rates (initial symptom removal, but reversal to sexual dysfunction during the subsequent five years), and overall failure-rate statistics obtained by combining the acute-treatment failures with the follow-up treatment reversal cases in a final classification to represent the incidence of program-treatment failures.

STATISTICS ON THE FIRST SIX YEARS OF THE CLINICAL POPULATION

In the original population of 215 marital units, there were 129 units with unilateral partner complaint of sexual inadequacy, and 86 units with bilateral partner distress. Therefore, a total of 301 cases of sexual dysfunction were treated in the 215 marital units referred for therapy for sexual inadequacy. There were, in addition, 12 single individuals (11 men, 1 woman) referred for treatment during the same clinical observation period. Thus, a total population of 313 individual cases of sexual inadequacy were accepted for treatment during the years 1959–64 inclusive.

There were 39 marital units in which failure of immediate treatment occurred (*F* column in Table 10). These units were arbitrarily removed from follow-up. There were 24 unilateral-partner-involvement and 15 bilateral-partner-involvement problems in these 39 marital units removed from follow-up because of initial failure

TABLE 10

Marital Units in Treatment Population, 1959–1964

Year	N	F	AFU	LFU	FU
1959	26	6	20	1	19
1960	34	6	28	2	26
1961	39	5	34	3	31
1962	40	8	32	6	26
1963	45	8	37	6	31
1964	31	6	25	3	22
Total	215	39	176	21	155

N = marital units referred for treatment.
F = immediate treatment failures.
AFU = marital units theoretically available to follow-up.
LFU = marital units lost to follow-up.
FU = marital units followed for five years.

in treatment success. Thus 54 individual cases were lost to the extended-observation series due to initial treatment failure.

Of clinical interest is the fact that although all 15 marital units with bilateral partner involvement in sexual dysfunction are reported as failures, in each unit there was reversal of inadequacy for one of the marital partners during the rapid-treatment program. There was no way to follow the partner whose symptoms were reversed without involving the one unsuccessfully treated; therefore, the 15 marital units were removed from follow-up procedures.

Thus 15 initially successful rapid-treatment cases were lost to follow-up by the arbitrary decision not to follow, for their own protection, marital units with a partner described as a clinical treatment failure. For example, a marital unit was referred in which the husband was a severe premature ejaculator and the wife had the complaint of primary orgasmic dysfunction. The husband's ejaculatory control was established but the wife was not orgasmic during the rapid-treatment phase. When this unit was not followed in order to protect the initial treatment failure (the wife), the initial treatment success (the husband) was immediately lost to statistical survey. There was no satisfactory way to avoid this loss of statistically positive follow-up material.

Of course, had there been an instance of dual failure to remove symptoms of sexual dysfunction with the rapid-treatment techniques in a single marital unit, the statistics in Column *F* would have been favorably prejudiced. Such a dual initial treatment failure did not occur in any marital unit during the six years under follow-up control. Therefore, all figures in the *F* column represent a single treatment failure, be it a marital partner or a single individual. Again, every effort has been made to establish a totally conservative approach toward the statistical analysis of the material to be presented.

The *LFU* column totals 21. This represents the marital units lost to follow-up during the five-year control period. In this clinical block of 21 marital units there were 12 with unilateral partner and 9 with bilateral partner sexual dysfunction that had been treated with apparent success during the rapid-treatment phase of the program. Lack of effective follow-up control thus has reduced the available control population by 30 more units.

There were 12 single units treated for sexual inadequacy (not shown in Table 10). Treatment failure with 2 single units was immediate, and one additional unit was lost to follow-up, thus reducing the total number of cases available for five-year evaluation by another three units.

RESULTS OF FIVE-YEAR FOLLOW-UP

Interim follow-up has been conducted by conference-call telephone interview. Although individual marital partners always are instructed to call the Foundation if they encounter sexual distress, there are regularly scheduled calls that include both members of the marital unit and both cotherapists. These calls continue on a specific schedule with lengthening intervals between conferences, unless sexual dysfunction redevelops. With severe difficulty, the units are, of course, encouraged to return for further treatment. In the first six years, 3 such marital units were retreated successfully and have continued without subsequent reversal to a sexually dysfunctional status. Statistically, however, these 3 units have been included in Table 11B in the treatment-reversal (TR) column because there was initial reversal to sexual dysfunction after treatment.

As an additional point of information, during the six years of five-year follow-up, there were 8 immediate treatment failures that have voluntarily informed Foundation personnel of spontaneous reversal of their symptoms of sexual inadequacy shortly after termination of the rapid-treatment program. Five women (3 primarily and 2 situationally nonorgasmic) reported orgasmic attainment in periods ranging from 72 hours to five months after treatment. Three men (1 primarily and 2 secondarily impotent) established patterns of successful sexual function within reported intervals of six weeks to six months after rapid-treatment program. None of these 8 individuals were exposed to other forms of psychotherapeutic support in the interim between termination of the two-week treatment program and their spontaneous symptom reversals. Whether there have been other spontaneous reversals of states of sexual dysfunction after failure to achieve a positive return during the acute phase of therapy is unknown. It will be recalled that Foundation policy denies the opportunity of follow-up for rapid-treatment failures.

Obviously, the 8 spontaneous reversals of sexual dysfunction within six months after termination of treatment must still be listed statistically as therapy failures, for there is no positive evidence that Foundation personnel contributed to their symptom removal.

The final five years' evaluation has been established on the basis of personal interviews conducted when possible in or near the marital unit's home environment. These interviews ranged from four-and-a-half to five-and-a-half years after termination of the rapid-treatment phase of the program and were conducted as the cotherapists' traveling schedules permitted. These personal interviews included 226 of the total of 313 sexually dysfunctional men and women to be presented for final review. The remaining 87 individuals were not followed successfully during the control period. However, at the five-year terminating interview period, regardless of prior policy, a specific attempt was made to contact these individuals by telephone. The results of this final follow-up effort were so unsatisfactory they will not be reported. It is on the basis of these final interviews that an ultimate decision as to treatment reversal (TR) was established and opportunity taken to describe the reversal rate (RR) percentage for the follow-up population.

TABLE 11A

Category Distribution of 313 Units Treated, 1959–1964

Complaint	N	KTR
Primary impotence	7	0
Secondary impotence	90	10
Premature ejaculation	74	1
Ejaculatory incompetence	5	0
Total treated male sexual inadequacy	176	11
Primary orgasmic dysfunction	77	2
Situational orgasmic dysfunction	60	3
Total treated female sexual inadequacy	137	5
Totals	313	16

N = units referred for treatment.
KTR = known treatment reversal.

TABLE 11B

Established Five-Year Follow-Up, 1959–1964

N	TR	RR (%)
226	16	7.1

N = total units with successful five-year follow-up.
TR = treatment reversal.
RR = reversal rate.

It is clear that once the sexual inadequacies of primary impotence, premature ejaculation, ejaculatory incompetence, primary and situational orgasmic dysfunction are reversed during the rapid-treatment phase of the therapy program, these inadequacies rarely return to distress the person previously sexually handicapped.

It is equally clear that the same clinical position cannot be supported when the initial complaint is secondary impotence. A reversal rate of 10–15 percent during five-year follow-up after treatment for any sexual dysfunction would indeed be a warning light for any clinician. This figure indicates that more work is needed to refine initial treatment techniques and establish levels of patient confidence in sexual performance well beyond the Foundation's current clinical return.

Inevitably, the basic clinical values returned from the long-range follow-up of treated patients emphasize errors in psychosocial conditioning of the patient and indicate shortcomings in clinical understanding and treatment concepts as well. There is no excuse for the lack of a long-maintained, professional "look-in-the-mirror" concept as an integral part of all investigations of new techniques of clinical treatment. *For that matter, long-range reviews of results returned from any established psychotherapeutic technique are always in order.*

For Foundation purposes, any rate of specific symptom recurrence above a 5 percent level during the five-year follow-up period is clinically unacceptable, if the number of treated individuals has reached the level of a statistically significant population. Statistical significance has not been attained in two of the treatment categories—primary impotence and ejaculatory incompetence.

It is obvious that with the exception of secondary impotence, there is not a significant sex-linked difference in treatment-reversal rates returned during the extended five-year observation.

TABLE 12

Failure Rate Summary

Complaint	N	F	IFR (%)	TR	OFR (%)
Primary impotence	32	13	40.6	0	40.6
Secondary impotence	213	56	26.3	10	30.9
Premature ejaculation	186	4	2.2	1	2.7
Ejaculatory incompetence	17	3	17.6	0	17.6
Male totals	448	76	16.9	11	19.4
Primary orgasmic dysfunction	193	32	16.6	2	17.6
Situational orgasmic dysfunction	149	34	22.8	3	24.8
Female totals	342	66	19.3	5	20.8
Male and female totals	790	142	18.9	16	20.0

N = units referred for treatment.   TR = treatment reversal.
F = immediate treatment failure.   OFR = overall failure rate.
IFR = initial failure rate.

OVERALL FAILURE RATE

The overall failure rate is presented (Table 12) by combining initial clinical failures (F) during the rapid-treatment phase with known reversals to sexual dysfunction in those patients initially judged as acceptable clinical treatment results (TR). Obviously, without total five-year follow-up of all patients exposed to the rapid-treatment techniques during the entire 11 years of the investigative program, this report is only a suggestive, *not* a statistically secure objective result.

In order to accomplish this material review, it is necessary to return to the original N for total program coverage.

When overall treatment results for the total program are reviewed, it is apparent that the concept suggested in the discussion of the initial-treatment-failure statistics earlier in the chapter is fully supported by 11 years of experience. If all types of referral for sexual dysfunction are considered conjointly, there obviously is no difference in effectiveness of treatment techniques between the sexually inadequate male and the sexually inadequate female, when considering overall treatment results.

However, there also is the specifically embarrassing fact that the overall failure rate in the treatment of secondary impotence for all males referred for treatment, regardless of age, is at the 31 percent level. This glaring evidence of treatment failure represents a specific challenge to Foundation personnel and, for that matter, to all others in the field. There must be marked reduction in this inexcusably high overall failure rate for treatment of secondary impotence.

A statistic that requires interpretation is that of the divorce incidence among the 155 marital units that continued to function effectively in sexual interchange for five years after termination of the acute treatment phase of the program. Nine of these units had either filed for legal separation (5) or were divorced (4) when seen in therapy. Eight of these 9 marital units described ongoing marriages at the final five-year interview.

Including the one failure to reconstitute a marriage from among the 9 legally separated marital partners seen in therapy, there were 4 marital units that had filed for legal separation (1) or were divorced (3) during the five years of follow-up. Both partners of one divorced unit had remarried and were sexually functional in their new marriages. The low divorce incidence in the sexually reconstituted marital units during their five-year observation period is of real interest, particularly when nationally reported levels of divorce incidence are contemplated.

The overall failure statistic for all individuals referred to the Foundation with symptoms of sexual inadequacy is at the 20 percent level. It must be emphasized again that in this suggestive overall review there are only 6, not 11, years of five-years follow-up statistics available. However, since there have been very few clinical reversals of the initial rapid-treatment techniques (except for the secondary impotence category) over the 6 years of five-year follow-up, the results are generally indicative of the return that might be expected for the total research population had sufficient time elapsed for a full review of the entire 11 years of intake. When treatment reversal did occur, it developed within the first 12 months after the acute therapy in at least three out of four cases.

Presuming sufficient financial support and adequate staffing, even if the clinical caseload were quadrupled, not a discernible reduction would be made in the level sea of clinical demand for treatment for human sexual inadequacy. Time and again the Foundation has not been able to meet the legitimate demands of clinical emergency. While there are no significant sociological studies relative to the incidence of sexual dysfunction in this country, a conservative estimate would indicate half the marriages as either presently sexually dysfunctional or imminently so in the future. The Foundation's clinical commitment is but an infinitesimal effort compared to what can and ought to be done to resolve the crippling societal problem of human sexual inadequacy.

Until such time as social mores and societal controls have successfully accepted the concept of the naturalness of sexual function instead of supporting taboo and fallacy-worn misconceptions, the only hope for population protection is a major postgraduate training program to develop seminar leaders for therapy training centers throughout the country.

15

TREATMENT FAILURES

Since there really is no acceptable excuse for failure, this section is written not in apology but in an attempt to underscore professional shortcomings and to emphasize problems of therapeutic judgment. As an integral part of every textbook dealing with therapeutic concepts and/or clinical techniques as methodological approaches to patient distress there should be a considered report of experience with limitations of concepts and technique, and of methodological failures. This chapter is such a report.

Inevitably, there were failed opportunities on both the patient's and the therapist's sides of the fence. There were instances of lack of sufficient patient motivation and/or psychosexual maturity to accept therapeutic direction. Total disaffection with mate, intense anxiety states, deliberate dissimulation, and revenge motifs clashed with therapeutic process. There were instances of therapist error in judgment, in clinical objectivity, and occasionally even in emotional control.

Foundation personnel have not been able to evaluate all failures (of patient or cotherapist) objectively. The intangibles of personal interaction preclude an unprejudiced review, but conscious effort has been made to profit from mistakes. Review sessions with personnel, discussion of clinical problems, and staff evaluations of therapeutic progress are indeed important sources of self-criticism. Such sessions are conducted as informal seminars on a daily basis by the professional staff of the Foundation.

One of the significant difficulties in the screening process is initial identification and subsequent elimination from admission to the Foundation's short-term educational program those marital units traumatized in such depth that there literally is no chance for reconstitution of an effective marital relationship (see Chapter

1). Time and again marital units have been referred that, in theory or in fact, have been moving toward legal separation when first seen in therapy and, time and again, these marital units have been reconstituted as psychosexually effective men and women with on-going marriages. There is an occasional situation, however, that escapes therapeutic endeavor. It is simply a question of entirely too little or much too late in the way of therapeutic contribution. No reliable measures to eliminate this type of referral have been established.

When a marital unit escapes protective screening and approaches the Foundation under the guise of an appeal for reversal of an established sexual dysfunction, frequently total disaffection with mate and revenge motifs are tied together by deliberate dissimulation. In order to illustrate areas of concern adequately, composite histories are presented to insure anonymity but not to prejudice factual material.

Mr. and Mrs. A joined the Foundation's treatment program with statement from referral source that there was a significant level of animosity between the two marital partners, their communication in and out of bed had been destroyed, and it was hoped that two weeks of mutual education and objective self-criticism might reconstitute the functional status of the marriage.

When seen in consultation, the husband was 43 and the wife 41 years of age. There were three children, a boy 15, and two girls, 12 and 10 years old. The unit, married 17 years, was in comfortable financial circumstances and socially quite active in their community.

Mr. A had been, and at consultation was, a premature ejaculator of severe proportion. Both husband and wife had a moderate degree of sexual experience before marriage. Mrs. A had been orgasmic with masturbatory techniques from early teenage years and on several occasions during intercourse in her late teens and her early twenties. She had been engaged for six months prior to meeting Mr. A, during which time she was routinely orgasmic with coital opportunity.

Mr. A's initial sexual exposures were of the usual time-pressured variety, so characteristic of the premature ejaculator's sexual history. But since no long-range personal commitment with coital opportunity had developed prior to marriage, he was unaware of any female-partner disaffection with his effectiveness of sexual functioning.

From onset there was no orgasmic return in the marriage for Mrs. A except that produced by her own masturbatory effort. She became progressively more frustrated attempting to cope with the consistently high degree of sexual dysfunction in her marriage. Finally, after ten years of marriage she was able to prevail upon her reluctant husband to seek professional consultation. A psychotherapeutic program was instituted and conducted for three years with only a moderate degree of cooperation from the husband. There was no significant change in his premature ejaculatory pattern.

Approximately four years before consultation with the Foundation, Mrs. A demanded separate bedrooms. Her reasons included a statement of facts: that her husband's sexual functioning had not improved under therapy, that continuation of sexual interchange provided her only with consistently high levels of sexual frustration, and that they both agreed that the three children represented sufficient size for their family. While declaring her bed off-limits, she stated that the only measure of physical recourse left was masturbation and that she preferred to establish the privacy necessary to accomplish her own tension release satisfactorily.

For two years Mr. A attempted to reconstitute an ongoing sexual relationship within the marriage, but ran into a blank wall of sexual rejection. He then sought sexual release outside the marriage. There were three different women involved over a six-months period before any sense of permanency in a sexual relationship was established. He evidenced incredibly poor judgment in establishing this semipermanent sexual connection with his wife's best friend, recently widowed. A few months later he committed the cardinal sin of getting caught. He was accidentally confronted by friends while leaving a local motel with his sexual partner. Needless to say, report of the embarrassing confrontation was immediately forwarded to his wife and eagerly disseminated in mutual social circles.

Mrs. A's fury knew no bounds. Her husband was peremptorily ejected from the home, and she sought both legal and psychotherapeutic support. After a period of time, a measure of superficial calm was restored. It was the psychotherapist, playing the mediator role, who reconstituted the marriage at a social level. Although Mr. A returned home, opportunity for sexual functioning was still denied. It was again this authority that referred them to the Foundation for treatment.

At onset, there was no clinical question of the depth of this wife's anger, resentment, and wounded pride. The vehemence of her response seemed pathological in its intensity. However, the cotherapists unrealistically accepted the concept that, if effectual sexual functioning could be reconstituted, other aspects of the marital disaffection might be forgiven or at least viewed from a less judgmental approach. The decision represented a combination of errors in objectivity and in judgment, for Mrs. A's resentment was unlimited, reflecting disillusion with the total of the marriage. The depth of her feeling was not evaluated properly by Foundation personnel.

She had joined the program with her husband specifically to extract her "pound of flesh." She wanted to be certain that he continued at a completely inadequate level sexually, not only in her eyes but also in the view of duly constituted authority; so she set about proving her point from onset of the first sessions in sensate focus. She was totally cooperative until after the application of the "squeeze technique" (Chapter 3), which produced relatively immediate results in ejaculatory control. Then her attitude literally changed overnight. Suddenly she could not understand or would not follow directions. The bemused cotherapists could not understand how such explicit directions, previously followed exactly, could either be misinterpreted or ignored by an obviously intelligent woman. There had been no previous clinical experience of similar nature.

The first positive inkling of the real depth of Mrs. A's resentment developed the third day the squeeze technique was employed. She stimulated penile erection as directed, but instead of helping her husband control the ejaculatory process with the squeeze technique, she manipulated forcefully, demanding full ejaculatory response rather than trying to establish control. Embarrassing as it is to relate, it was the third time this deliberate perversion of carefully explained procedural technique had occurred before the clinical realization dawned.

Mrs. A readily admitted to the cotherapists when faced in private session that her main reason for coming to the Foundation was to prove to her husband that he was and always would be sexually inadequate, so that when she chose to divorce him, as she had every intention of doing at her discretion, he would be most hesitant to consider remarriage in view of his established sexual disability. If Mr. A had not been making significant progress toward ejaculatory control, she would not have made any move that would give her intent away, but with obvious therapeutic progress came demand for decision, and from her point of view there could be only one decision.

Her disaffection was endlessly deep. She considered her husband less than a man because he had not been able to satisfy her sexually, and nothing could shake this conviction. In her eyes his adultery was completely inexcusable, particularly because he had been caught with her best friend, and to her complete embarrassment word had been widely circulated socially. That her husband had chosen her best friend for continuing sexual companionship was, to her, a deliberate attempt to belittle and to degrade her as a woman. She was convinced that he had really planned the series of events, including the motel encounter, as a means of revenge for her closed bedroom door.

Even following her voluntary public confession of resentment, anger, and desire for revenge, and the involuntary exposure of her paranoid tendencies, she could not be reached in therapy. Every effort was made to reconstitute an ongoing relationship within the marriage, but failure was complete. Mrs. A was adamant that she would have no part of reconstituting the marriage. She wanted termination at all costs plus the "pleasure" of the ultimate destruction of her husband's masculinity. Her only real frustration during the unit's visit to the Foundation was the fact that she was not able to convince her husband that his sexual dysfunction was of such magnitude he should not consider remarriage in the future. The cotherapists made it clear to him that his premature ejaculatory status need not remain a permanent disability.

From a therapeutic point of view, there were two basic errors in this situation. First, the total degree of Mrs. A's psychosexual disaffection with her husband and her presenting levels of psychopathology were not evaluated properly by Foundation personnel. Despite numerous interview opportunities, no significant level of clinical suspicion was generated. She quietly verbalized interest in establishing effective sexual function in the marriage and so confused the cotherapists that it was much too long after onset of the clinical program before their lulled suspicions were finally awakened. Second, there must have been premonitory signs; there must have been keys to this problem; there must have been some way to reach her, if not to develop marital confidence, at least for future consideration of her own mental health. But Foundation personnel were unsuccessful in any of these directions.

Although the referral source was briefed at length when the treatment program arbitrarily was terminated, Mrs. A refused to return to her prior means of psychotherapeutic support. She divorced her husband, remarried within six months, and was again divorced less than two years later. She has been lost to even casual follow-up since her second divorce. This woman needed help that the Foundation did not provide, although there was every opportunity to do so.

Mr. A remarried approximately 18 months after the divorce. After six months of marriage, the premature ejaculatory tendency was brought under control with a long-weekend visit to the Foundation by the newly constituted marital unit.

One of the Foundation's serious therapeutic problems is that of relieving individual anxiety without medicating the patient. For many individuals, any tranquilizing medication can be a depressant to effective sexual function (see Chapter 6). As stated, approximately 90 percent of the patients referred for treatment have come from outside of the St. Louis area (see Chapters 1 and 14). Usually appointments for treatment necessitate a waiting period of several months. Under these circumstances, progressively increasing anxieties become an integral part of the daily life of a marital unit-in-waiting. Innumerable expressions of concern arise, such as: "How can anyone help us?" "How can we get away from family or business?" "How can we keep our friends from knowing where we are going?" "What excuses can we give?" "How can we afford it?" "If we just wait a little longer maybe things will get better." "How can it be done in two weeks?" And so on.

At least 75 percent of the time the complainee in the marital unit—i.e., the impotent male or the nonorgasmic female—seriously considers withdrawal from the formal commitment to therapy during the waiting period. The remainder of the time the theoretically noninvolved partner usually expresses his or her doubts as to the reasonableness of two weeks of intensive therapy. In short, husband and wife are consistently compounding each other's fears and anxieties. This is particularly true as appointment time is imminent and the die is to be cast.

The strained, drawn faces of men and women approaching Foundation personnel for the first time are graphic indications of the internal tensions created by these fears and anxieties. Voices crack, hands shake and sweat—evidence of the intensity of their self-created tensions. Unfortunately, among these naturally concerned people whose tensions can be resolved, there are occasional individuals that simply cannot be rescued from their anxieties. Their fears of performance are of such magnitude that there seems no way to shake their absolute surety that the particular form of sexual dysfunction cannot be resolved.

The concept that nothing can be done to help is so explicit for many applicants that they may be totally impervious to interpersonal discussions the first two days of actual therapy (following the Roundtable discussion). Usually these situations can be completely relieved or at least markedly alleviated during the first week. There remain, however, occasional individuals whom the cotherapists simply cannot reach and who ultimately must be listed as therapeutic failures. Obviously there are fears and pressures of performance artificially elevated to such extent that therapists cannot break through to reorient functional concepts.

Severe anxieties center upon grave fears that material of sexual connotation, personally considered as totally restrictive in content, might be initially unearthed and subsequently inadvertently released to one's husband or wife by the cotherapists. Occasionally the therapy program may be slowed almost to a standstill before it is apparent that there has been withholding of vital information. Such an occurrence means that the cotherapists have not caught the signals emanating from the beleaguered sexual partner striving to retain his or her confidential information at all costs. When routine history-taking explores attitudinal concepts, sexual confidence, and sexual experience (see Chapter 2), the patient's sensitive areas are inevitably touched upon. His increased anxiety, as presumably he is threatened by the investigator, should alert the experienced observer. There is no need, however, to rush in pursuit of the elusive material. The area in question can be returned to in a dozen different ways, giving the patient encouragement to provide the key to his or her confidential information before ultimately there is authoritative need for confrontation. If such withholding is suspected, there must be a private confrontation before significant therapeutic progress can be anticipated.

At this point in time the involved partner may have to decide whether to release his or her presumedly inadmissible material or to have the Foundation personnel acknowledge inadequacy to deal with the particular problem and terminate the therapeutic program. There have been only four instances of the latter choice.

Having established the existence and quality of the material creating the stumbling-block, it may be relatively easy for authority to work around the restricted information, and continue therapy while protecting the concerned marital partner. At least two-thirds of the time it is possible to circumnavigate the area of personal concern, protecting material and sources, and still attain a positive treatment result. Nevertheless, there are times when this restrictive material must be exchanged between marital partners, if there is to be therapeutic progress. This is a crucial stage in the therapy program. Obviously the confidential information cannot be exchanged without the specifically involved patient's full permission. The question that inevitably arises to confront the beleaguered wife or husband is whether the sexual continuity of the marriage is more important than protecting the confessional material. At this stage of therapy, severe levels of anxiety and fears for self-image and for marital future loom enormously in fantasy and are most difficult to assuage.

The decision confronting the cotherapists is made more complex by the necessity of going beyond theoretical concept. The fearful partner potentially has more conclusive knowledge of the husband's (wife's) ability to accept the restricted information with objectivity. This fact must be given consideration by the cotherapists.

For 7 years before her marriage at the age of 23, Mrs. B had been living in an incestuous relationship with her father, presumably appeasing his sexual demands to prevent similar abuse of a younger sister. It is to be expected that she might find her husband's sexual approaches frightening, unstimulating, or even revolting after eight years of marriage. She was terrified at the thought of having the protectively raised, well-educated, professional man that was her husband try to cope with the knowledge of long-established incest.

Mr. C, a 33-year-old businessman with acknowledged homosexual response patterns dating back to his twelfth year, married primarily as social protection a virginal girl, obviously sincerely in love with him. It is not surprising that he has been primarily impotent and unable to consummate a five-year marriage.

Yet both marriages were referred for therapy. The professional man's wife (Mrs. B) with total rejection of male sexual approach, and the young businessman (Mr. C) with primary impotence, are indeed serious problems in sexual dysfunction. If there can be no release of the background information, how does one constitute a continuing pattern of effective sexual functioning? How can the sexually rejected and sexually frustrated marital partners come to understand the years of rejection by their mates and look with some confidence for relief of their own frustrating sexual tensions if no information is exchanged? There is little to be gained by dissimulation with intelligent people when sexual responsivity is concerned, and yet so much can be lost for all parties if no therapeutic progress can be made after release of confidential information. Each therapeutic gamble must be individualized and evaluated carefully; not to gamble at times is indeed poor therapy.

When unshared confidential information creates fears of performance, how does one educate to sexual effectiveness without considering all factors involved? How can individual marriages be judged sufficiently stable and of significant value to warrant an open discussion? When should the cotherapists beg the question and admit inability to resolve the problem of sexual dysfunction in order to protect the security information?

The businessman (Mr. C) and his wife are from a moderate-sized town where one of the larger industries is owned by the girl's father. The husband's family also is well-established in the community. Almost all his homosexual experiences have been outside the local area, in schools or during vacation. Can he now risk local spread of knowledge of his homophile orientation by a frustrated wife if, after a confrontation session, she either rejects him as a marital partner or the therapeutic program proves unsuccessful and the marriage is not consummated satisfactorily? If she withdraws from the union for any reason, she may feel free to discuss "their problem" presumably in self-defense before the inevitable judgment of the local community. These are subtleties that build anxieties of major proportion for any individual.

If the professional man (Mr. B) discovers that his presumedly virginal bride had been having intercourse with her father for years before their marriage, can he tolerate the ego-shattering impact of the basic reason for his wife's sexual rejection of him as a male or deal with his own visceral reaction to the nature of the information? Is he stable enough as an individual personality to be objective in this situation? From a therapeutic point of view, it is of vital import to decide whether to demand information exchange or whether to admit therapeutic inadequacy to reverse the symptomatology of the specific sexual dysfunction, allowing the unit to return to their home as therapeutic failures from a sexual functioning point of view, but with the information protected and the marriage presumably intact. After all, the Foundation's primary goal is to treat the marital relationship. Either way, risks are great but costs may be even greater. It is so easy to make the wrong decision. The easy way out, of course, is to declare the treatment inadequate and beg the question.

Although the frightened woman (Mrs. B) finally gave permission to release her story of incest, it was arbitrarily decided that her husband might not have enough confidence in his own sexuality or sexual functioning to accept his wife's restricted information in a mature manner. Her abject terror at the possibility of information exchange obviously was a determining factor and the source of professional loss of objectivity. Thus there was reported clinical failure to accomplish orgasmic return. There was no way to orient the sexually repelled wife to adequacy of sexual function without discussing her ever-present fantasy of coition with her father whenever her husband approached.

In retrospect, the decision seems to have been the wrong one. The wife's status as a sexually nonresponsive woman has been unacceptable to her husband. Mr. B, like so many other men, considers a sexually nonresponsive wife as not only a source of personal rejection, but continuing evidence of his own failure to function effectively in a masculine role. To relieve his own sense of sexual inadequacy there has been a succession of women openly led to bed to prove his masculinity. Mrs. B, tragically enough, is pathetically grateful for his acceptance of her even as a second-class wife.

The cotherapists should not have been swayed by Mrs. B's abject terror and allowed the situation to escape control. When a cotherapist's lack of objectivity plays a part in a decision, he can only hope for the best because he certainly no longer can claim a nonprejudiced viewpoint. This woman might have been salvaged as an effective human being and the marriage constituted on a secure basis had Foundation personnel taken a more positive attitude. Instead, the easy way out was taken. As a result, Mr. B got little from therapy, his wife got even less, and the marriage exists on a social basis only.

The decision was made to discuss Mr. C's past homosexual experiences openly after reluctant permission finally was granted by the highly anxious husband. Mrs. C accepted the situation with equanimity. The background of his homophile orientation was explained and understood, and her cooperation while in the rapid-treatment program was total. He developed real interest in heterosexual functioning and the mariage was consummated during the acute phase of therapy. There are now children in the home and the husband is functioning most effectively in a heterosexual manner without return of homosexual demand. This short-term result supports the decision to put the restricted information before the wife and ask her immediate understanding, support, and long-term cooperation. How she will react when her son grows into adolescence and she recalls her husband's penchant for homosexual relations with young boys is yet another matter. There must be long-term follow-up in such a situation.

A 20-year marriage of a middle-aged man and wife (Mr. and Mrs. D) was destroyed by allowing both of the concerned partners to influence therapeutic procedure. The wife had never been orgasmic. The husband, aware of his poor record as an effective sexual performer in the marriage, additionally reported occasions of impotence in the last few years before consultation. However, he continued to be most interested in his wife as a sexual entity. His was a restrictive background; he had been virginal at marriage and his knowledge of sexual functioning was frighteningly inadequate. The wife, also with negligible sexual experience before marriage, had expected her husband to be the expert. Over the years they had been mutually frustrated by their sexual inadequacy. There had been no children, but there had been a real warmth between these two people until their sexually dysfunctional status gradually tore them apart.

Following the usual pattern, there developed, from a postcoital state of frequent tears from the wife and repeated apologies by the husband, multiple excuses to avoid sexual opportunity and, of course, progressive loss of interpersonal communication. Yet, the only true sexual difficulty for this marital unit was lack of knowledge necessary for effective sexual functioning.

In the three or four years before referral to the Foundation, both partners in desperation had sought sexual release outside the marriage with more experienced partners. For the husband there were several different women without any significant personal identification and therefore little improvement in psychosexual attitudes. His sexual gratification had always been of paramount importance, and this was accomplished. For the wife, however, there was one continuing extramarital episode with very real personal identification in that a sense of permanency was established in the relationship, even though there was no opportunity for marriage since the man involved was her religious adviser. She was consistently orgasmic in this extramarital relationship.

Both Mr. and Mrs. D, living with severe levels of guilt, finally sought professional advice in the hope of developing some effectiveness of mutual sexual functioning and of reconstituting their marriage—something they both sincerely wanted. When referred to the Foundation by a local professional, each marital partner was afraid that the other would come to know of the adulterous behavior. Each blindly refused the cotherapists permission to discuss the background of the reasons, causes, and events leading to the visitation of other bedrooms. Yet, when they were seen in referral, both local professional and Foundation personnel were fully convinced that theirs was a potentially effective marriage and that both partners sincerely wanted some direction that would enable them to give of themselves fully in their interpersonal relationships.

The Foundation made the mistake of attempting detailed therapy for sexual dysfunction while allowing each patient to maintain his or her own informational security. The failure to constitute effectiveness of sexual functioning was indeed complete. No stable interpersonal communication was ever established. During every therapy session each severely anxious partner was constantly concerned with protecting his or her own experiential isolation rather than moving toward one another in a free exchange of vulnerabilities. While responding to communicative exchange in a pattern of anxious self-protection, the partners developed no mutuality of sexual expression. Each fantasied the extramarital sexual partner when attempting to respond to sexual direction at the Foundation. As a result of a constant "I–me" desire for personal attention in therapy, the wife has not been orgasmic within the marriage in the several years that have followed visitation to the Foundation and has lost much of her original level of response to her religious adviser. The husband has noted definite increase in frequency of episodes of erective failure both in and out of marriage.

The marriage slowly disintegrated and moved to the divorce courts. In retrospect, had sufficient information been exchanged to relieve their intense anxieties and to enlist a return of interpersonal communication, there is every reason to believe that in view of their mutual level of sexual responsivity outside the marriage and the definitive residual of interpersonal concern present at the time of therapy, the innate levels of their mutual responsivity could have been concentrated in the marital bed. Each partner requested and received permission to remain in contact with the Foundation. From these talks came the information stated above.

Mr. and Mrs. D had a great deal to lose by maintaining their informational security, and they were allowed to lose it by the cotherapists involved. Foundation personnel should have been able to get through to both members of this marital unit the full concept of what they were doing to themselves, let alone to each other. In large measure inadequacy of clinical judgment evidenced by Foundation personnel terminated a marriage.

Occasionally, excellence of a patient response can obscure professional objectivity just as apparent personal failure can influence therapeutic judgment.

Mr. and Mrs. E, 37 and 34 years of age, respectively, married 10 years with two girls aged 8 and 5, were referred to the Foundation. There were dysfunctional complaints of severe premature ejaculation and primary nonorgasmic status.

These marital partners, both college graduates, felt that they had a basically good marriage with the exception of the wife's high level of postcoital frustration and the husband's very real sense of sexual inadequacy. He was well aware of his premature ejaculatory status and had tried every means known to him in an effort to slow the ejaculatory process. As usual, his ploys had been unsuccessful.

This most cooperative couple progressed excellently. They had attained from 30 to 45 minutes of ejaculatory control with intravaginal containment five to six days after joining the Foundation. Eight days after the initial intake interview, Mrs. E was orgasmic with coital activity for the first time in her life. These two people were delighted with the results and were discharged from the Foundation's rapid-treatment program nine days after their arrival. This was a major error in judgment by Foundation personnel; for the husband became secondarily impotent within 48 hours after dismissal from the program.

Experience has taught that occasionally, as an established premature ejaculator develops control to the extent that he is able to satisfy his sexual partner completely during coital functioning, he may go through a transitory phase of secondary impotence (see Chapter 3). When under the psychological stress of recovery from a long-continued state of sexual inadequacy, his fears of performance may be fleetingly transferred from concern for control to concern for erection. In sexual dysfunction, years of established fears for performance are not necessarily lost with rapid symptom reversal.

After a premature ejaculator gains control, there still must be a period of transition before full sexual functioning is assured. This episode of excitement and pleasure with newly gained control also is a period when secondary impotence can develop rapidly if the marital unit is not forewarned of a possible pitfall they might face. Delighted with the mutuality of their newly established physical responsivity, both husband and wife may cohabit so frequently that the male partner temporarily may lose his facility for erection because of the satiation involved in functioning at previously unaccustomed levels of coital frequency.

Had Mr. and Mrs. E been retained under Foundation control for another three or four days, or forewarned of the possibility of circumstantial erective distress, the episodic secondary impotence would have been detected when it occurred and probably resolved without incident by adequate explanation. As it was, the secondary impotence developed two days after the unit's return home. Despite warnings to call if trouble developed, it was another ten days before husband and wife sought help, during which time Mr. E was repetitively impotent when attempting to respond to his wife's enthusiastic sexual demands. Both individuals worked frantically to accomplish erection and, frightened that something had gone seriously wrong, developed mutual fears of performance. They thought the impotence might be a permanent result of learning ejaculatory control, and by the time they notified the Foundation of their particular distress they were indeed terror-stricken.

Despite return to the Foundation for supplemental treatment for the secondary impotence, Mr. E's fears of performance have continued. He is fully impotent on occasion and has less than full erection at other opportunities. Mrs. E firmly believes that her period of uncontrolled sexual demand is fully responsible for her husband's developing symptoms of secondary impotence despite hours spent in post-factum explanation to the marital unit. As a result, added to Mr. E's stressful situation is the reduction in direct stimulative approach from his partner caused by her fear of showing any response which she feels might be construed as demand. Had these people been retained in therapy for a satisfactory length of time or forewarned of possible complications, symptoms of secondary impotence, as they developed, could have been easily explained and effectively counterbalanced. There need not have been an unfortunate residual to therapy.

Foundation personnel learned the valuable lesson that clinical judgment must not be swayed by mutual delight with a rapid "cure." Certainly the less-than-effective treatment result is directly attributable to professional judgmental error. It remains a necessary rule of therapeutic procedure that the "cure" must be developed within the psychosexual context of the patients' own lives and that they must understand fully the nature of the biophysical and psychosocial changes made. When both patient and therapist are influenced by mere symptom reversal and forget that there is a man, a woman, and a marital state to treat in addition to the overt symptomatology of sexual dysfunction, less than satisfactory results inevitably accrue.

One of the major problems in rapid treatment to reverse symptoms of sexual dysfunction is contending with an antipathy toward therapists in general and to those in authority at the Foundation in particular. Many of the sexually dysfunctional men and women have had major degrees of psychotherapy before referral for symptom removal (see Chapter 14) and they may have become therapeutic nihilists.

In one such situation, Dr. and Mrs. F were both in their midforties, with one child, an 18-year-old daughter from a 22-year marriage, when referred for primary nonorgasmic status. He was a physician with a tremendously demanding practice. Although he was basically quite adequate sexually, over a period of years many other areas of concern had been given more attention than marital sexual functioning. Before marriage there were several casual sexual opportunities but no personal identification. After marriage there was no significant history other than complete dedication to his work with concomitant reduction of time to devote to his family and his wife.

Mrs. F had two years of college and was quite active in the social activities of the city in which they live. Before marriage she had intercourse on two occasions without orgasmic return. After marriage she busied herself with many community projects to distract from a constantly maintained level of sexual frustration. She sought relief from four different psychotherapists (two psychiatrists, a psychologist, and a religious adviser) in the course of the marriage, moving from one to the other seeking "the secret" of orgasmic release. There had been no treatment success.

As her negative exposure to therapists developed, paralleling her negative experience with the time-consuming demands of the medical profession, her antipathy increased to all things authoritative, particularly those with a medical background. She blamed the profession of medicine (probably correctly) for her sexual dysfunction, presumably because it made excessive demands of time and personal commitment upon her husband.

When Dr. and Mrs. F were seen in consultation, she had completely rejected him as a man and as a husband, feeling that he had no interest in her as an individual. In addition, apparently sensitized by a traumatic experience in prior psychotherapy, she was certain that medical authority would immediately take her husband's side in any therapeutic approach to their mutual problem of sexual dysfunction.

Antipathy toward psychotherapy had reached such a degree that she came to the Foundation with extreme reluctance, yielding ultimately, but with little grace, to her husband's many requests for a final attempt to establish an effective pattern of sexual functioning in the marriage. During the intake interviews she was barely civil, lashing out at the medical profession in general and her cotherapists in particular; during roundtable discussion she expressed her resentment of all things professional in a vehement tirade, a good deal of which probably was well-founded. The atmosphere was of uncontrolled emotion and deepseated prejudice. The specific therapeutic difficulties involved acknowledging and understanding her resentment, not taking sides with the husband, and yet not losing all authoritative balance.

Personnel at the Foundation, understanding her prejudicial background, tried to temporize and to continue the therapeutic program with objectivity despite the woman's constant attacks. As therapy progressed, Mrs. F initially was encouraged in the fact that her sexual tensions were elevating and her physical responsivity obviously increasing. On the eighth day, having fallen into a violent argument with her husband over a trivial matter, she immediately returned to her previously rigid, unresponsive, castigating attitude toward sexual function.

By the next day she was fully convinced that there was no hope for her as a sexually responsive individual and was totally unreceptive to the concept that mistakes had to be made during the two-week period at the Foundation if lessons were to be learned (see Chapter 1). Suspecting the motives of the cotherapists involved, Mrs. F, in the bitterness of her disappointment, viciously attacked them as charlatans and accused them of taking sides with her husband in the therapeutic program.

Instead of quietly accepting the attack, understanding the motivation and attempting to get through to the patient, Foundation personnel, caught up in the emotional storm, possibly sensitized by the consistency of prior attack, lost professional objectivity and discharged the patients.

This was an inexcusable professional blunder, for had some objectivity been retained this marital unit probably could have been helped to effective sexual responsivity. Regardless of the emotional tirade and the level of vituperation, and particularly in view of the obvious degree of exposed psychopathology, there is no excuse for the cotherapist's losing emotional control in response to attack. This is exactly what happened and, embarrassingly, professional loss of emotional equanimity may have cost this marital unit their opportunity for effectiveness of sexual responsivity and an ongoing marriage. This marriage ended in divorce.

There is a category that must be listed as therapeutic malpractice. In some instances malpractice is indeed a kind word. This category has been divided into two general divisions: first, those therapists referring patients but requesting or insisting upon frequent reports from the patients during the therapy, then taking advantage of the opportunity by telephone to provide their own personal interpretation of therapeutic progress or failure; second, those therapists, male and female alike, that take gross advantage of their authoritative role to seduce their patients into sexual interchange.

Mr. and Mrs. G were 46 and 41, respectively, when referred for therapy. They had two children, a girl 18 and a boy 15, in a 20-year marriage. Mrs. G had never been orgasmic. Neither husband nor wife provided a positive history of extramarital sexual exposure. The husband, a successful businessman, had functioned adequately within the sexual context of the marriage. He had real need of knowledge of effective sexual functioning, as he was uninformed and inexperienced when married, but otherwise could not be specifically faulted as the primary cause of his wife's nonorgasmic status.

Mrs. G was the only child of a wealthy family. Her mother committed suicide when she was 13; her father remarried a woman with whom Mrs. G could not or would not establish an ongoing relationship. In retrospect, the fault in the constant combat between the only female child and the second wife seemed to be equally divided between them. At age 15 the girl lost a year of school while being treated for a "nervous breakdown."

Mrs. G had never masturbated, had few acquaintances of either sex, and was totally uncomfortable with any manner of sexual material. She was a markedly introverted, socially insecure, 21-year-old virgin at marriage. She married an attractive extrovert with a good education, little money, and a driving ambition for success in the business world.

Mrs. G's wedding night was her first exposure to the sexual realities. She was painfully penetrated, reacted with fear, tried to withdraw but was repetitively mounted by a sexually demanding husband. After a month of repeated painful coital connection, although refusing to see a physician, she began avoiding sexual exposure as much as possible. The two children were planned, but there was little else in their interpersonal relationship designed to maintain any constancy of sexual interchange.

In a short time, Mr. G lost most of his sexual interest in his wife, feeling that the sexual return from the inevitable battle to coerce her into bed was not worth the effort involved. Over the next decade he concentrated on a successful business career to the exclusion of his wife and thereby compounded her obvious lack of personal security into complete loss of self-confidence. She was fully convinced that she would never be able to function adequately as the wife of an ambitious, successful young man. The marriage degenerated into a friendly "roommate" type of relationship, with Mrs. G avoiding a woman's role in social and sexual exposure as much as possible.

After approximately 15 years of marriage, her husband had achieved a significant amount of professional recognition and then turned again to his marriage. As many men before him, he expected the marriage to mature on order and to function to mutual enhancement of husband and wife when he so ordained. Nothing like this occurred, for by this time Mrs. G, seeking help from her third psychotherapist, had achieved with this professional a significant amount of personal security and a sense of protection. With psychotherapeutic sessions several times a week devoted to alleviating her insecurities and her sexual frustrations, she developed a tremendous level of personal identification with her therapist. The following four years were devoted to psychotherapeutic attempts to reconstitute a personality and to provide her with strength to cope with her concerns for personal inadequacy.

Finally Mr. G consulted his own psychotherapist in the hope of constituting effective sexual functioning in the marriage and was referred with his wife to the Foundation. Mrs. G's therapist would not approve the referral; therefore the Foundation did not accept the patients in therapy. After six months of discussion between the two therapists, the wife's therapist agreed that she should accompany her husband in an attempt to constitute effective sexual functioning within the marriage.

However, a private arrangement between patient and therapist had been established without knowledge of Foundation personnel. Mrs. G was to report to her psychotherapist daily at termination of her sessions with Foundation professionals to seek guidance and an interpretation of the therapy as it progressed. Several times in the course of the first 11 days of treatment cotherapists were amazed at the new interpretations Mrs. G would place on material reviewed and discussed to all parties' satisfaction on the previous day. The new interpretations frequently would be followed by alternative suggestions as to proper therapeutic approaches to effectiveness of sexual functioning. In certain situations she refused sexual cooperation, never suggesting refusal during conferences, but always taking a stand when alone with her husband. At other times, her demands for immediate psychosexual return were far beyond her stage of capability.

Still the cotherapists did not arrive at causation for this marked variation in behavior pattern from that expected of the particular personality. Time and again the cotherapists asked themselves what they had missed in their conceptualization of the individual. It was only during an occasion when her usual belated objections to the Foundation's professional approach to the marital unit's problems were couched in psychotherapeutic terms that should have been somewhat foreign to her that the cotherapists became suspicious that there were three therapists attempting to treat Mrs. G simultaneously. Once this possibility was suggested, she confirmed professional suspicions freely with open admission of daily consultation with her psychotherapist. Consequently, the therapeutic program with the Foundation was terminated, and she was returned to prior therapeutic control.

Early in treatment, Foundation personnel were aware that there was an unexplained extraneous influence on Mrs. G's interpretation and response to many therapeutic suggestions. In reporting one daily session, a cotherapist wrote, "She acts like she's on the other team—I wonder who her coach is?" This was on the fifth day of therapy, but it took essentially another week for the suspicions of the professional staff to surface clinically. When the tapes of her interviews were reviewed, there literally was daily evidence of the degree of the extraneous professional influence, but the staff was not receptive to the many hints that developed in the course of each therapeutic session.

There should never be such castration of authority and confusion of patient. It was this case that established a minor point in Foundation policy. If both members of the marital unit are under care of individual psychotherapists, the marital unit will not be received in therapy without verbal and/or written release from both psychotherapists, plus the opportunity for direct interviews by Foundation personnel with both of these professionals.

That every therapist has the primary responsibility for protecting his patient goes without argument. However, when patients are the responsibility of the Foundation, its duly accredited personnel must be in complete control of the projected therapeutic program. Many times patients are referred for symptom removal while in the process of either analysis or long-continued psychotherapy. The Foundation is pleased to cooperate with such programs, and every effort is made to report in detail to the referral sources. But once the patients enter Foundation influence there cannot be "coaches" until termination of the acute phase of therapy. One of the greatest disservices that can be done to patients is to have them pulled by authority in first one direction and then another. Nothing is accomplished except a high level of frustration for the patients involved. Obviously, the established areas of authority for all professionals involved must be identified. Needless to say, therapeutic return in the situation reported above was negligible from a Foundation point of view and, of course, the unit was reported as a failure in treatment for orgasmic dysfunction.

Unfortunately, Foundation personnel frequently encounter during their in-depth interviews reports of tragic psychotherapeutic malpractice, that of the therapist seducing the essentially defenseless patient into mutual sexual experience. While this occurrence is presented under a listing of psychotherapeutic failures, this does not imply that such a situation has developed under Foundation jurisdiction teams; it has not. However, this problem is of such serious import and is encountered by the Foundation with such frequency in patient's histories that it must be mentioned. There is no good place to include consideration of it in textbook format. Therefore, the discussion is arbitrarily placed under the general heading of therapeutic failure, for that certainly is the usual result of such an approach, at least from the patient's point of view.

When this type of confidential information is obtained from patients, it obviously must be protected at all costs. And the costs certainly have been great to the individuals involved. Marriages have been dissolved, and positive psychotherapeutic return to participation in the Foundation program has been negated. Many marital units have been committed to indefinite continuation of their complaints of sexual dysfunction because a unit member's primary psychosexual commitment was directed toward his or her therapist, professional consultant, or accepted authority rather than toward the marital partner. There are on record an unfortunately large number of reasonably documented cases to support the necessity for a plea for personal and professional integrity among those individuals counseling for sexual inadequacy.

It is easy for psychotherapists to seduce or accede to seduction by their patients, particularly when these patients are under treatment for sexual dysfunction. For therapists have every advantage— the extremely vulnerable patient, the forces of transference and countertransference, the subject matter per se, are all significant elements influencing these psychosocial tragedies. There is no greater negation of professional responsibility than taking sexual advantage of an essentially defenseless patient; yet this often happens.

On record at the Foundation are histories recording direct statements of sexual exchange between patients and therapists from every conceivable level of professional discipline involved in consultation and/or treatment of a sexually inadequate individual. Listed specifically by patients are physicians of every established discipline treating sexually inadequate men or women, behaviorists (the major disciplines), theologians (the major religions), and legal advisers. Representatives of each of these disciplines have been recorded in histories as participants in a variety of sexual activity with men and women seeking their professional support.

Patients fantasy many sexual episodes with their therapists that have not occurred. These fantasied sexual interchanges between patient and therapist represent yet another great bulk of material collected during the last 11 years. This material may in time be published as a separate monograph. It is of such magnitude that it has no place in a general textbook on the treatment of sexual dysfunction.

After a period of time, however, the experienced cotherapist learns to separate fact from fiction in a large percentage of cases. In the situations described above, the details are too specific, the orientation too real, the material too well supported to be questioned. Whenever the slightest question of authenticity arises in the minds of the Foundation's personnel, the reported material is negated. However, there have been entirely too many instances in which there was no question raised in the minds of these professionals.

The pattern with the highest single incidence is that of the female patient who, contending with a sexually inadequate husband, moves toward the male therapist for sexual support. Since most therapists are male, it is to be expected that this type of situation is the most frequently encountered.

Little is to be gained in providing the distressed patient with personal sexual experience, for there usually is strong personal identification on the woman's part so that even if she is successful in orgasmic return with her therapist, there is no assurance of ability to transfer this facility in due course to the rejected husband. Any woman's inherent demand for exchange of vulnerabilities is markedly enhanced by this presumed therapeutic procedure, particularly when the subject is sexual dysfunction, and many therapists take advantage of this vulnerability.

There are, in addition, recorded histories of male patients seduced by male therapists into homosexual activity and of female patients led into similar situations at the direction of female therapists. There are also on record histories of two female therapists who have joined male patients in sexual intercourse.

Despite occasional reports in the psychiatric literature, no real issue has seriously been raised in this exquisitely sensitive area, but it is long overdue. Obviously, Foundation personnel could not provide even a composite history for professional consumption, because a patient-therapist sexual relationship might be identified by suggestion if nothing else. Suffice it to say that time and time again, year in and year out, male and female patients have reported sexual experience with their therapists (old or new, ongoing or rejected), and that the specifics of the material as reported are far and away too real for the Foundation's personnel to credit patient fantasy in most cases. Even if only 25 percent of these specific reports were correct, there still would be an overwhelming issue confronting those professionals serving as therapists in the field of human sexual dysfunction.

A significant pitfall in psychotherapeutic procedure has been specifically pinpointed. One of the great advantages of the dual-sex team and the Foundation policy to treat both members of the marital unit is that even though there might be a moment of opportunity, there certainly is a built-in mutual protection and defense for both patients and cotherapists. The primary responsibility of the dual-sex team in therapy is to focus the psychosexual attention of the marital partners upon each other and not on the therapeutic team or the members thereof. This innate form of patient protection may be one of the stronger arguments for the dual-sex team when professionals are dealing consistently with the vulnerability of men and women lost in the maze of human sexual inadequacy.

BIBLIOGRAPHY

This bibliography is but a point of departure. It is representative only of the information potential employed during the past 11 years by Foundation personnel in developing treatment programs for sexual inadequacy. Discussions are listed that have been of immense value, and there are some of little concern. Rather than underscore a prejudicial preference, it seemed more the procedure of choice to make the referral index available to the professions without comment. From these references there is full opportunity for in-depth evaluation of source material and current opinion on any phase of the multidisciplinary approach to the study of human sexual function and dysfunction.

No attempt has been made to cite these references in the text. Since there frequently were a multiplicity of subjects covered in the same paper, such citing would have been a herculean task with minimal return other than an impressive maze of essentially valueless numbers strewn throughout the text.

It is impossible to credit all the authors in the many disciplines responsible for the immense literature on sex and sexuality that has contributed to various aspects of this text. This bibliography is not intended to be definitive but rather is meant to provide nothing more than a means to become familiar with and oriented to the psychology and physiology of human sexual behavior.

Abraham, H. C.   A contribution to the problem of female sexuality. *Int. J. Psychoanal.* 37:351–353, 1956.

Abraham, H. C.   Therapeutic and psychological approach to cases of unconsummated marriage. *Brit. Med. J.* 1:837–839, 1956.

Abraham, K.   Ejaculatio praecox. In *Selected Papers of Karl Abraham, M.D.* (Bryan and Strachey, Trans.). London: Hogarth Press, 1948.

Abse, D. W.   Sexual disorder and marriage. In *Marriage Counseling in Medical Practice* (E. M. Nash, N. L. Jessner, and D. W. Abse, Eds.). Chapel Hill: University of North Carolina Press, 1964.

Ackerman, N. W.   *The Psychodynamics of Family Life: Diagnosis and Treatment of Family Relationships.* New York: Basic Books, 1958.

393

Adrian, E. D. *The Basis of Sensation: The Action of the Sense Organs.* New York: W. W. Norton, 1928.

Afrodex and impotence. *Med. Lett. Drugs Ther.* 10:97–98, 1968.

Agoston, T. Fear of post-orgastic emptiness. *Psychoanal. Rev.* 33:197–214, 1946.

Ahmed, S. H. Treatment of premature ejaculation. *Brit. J. Psychiat.* 114:1197–1198, 1968.

Allen, C. *A Textbook of Psychosexual Disorders.* London: Oxford University Press, 1962.

Allen, F. H. Psychiatry and social work in cooperation. *Amer. J. Psychiat.* 104:554–557, 1948.

Allen, W. M., and Masters, W. H. Traumatic laceration of uterine support: The clinical syndrome and the operative treatment. *Amer. J. Obstet. Gynec.* 70:500–513, 1955.

Alvarez, W. C. Sexual deficiency. *Clin. Med.* 54:158–159, 1947.

Amoore, J. E., and Venstrom, D. Correlations between stereo-chemical assessments and organoleptic analysis of odorous compounds. In *Olfaction and Taste.* (T. Hayashi, Ed.). Oxford: Pergamon Press, 1967. Vol. II.

Amulree, L. Sex and the elderly. *Practitioner* 172:431–435, 1954.

Andersen, A. P. Androgenic treatment of frigidity. *Geburtsh. Frauenheilk.* 18:632, 1958.

Andersen, T. Digitalis-induced impotence. *Nord. Med.* 75:334, 1966.

Appel, K. E. Problems with which people want help in sex and marriage. In *Man and Wife* (E. H. Mudd and A. Krich, Eds.). New York: W. W. Norton, 1957.

Aresin, L. Practical experiences with marital and sex counseling. *Deutsch. Gesundh.* 20:1692–1696, 1965.

Aresin, L. Sexual problems in young marriages. *Psychiat. Neurol. Med. Psychol.* 20:3–7, 1968.

Armstrong, E. B. The possibility of sexual happiness in old age. In *Advances in Sex Research* (H. G. Beigel, Ed.). New York: Hoeber-Harper, 1963.

Ascenzo Cabello, J., et al. Impotentia coeundi caused by narrow vaginal introit. *Acad. Peru Cir.* 17:325–328, 1964.

Aycock, L. Medical management of premature ejaculation. *J. Urol.* 62:361–362, 1949.

Babbott, D., Rubin, A., and Ginsburg, S. J. The reproductive characteristics of diabetic men. *Diabetes* 7:33–35, 1958.

Bailey, D. S. *The Mystery of Love and Marriage: A Study in the Theology of Sexual Relation.* New York: Harper & Brothers, 1952.

Bailey, D. S. *Sexual Relations in Christian Thought*. New York: Harper & Brothers, 1959.

Bailey, D. S. *Common Sense About Sexual Ethics: A Christian View*. New York: Macmillan, 1962.

Bainton, R. H. *What Christianity Says About Sex, Love, and Marriage*. New York: Association Press, 1957.

Ballenger, E. G., Elder, O. F., and McDonald, H. P. Impotence. *J. Urol.* 36:250–254, 1936.

Bandura, A. Behavioral psychotherapy. *Scientific American* 216:78–86, 1967.

Barker, W. J. Female sexuality. *J. Amer. Psychoanal. Ass.* 16:123–145, 1968.

Barnes, J. The unmarried woman. *Practitioner* 172:405–410, 1954.

Barnett, M. C. Vaginal awareness in the infancy and childhood of girls. *J. Amer. Psychoanal. Ass.* 14:129–141, 1966.

Barnett, M. C. 'I can't' versus 'he won't': Further considerations of the psychical consequences of the anatomic and physiological differences between the sexes. *J. Amer. Psychoanal. Ass.* 16:588–600, 1968.

Barnouw, V., and Stern, J. A. Some suggestions concerning social and cultural determinants of human sexual behavior. In *Determinants of Human Sexual Behavior* (G. Winokur, Ed.). Springfield, Ill.: Charles C Thomas, 1963.

Barros, J. M. de. Female orgasm: Its determination on the physiology of the tonus property in muscular contraction, principally in the smooth fiber, and histology of the vaginal canal. *Rev. Brasil. Med.* 21:327–336, 1964.

Bartlett, R. G., Jr. Physiologic responses during coitus. *J. Appl. Physiol.* 9:469–472, 1956.

Bártová, D., et al. Thioridazine treatment of ejaculatio praecox. *Activ. Nerv. Sup.* (Praha) 7:244–245, 1965.

Baruch, D. W., and Miller, H. *Sex in Marriage*. New York: Hoeber-Harper, 1962.

Bash, E. *Love and Sexuality: A Place to Walk*. A Syllabus for Group Study. Minneapolis, Minn.: American Lutheran Church, 1966.

Bassett, M. *A New Sex Ethics and Marriage Structure*. New York: Philosophical Library, 1961.

Bauer, B. A. *Woman and Love* (E. Paul and C. Paul, Trans.). New York: Boni & Liveright, 1927.

Beach, F. A. A review of physiological and psychological studies of sexual behavior in mammals. *Physiol. Rev.* 27:240–307, 1947.

Beach, F. A. *Hormones and Behavior*. New York: Harper & Brothers, 1948.

Beach, F. A. (Ed.). *Sex and Behavior*. New York: John Wiley, 1965.

Beasley, B. T. Dyspareunia. *Southern Med. J.* 40:646–653, 1947.

Beauvoir, S. de. *The Second Sex*. New York: Alfred A. Knopf, 1955.

Beck, A. T. Sexuality and depression. *Med. Asp. Human Sexuality* 2(7):44–51, 1968.

Behrman, S. J., and Gosling, J. R. G. *Fundamentals of Gynecology*. New York: Oxford University Press, 1959.

Beier, E. G. *The Silent Language of Psychotherapy: Social Reinforcement of Unconscious Processes*. Chicago: Aldine Publishing, 1966.

Beiser, H. R. Self-listening during supervision of psychotherapy. *Arch. Gen. Psychiat.* (Chicago) 15:135–139, 1966.

Békésy, G. von. Can we feel the nervous discharges of the end organs during vibratory stimulation of the skin? *J. Acoust. Soc. Amer.* 34: 124, 1962.

Békésy, G. von. Interaction of paired sensory stimuli and conduction in peripheral nerves. *J. Appl. Physiol.* 18:1276–1284, 1963.

Békésy, G. von. Modification of sensory localization as a consequence of oxygen intake and reduced blood flow. *J. Acoust. Soc. Amer.* 35: 1183–1187, 1963.

Békésy, G. von. *Sensory Inhibition*. Princeton: Princeton University Press, 1967.

Belfrage, S. H. Medical aspects of law on nullity of marriage (on grounds of sexual incapacity). *Med. Press* 211:358–361, 1944.

Bell, A. I. Some observations on the role of the scrotal sac and testicles. *J. Amer. Psychoanal. Ass.* 9:261–286, 1961.

Bell, D. S., and Trethowan, W. H. Amphetamine addiction and disturbed sexuality. *Arch. Gen. Psychiat.* (Chicago) 4:74–78, 1961.

Bell, W. B. *The Sex Complex. A Study of the Relationships of the Internal Secretions to the Female Characteristics and Functions in Health and Disease*. New York: W. Wood, 1916.

Benedek, T. Psychosexual functions in women. In *The Encyclopedia of Psychology* (P. Harriman, Ed.). New York: Philosophical Library, 1946.

Benedek, T. The functions of the sexual apparatus and their disturbances. In *Psychosomatic Medicine* (F. Alexander, Ed.). New York: W. W. Norton, 1950.

Benedek, T. *Studies in Psychosomatic Medicine: Psychosexual Functions in Women*. New York: Ronald Press, 1952.

Benedek, T. Sexual functions in women and their disturbances. In *American Handbook of Psychiatry* (S. Arieti, Ed.). New York: Basic Books, 1959.

Benedek, T. Über Orgasmus und Frigidität. *Jahrbuch der Psycho-analyse* 3:11–29, 1964.

Benedek, T. Benedek's discussion of Sherfey's paper on female sexuality. *J. Amer. Psychoanal. Ass.* 16:424–428, 1968.

Benjamin, H. A survey of the problem of impotence and a realistic approach to its management. *Urol. Cutan. Rev.* 47:567–571, 1943.

Benjamin, H. Endocrine aspect of problem: 39 cases. *Urol. Cutan. Rev.* 50:139–143, 1946.

Benjamin, H. Outline of a method to estimate the biological age with special reference to the role of the sexual functions. *Int. J. Sexology* 3:34–37, 1949.

Benjamin, H. Problems of old age and their treatment. *J. Dent. Med.* 6:79–85, 1951.

Benjamin, H. Impotence and aging. *Sexology* 26:238–243, 1959.

Benjamin, H. The role of the physician in the sex problems of the aged. In *Advances in Sex Research* (H. G. Beigel, Ed.). New York: Hoeber-Harper, 1963.

Bente, D., and Kluge, E. States of sexual excitement associated with uncinate gyrus syndrome: Clinical contribution to pathophysiology and pathobiology of the archipallium. *Arch. Psychiat. Nervenkr.* 190:357–376, 1953.

Bergler, E. Some special varieties of ejaculatory disturbance not hitherto described. *Int. J. Psychoanal.* 16:84–95, 1935.

Bergler, E. Further observations on the clinical picture of 'psychogenic oral aspermia.' *Int. J. Psychoanal.* 18:196–234, 1937.

Bergler, E. *Psychic Impotence in Men.* Monograph, Medical Edition. Berne: Huber, 1937.

Bergler, E. Some recurrent misconceptions regarding impotence. *Psychoanal. Rev.* 27:450–466, 1940.

Bergler, E. The problem of frigidity. *Psychiat. Quart.* 18:374–390, 1944.

Bergler, E. A short genetic survey of psychic impotence. I. Terminology and the facts behind it. *Psychiat. Quart.* 19:412–416, 1945.

Bergler, E. A short genetic survey of psychic impotence. II. 20 informative questions. *Psychiat. Quart.* 19:416–437, 1945.

Bergler, E. A short genetic survey of psychic impotence. III. Types of penis neurosis. *Psychiat. Quart.* 19:657–676, 1945.

Bergler, E. New genetic investigations on impotence and frigidity. *Bull. Menninger Clin.* 11:50–59, 1947.

Bergler, E. Frigidity in the female: Misconceptions and facts. *Marriage Hygiene* 1:16–21, 1947.

Bergler, E. Premature ejaculation. *Int. J. Sexology* 4:14, 1950.

Bergler, E. *Neurotic Counterfeit-Sex*. New York: Grune & Stratton, 1951.

Bergler, E. Some a-typical forms of impotence and frigidity. *Psychoanal. Rev.* 41:29–47, 1954.

Bergler, E., and Kroger, W. S. Dynamic significance of vaginal lubrication to frigidity. *Western J. Surg. Obstet. Gynec.* 61:711–176, 1953.

Bergler, E., and Kroger, W. S. *Kinsey's Myth of Female Sexuality*. New York: Grune & Stratton, 1954.

Berry, A. N. Recognition and management of sexual maladjustment. *Amer. J. Obstet. Gynec.* 64:581–586, 1952.

Best, C. H., and Taylor, N. B. (Eds.). *The Physiological Basis of Medical Practice*, 7th ed. Baltimore: Williams & Wilkins, 1961.

Beukenkamp, C. The noncommunication between husbands and wives as revealed in group psychotherapy. *Int. J. Group Psychother.* 9:308–313, 1959.

Beyme, F. Archetypal dreams and frigidity. *J. Anal. Psychol.* 12:3–22, 1967.

Bieber, I. Olfaction in sexual development and adult sexual organization. In *Science and Psychoanalysis: Psychoanalysis and Human Values* (J. H. Masserman, Ed.). New York: Grune & Stratton, 1960. Vol. III.

Bieren, R. Dyspareunia. *Med. Ann. D.C.* 19:608–611, 1950.

Bieren, R. Painful sex in women. *Sexology* 30:88–90, 1963.

Bilikiewicz, T. The effects of sexual disturbances on family life. *J. Fam. Welfare* 9:25–40, 1962.

Biran, S. Dynamic psychology of male sexual neurosis. *Z. Psychosom. Med.* 7:267–279, 1961.

Bird, H. W., and Martin, P. A. Countertransference in psychotherapy of marriage partners. *Psychiatry* 19:353–360, 1956.

Bird, J. W. *The Freedom of Sexual Love*. Garden City: Doubleday, 1967.

Bishop of Rochester. The church and sex. *Practitioner* 172:350–354, 1954.

Biskind, M. S. Relation of nutritional deficiency to impaired libido and potency in male. *J. Geront.* 2:303–314, 1947.

Biskind, M. S. Nutritional deficiency in the etiology of certain sex-endocrine disorders. In *Sex, Society, and the Individual* (A. P. Pillay & A. Ellis, Eds.). London: Delisle, 1953.

Bleuler, M. *Endokrinologische Psychiatrie*. Stuttgart: Georg Thieme, 1954.

Bliss, E. L. (Ed.). *Roots of Behavior*. New York: Hoeber-Harper, 1962.

Bloch, I. *The Sexual Life of Our Time in Its Relation to Modern Civilization*. London: Rebman, 1908.

Bloch, I. *Sex Life in England*. New York: Panurge Press, 1934.

Blood, R. O., Jr. *Marriage*. New York: Free Press of Glencoe, 1962.

Blood, R. O., Jr., and Wolfe, D. M. *Husbands and Wives*. Glencoe, Ill.: Free Press, 1960.

Blumer, D., and Walker, A. E. Sexual behavior in temporal lobe epilepsy: A study of the effects of temporal lobectomy on sexual behavior. *Arch. Neurol.* (Chicago) 16:37–43, 1967.

Bohnenstengel, G. Choriostimon therapy in impotentia coeundi and impotentia generandi. *Derm. Wschr.* 153:1049–1057, 1967.

Bonaparte, M. Passivity, masochism, and femininity. *Int. J. Psychoanal.* 16:325–333, 1935.

Bonaparte, M. *Female Sexuality*. New York: International Universities Press, 1953.

Book, J. C. Role-divided three-cornered therapy. *Psychiatry* 17:277, 1954.

Borelli, S. On the prescription of sex hormones in male sex disorders (impotentia coeundi). *Landarzt* 43:476–477, 1967.

Bors, E., and Comarr, A. E. Neurological disturbances of sexual function with special references to 529 patients with spinal cord injury. *Urol. Survey* 10:191–222, 1960.

Bosselman, B. C. Castration anxiety and phallus envy: A reformulation. *Psychiat. Quart.* 34:252–259, 1960.

Bowers, L. M., Cross, R. R., and Lloyd, F. A. Sexual function and urologic disease in the elderly male. *J. Amer. Geriat. Soc.* 11:647–652, 1963.

Bowlby, J. Symposium on the contribution of current theories to an understanding of child development. *Brit. J. Med. Psychol.* 30:230, 1957.

Bowman, C. C. Social factors opposed to the extension of heterosexuality. *Amer. J. Psychiat.* 106:441–447, 1949.

Bowman, K. M. The sex life of the aging individual. *Geriatrics* 9:83–84, 1954.

Bowman, K. M. The sex life of the aging individual. In *Sexual Behavior and Personality Characteristics* (M. F. DeMartino, Ed.). New York: Citadel Press, 1963.

Boyer, C. L. Group therapy with married couples. *Marr. Fam. Living* 22:21–24, 1960.

Brady, J. P. Breviatal-relaxation treatment of frigidity. *Behav. Res. Ther.* 4:71–77, 1966.

Brady, J. P., Mudd, E. H., Wagenheim, H. S., Lazarus, A. A., and

Rugart, K. F.   Roundtable: Frigidity. *Med. Asp. Human Sexuality* 2(2): 26–40, 1968.

Brecher, R., and Brecher, E. (Eds.).   *An Analysis of Human Sexual Response.* Boston: Little, Brown, 1966.

Bricaire, H. Dreyfus-Moreau, J., Azerod, E., Derot, M., Hamburger, J., Netter, A., and Pequignot, H.   Comment traiter l'impuissance sexuelle? *Presse Med.* 71:1653–1655, 1963.

Brierley, M.   Some problems of integration in women. *Int. J. Psychoanal.* 13:433–447, 1932.

Brierley, M.   Specific determinants in feminine development. *Int. J. Psychoanal.* 7:163–180, 1936.

Brill, A. A.   The sense of smell in the neurosis and psychoses. *Psychoanal. Quart.* 1:7–42, 1932.

Broadbent, D. E.   *Perception and Communication.* London: Pergamon Press, 1958.

Brothers, J.   *Woman.* New York: Doubleday, 1961.

Brown, D. G.   Female orgasm and sexual inadequacy. In *An Analysis of Human Sexual Response* (R. Brecher and E. Brecher, Eds.). Boston: Little, Brown, 1966.

Brown, F., and Kempton, R. T.   *Sex Questions and Answers.* New York: McGraw-Hill, 1950.

Brown, H. G.   *Sex and the Single Girl.* New York: Bernard Geis, 1962.

Browne, F. J., and Browne, J. C. M.   *Postgraduate Obstetrics and Gynecology.* Washington, D.C.: Butterworth, 1964.

Browning, W. J.   Male climacteric and impotence. *Int. Rec. Med.* 173:690–694, 1960.

Bruhl, D. E., and Leslie, C. H.   Afrodex, double blind test in impotence. *Med. Rec. Ann.* 56:22, 1963.

Bryan, D.   Scent in a symptomatic act. *Int. J. Psychoanal.* 8:403–405, 1927.

Buck, P. S.   Changing relationships between men and women. In *American Women: The Changing Image* (B. B. Cassara, Ed.). Boston: Beacon Press, 1962.

Bues, E., Alnor, P., and Peter, D.   Disturbances in the sexual functions after lumbar sympathectomy. *Chirurg.* 28:103–107, 1957.

Burdine, W. E., Shipley, T. E., and Papas, A. T.   Delatestryl, a long-acting androgenic hormone: Its use as an adjunct in the treatment of women with sexual frigidity. *Fertil. Steril.* 8:255–259, 1957.

Burgess, E. W., and Wallin, P.   *Engagement and Marriage.* Philadelphia: J. B. Lippincott, 1953.

Burnap, D. W., and Golden, J. S.   Sexual problems in medical practice. *J. Med. Educ.* 42:673–680, 1967.

Burton, G., and Kaplan, H. M. Sexual behavior and adjustment of married alcoholics. *Quart. J. Stud. Alcohol* 29:603–609, 1968.

Butterfield, O. M. *Marriage and Sexual Harmony.* New York: Emerson Books, 1946.

Bychowski, G. Some aspects of psychosexuality in psychoanalytic experience. In *Psychosexual Development in Health and Disease* (P. H. Hoch and J. Zubin, Eds.). New York: Grune & Stratton, 1949.

Bychowski, G. Frigidity and object relationship. *Int. J. Psychoanal.* 44:57–62, 1963.

Calderone, M. S. *Release from Sexual Tensions.* New York: Random House, 1960.

Calderone, M. S. Sexual problems in medical practice. *J. Amer. Med. Wom. Ass.* 23:140–146, 1968.

Caldwell, B. M., and Watson, R. I. An evaluation of psychologic effects of sex hormone administration in aged women. I. Results of therapy after six months. *J. Geront.* 7:228–244, 1952.

Cameron, D. E. Sexuality and the sexual disorders. In *Modern Practice in Psychological Medicine.* New York: Hoeber-Harper, 1949.

Campbell, D., Daly, M. J., Winn, H., and Holmes, D. Roundtable: Sex and the menstrual cycle. *Med. Asp. Human Sexuality* 2(7):12–17, 1968.

Cantor, A. J. Hemorrhoidal-prostatic-impotence syndrome. *New York J. Med.* 46:1455–1456, 1946.

Cantor, M. B. Karen Horney on the psychoanalytic technique: The initial interview. *Amer. J. Psychoanal.* 17:39–44, 1957.

Caprio, F. S. *The Sexually Adequate Male.* New York: Grune & Stratton, 1950.

Caprio, F. S. *The Sexually Adequate Female.* New York: Citadel Press, 1953.

Carmichael, H. T., Noonan, W. J., and Kenyon, A. T. The effects of testosterone propionate in impotence. *Amer. J. Psychiat.* 97:917–943, 1941.

Castallo, M. A., and Schulz, C. L. *Woman's Inside Story.* New York: Macmillan, 1948.

Castelnuovo-Tedesco, P. *The Twenty-Minute Hour.* Boston: Little, Brown, 1965.

Cauldwell, D. O. When does sex life end? *Sexology* 25:250–253, 1958.

Cautela, J. R., and Wisocki, P. A. The use of male and female therapists in the treatment of homosexual behavior. Paper presented to Association for the Advancement of Behavior Therapies at American Psychological Association Convention, Aug. 31, 1968.

Cavanagh, J. R.   Rhythm of sexual desire in women. *Med. Asp. Human Sexuality* 3(2):29–39, 1969.

Cervantes, L. F.   *And God Made Man and Woman.* Chicago: Henry Regnery, 1959.

Chapman, J. D.   *The Feminine Mind and Body: The Psychosexual and Psychosomatic Reactions of Women.* New York: Philosophical Library, 1967.

Chappell, B. S.   Relief of impotency by cartilage implants: Presentation of technique. *J. S. Carolina Med. Ass.* 48:31–34, 1952.

Chesser, E.   *The Sexual, Marital, and Family Relationships of the English Woman.* New York: Roy Publishers, 1956.

Chokyu, K.   Studies on diabetes mellitus and functions of the male sexual glands. *Acta Urol. Jap.* 11:850–876, 1965.

Christenson, C. V., and Gagnon, J. H.   Sexual behavior in groups of older women. *J. Geront.* 20:351–356, 1965.

Claman, A. D.   Sexual difficulties after 50. *Canad. Med. Ass. J.* 94:207, 1966.

Clark, L.   *Emotional Adjustment in Marriage.* Saint Louis: C. V. Mosby, 1937.

Clark, L.   *The Enjoyment of Love in Marriage.* New York: New American Library, 1969.

Clark, L.   Sexual adjustment in marriage. In *The Encyclopedia of Sexual Behavior* (A. Ellis and A. Abarbanel, Eds.). New York: Hawthorn Books, 1961.

Claye, A. M.   The problem of dyspareunia. *New Zeal. Med. J.* 54:297–306, 1955.

Cleaver, E. C.   *Soul on Ice.* New York: Dell Publishing, 1968.

Clemens, A. H.   *Marriage and the Family: An Integrated Approach for Catholics.* Englewood Cliffs, N.J.: Prentice-Hall, 1957.

Coburn, W. A.   Physical examination for marriage problems. *Med. Asp. Human Sexuality* 3(6):52–60, 1969.

Cohen, A.   *Everyman's Talmud.* New York: E. P. Dutton, 1949.

Cohen, R. A., and Cohen, M. B.   Research in psychotherapy: A preliminary report. *Psychiatry* 24:46–61, 1961.

Colby, F. H.   *Essential Urology.* Baltimore: Williams & Wilkins, 1961.

Colby, K. M.   Psychotherapeutic processes. *Ann. Rev. Psychol.* 15:347–370, 1964.

Cole, W. G.   *Sex in Christianity and Psychoanalysis.* New York: Oxford University Press, 1955.

Cole, W. G.   *Sex and Love in the Bible.* New York: Association Press, 1959.

Collier, J. L. *The Hypocritical American. An Essay on Sex Attitudes in America.* Indianapolis: Bobbs-Merrill, 1964.

Comfort, A. *The Nature of Human Nature.* New York: Harper & Row, 1966.

Comfort, A. *Sex in Society.* New York: Citadel Press, 1966.

Comfort, A. Disorders of sex and reproduction: Psychosomatic aspects. Summing up. *J. Psychosom. Res.* 12:117–120, 1968.

Condamin, R. Dyspareunie et frigidité dans leurs rapports avec la douglassite. *Lyon Med.* 138:523–531, 1926.

Condamin, R. Essai de pathogénie de l'ovarite scléro-kystique; ses relations étiologiques avec la douglassite. *Lyon Med.* 144:681–691, 1929.

Condrau, G. On the psychotherapy of male impotence. *Praxis* 49:641–644, 1960.

Connery, M. F. Problems in teaching the team concept. *J. Psychiat. Soc. Work* 21:81–89, 1951.

Conti, G. L'erection du penis humain et ses bases morphologicovasculaires. *Acta Anat.* 14:217–262, 1952.

Cook, E. N. Premature ejaculation. *J.A.M.A.* 181:278, 1962.

Cooper, A. *The Sexual Disabilities of Man and Their Treatment.* New York: Harper & Brothers, 1915.

Cooper, A. J. Hostility and male potency disorders. *Compr. Psychiat.* 9:621–626, 1968.

Cooper, A. J. 'Neurosis' and disorders of sexual potency in the male. *J. Psychosom. Res.* 12:141–144, 1968.

Cooper, A. J. A factual study of male potency disorders. *Brit. J. Psychiat.* 114:719–731, 1968.

Cooper, A. J. A clinical study of 'coital anxiety' in male potency disorders. *J. Psychosom. Res.* 13:143–147, 1969.

Cordonnier, J. J. *Clinical Urology for General Practice.* Saint Louis: C. V. Mosby, 1956.

Corsini, R., and Putzer, L. *Bibliography of Group Psychotherapy.* New York: Beacon House, 1947.

Courtenay, M. *Sexual Discord in Marriage: A Field for Brief Psychotherapy.* Philadelphia: Lippincott, 1968.

Cox, W. M., Karafin, L., Kaufman, J. J., Parker, C. R., and Shirley, S. W. What do you advise patients with premature ejaculation? *Med. Asp. Human Sexuality* 3(2):6–10, 1969.

Crawshaw, R., and Key, W. Psychiatric teams: A selective review of the literature. *Arch. Gen. Psychiat.* (Chicago) 5:397–405, 1961.

Creevy, C. D., and Rea, C. E. The treatment of impotence by male sex hormone. *Endocrinology* 27:392–394, 1940.

Crossen, H. S., and Crossen, R. J. *Diseases of Women*. Saint Louis: C. V. Mosby, 1944.

Cuber, J. F. The sexless marriage. *Med. Asp. Human Sexuality* 3(11): 19–33, 1969.

Cuber, J. F., and Harroff, P. B. *The Significant Americans: A Study of Sexual Behavior Among the Affluent*. New York: Appleton-Century-Crofts, 1965.

Cutler, R. L. Countertransference effects in psychotherapy. *J. Consult. Psychol.* 22:349–356, 1958.

Dahlen, C. P., and Goodwin, W. E. Sexual potency after perineal biopsy. *J. Urol.* 77:660–669, 1957.

Daly, C. D., and White, R. S. Psychic reactions to olfactory stimuli: A preliminary paper. *Brit. J. Med. Psychol.* 10:70–87, 1930.

Daly, M. J. Sexual attitudes in menopausal and postmenopausal women. *Med. Asp. Human Sexuality* 2(5):48–53, 1968.

Damon, V. G., and Taves, I. *I Learned about Women from Them*. New York: David McKay, 1962.

Damrau, F. Premature ejaculation: Use of ethyl aminobenzoate to prolong coitus. *J. Urol.* 89:936–939, 1963.

Danesino, V., and Martella, E. Modern concepts of functioning of cavernous bodies of vagina and clitoris. *Arch. Ostet. Ginec.* 60:150–167, 1955.

Daniels, A. K. *It's Never Too Late To Love*. New York: Pyramid Books, 1953.

Dannreuth, W. T. Vaginal dyspareunia. *Amer. J. Obstet. Gynec.* 74:747–752, 1957.

Daruvala, R. B. Sex inefficiency. *Indian Med. J.* 60:111–112, 1966.

Davis, K. B. *Factors in the Sex Life of 2200 Women*. New York: Harper & Brothers, 1929.

Davis, M. *The Sexual Responsibility of Women*. New York: Dial Press, 1956.

Davis, M. *Sexual Responsibility in Marriage*. New York: Dial Press, 1963.

Dawkins, S., and Taylor, R. Non-consummation of marriage: A survey of seventy cases. *Lancet* 2:1029–1033, 1961.

DeMartino, M. F. (Ed.). *Sexual Behavior and Personality Characteristics*. New York: Grove Press, 1966.

Dember, W. N., and Earl, R. W. Analysis of exploratory, manipulatory, and curiosity behaviors. *Psychol. Rev.* 64:91–96, 1957.

Denber, H. C. Sexual problems in the mature female. *Psychosomatics* 9(Suppl.):40–43, 1968.

Dengrove, E.   Behavior therapy of the sexual disorders. *J. Sex Res.* 3:49–61, 1967.

Dengrove, E., Marcus, D. M., and Cook, E. N.   Premature ejaculation. *J.A.M.A.* 183:389–390, 1963.

Deutsch, H.   The psychology of women in relation to the functions of reproduction. *Int. J. Psychoanal.* 6:405–418, 1925.

Deutsch, H.   Motherhood and sexuality. *Psychoanalysis* 2:476–488, 1933.

Deutsch, H.   *The Psychology of Women.* New York: Grune & Stratton, 1945. Vols. I, II.

Deutsch, H.   Frigidity in women. In *Neurosis and Character Types.* New York: International Universities Press, 1965.

Devereux, G.   The significance of the external female genitalia and of female orgasm for the male. *J. Amer. Psychoanal. Ass.* 6:278–286, 1958.

Diamond, M. (Ed.).   *Perspectives in Reproduction and Sexual Behavior.* Bloomington: Indiana University Press, 1968.

Dickinson, R. L.   *Human Sex Anatomy.* Baltimore: Williams & Wilkins, 1933.

Dickinson, R. L.   Medical reflections upon some life histories. In *The Sex Life of the Unmarried Adult* (I. S. Wile, Ed.). New York: Vanguard Press, 1940.

Dickinson, R. L., and Beam, L.   *A Thousand Marriages.* Baltimore: Williams & Wilkins, 1931.

Dickinson, R. L., and Beam, L.   *The Single Woman.* Baltimore: Williams & Wilkins, 1934.

Dickinson, R. L., and Pierson, H. H.   The average sex life of American women. *J.A.M.A.* 85:1113–1117, 1925.

Dicks, H. V.   Clinical studies in marriage and the family: A symposium on methods. *Brit. J. Med. Psychol.* 26:181–196, 1953.

Diethelm, O.   *Treatment in Psychiatry.* New York: Macmillan, 1936.

Dingman, J.   Endocrine aspects of impotence. *Med. Asp. Human Sexuality* 3:57–66, 1969.

Ditman, K. S.   Inhibition of ejaculation by chlorprothixene. *Amer. J. Psychiat.* 120:1004–1005, 1964.

Doepfmer, R.   Über eine neuartige Behandlung der ejaculatio praecox. *München. Med. Wschr.* 106:1103–1107, 1964.

Dollard, J., and Auld, F.   *Scoring Human Motives: A Manual.* New Haven, Conn.: Yale University Press, 1959.

Dollard, J., and Miller, N. E.   *Personality and Psychotherapy.* New York: McGraw-Hill, 1950.

Dreikurs, R. The psychological interview in medicine. *Amer. J. Individ. Psychol.* 10:99–122, 1952.

Drellich, M. G., and Bieber, I. The psychologic importance of the uterus and its functions: Some psychoanalytic implications of hysterectomy. *J. Nerv. Ment. Dis.* 126:322–336, 1958.

Dreyfus-Moreau, J. Apropos of various factors favoring impotence. *Evolut. Psychiat.* (Paris) 29:437–462, 1964.

Dreyfus-Moreau, J. The treatment of psychogenic impotence. *Sem. Ther.* 40:117–118, 1964.

Duffy, J. Masturbation and clitoridectomy: A nineteenth-century view. *J.A.M.A.* 186:246–248, 1963.

Durant, W., and Durant, A. *The Lessons of History.* New York: Simon and Schuster, 1968.

Duvall, E. M., and Duvall, S. M. (Eds.). *Sex Ways—In Fact and Faith: Bases for Christian Family Policy.* New York: Association Press, 1961.

Duvall, E. M., and Duvall, S. M. *Sense and Nonsense About Sex.* New York: Asosciation Press, 1962.

Echtman, J. Diathermy treatment in impotency: A new method. *Urol. Cutan. Rev.* 34:727–728, 1930.

Eeman, P. D. Physiology of the orgasm and of psychoanalysis. *Int. J. Sexology* 3:92–98, 1949.

Ehrmann, W. Some knowns and unknowns in research into human sex behavior. *Marr. Fam. Living* 19:16–24, 1957.

Ehrmann, W. Social determinants of human sexual behavior. In *Determinants of Human Sexual Behavior* (G. Winokur, Ed.). Springfield, Ill.: Charles C Thomas, 1963.

Eickhoff, A. R. *A Christian View of Sex and Marriage.* New York: Free Press of Glencoe, 1966.

Eisenstein, V. W. (Ed.). *Neurotic Interaction in Marriage.* New York: Basic Books, 1956.

Eissler, K. On certain problems of female sexual development. *Psychoanal. Quart.* 8:191–210, 1939.

Ekstein, R., and Wallerstein, R. X. *The Teaching and Learning of Psychotherapy.* New York: Basic Books, 1958.

Elgosin, R. B. Premarital counseling and sexual adjustment in marriage. *Conn. Med. J.* 15:999–1002, 1951.

Eliasberg, W. Disorders of male sexuality as encountered in practitioner's office. *Psychiat. Quart.* 18:567–581, 1944.

Elkan, E. Evolution of female orgastic ability: A biological survey. *Int. J. Sexology* 2:1–13; 84–93, 1948.

Elkan, E.   Orgasm inability in women. *Int. J. Sexology* 4:243, 1951.

Elkasberg, W.   Marital disorders erroneously called male sexual disorders. *J. Amer. Med. Wom. Ass.* 51:27–29, 1944.

Ellery, R. S.   Frigidity and dyspareunia. *Med. J. Aust.* 2:626–628, 1954.

Ellis, A.   Is the vaginal orgasm a myth? In *Sex, Society, and the Individual* (A. P. Pillay and A. Ellis, Eds.). London: Delisle, 1953.

Ellis, A.   Marriage counseling with couples indicating sexual incompatibility. *Marr. Fam. Living* 15:53–59, 1953.

Ellis, A.   Psychosexual and marital problems. In *An Introduction to Clinical Psychology* (L. A. Pennington and I. A. Berg, Eds.). New York: Ronald Press, 1954.

Ellis, A. (Ed.).   *Sex Life of the American Woman and the Kinsey Report.* New York: Greenberg, 1954.

Ellis, A.   Marriage counseling with couples indicating sexual incompatibility. In *Readings in Marriage Counseling* (C. E. Vincent, Ed.). New York: Thomas Y. Crowell, 1957.

Ellis, A.   Sex problems of couples seen for marriage counseling. *J. Fam. Welfare* 3:81–84, 1957.

Ellis, A.   Guilt, shame, and frigidity. *Quart. Rev. Surg. Obstet. Gynec.* 16:259–261, 1959.

Ellis, A.   *The Art and Science of Love.* New York: Lyle Stuart, 1960.

Ellis, A.   Frigidity. In *The Encyclopedia of Sexual Behavior* (A. Ellis and A. Abarbanel, Eds.). New York: Hawthorn Books, 1961.

Ellis, A.   Coitus. In *The Encyclopedia of Sexual Behavior.* (A. Ellis and A. Abarbanel, Eds.). New York: Hawthorn Books, 1961.

Ellis, A.   *The American Sexual Tragedy.* New York: Lyle Stuart, 1962.

Ellis, A.   *Sex Without Guilt.* New York: Lyle Stuart, 1966.

Ellis, A., and Abarbanel, A. (Eds.).   *The Encyclopedia of Sexual Behavior.* New York: Hawthorn Books, 1961. Vols. I, II.

Ellis, H.   *Little Essays of Love and Virtue.* New York: Doran, 1922.

Ellis, H.   *Studies in the Psychology of Sex.* Philadelphia: F. A. Davis, 1928. Vols. I–VII.

Ellis, H.   *Psychology of Sex.* New York: Emerson, 1954.

Ellis, W. J., and Grayhack, J. T.   Sexual function in aging males after orchiectomy and estrogen therapy. *J. Urol.* 89:895–899, 1963.

Ellison, C.   Psychosomatic factors in the unconsummated marriage. *J. Psychosom. Res.* 12:61–65, 1968.

El-Masri, D.   Prothèse en polyéthylène des corps caverneux. *J. Med. Liban.* 18:365–369, 1965.

El Senoussi, A., Coleman, D. R., and Tauber, A. S.   Factors in male impotence. *J. Psychol.* 48:3–46, 1959.

Engle, E. T., and Pincus, G. (Eds.). *Hormones and the Aging Process.*
New York: Academic Press, 1956.

English, O. S. Three common sexual problems: Masturbation, homosexuality, and impotence and frigidity. In *Man and Wife* (E. H.
Mudd and A. Krish, Eds.). New York: W. W. Norton, 1957.

English, O. S., and Pearson, G. H. J. *Emotional Problems of Living.*
New York: W. W. Norton, 1945.

Epstein, A. W. Disordered human sexual behavior associated with
temporal lobe dysfunction. *Med. Asp. Human Sexuality* 3:62–68, 1969.

Erikson, E. H. Inner and outer space: Reflections on womanhood.
Daedalus 93(2):582–606, 1964.

Etter, E. A. Hypogonadal impotence in middle-aged men. *Arizona
Med.* 17:217–220, 1960.

Farson, R. E. (Ed.). *Science and Human Affairs.* Palo Alto, Cal.:
Science and Behavior Books, 1965.

Fast, J. *What You Should Know About Human Sexual Response.*
New York: Berkley Publishing, 1966.

Feldman, S. S. Anxiety and orgasm. *Psychoanal. Quart.* 20:528–549,
1951.

Fenichel, O. *The Psychoanalytic Theory of Neurosis.* New York:
W. W. Norton, 1945.

Ferber, A. S., Tietze, C., and Lewitt, S. Men with vasectomies: A
study of medical, sexual, and psychosocial changes. *Psychosom. Med.*
29:354–366, 1967.

Ferenczi, S. Paraesthesias of the genital region in impotence. In *Further Contributions to the Theory and Technique of Psychoanalysis.*
New York: Basic Books, 1952.

Ferenczi, S. The analytic interpretation and treatment of psychosexual impotence. In *Sex in Psychoanalysis.* New York: Dover Publications, 1956.

Ferguson, L. W. Correlates of woman's orgasm. *J. Psychol.* 6:295–302,
1938.

Finkle, A. L. Sexual potency and the physician. *Med. Times* 88:557–
559, 1960.

Finkle, A. L. Sexual potency after perineal prostatectomy. *Western J.
Surg. Obstet. Gynec.* 70:55–57, 1962.

Finkle, A. L. Trauma and sexual impotence. *J. Trauma* 4:60–97, 1962.

Finkle, A. L. Diagnosis of sexual problems in urology. In *Advances
in Diagnostic Urology* (J. J. Kaufman, Ed.). Boston: Little, Brown,
1964.

Finkle, A. L. Sex problems in later years. *Med. Times* 95:416–419,
1967.

Finkle, A. L. Sex after prostatectomy. *Med. Asp. Human Sexuality* 2(3):40–41, 1968.

Finkle, A. L., and Moyers, T. G. Sexual potency in aging males. IV. Status of private patients before and after prostatectomy. *J. Urol.* 84:152–157, 1960.

Finkle, A. L., and Moyers, T. G. Sexual potency in aging males. V. Coital ability following open perineal prostatic biopsy. *J. Urol.* 84:649–653, 1960.

Finkle, A. L., Moyers, T. G., Tobenkin, M. I., and Karg, S. J. Sexual potency in aging males. I. Frequency of coitus among clinic patients. *J.A.M.A.* 170:1391–1393, 1951.

Finkle, A. L., and Prian, D. V. Sexual potency in elderly men before and after prostatectomy. *J.A.M.A.* 196:139–143, 1966.

Fisher, C., Gross, J., and Zuch, J. Cycle of penile erection synchronous with dreaming (REM) sleep. *Arch. Gen. Psychiat.* (Chicago) 12:29–45, 1965.

Fisher, S., and Osofsky, H. Sexual responsiveness in women: Psychological correlates. *Arch. Gen. Psychiat.* (Chicago) 17:214–226, 1967.

Fiske, D. W., et al. Planning of research on effectiveness of psychotherapy. *Arch. Gen. Psychiat.* (Chicago) 22:22–32, 1970.

Fitzherbert, J. Scent and the sexual object. *Brit. J. Med. Psychol.* 32:206–209, 1959.

Fleck, L. Evaluation of the female orgastic capacity and its disorders from the psychoanalytic point of view. *Psyche* (Stuttgart) 23:58–74, 1969.

Fleischmann, O. A method of teaching psychotherapy. *Bull. Menninger Clin.* 19:160–172, 1955.

Fleming, J. Teaching the basic skills of psychotherapy. *Arch. Gen. Psychiat.* (Chicago) 16:417–426, 1967.

Fletcher, P., and Walker, K. Non-sexual factors in impotence. *Med. World* 78:596–601, 1953.

Fliess, R. *Erogeneity and Libido.* New York: International Universities Press, 1956.

Ford, C. S., and Beach, F. A. *Patterns of Sexual Behavior.* New York: Harper & Brothers, 1951.

Foss, G. L. The influence of androgens on sexuality in women. *Lancet* 260:667–669, 1951.

Francis, W. J. A., and Jeffcoate, T. N. A. Dyspareunia following vaginal operations. *J. Obstet. Gynaec. Brit. Comm.* 68:1–10, 1961.

Frank, L. K. *The Conduct of Sex.* New York: William Morrow, 1961.

Frank, R. T. Dyspareunia: A problem for the general practitioner. *J.A.M.A.* 136:361–365, 1948.

Frankl, V. E.   Psychogene Potenzstörungen. *Wien. Med. Wschr.* 108: 477–481, 1958.

Franks, C. M.   Reflections upon the treatment of sexual disorders by the behavioral clinician: An historical comparison with the treatment of the alcoholic. *J. Sex Res.* 3:212–222, 1967.

Fraschini, A.   Contribution to therapeutics of ejaculatio praecox and of some forms of sexual impotence. *G. Geront.* 14:1205–1207, 1966.

Freedman, A. M., and Kaplan, H. I. (Eds.).   *Comprehensive Textbook of Psychiatry.* Baltimore: Williams & Wilkins, 1967.

Freeman, J. T.   Sexual capacities in the aging male. *Geriatrics* 16:37–43, 1961.

Freeman, S. K.   Odor. *Int. Science Technology* No. 69, pp. 70–80, 1967.

Freud, S.   *Beyond the Pleasure Principle.* London: Hogarth Press, 1922.

Freud, S.   Some psychological consequences of the anatomical distinction between the sexes. *Int. J. Psychoanal.* 8:133–142, 1927.

Freud, S.   Concerning the sexuality of woman. *Psychoanal. Quart.* 1:191–209, 1932.

Freud, S.   Female sexuality. *Int. J. Psychoanal.* 13:281–297, 1932.

Freud, S.   *New Introductory Lectures on Psychoanalysis.* New York: W. W. Norton, 1933.

Freud, S.   Three contributions to the theory of sex. In *The Basic Writings of Sigmund Freud* (A. A. Brill, Ed. and Trans.). New York: Modern Library, 1938.

Freud, S.   *A General Introduction to Psychoanalysis* (J. Riviere, Trans.). New York: Garden City Publishing, 1943.

Freud, S.   *Sexuality and the Psychology of Love.* New York: Collier Books, 1963.

Freud, S.   *Three Essays on the Theory of Sexuality* (J. Strachey, Ed. and Trans.). New York: Basic Books, 1963.

Freyhan, F. A.   Loss of ejaculation during Mellaril treatment. *Amer. J. Psychiat.* 118:171–172, 1961.

Fried, E.   Clinical aspects of adult therapy. II. Some connections between sexuality and ego organization. *Amer. J. Orthopsychiat.* 29:391–401, 1959.

Fried, E.   *The Ego in Love and Sexuality.* New York: Grune & Stratton, 1960.

Friedan, B.   *The Feminine Mystique.* New York: W. W. Norton, 1963.

Friedman, L. J.   *Virgin Wives: A Study of Unconsummated Marriages.* London: Tavistock Publishing, 1962.

Friedman, P.   Some observations on the sense of smell. *Psychoanal. Quart.* 28:307–329, 1959.

Frith, K. M. An unusual cause of dyspareunia. *J. Obstet. Gynaec. Brit. Comm.* 67:303–304, 1960.

Frith, K. M. Some observations on vaginismus. *J. Obstet. Gynaec. Brit. Comm.* 68:1033–1037, 1961.

Fromm, E. Sex and character. *Psychiatry* 6:21–31, 1943.

Fromm, E. *The Art of Loving.* New York: Harper & Brothers, 1956.

Fromme, A. *Understanding the Sexual Response in Humans.* New York: Pocket Books, 1966.

Fromm-Reichmann, F. *Principles of Intensive Psychotherapy.* Chicago: University of Chicago Press, 1950.

Gagnon, J. H. Sexuality and sexual learning in the child. *Psychiatry* 25:212–228, 1965.

Gallant, D. M. The effect of alcohol and drug abuse on sexual behavior. *Med. Asp. Human Sexuality* 2(1):30–36, 1968.

Gallichan, W. M. *Sexual Apathy and Coldness in Women.* Boston: Stratford, 1928.

Garber, R. S. A psychiatrist's view of remotivation. *Ment. Hosp.* 16:219–221, 1965.

Garner, H. H. Passivity and activity in psychotherapy. *Arch. Gen. Psychiat.* (Chicago) 5:411–417, 1961.

Garrison, P. L., and Gamble, C. J. Sexual effects of vasectomy. *J.A.M.A.* 144:293–295, 1950.

Gastaut, H., and Collomb, H. Étude du comportement sexuel chez les épileptiques psychomoteurs. *Ann. Medicopsychol.* 112:657–696, 1954.

Gebhard, P. H. Factors in marital orgasm. *Med. Asp. Human Sexuality* 2(7):22–25, 1968.

Gebhard, P. H. Human sex behavior research. In *Perspectives in Reproduction and Sexual Behavior* (M. Diamond, Ed.). Bloomington: Indiana University Press, 1968.

Geddes, D. P. (Ed.). *An Analysis of the Kinsey Reports on Sexual Behavior in the Human Male and Female.* New York: Dutton, 1954.

Geist, S. H., and Salmon, U. J. Androgen therapy in gynecology. *J.A.M.A.* 117:2207–2215, 1941.

Geist, S. H., Salmon, U. J., Gaines, J. A., and Walter, R. I. The biological effects of androgen (testosterone propionate) in women. *J.A.M.A.* 114:1539–1544, 1940.

Geldard, F. A. *The Human Senses.* New York: John Wiley, 1953.

Gelma, E. L'érotisme de l'âge avancé. *Paris Med.* 4:1, 1938.

Gennser, G., et al. Retention of the seminal fluid as a cause of sterility. *Lakartidningen* 66:2307–2315, 1969.

Gibert, H. *The Meaning and Practice of Sexual Love in Christian Marriage* (A. Humbert, Trans.). New York: Hawthorn Books, 1964.

Giese, H. Über die menschliche Sexualität. *Psychiat. Neurol. Med. Psychol.* (Leipzig) 10:137–141, 1958.

Gildea, E. F., and Robins, L. N. Suggestions for research in sexual behavior. In *Determinants of Human Sexual Behavior* (G. Winokur, Ed.). Springfield, Ill.: Charles C Thomas, 1963.

Giovacchini, P. L. Treatment of marital disharmonies: The classical approach. In *The Psychotherapies of Marital Disharmony* (B. L. Greene, Ed.). New York: Free Press of Glencoe, 1965.

Girard, P. F. Male impotence. *Acta Neurol. Belg.* 65:587–597, 1965.

Glassberg, I. J. Sexual impotence. *J. Louisiana Med. Soc.* 107:457–460, 1955.

Glenn, J. F. (Ed.). *Diagnostic Urology*. New York: Hoeber-Harper, 1964.

Glenn, J., and Kaplan, E. H. Types of orgasm in women: A critical review and redefinition. *J. Amer. Psychoanal. Ass.* 16:549–564, 1968.

Goldberg, M. Counseling sexually incompatible marriage partners. *Postgrad. Med.* 42:62–68, 1967.

Goldberg, M. Marital sexual problems in medical practice. *J. Amer. Med. Wom. Ass.* 23:158–162, 1968.

Golden, M. M. The acute attack of impotence. *New York J. Med.* 61: 3785–3786, 1961.

Goldman, S. F., and Markham, M. J. Clinical use of testosterone in the male climacteric. *J. Clin. Endocr.* 2:237–242, 1942.

Goldstein, A. P. *Therapist-Patient Expectancies in Psychotherapy*. New York: Pergamon Press, 1962.

Goldstein, A. P., and Dean, S. J. (Eds.). *The Investigation of Psychotherapy: Commentaries and Readings*. New York: John Wiley, 1966.

Goldstein, A. P., Heller, K., and Sechrest, L. B. *Psychotherapy and the Psychology of Behavior Change*. New York: John Wiley, 1966.

Goldzieher, M., and Goldzieher, J. W. The male climacteric and the post-climacteric states. *Geriatrics* 8:1–10, 1953.

Gottlieb, A., and Pattison, E. M. Married couples group psychotherapy. *Arch. Gen. Psychiat.* (Chicago) 14:143–152, 1966.

Gould, W. L. The male climacteric: Report of a series of 120 cases using fortified pituitary gonadotropic hormone. *Med. Times* 79:154–161, 1951.

Gould, W. L. New therapeutic approach to aging. *Clin. Med.* 64:865–868, 1957.

Graber, E. A., Barber, H. K., and O'Rourke, J. J. Newlywed apareunia. *Obstet. Gynec.* 33:418–421, 1969.

Grafenberg, E.   The role of the urethra in female orgasm. *Int. J. Sexology* 3:145–148, 1950.

Graham, S. R.   The effects of psychoanalytically oriented psychotherapy on levels of frequency and satisfaction in sexual activity. *J. Clin. Psychol.* 16:94–95, 1960.

Grant, V. W.   *The Psychology of Sexual Emotion*. New York: Longmans, Green, 1957.

Green, M.   Inhibition of ejaculation as a side-effect of Mellaril. *Amer. J. Psychiat.* 118:172–173, 1961.

Green, M., and Berman, S.   Failure of ejaculation produced by Dibenzyline. *Conn. Med.* 18:30–33, 1954.

Green, Z. B.   *Christian Male-Female Relationships*. Grand Rapids, Mich.: Baker Book House, 1967.

Greenacre, P.   Special problems of early female sexual development. *Psychoanal. Stud. Child* 5:122–138, 1950.

Greenbank, R. K.   Are medical students learning psychiatry? *Penn. Med. J.* 64:989–992, 1961.

Greenbank, R. K.   Psychotherapy using two therapists. *Amer. J. Psychother.* 18:488–499, 1964.

Greenbank, R. K.   Patients who talk without words. *Psychosomatics* 6:210–214, 1965.

Greenberg, H. R.   Erectile impotence during the course of Trofranil therapy. *Amer. J. Psychiat.* 121:1021, 1965.

Greenblatt, R. B.   Hormone factors in libido. *J. Clin. Endocr.* 3:305–306, 1943.

Greenblatt, R. B.   *Search the Scriptures*. Philadelphia: J. B. Lippincott, 1963.

Greenblatt, R. B., Mortara, F., and Torpin, R.   Sexual libido in the female. *Amer. J. Obstet. Gynec.* 44:658–663, 1942.

Greenblatt, R. B., and Scarpa-Smith, C. J.   Nymphomania in postmenopausal women. *J. Amer. Geriat. Soc.* 7:339–342, 1959.

Greenblatt, R. B., and Wilcox, E. A.   Hormonal therapy of fibromyomas of the uterus. *South. Surgeon* 10:339–346, 1941.

Greene, B. L.   Marital disharmony: Concurrent analysis of husband and wife. A preliminary report. *Dis. Nerv. Sys.* 21:73–78, 1960.

Greene, B. L. (Ed.).   *The Psychotherapies of Marital Disharmony*. New York: Free Press of Glencoe, 1965.

Greene, B. L., Solomon, A. P., and Lustig, N.   The psychotherapies of marital disharmony: With special reference to marriage counseling. *Med. Times* 91:243–256, 1963.

Greene, L. F., and Kelalis, P. P.   Retrograde ejaculation of semen due to diabetic neuropathy. *J. Urol.* 98:693–696, 1967.

Greenhill, J. P.   Frigidity in females. *Postgrad. Med.* 12:145–151, 1952.

Greenhill, J. P.   Traitement de la frigidité chez la femme. *Gynec. Prat.* 8:139, 1957.

Grimm, R.   *Love and Sexuality* (D. R. Mace, Trans.). New York: Association Press, 1964.

Groome, J. R.   A local use for testoterone. *Lancet* 2:722, 1939.

Gross, S.   *Practical Treatise on Impotence and Sterility.* Edinburgh: Y. J. Pentland, 1887.

Grossberg, J. M.   Behavior therapy: A review. *Psychol. Bull.* 62:73–88, 1964.

Grotjahn, M.   Problems and techniques of supervision. *Psychiatry* 18: 9–15, 1955.

Grotjahn, M.   *Psychoanalysis and the Family Neurosis.* New York: W. W. Norton, 1960.

Guitarte, A.   Sexual impulse in unmarried woman. *Bol. Inst. Matern.* 15:184–191, 1946.

Gulevich, G., and Zarcone, V.   Nocturnal erection and dreams. *Med. Asp. Human Sexuality* 3(4):105–109, 1969.

Gullerud, E. N., and Harlan, V. L. Four-way joint interviewing in marital counseling. *Social Casework* 43:10, 1962.

Gutheil, E. H.   Sexual dysfunctions in men. In *American Handbook of Psychiatry* (S. Arieti, Ed.). New York: Basic Books, 1959.

Guttmacher, A., et al.   *Birth Control and Love.* London: Macmillan, 1969.

Guyon, R.   *The Ethics of Sexual Acts.* New York: Alfred A. Knopf, 1948.

Hagan, P. J.   Posttraumatic anosmia. *Arch. Otolaryng.* (Chicago) 85: 85–89, 1967.

Haire, N.   *Encyclopedia of Sexual Knowledge.* New York: Eugenics Publishing, 1937.

Haire, N.   *Everyday Sex Problems.* London: Frederick Muller, 1948.

Haley, J.   Marriage therapy. *Arch. Gen. Psychiat.* (Chicago) 8:3, 1963.

Haley, J., and Hoffman, L. (Eds.).   *Techniques of Family Therapy.* New York: Basic Books, 1967.

Hall, S. P.   Vaginismus as cause of dyspareunia: Report of cases and method of treatment. *Western J. Surg. Obstet. Gynec.* 60:117–120, 1952.

Hamilton, E. G.   Frigidity in the female. *Missouri Med.* 58:1040–1051, 1961.

Hamilton, G. V.   *A Research in Marriage.* New York: Albert and Charles Boni, 1929.

Hamilton, J. B. Induction of penile erection by male hormone substances. *Endocrinology* 21:744–749, 1937.

Hamm, F. C., and Weinberg, S. R. (Eds.). *Urology in Medical Practice.* Philadelphia: J. B. Lippincott, 1962.

Hammerman, S. Masturbation and character. *J. Amer. Psychoanal. Ass.* 9:287–311, 1961.

Hammond, W. A. *Sexual Impotence in the Male.* New York: Bermingham, 1883.

Hampson, J. L., and Hampson, J. G. The ontogenesis of sexual behavior in man. In *Sex and Internal Secretions* (W. C. Young, Ed.). Baltimore: Williams & Wilkins, 1961.

Hardenbergh, E. W. The psychology of feminine sex experience. *Int. J. Sexology.* 2:224–228, 1949.

Hardenbergh, E. W. The psychology of feminine sex experience. In *Sex, Society, and the Individual* (A. P. Pillay and A. Ellis, Eds.). London: Delisle, 1953.

Hardy, K. R. An appetitional theory of sexual motivation. *Psychol. Rev.* 71:1–17, 1964.

Harlfinger, H. The psychosomatic case. II. Vaginismus and anorgasmy. *Geburtsh. Frauenheilk.* 28:1126–1131, 1968.

Harlow, H. F. The nature of love. *Amer. Psychol.* 13:673–685, 1958.

Harrison, S. I., and Carek, D. J. *A Guide to Psychotherapy.* Boston: Little, Brown, 1966.

Haslam, M. T. The treatment of psychogenic dyspareunia by reciprocal inhibition. *Brit. J. Psychiat.* 111:280–282, 1965.

Hastings, D. W. *Impotence and Frigidity.* Boston: Little, Brown, 1963.

Hastings, D. W. Problems of impotence. *Sexology* 31:90–92, 1964.

Havemann, E. *Men, Women and Marriage.* Garden City: Doubleday, 1962.

Hayashi, T. (Ed.). *Olfaction and Taste.* Oxford: Pergamon Press, 1967. Vol. II.

Heath, R. G. (Ed.). *The Role of Pleasure in Behavior.* New York: Harper & Row, 1964.

Heaver, L. Psychosemantic aspects of nonverbal communication. *Logos: Bull. Nat. Hosp. Speech Disorders* 5:60–70, 1962.

Hegar, A. Diagnose der frühesten Schwangerschaftsperiode. *Deutsch. Med. Wschr.* 21:565–567, 1895.

Heiman, M. Sexual response in women: A correlation of psysiological findings with psychoanalytic concepts. *J. Amer. Psychoanal. Ass.* 11:360–387, 1963.

Heiman, M. Heiman's discussion of Sherfey's paper on female sexuality, *J. Amer. Psychoanal. Ass.* 16:406–416, 1968.

Heiman, M. Female sexuality: Introduction. *J. Amer. Psychoanal. Ass.* 16:565–568, 1968.

Held, R. R. Psychotherapie de l'impuissance sexuelle. *Evolut. Psychiat.* (Paris) 3:489, 1957.

Held, R. R. Further views on psychotherapy of sexual impotence. *Sem. Ther.* 41:300–304, 1965.

Heller, C. G., and Myers, G. B. Male climacteric: Its symptomatology, diagnosis and treatment; use of therapeutic test with testosterone propionate (androgen) and testicular biopsies in delineating male climacteric from psychoneurosis and psychogenic impotence. *J.A.M.A.* 126:472–477, 1944.

Heller, J. Another case of inhibition of ejaculation as a side effect of Mellaril. *Amer. J. Psychiat.* 118:173, 1961.

Hellerstein, H. K., and Friedman, E. H. Sexual activity and the post-coronary patient. *Med. Asp. Human Sexuality* 3(3):70–96, 1969.

Henderson, V. E., and Roepke, M. H. On mechanism of erection. *Amer. J. Physiol.* 106:441–448, 1933.

Hendrick, I. Psychosexuality. In *The Anatomy of Love* (A. M. Krich, Ed.). New York: Dell, 1960.

Henkin, R. I. The definition of primary and accessory areas of olfaction as the basis for a classification of decreased olfactory acuity. In *Olfaction and Taste* (T. Hayashi, Ed.). Oxford: Pergamon Press, 1967. Vol. II.

Herman, M. Role of somesthetic stimuli in the development of sexual excitation in man. *Arch. Neurol. Psychiat.* 64:42–56, 1950.

Herrick, E. H. Sex changes in aging. *Sexology* 24:248–253, 1957.

Hettlinger, R. F. *Living with Sex: The Student's Dilemma.* New York: Seabury Press, 1966.

Hierons, R., and Saunders, M. Impotence in patients with temporal-lobe lesions. *Lancet* 2:761–763, 1966.

Hilse, W. C. Management of sexual conflicts in general practice. *J.A.M.A.* 150:846–849, 1952.

Hiltner, S. A contemporary Christian view of sex. *Pastoral Psychol.* 4:43–52, 1953.

Hirsch, E. W. Sexual impotence: Plea for more descriptive terminology. *Med. Rec.* 157:611–612, 1944.

Hirsch, E. W. *The Power to Love.* New York: Citadel Press, 1948.

Hirsch, E. W. *How to Improve Your Sexual Relations.* Chicago: Zeco, 1951.

Hirsch, E. W. The role of the female partner in premature ejaculation. *Int. J. Sexology* 5:1–6, 1951.

Hirsch, E. W. Coital and non-coital sex techniques. In *Sex Life of the*

American Woman and the Kinsey Report (A. Ellis, Ed.). New York: Greenberg, 1954.

Hirschfeld, M. *Sexual Pathology.* New York: Emerson Books, 1939.

Hirt, N. B. Sexual difficulties after 50: Psychiatrist's view. *Canad. Med. Ass. J.* 94:213–214, 1966.

Hitschmann, E., and Bergler, E. *Frigidity in Women: Its Characteristics and Treatment* (P. L. Weil, Trans.). Washington: Nervous and Mental Disease Publishing, 1936.

Hitschmann, E., and Bergler, E. Frigidity in women: Restatement and renewed experiences. *Psychoanal. Rev.* 36:45–53, 1949.

Hoenig, J., and Hamilton, C. M. Epilepsy and sexual orgasm. *Acta Psychiat. Scand.* 35:448, 1960.

Hohman, L. B., and Scott, W. W. A combined psychiatric and urologic study of sexual impotence. *J. Urol.* 29:59–76, 1933.

Hollender, M. H. Women's fantasies during sexual intercourse. *Arch. Gen. Psychiat.* (Chicago) 8:86–90, 1963.

Hollender, M. H. Hysterectomy and feelings of femininity. *Med. Asp. Human Sexuality* 3(7):6–15, 1969.

Hollender, M. H., Luborsky, L., and Scaramella, T. J. Body contact and sexual enticement. *Arch. Gen. Psychiat.* (Chicago) 20:188–191, 1969.

Hollis, F. *Women in Marital Conflict.* New York: Family Service Association of America, 1949.

Holloway, H. J. Cervicitis and endocervicitis in relation to gynecologic symptomatology. *Amer. J. Obstet. Gynec.* 32:304–307, 1936.

Holtgrewe, H. L., and Valk, W. L. Late results of transurethral prostatectomy. *J. Urol.* 92:51–55, 1964.

Horney, K. The flight from womanhood: The masculinity complex in women as viewed by men and women. *Int. J. Psychoanal.* 7:324–339, 1924.

Horney, K. On the genesis of the castration complex in women. *Int. J. Psychoanal.* 5:50–65, 1924.

Horney, K. The dread of woman: Observations on a specific difference in the dread felt by men and by women respectively for the opposite sex. *Int. J. Psychoanal.* 13:348–360, 1932.

Horney, K. The denial of the vagina. *Int. J. Psychoanal.* 14:57–70, 1933.

Horney, K. Psychogenic factors in functional female disorders. *Amer. J. Obstet. Gynec.* 25:694–704, 1933.

Horney, K., and Kelman, H. *Feminine Psychology.* New York: W. W. Norton, 1967.

Hornstein, F. X. von, and Faller, A. *Sex, Love, Marriage: A Handbook and Guide for Catholics.* (A. V. O'Brien and W. J. O'Hara, Eds.). New York: Herder & Herder, 1964.

Horrobin, D. F.   *The Communication Systems of the Body.* New York: Basic Books, 1964.

Horton, R., and Tait, J. F.   Androstenedione production and interconversion rates measured in peripheral blood and studies on the possible site of its conversion to testosterone. *J. Clin. Invest.* 45:301–313, 1966.

Horton, R., and Tait, J. F.   In vivo conversion of dehydroisoandrosterone to plasma androstenedione and testosterone in man. *J. Clin. Endocr.* 27:79–88, 1967.

Huddleston Slater, W. B.   Vaginisme. *Nederl. T. Geneesk.* 93:4309–4313, 1949.

Huffman, J. W.   The effect of gynecologic surgery on sexual relations. *Amer. J. Obstet. Gynec.* 59:915–917, 1950.

Huffman, J. W.   *Gynecology and Obstetrics.* Philadelphia: W. B. Saunders, 1962.

Huffman, J. W.   Sexual reactions after gynecologic surgery. *Med. Asp. Human Sexuality* 3(11):48–57, 1969.

Hughes, J. M.   Failure to ejaculate with chlordiazepoxide. *Amer. J. Psychiat.* 121:610–611, 1964.

Huhner, M.   *A Practical Treatise on Disorders of the Sexual Function in the Male and Female.* Philadelphia: F. A. Davis, 1916.

Huhner, M.   Diagnosis and treatment of impotence in the male and female. *Amer. Med.* 38:144–152, 1932.

Huhner, M.   Masturbation and impotence from a urologic standpoint. *J. Urol.* 36:770–785, 1936.

Huhner, M.   Impotence in the male. *Med. Rec.* 149:366–370, 1939.

Huhner, M.   *Sexual Disorders.* Philadelphia: F. A. Davis, 1942.

Huhner, M.   *The Diagnosis and Treatment of Sexual Disorders in the Male and Female Including Sterility and Impotence.* Philadelphia: F. A. Davis, 1945.

Hulme, W. E.   *The Pastoral Care of Families.* New York: Abingdon Press, 1962.

Hulse, W. C.   Management of sexual conflicts in general practice. *J.A.M.A.* 150:846–849, 1952.

Hummer, W. K.   Frigidity in women: A symptom, not a diagnosis. *Minn. Med.* 49:1879–1884, 1966.

Hunt, M. M.   *The Natural History of Love.* New York: Alfred A. Knopf, 1959.

Hunt, M. M.   *Her Infinite Variety: The American Woman as Lover, Mate and Rival.* New York: Harper & Row, 1962.

Hurvitz, N. Marital problems following psychotherapy with one spouse. *J. Consult. Psychol.* 31:38–47, 1967.

Hutton, I. E. *The Sex Technique in Marriage.* New York: Emerson Books, 1942.

Huxley, A. *The Doors of Perception.* New York: Harper & Row, 1964.

Hynie, J. The sexological aspects of hypospadias. *Acta Chir. Plast.* (Praha) 8:232–234, 1966.

Imielinski, K. Männliche Sexualneurose: Analyse von 146 Fällen. *Psychiat. Neurol.* (Basel) 143:398–406, 1962.

Irisawa, S., et al. Sexual disturbances in diabetes. *Tohoku J. Exp. Med.* 88:311–326, 1966.

Israel, S. L. Premenstrual tension. *J.A.M.A.* 110:1721–1723, 1938.

Jackson, D. D., and Weakland, J. H. Conjoint family therapy. *Psychiatry* 24:30–45, 1961.

Jacobs, E. C. Effects of starvation on sex hormones in the male. *J. Clin. Endocr.* 8:227–232, 1948.

Jarvik, L. F. Sex differences in longevity. In *Advances in Sex Research* (H. G. Beigel, Ed.). New York: Hoeber-Harper, 1963.

Jaspers, K. *The Nature of Psychotherapy* (J. Hoenig and M. W. Hamilton, Trans.). Chicago: Phoenix Books, 1965.

Jensen, O. *The Revolt of American Women.* New York: Harcourt, Brace, 1952.

Johnson, D. *Marriage Counseling: Theory and Practice.* Englewood Cliffs, N.J.: Prentice-Hall, 1961.

Johnson, J. Disorders of sexual potency in the male. Unpublished M.D. thesis. University of Manchester, 1964.

Johnson, J. Androgyny and disorders of sexual potency. *Brit. Med. J.* 5461:572–573, 1965.

Johnson, J. Prognosis of disorders of sexual potency in the male. *J. Psychosom. Res.* 9:195–200, 1965.

Johnson, J. Sexual impotence and the limbic system. *Brit. J. Psychiat.* 111:300–303, 1965.

Johnson, V. E., and Masters, W. H. Treatment of the sexually incompatible family unit. *Minn. Med.* 44:466–471, 1961.

Johnson, V. E., and Masters, W. H. Sexual incompatibility: Diagnosis and treatment. In *Human Reproduction and Sexual Behavior* (C. W. Lloyd, Ed.). Philadelphia: Lea & Febiger, 1964.

Johnson, V. E., and Masters, W. H. A team approach to the rapid diagnosis and treatment of sexual incompatibility. *Pacif. Med. Surg.* 72:371–375, 1964.

Johnston, J. W., Jr. Experiments on the specificities of human olfaction. Part 2. In *Olfaction and Taste* (T. Hayashi, Ed.). Oxford: Pergamon Press, 1967. Vol. II.

Jones, E.   The early development of female sexuality. *Int. J. Psychoanal.* 8:459–472, 1927.

Jones, E.   Early female sexuality. *Int. J. Psychoanal.* 16:263–273, 1935.

Kagan, J.   Differential reward value of incomplete and complete sexual behavior. *J. Comp. Physiol. Psychol.* 48:59–64, 1955.

Kalliomaki, J. L., Markkanen, T. K., and Mustonen, V. A.   Sexual behavior after cerebral vascular accident: A study on patients below the age of 60 years. *Fertil. Steril.* 12:156–158, 1961.

Kalogerakis, M. G.   The role of olfaction in sexual development. *Psychosom. Med.* 25:420–432, 1963.

Kamiat, A. H.   *Feminine Superiority*. New York: Bookman, 1960.

Kamlp, H., and Thor, R.   Vaginisme og frigiditet behandlet med afspaending. *Ugeskr. Laeg.* 115:1363–1367, 1953.

Kaplan, A. H., and Abrams, M.   Ejaculatory impotence. *J. Urol.* 79: 964–968, 1958.

Karacan, I., Goodenough, D. R., Shapiro, A., and Starker, S.   Erection cycle during sleep in relation to dream anxiety. *Arch. Gen. Psychiat.* (Chicago) 15:183–189, 1966.

Kardiner, A.   *Sex and Morality*. Indianapolis: Bobbs-Merrill, 1954.

Kargman, M. W.   The clinical use of social system theory in marriage counseling. *Marr. Fam. Living* 19:263–269, 1957.

Katz, R. L.   *Empathy: Its Nature and Uses*. New York: Free Press of Glencoe, 1963.

Kaufman, J. J. (Ed.).   *Advances in Diagnostic Urology*. Boston: Little, Brown, 1964.

Kaufman, J. J., and Borgeson, G.   *Man and Sex*. New York: Simon and Schuster, 1961.

Kaydis, A.   Group psychotherapy with married couples. *Int. Ment. Health News* 6:4–6, 1964.

Kaye, H. E.   Mythology of the genitalia. *Med. Asp. Human Sexuality* 3(6):61–69, 1969.

Kegel, A. H.   Sexual functions of the pubococcygeus muscle. *Western J. Surg. Obstet. Gynec.* 60:521, 1952.

Keiser, S.   On the psychopathology of orgasm. *Psychoanal. Quart.* 16: 378–390, 1947.

Keiser, S.   Body ego during orgasm. *Psychoanal. Quart.* 21:153–166, 1952.

Keiser, S.   Female sexuality. *J. Amer. Psychoanal. Ass.* 4:563–574, 1956.

Keiser, S.   Keiser's discussion of Sherfey's paper on female sexuality. *J. Amer. Psychoanal. Ass.* 16:449–456, 1968.

Keith, C.   Multiple transfers of psychotherapy patients. *Arch. Gen. Psychiat.* (Chicago) 14:185–189, 1966.

Kelly, G. L.   *Sexual Feeling in Woman.* Kingsport: Kingsport Press, 1930.

Kelly, G. L.   Problems of impotence in aging males. *J. Amer. Geriat. Soc.* 3:883–889, 1955.

Keshin, J. G.   Dislocation of penis complicated by neurogenic bladder, fistula from bladder to thigh, and impotence. *J. Urol.* 82:342–346, 1959.

Keshin, J. G., and Pinck, B. D.   Impotentia. *New York J. Med.* 49:269–272, 1949.

Kestenberg, J. S.   On the development of maternal feelings in early childhood. *Psychoanal. Stud. Child* 11:257–291, 1956.

Kestenberg, J. S.   Vicissitudes of female sexuality. *J. Amer. Psychoanal. Ass.* 4:453–476, 1956.

Kestenberg, J. S.   Kestenberg's discussion of Sherfey's paper on female sexuality. *J. Amer. Psychoanal. Ass.* 16:417–423, 1968.

Kestenberg, J. S.   Outside and inside, male and female. *J. Amer. Psychoanal. Ass.* 16:457–520, 1968.

Kiev, A., and Hackett, E.   The chemotherapy of impotence and frigidity. *J. Sex Res.* 4:220–224, 1968.

Kinch, R. A.   Sexual difficulties after 50: The gynecologist's view. *Canad. Med. Ass. J.* 94:211–212, 1966.

Kinsey, A. C.   Sex behavior in the human animal. *Ann. N.Y. Acad. Sci.* 47:635–637, 1947.

Kinsey, A. C., Pomeroy, W. B., and Martin, C. E.   *Sexual Behavior in the Human Male.* Philadelphia: W. B. Saunders, 1948.

Kinsey, A. C., Pomeroy, W. B., Martin, C. E., and Gebhard, P. H.   Concepts of normality and abnormality in sexual behavior. In *Psychosexual Development in Health and Disease* (P. Hoch and J. Zubin, Eds.). New York: Grune & Stratton, 1949.

Kinsey, A. C., Pomeroy, W. B., Martin, C. E., and Gebhard, P. H.   *Sexual Behavior in the Human Female.* Philadelphia: W. B. Saunders, 1953.

Kirkendall, L. A.   Toward a clarification of the concept of male sex drive. *Marr. Fam. Living* 20:367–372, 1958.

Kirkendall, L. A.   Sex drive. In *The Encyclopedia of Sexual Behavior* (A. Ellis and A. Abarbanel, Eds.). New York: Hawthorn Books, 1961.

Kirsner, J., Ford, H., and Kassriel, R.   Anticholinergic drugs in peptic ulcer. *Med. Clin. N. Amer.* 41:495–520, 1957.

Kisch, E. H.   *The Sexual Life of Women in Its Physiological, Pathological, and Hygienic Aspects* (N. E. Paul, Trans.). New York: Allied Book, 1926.

Kleegman, S. J. Frigidity in women. *Quart. Rev. Surg. Obstet. Gynec.* 16:243–248, 1959.

Kleegman, S. J. Female sex problems. *Sexology* 31:226–229, 1964.

Kleegman, S. J. How women respond. *Sexology* 31:159–162, 1964.

Kleemeier, R. W., and Kantor, M. B. Methodological considerations in the study of human sexual behavior. In *Determinants of Human Sexual Behavior* (G. Winokur, Ed.). Springfield, Ill.: Charles C Thomas, 1963.

Klemer, R. H. (Ed.). *Counseling in Marital and Sexual Problems: A Physician's Handbook.* Baltimore: Williams & Wilkins, 1965.

Klemer, R. H. Talking with patients about sexual problems. In *Counseling in Marital and Sexual Problems.* (R. H. Klemer, Ed.). Baltimore: Williams & Wilkins, 1965.

Klingensmith, P. O. Sexual adjustment as seen by the gynecologist and obstetrician. In *Man and Wife* (E. H. Mudd and A. Krich, Eds.). New York: W. W. Norton, 1957.

Klumbies, G. Das Herz im Orgasmus. *Med. Klin.* 3:952, 1950.

Klumbies, G., and Kleinsorge, H. Circulating dangers and prophylaxis during orgasm. *Int. J. Sexology* 4:61–66, 1950.

Knight, R. P. Functional disturbances in the sexual life of women: Frigidity and related disorders. *Bull. Menninger Clin.* 7:25–35, 1943.

Kohlmeyer, W. Sexually frustrated patients: A common misconception. *Delaware Med. J.* 27:189–191, 1955.

Koll, I. S. *Diseases of the Male Urethra.* London: W. B. Saunders, 1918.

Korenman, S. G., Wilson, H., and Lipsett, M. B. Testosterone production rates in normal adults. *J. Clin. Invest.* 42:1753–1760, 1963.

Kraft, T., and Al-Issa, I. Behavior therapy and the treatment of frigidity. *Amer. J. Psychother.* 21:116–120, 1967.

Kramer, E. Judgment of personality characteristics and emotions from non-verbal properties of speech. *Psychol. Bull.* 60:408–420, 1963.

Kramer, P. Early capacity for orgastic discharge and character formation. *Psychoanal. Stud. Child* 9:128–141, 1954.

Kretschmer, H. L. Medical management of chronic prostatitis. *Wisconsin Med. J.* 38:363–372, 1939.

Kroger, W. S. Psychosomatic aspects of frigidity and impotence. *Int. Rec. Med.* 171:469–478, 1958.

Kroger, W. S., and Freed, S. C. Psychosomatic aspects of frigidity. *J.A.M.A.* 143:526–532, 1950.

Kroger, W. S., and Freed, S. C. *Psychosomatic Gynecology.* Philadelphia: W. B. Saunders, 1951.

Kronhausen, P., and Kronhausen, E. *Sex Histories of American College Men.* New York: Ballantine Books, 1960.

Kubie, L. S. Psychiatric implications of the Kinsey report. In *Sexual Behavior in American Society* (J. Himelhoch and S. Fava, Eds.). New York: W. W. Norton, 1955.

Kubie, L. S. Research into the process of supervision in psychoanalysis. *Psychoanal. Quart.* 27:226–236, 1958.

Kupperman, H. S. Hormonal aspects of frigidity. *Quart. Rev. Surg. Obstet. Gynec.* 16:254–257, 1959.

Kupperman, H. S. Sex hormones. In *The Encyclopedia of Sexual Behavior* (A. Ellis and A. Abarbanel, Eds.). New York: Hawthorn Books, 1961.

Kurland, M. L., Layman, W. A., and Rozan, G. H. Impotence in the male. *GP* 32:113–116, 1965.

Laidlaw, R. W. The psychiatrist as a marriage counselor. *Amer. J. Psychiat.* 106:732–736, 1950.

Laird, D. A. Some normal odor effects and associations of psychoanalytic significance. *Psychoanal. Rev.* 21:194–200, 1934.

Lampl De Groot, J. Problems of femininity. *Psychoanal. Quart.* 2: 489–518, 1933.

Lamson, H. D. Are American women frigid? *Int. J. Sexology* 3:162–167, 1950.

Lanval, M. General anesthesia and female frigidity. *Marriage Hygiene* 1:236–237, 1948.

Lash, H. Silicone implant for impotence. *J. Urol.* 100:709–710, 1968.

Lash, H., Zimmerman, D. C., and Loeffler, R. A. Silicone implantation: Inlay method. *Plast. Reconstr. Surg.* 34:75–80, 1964.

Layman, W. A., Rozan, G. H., and Kurland, M. L. Frigidity in the female. *GP* 34:103–106, 1966.

Lazarus, A. A. The treatment of chronic frigidity by systematic desensitization. *J. Nerv. Ment. Dis.* 136:272–278, 1963.

Lazarus, A. A. Modes of treatment for sexual inadequacies. *Med. Asp. Human Sexuality* 3:53–58, 1969.

Leader, A. J. Chronic vesiculoprostatitis: a reorientation. *J.A.M.A.* 168: 995–999, 1958.

Leckie, F. H. Hypnotherapy in gynecological disorders. *Int. J. Clin. Exp. Hypn.* 12:121–146, 1964.

Lehfeldt, H. Coitus interruptus. *Med. Asp. Human Sexuality* 2(11): 29–31, 1968.

Leriche, R., and Morel, A. The syndrome of thrombotic obliteration of the aortic bifurcation. *Ann. Surg.* 127:193–206, 1948.

Leslie, C. H., and Bruhl, D. E.   An effective anti-impotence agent: Statistical evaluation of 1000 reported cases. *Memphis Mid South Med. J.* 38:379–385, 1963.

Leuba, C.   *The Sexual Nature of Man and Its Management.* New York: Doubleday, 1954.

Levie, L. H.   Vaginal orgasm. *Int. J. Sexology* 3:122, 1949.

Levie, L. H.   Disturbances in male potency. In *Sex, Society, and the Individual* (A. P. Pillay and A. Ellis, Eds.). London: Delisle, 1953.

Levie, L. H.   Impotentia ejaculandi. *Nederl. T. Geneesk.* 101:1900–1907, 1957.

Levine, J.   The sexual adjustment of alcoholics: A clinical study of a selected sample. *Quart. J. Stud. Alcohol* 16:675–680, 1955.

Levine, J., and Albert, H.   Sexual behavior after lobotomy. *J. Nerv. Ment. Dis.* 113:332–341, 1951.

Levine, L.   Orgasm capacity of women. *Marriage Hygiene* 1:172–173, 1948.

Levine, L.   A criterion for orgasm in the female. *Marriage Hygiene* 1: 173–174, 1948.

Lewin, S. A., and Gilmore, J.   *Sex after Forty.* New York: Medical Research Press, 1952.

Lewis, J. M.   Impotence as a reflection of marital conflict. *Med. Asp. Human Sexuality* 3(6):73–78, 1969.

Leznenko, V. N.   On a method of group psychotherapy of various forms of functional impotence in men. *Zh. Nevropat. Psikhiat. Korsakov.* 68:775–778, 1968.

Lichtenstein, H.   Identity and sexuality: A study of their interrelationship in man. *J. Amer. Psychoanal. Ass.* 9:179–260, 1961.

Lief, H. I.   What medical schools teach about sex. *Bull. Tulane Univ. Med. Fac.* 22:161–168, 1963.

Lief, H. I.   Sex education of medical students and doctors. *Pacif. Med. Surg.* 73: 52–58, 1965.

Lief, H., Dingman, J. F., and Bishop, M. P.   Psychoendocrinologic studies in a male with cyclic changes in sexuality. *Psychosom. Med.* 24:357–368, 1962.

Lief, H. I., and Reed, D. M.   Normal psychosexual functioning. In *Comprehensive Textbook of Psychiatry* (A. M. Freedman and H. I. Kaplan, Eds.). Baltimore: Williams & Wilkins, 1967.

Lindsay, H. B.   The male and female climacteric. *Dis. Nerv. Syst.* 23: 149–151, 1962.

Liswood, R.   Variety: The spice of marital sex. *Med. Asp. Human Sexuality* 3(11):105–112, 1969.

Lloyd, C. W. *Human Reproduction and Sexual Behavior.* London: Henry Kimpton, 1964.

Locke, H. J. *Predicting Adjustment in Marriage.* New York: Holt, Rinehart and Winston, 1951.

Loeffler, R. A., and Sayegh, E. S. Perforated acrylic implants in the management of organic impotence. *J. Urol.* 84:559, 1960.

Loeffler, R. A., Sayegh, E. S., and Lash, H. The artificial os penis. *Plast. Reconstr. Surg.* 34:71–74, 1964.

Loeser, A. A. Subcutaneous implantation of female and male hormone in tablet form in women. *Brit. Med. J.* 1:479–482, 1940.

Loewe, S. Influence of autonomic drugs on ejaculation. *J. Pharmacol. Exp. Ther.* 63:70–75, 1938.

Loewe, S., and Puttuck, S. L. Anti-ejaculatory effect of sympatholytic, gangliolytic and spasmolytic drugs. *J. Pharmacol. Exp. Ther.* 107:379, 1953.

Loewenstein, J. Treatment of impotence: A coitus-training apparatus. *Brit. Med. J.* 2:49–50, 1941.

Loewenstein, J. Mechanotherapy: Recent experiences with C. T. (coitus-training) apparatus. *Med. Press* 211:381–384, 1944.

Loewenstein, J. Disorders of erection. No. 1. *Marriage Hygiene* 1:35–40, 1947.

Loewenstein, J. Disorders of erection. No. 2. *Marriage Hygiene* 1:92–97, 1947.

Loewenstein, J. *The Treatment of Impotence: With Special Reference to Mechanotherapy.* London: Hamish Hamilton, 1947.

Lomax-Simpson, J. Dyspareunia. *Brit. Med. J.* 2:744, 1958.

Lorand, S. Contribution to the problem of vaginal orgasm. *Int. J. Psychoanal.* 20:432–438, 1939.

Lorenz, K. Z. *King Solomon's Ring: New Light on Animal Ways.* New York: Thomas Y. Crowell, 1952.

Lott, G. M. The training of non-medical cooperative psychotherapists by multiple psychotherapy. *Amer. J. Psychother.* 6:440, 1952.

Lowen, A. Frigidity: A bioenergetic study. *Quart. Rev. Surg. Obstet. Gynec.* 16:258, 1959.

Lowrie, R. J. Frigidity in women. *Western J. Surg.* 60:458–462, 1960.

Lowsley, O. S., and Bray, J. L. Surgical relief of impotence. *J.A.M.A.* 107:2029, 1936.

Lowsley, O. S., and Cangelosi, J. T. Ten years' experience with operation for cure of certain types of impotence. *Southern Med. J.* 39:67–69, 1946.

Lowsley, O. S., and Kerwin, T. J. *Clinical Urology*. Baltimore: Williams & Wilkins, 1956.

Lowsley, O. S., and Rueda, A. Further experience with an operation for the cure of certain types of impotence. *J. Int. Coll. Surg.* 19(1): 69–77, 1953.

Lundberg, F., and Farnham, M. F. *Modern Woman, the Lost Sex*. New York: Harper & Brothers, 1947.

Lundin, W. H., and Aranov, B. M. Use of co-therapists in group psychotherapy. *J. Consult. Psychol.* 16:176, 1952.

Lydston, G. F. Surgical treatment of impotence. *Amer. J. Clin. Med.* 15:1571, 1908.

Ma, J. Y. C. Lowsley plastic operation for cure of certain types of sexual impotence with two case reports. *Chin. Med. J.* 67:143–146, 1949.

Mace, D. R. *Hebrew Marriage: A Sociological Study*. London: Epworth Press, 1953.

Mace, D. R. *Success in Marriage*. Nashville: Abingdon Press, 1958.

Mace, D. R., Liswood, R., Bloch, D., Tate, F., and Kleegman, S. J. Roundtable: What makes a happy marriage? *Med. Asp. Human Sexuality* 3(7):29–49, 1969.

Maclean, P. D. Cerebral representation of penile erection. *J. Neurophysiol.* 25:29, 1962.

Madsen, C. H., Jr., and Ullmann, L. P. Innovations in the desensitization of frigidity. *Behav. Res. Ther.* 5:67–68, 1967.

Maizlish, L., and Hurley, J. R. Attitude changes of husbands and wives in time-limited group psychotherapy. *Psychiat. Quart.* 37:230–249, 1963.

Makizumi, I. A study on the male sexual impotence. *Jap. J. Urol.* 59:16–47, 1968.

Malleson, J. Vaginismus: Its management and psychogenesis. *Brit. Med. J.* 2:213–216, 1942.

Malleson, J. Sexual disorders in women: Their medical significance. *Brit. Med. J.* 2:1480–1483, 1951.

Malleson, J. *Any Wife or Any Husband*. New York: Random House, 1952.

Malleson, J. Sex problems in marriage with particular reference to coital discomfort and the unconsummated marriage. *Practitioner* 172: 389–396, 1954.

Mandell, A. J. The management of sexual impotence. *GP* 28(3):108–112, 1963.

Mandy, A. J. Frigidity. In *Sex Life of the American Woman and the Kinsey Report* (A. Ellis, Ed.). New York: Greenberg, 1954.

Mann, E. C.   Frigidity. *Clin. Obstet. Gynec.* 3:739–758, 1960.

Mann, T.   Effects of pharmacological agents on male sexual functions. *J. Reprod. Fertil.* 4 (Suppl.): 101–114, 1968.

Marcelli, F., et al.   Frigidity and sterility. *Clin. Obstet. Gynec.* 66:580–589, 1964.

Margolis, R., and Leslie, C. H.   Review of studies on a mixture of nux vomica, yohimbine and methyl testosterone in the treatment of impotence. *Curr. Ther. Res.* 8:280–284, 1966.

Margolis, R., Sangree, H., Prieto, P., Stein, L., and Chinn, S.   Clinical studies on the use of Afrodex in the treatment of impotence: Statistical summary of 4000 cases. *Curr. Ther. Res.* 9:213–219, 1967.

Marmor, J.   Some considerations concerning orgasm in the female. *Psychosom. Med.* 16:240–245, 1954.

Marsh, E. M., and Vollmer, A. M.   Possible psychogenic aspects of infertility. *Fertil. Steril.* 2:70–79, 1951.

Marshall, V. F.   *Textbook of Urology.* New York: Hoeber-Harper, 1964.

Martin, C. B.   Sex during the menstrual period. *Med. Asp. Human Sexuality* 3(6):37–49, 1969.

Martin, M. J.   Frigidity, impotence and the family. *Psychosomatics* 9: 225–228, 1968.

Martin, P. A., and Bird, H. W.   An approach to the psychotherapy of marriage partners: The stereoscopic technique. *Psychiatry* 16:123–127, 1953.

Maslow, A.   Self-esteem, dominance feeling, and sexuality in women. *J. Soc. Psychol.* 16:259–294, 1942.

Maslow, A.   *Motivation and Personality.* New York: Harper & Brothers, 1954.

Maslow, A. H.   *Toward a Psychology of Being.* Princeton: D. Van Nostrand, 1962.

Maslow, A. H.   *Religions, Values, and Peak-Experiences.* Columbus: Ohio State University Press, 1964.

Mason, I.   Headaches and vertigo and their correlations to derangement of sexual function. *Ohio Med. J.* 41:132–136, 1945.

Masserman, J. H.   Historical, comparative and experimental roots of short-term therapy. In *Brief Psychotherapy* (L. Wolberg, Ed.). New York: Grune & Stratton, 1965.

Masserman, J. H.   *Modern Therapy of Personality Disorders.* Dubuque, Iowa: Wm. C. Brown, 1966.

Masserman, J. H. (Ed.).   *Science and Psychoanalysis: Sexuality of Women.* New York: Grune & Stratton, 1966. Vol. X.

Masters, W. H. The rationale and technique of sex hormone replacement in the aged female and a preliminary result report. *S. Dakota J. Med.* 4:296–300, 1951.

Masters, W. H. Long range sex steroid replacement: Target organ regeneration. *J. Geront.* 8:33–39, 1953.

Masters, W. H. Rationale of sex steroid replacement in the "neutral gender." *Geriatrics* 3:389–395, 1955.

Masters, W. H. Sex life of the aging female. In *Sex in Our Culture* (G. Groves and A. Stone, Eds.). New York: Emerson Books, 1955.

Masters, W. H. Endocrine therapy in the aging individual. *Obstet. Gynec.* 8:61–67, 1956.

Masters, W. H. Sex steroid replacement in the aging individual. In *Hormones and the Aging Process.* New York: Academic Press, 1956.

Masters, W. H. Sex steroid influence on the aging process. *Amer. J. Obstet. Gynec.* 74:733–746, 1957.

Masters, W. H. The sexual response cycle of the human female. I. Gross anatomic considerations. *Western J. Surg. Obstet. Gynec.* 68: 57–72, 1960.

Masters, W. H. Clinical significance of the study of human sexual response. *Med. Asp. Human Sexuality* 1:14–20, 1967.

Masters, W. H., and Allen, W. M. Female sex hormone replacement in the aged woman. *J. Geront.* 3:183–190, 1948.

Masters, W. H., and Ballew, J. W. The third sex. *Geriatrics* 10:1–4, 1955.

Masters, W. H., and Grody, M. H. Estrogen-androgen substitution therapy in the aged female. II. Clinical response. *Obstet. Gynec.* 2: 139–147, 1953.

Masters, W. H., and Johnson, V. E. The sexual response cycle of the human female. II. Vaginal lubrication. *Ann. N.Y. Acad. Sci.* 83:301–317, 1959.

Masters, W. H., and Johnson, V. E. The human female: Anatomy of sexual response. *Minn. Med.* 43:31–36, 1960.

Masters, W. H., and Johnson, V. E. The artificial vagina: Anatomic, physiologic, psychosexual function. *Western J. Surg. Obstet. Gynec.* 69:192–212, 1961.

Masters, W. H., and Johnson, V. E. The physiology of the vaginal reproductive function. *Western J. Surg. Obstet. Gynec.* 69:105–120, 1961.

Masters, W. H., and Johnson, V. E. Anatomy of the female orgasm. In *The Encyclopedia of Sexual Behavior* (A. Ellis and A. Abarbanel, Eds.). New York: Hawthorn Books, 1961.

Masters, W. H., and Johnson, V. E.   The sexual response cycle of the human female. III. The clitoris: Anatomic and clinical considerations. *Western J. Surg. Obstet. Gynec.* 70:248–257, 1962.

Masters, W. H., and Johnson, V. E.   The sexual response cycle of the human male. I. Gross anatomic considerations. *Western J. Surg. Obstet Gynec.* 71:85–95, 1963.

Masters, W. H., and Johnson, V. E.   The clitoris: An anatomic baseline for behavioral investigation. In *Determinants of Human Sexual Behavior* (G. Winokur, Ed.). Springfield, Ill.: Charles C Thomas, 1963.

Masters, W. H., and Johnson, V. E.   Sexual response. Part II. Anatomy and physiology. In *Human Reproduction and Sexual Behavior* (C. W. Lloyd, Ed.). Philadelphia: Lea & Febiger, 1964.

Masters, W. H., and Johnson, V. E.   The sexual response cycles of the human male and female: Comparative anatomy and physiology. In *Sex and Behavior* (F. A. Beach, Ed.). New York: John Wiley, 1965.

Masters, W. H., and Johnson, V. E.   The sexual response cycle of the human female. I. Gross anatomic considerations. In *Sex Research: New Developments* (J. Money, Ed.). New York: Holt, Rinehart and Winston, 1965.

Masters, W. H., and Johnson, V. E.   The sexual response cycle of the human female. II. The clitoris: Anatomic and clinical considerations. In *Sex Research: New Developments* (J. Money, Ed.). New York: Holt, Rinehart and Winston, 1965.

Masters, W. H., and Johnson, V. E.   Counseling with sexually incompatible marriage partners. In *Counseling in Marital and Sexual Problems: A Physician's Handbook* (R. H. Klemer, Ed.). Baltimore: Williams & Wilkins, 1965.

Masters, W. H., and Johnson, V. E.   *Human Sexual Response*. Boston: Little, Brown, 1966.

Masters, W. H., and Johnson, V. E.   Human sexual inadequacy and some parameters of therapy. In *Perspectives in Reproduction and Sexual Behavior* (M. Diamond, Ed.). Bloomington: Indiana University Press, 1968.

Masters, W. H., and Johnson, V. E.   Human sexual response: The aging female and the aging male. In *Middle Age and Aging* (B. L. Neugarten, Ed.). Chicago: University of Chicago Press, 1968.

Masters, W. H., and Magallon, D. T.   Androgen administration in the postmenopausal woman. *J. Clin. Endocr.* 10:348–358, 1950.

Masters, W. H., and Magallon, D. T.   Hormone replacement therapy in the aged female: Estrogen bioassay. *Proc. Soc. Exp. Biol. Med.* 73:672–676, 1950.

May, A. G., DeWeese, J. A., and Rob, C. G. Changes in sexual function following operation on the abdominal aorta. *Surgery* 65:41–47, 1969.

Mayer, M. D. Classification and treatment of dyspareunia. *Amer. J. Obstet. Gynec.* 24:751–755, 1932.

Mayer, M. D. Status of psychotherapy in gynecologic practice. *Amer. J. Obstet. Gynec.* 34:47–57, 1937.

McCall, G. J., and Simmons, J. L. *Identities and Interactions.* New York: Free Press of Glencoe, 1966.

McClean, P. D. New findings relevant to the evolution of psychosexual functions of the brain. *J. Nerv. Ment. Dis.* 135:289–301, 1962.

McDowell, F. H. Sexual manifestations of neurologic disease. *Med. Asp. Human Sexuality* 2:13–21, 1968.

McGavack, T. H. The male climacterium. *J. Amer. Geriat. Soc.* 3: 639–655, 1955.

McGuire, T. F., and Steinhilber, R. M. Sexual frigidity. *Mayo Clin. Proc.* 39:416–426, 1964.

McKegney, F. P. The medical treatment of sexual problems. *Conn. Med.* 30:611–612, 1966.

Mead, B. T. Sexual problems. *Med. Times* 90:1033, 1962.

Mead, M. *Male and Female.* New York: William Morrow, 1949.

Mears, E. Dyspareunia. *Brit. Med. J.* 2:443–445, 1958.

Medrano, R. S. Relation between abortion and lack of orgasm: A preliminary report. *Bol. Col. Med. Camaguey* 11:160–181, 1948.

Meerloo, J. A. M. *Conversation and Communication.* New York: International Universities Press, 1952.

Meerloo, J. A. M. Communication and the therapeutic encounter. *Logos: Bull. Nat. Hosp. Speech Disorders* 2:55–60, 1959.

Meerloo, J. A. M. *Unobtrusive Communication.* Assen: Koninklijke Van Gorcum & Co. N.V., 1964.

Melicow, M. M. Coitus, impotence and angina pectoris. *New York Med. J.* 45:1325–1328, 1945.

Mellan, J. Psychotherapy of sexual disturbances in single men. *Psychiat. Neurol. Med. Psychol.* (Leipzig) 20:19–21, 1968.

Mellgren, A. On a modified hypnosis therapy of impotentia erectionis. *Derm. Wschr.* 153:897-899, 1967.

Menaker, E. A. Note on some biologic parallels between certain innate animal behavior and moral masochism. *Psychoanal. Rev.* 43:31, 1956.

Menninger, K. A. Impotence and frigidity from the standpoint of psychoanalysis. *J. Urol.* 34:166–183, 1935.

Menninger, K. A. Impotence and frigidity. *Bull. Menninger Clin.* 1: 251–260, 1937.

Menninger, K. A. Impotence and frigidity. In *Man Against Himself*. New York: Harcourt, Brace, 1938.

Menninger, K. A. Somatic correlations with the unconscious repudiation of femininity in women. *J. Nerv. Ment. Dis.* 89:514–527, 1939.

Menninger, K. A. *Theory of Psychoanalytic Technique.* New York: Basic Books, 1958.

Mertz, P. Therapeutic considerations in masturbation. *Amer. J. Psychother.* 9:630–639, 1955.

Meyers, R. Evidence of a locus of the neural mechanisms for libido and penile potency in the septo-fornico-hypothalamic region of the human brain. *Trans. Amer. Neurol. Ass.* 86:81–85, 1961.

Michael, S. T. Impotence during electric-shock therapy. *Psychiat. Quart.* 25:24–31, 1951.

Mikulicz-Radecki, F. von. Difficulties during coitus. *Geburtsh. Frauenheilk.* 8:409–423, 1948.

Miller, N. E., Hubert, G., and Hamilton, J. B. Mental and behavioral changes following male hormone treatment of adult castration, hypogonadism, and psychic impotence. *Proc. Soc. Exp. Biol. Med.* 38:538–540, 1938.

Millin, T. Impotence and its surgical treatment: With reference to new operative procedure. *Proc. Roy. Soc. Med.* 29:817–824, 1936.

Mirowitz, J. M. The utilization of hypnosis in psychic impotence. *Brit. J. Med. Hypn.* 17:25–32, 1966.

Mitsuya, H., Asai, J., Suyama, K., Ushida, T., and Hosoe, K. Application of X-ray cinematography in urology: I. Mechanism of ejaculation. *J. Urol.* 83:86–92, 1960.

Mittlemann, B. Complementary neurotic reactions in intimate relationships. *Psychoanal. Quart.* 13:479–491, 1944.

Mittlemann, B. The concurrent analysis of married couples. *Psychoanal. Quart.* 17:182–197, 1948.

Molčan, J. On the treatment of male sexual function disorders with mesoridazine. *Activ. Nerv. Sup.* (Praha) 10:261–262, 1968.

Molchow, C. W. *The Sexual Life.* Saint Louis: C. V. Mosby, 1923.

Money, J. Phantom orgasm in the dreams of paraplegic men and women. *Arch. Gen. Psychiat.* (Chicago) 3:373–383, 1960.

Money, J. Components of eroticism in man. I. The hormones in relation to sexual morphology and sexual desire. *J. Nerv. Ment. Dis.* 132:239–248, 1961.

Money, J. Components of eroticism in man. II. The orgasm and genital somesthesia. *J. Nerv. Ment. Dis.* 132:289–297, 1961.

Money, J. Sex hormones and other variables in human eroticism. In

Sex and Internal Secretions (W. C. Young, Ed.). Baltimore: Williams & Wilkins, 1961.

Money, J. (Ed.). *Sex Research: New Developments*. New York: Holt, Rinehart and Winston, 1965.

Money, J. Psychosexual differentiation. In *Sex Research: New Developments* (J. Money, Ed.). New York: Holt, Rinehart and Winston, 1965.

Money, J. The sex instinct and human eroticism. *J. Sex Res.* 1:3–16, 1965.

Money, J., Hampson, J. G., and Hampson, J. L. Imprinting and the establishment of gender role. *A.M.A. Arch. Neurol. Psychiat.* 77:333–336, 1957.

Money, J., and Hirsch, S. After priapism: Orgasm retained, erection lost. *J. Urol.* 94:152–157, 1965.

Money, J., and Yankowitz, R. The sympathetic-inhibiting effects of the drug Ismelin on human male eroticism with a note on Mellaril. *J. Sex Res.* 3:69–82, 1967.

Monro, D., Horne, H. W., Jr., and Paull, D. P. Effect of spinal cord injury on male sexual potency. *New Eng. J. Med.* 239:903, 1948.

Moore, B. E. Frigidity in women. *J. Amer. Psychoanal. Ass.* 9:571–584, 1961.

Moore, B. E. Frigidity: A review of psychoanalytic literature. *Psychoanal. Quart.* 33:323–349, 1964.

Moore, B. E. Psychoanalytic reflections on the implications of recent physiological studies of female orgasm. *J. Amer. Psychoanal. Ass.* 16:569–587, 1968.

Moraes, J. B. de. Clinical trial of a drug combination composed of gamma-aminobutyric acid with methyltestosterone used in the treatment of psychoneuroendocrine disorders. *Hospital* (Rio) 68:1423–1429, 1965.

Morris, J. K. *Marriage Counseling: A Manual for Ministers*. Englewood Cliffs, N.J.: Prentice-Hall, 1965.

Moser, A. Use of dibucaine in obstetrics, gynecology, and marriage counseling. *Wien. Med. Wschr.* 103:814–816, 1953.

Mozes, E. B. Impotence: What the wife can do. *Sexology* 26:176–181, 1959.

Mudd, E. H. *The Practice of Marriage Counseling*. New York: Association Press, 1951.

Mudd, E. H. Sex problems in marriage counseling. In *An Analysis of Human Sexual Response* (R. Brecher and E. Brecher, Eds.). New York: Signet Books, 1966.

Mudd, E. H., and Krich, A. (Eds.). *Man and Wife: A Sourcebook of*

Family Attitudes, Sexual Behavior and Marriage Counseling. New York: W. W. Norton, 1957.

Mudd, E. H., Stein, M., and Mitchell, H. C. Paired reports of sexual behavior of husbands and wives in conflicted marriages. *Compr. Psychiat.* 2:149–156, 1961.

Mudd, E. H., and Von Minckwitz, K. Sex problems in marriage counseling. In *Sex in Our Culture* (G. Groves and A. Stone, Eds.). New York: Emerson Books, 1961.

Mueller, G. O. W. Toward ending the double-standard of sexual morality. *J. Offender Therapy* Vol. 8, No. 1, 1964.

Mullen, E. A. Impotence treated by muscle plication. *Urol. Cutan. Rev.* 42:351, 1938.

Munro, D., Horne, H. W., Jr., and Paull, D. P. Effect of injury to spinal cord and cauda equina on sexual potency of men. *New Eng. J. Med.* 239:903–911, 1948.

Nardelli, L. "Ejaculatio praecox," a rarely noticed disease. (Thoughts on an etiopathogenic connection between ejaculation praecox and nonspecific urethritis.) *Hautarzt* 11:548–549, 1960.

Narramore, C. M. *Life and Love. A Christian View of Sex: Dating, Marriage, Human Birth, Physical Development, Sex Problems, Youth Opinions, Definition.* Grand Rapids: Zondervan Publishing House, 1956.

Nayar, R. Impotence in the male. *Indian. Med. J.* 43:274–280, 1949.

Nedoma, K., Bartak, V., Raboch, J., and Dana, R. Sexual life in sterile marriage. *Int. J. Sexology* 8:142, 1955.

Negri, V. *Psychoanalysis of Sexual Life.* Los Angeles: Western Institute of Psychoanalysis, 1949.

Neubeck, G. Factors affecting group therapy with married couples. *Marr. Fam. Living* 16:216–220, 1954.

Newman, G., and Nichols, C. R. Sexual activities and attitudes in older persons. *J.A.M.A.* 173:33–35, 1960.

Newton, N. *Maternal Emotions.* New York: Paul B. Hoeber, 1955.

Niederland, W. G. Some psychological disorders of femininity and masculinity. In *The Way of Woman* (J. E. Fairchild, Ed.). New York: Fawcett, 1956.

Northcote, H. *Christianity and Sex Problems.* Philadelphia: F. A. Davis, 1916.

Novak, E. R., and Jones, G. S. *Novak's Textbook of Gynecology.* Baltimore: Williams & Wilkins, 1961.

Novak, J. Nature and treatment of vaginismus. *Urol. Cutan. Rev.* 52:128–130, 1948.

Novell, H. A. The change. *Amer. J. Obstet. Gynec.* 78:908–914, 1959.

Noy, P., Wollstein, S., and Kaplan-De-Nour, A. Clinical observations on the psychogenesis of impotence. *Brit. J. Med. Psychol.* 39:43–53, 1966.

Oberndorf, C. P. Psychoanalysis of married couples. *Psychoanal. Rev.* 25:453–475, 1938.

O'Conor, V. J., Jr. Impotence and the Leriche syndrome: An early diagnostic sign; consideration of the mechanism; relief by endarterectomy. *J. Urol.* 80:195–198, 1958.

O'Hare, H. The normal women. *Int. J. Sexology* 4:117–118, 1950.

O'Hare, H. Vaginal versus clitoral orgasm. *Int. J. Sexology* 4:243–246, 1951.

Oliven, J. F. *Sexual Hygiene and Pathology.* Philadelphia: J. B. Lippincott, 1955.

Oltman, J. E., and Friedman, S. Acute heterosexual inadequacy. I. In the male. *Psychiat. Quart.* 12:669–678, 1938.

Oltman, J. E., and Friedman, S. Acute heterosexual inadequacy. II. In the female. *Psychiat. Quart.* 14:194–204, 1940.

O'Malley, P. P. Impotence: A clinical study. *J. Irish Med. Ass.* 61:85–93, 1968.

O'Neal, P., and Wessen, A. F. Frigidity: A suggested study of human sexual behavior. In *Determinants of Human Sexual Behavior* (G. Winokur, Ed.). Springfield, Ill.: Charles C Thomas, 1963.

Orr, D. W. Anthropological and historical notes on the female sexual role. *J. Amer. Psychoanal. Ass.* 16:601–612, 1968.

Ostow, M. The erotic instincts: A contribution to the study of instincts. *Int. J. Psychoanal.* 38:305, 1957.

Ovesey, L., et al. Retarded ejaculation: Psychodynamics and psychotherapy. *Amer. J. Psychother.* 22:185–201, 1968.

Palozzali, M. Coital reflexes and their disorders. *Presse Med.* 66:1633–1636, 1958.

Parkes, A. S., and Bruce, H. M. Olfactory stimuli in mammalian reproduction. *Science* 134:1049–1054, 1961.

Parloff, M. B. The family in psychotherapy. *Arch. Gen. Psychiat.* (Chicago) 4:445–451, 1961.

Pasmore, J. Sex and its problems. V. The frigid female. *Practitioner* 198:730–734, 1967.

Patterson, R. M., and Craig, J. B. Misconceptions concerning the psychological effects of hysterectomy. *Amer. J. Obstet. Gynec.* 85:105–111, 1963.

Payne, S. M. A concept of femininity. *Brit. J. Med. Psychol.* 15:18–33, 1936.

Pearman, R. O.   Treatment of organic impotence by implantation of a penile prosthesis. *J. Urol.* 97:716–719, 1967.

Peberdy, G.   Sex and its problems. X. Sexual adjustment at the climacteric. *Practitioner* 119:564–571, 1967.

Peck, M. W., and Wells, F. L.   Further studies in psycho-sexuality of college graduate men. *Ment. Hyg.* 9:502–520, 1925.

Pedersen-Bjergaard, K., and Tonnesen, M.   Sex hormone analysis: Excretion of sexual hormones by normal males, impotent males, polyarthritics and prostatics. *Acta Med. Scand.* 131 (Suppl. 213):284–297, 1948.

Perelman, J. L.   Problems affecting group therapy with married couples. *Int. J. Group Psychother.* 10:136–142, 1960.

Perloff, W. H.   Role of the hormones in human sexuality. *Psychosom. Med.* 11:133, 1949.

Petó, E.   Contribution to the development of smell feeling. *Brit. J. Med. Psychol.* 15:314–320, 1936.

Pfeiffer, E.   Geriatric sex behavior. *Med. Asp. Human Sexuality* 3(7): 19–28, 1969.

Pfeiffer, E., Verwoerdt, A., and Wang, H. S.   Sexual behavior in aged men and women. I. Observations on 254 community volunteers. *Arch. Gen. Psychiat.* (Chicago) 19:753–758, 1968.

Pfeiffer, E., Verwoerdt, A., and Wang, H. S.   The natural history of sexual behavior in biologically advantaged group of aged individuals. *J. Geront.* 24:193–198, 1969.

Phillip, E. E.   *Obstetrics and Gynaecology.* London: H. K. Lewis, 1962.

Pillay, A. P., and Ellis, A. (Eds.).   *Sex, Society, and the Individual.* London: Delisle, 1953.

Pincus, L. (Ed.).   *Marriage: Studies in Emotional Conflict and Growth.* London: Methuen, 1960.

Pines, M.   "Human Sexual Response": A discussion of the work of Masters and Johnson. *J. Psychosom. Res.* 12:39–49, 1968.

Podolsky, E.   *What You Should Know About Sexual Impotence.* New York: Pelton, 1900.

Podolsky, E.   Relation of nose to sexual activity. *Eye Ear Nose Throat Monthly* 25:193–195, 1946.

Polatin, P., and Douglas, D. B.   Spontaneous orgasm in a case of schizophrenia. *Psychoanal. Rev.* 40:17–26, 1953.

Pomeroy, W. B.   *Boys and Sex.* New York: Delacourt Press, 1968.

Pomeroy, W. B.   *Girls and Sex.* New York: Delacourt Press, 1969.

Porter, R. (Ed.).   *The Role of Learning in Psychotherapy.* Boston: Little, Brown, 1968.

Post, F. Sex and its problems. IX. Disorders of sex in the elderly. *Practitioner* 199:377–382, 1967.

Potts, I. F. The mechanism of ejaculation. *Med. J. Aust.* 1:495–497, 1957.

Powers, D. F. Psychic impotence in the male: Report of a case. *W. Virginia Med. J.* 50:48–50, 1954.

Pratt, J. Notes on the unconscious significance of perfume. *Int. J. Psychoanal.* 23:80–83, 1942.

Pullias, E. V. Masturbation as a mental hygiene problem: A study of the beliefs of 75 young men. *J. Abnorm. Soc. Psychol.* 32:216–222, 1937.

Puxom, M., and Dawkins, S. Non-consummation of marriage. *Med. Sci. Law* 4:15–21, 1964.

Rabiner, A. M., and Rubinstein, H. S. Dorsal nerve of penis as factor in potency. *Trans. Amer. Neurol. Ass.* 70:177, 1944.

Raboch, J., et al. Contribution to the study of sexual frigidity in women with menstruation disorders. *Cesk. Gynek.* 31:616–618, 1966.

Raboch, J., et al. The sexual life of frigid women. *Psychiat. Neurol. Med. Psychol.* (Leipzig) 20:368–373, 1968.

Raboch, J., Bartak, V., and Nedoma, K. Types of sexual reactivity in gynecological patients. *J. Sex Res.* 4:282–287, 1968.

Rachman, S. Sexual disorders and behavior therapy. *Amer. J. Psychiat.* 118:235–240, 1961.

Rado, S. Fear of castration in women. *Psychoanal. Quart.* 2:425–475, 1933.

Rado, S. An adaptational view of sexual behavior. In *Psychosexual Development in Health and Disease* (P. H. Hoch and J. Zubin, Eds.). New York: Grune & Stratton, 1949.

Rado, S. Sexual anesthesia in the female. *Quart. Rev. Surg. Obstet. Gynecol.* 16:249–253, 1959.

Rainer, J., and Rainer, J. *Sexual Pleasure in Marriage.* New York: Messner, 1959.

Rao, A. V. Impotence: Some psychiatric aspects of aetiology and treatment. *J. Indian Med. Ass.* 51:177–180, 1968.

Raspadori, F., and Selmi, G. Study of male sexual impotence from antiquity to today. *Clinica* (Bologna) 24:16–37, 1964.

Raspadori, F., and Selmi, G. Male and female impotentia coeundi et generandi and its significance to social medicine. *Minerva Med.* 56: 654–658, 1965.

Rattner, J. Disorders of sex life and love life. *Landarzt* 42:856–862, 1966.

Reding, G. R., and Ennis, B.   Treatment of the couple by a couple. *Brit. J. Med. Psychol.* 37:325, 1964.

Reding, G. R., Charles, L. A., and Hoffman, M. B.   Treatment of the couple by a couple. II. Conceptual framework, case presentation and follow-up study. *Brit. J. Med. Psychol.* 40:243–252, 1967.

Reed, D. M.   What is the norm for sexual relations in marriage? *Med. Asp. Human Sexuality* 1:6–9, 1967.

Reed, W. A., and Lally, J. F., Jr.   A clinical trial with testosterone cyclopentylpropionate. *J. Louisiana Med. Soc.* 105:172–174, 1953.

Reed, W. A., and McMillan, T. E.   Testosterone propionate in impotence. *New Orleans Med. Surg. J.* 93:634–637, 1941.

Reich, W.   *Die Funktion des Orgasmus.* Vienna: Internationaler Psychoanalytischer, 1927.

Reichert, P.   Does heart disease end sex activity? *Sexology* 29:76–81, 1962.

Reik, T.   *Psychology of Sex Relations.* New York: Farrar, 1945.

Reiss, I. L.   Sociological studies of sexual standards. In *Determinants of Human Sexual Behavior* (G. Winokur, Ed.). Springfield, Ill.: Charles C Thomas, 1963.

Renaud, J.   Frigidity. *Rev. Franc. Gynec. Obstet.* 61:501–512, 1966.

Retief, P. J. M.   Physiology of micturition and ejaculation. *S. Afr. Med. J.* 13:91–102, 1950.

Reynolds, S. R. M.   *Physiological Bases of Gynecology and Obstetrics.* Springfield, Ill.: Charles C Thomas, 1952.

Rhymes, D. A.   *No New Morality: Christian Personal Values and Sexual Morality.* Indianapolis: Bobbs-Merrill, 1964.

Richardson, T. A.   Hypnotherapy in frigidity. *Amer. J. Clin. Hypn.* 5:194–199, 1963.

Richter, D.   *Aspects of Learning and Memory.* New York: Basic Books, 1966.

Riffenburgh, R. S., and Strassman, H. D.   A curriculum in sexual education for medical students. *J. Med. Educ.* 42:1031–1036, 1967.

Riondel, A., Tait, J. F., Gut, M., Tait, S. A. S., Joachim, E., and Lillie, B.   Estimation of testosterone in human peripheral blood using S^{35}-thiosemicarbazide. *J. Clin. Endocr.* 23:620–628, 1963.

Riviere, J.   Womanliness as a masquerade. *Int. J. Psychoanal.* 10:303–313, 1929.

Robinson, H. R.   Gonadal stimulation for impotence. *Med. Rec. Ann.* 53:94–96, 1960.

Robinson, M. N.   *The Power of Sexual Surrender.* Garden City: Doubleday, 1959.

Robinson, W. J. A *Practical Treatise on the Causes, Symptoms, and Treatment of Sexual Impotence and Other Sexual Disorders in Men and Women*. New York: Critic & Guide, 1915.

Robinson, W. J. *Treatment of Sexual Impotence*. New York: Eugenics Publishing, 1933.

Robinson, W. J. *Woman: Her Sex and Love Life*. New York: Eugenics Publishing, 1939.

Rockberger, H. On the search for the orgiastic experience. *J. Sex Res.* 5:57–64, 1969.

Roderick, W. R. Current ideas on the chemical basis of olfaction. *J. Chem. Educ.* 43:510–520, 1966.

Rodgers, D. A., and Ziegler, F. J. Changes in sexual behavior consequent to use of noncoital procedures of contraception. *Psychosom. Med.* 30:495–505, 1968.

Roen, P. R. Impotence: A concise review. *New York J. Med.* 65:2576–2582, 1965.

Roen, P. R. Urologic causes of frigidity. *Med. Asp. Human Sexuality* 2(8):20–21, 1968.

Rose, R. B., and Kimbrough, J. C. Study of incontinence and impotence following prostatic surgery. *Military Surg.* 108:481–483, 1951.

Rosecan, M., Glaser, R. J., and Goldman, M. L. Orthostatic hypotension, anhidrosis and impotence. *Circulation* 6:30–40, 1952.

Rosen, I. The male response to frigidity. *J. Psychosom. Res.* 10:135–141, 1966.

Rosenbaum, J. B. The significance of the sense of smell in the transference. *J. Amer. Psychoanal. Ass.* 9:312–324, 1961.

Rosenfeld, A. *The Second Genesis: The Coming Control of Life*. Englewood Cliffs, N.J.: Prentice-Hall, 1969.

Rosenzweig, S. *Psychodiagnosis*. New York: Grune & Stratton, 1949.

Rouband, F. *Traite de l'Impuissance et de la Stérilité Chez l'Homme et Chez la Femme*. Paris: J. B. Baillière, 1876.

Rougelot, R. E. The problem of dyspareunia and frigidity. *J. Louisiana Med. Soc.* 107:156–159, 1955.

Rowan, R. L., and Howley, T. F. Premature ejaculation. *Fertil. Steril.* 14:437–440, 1963.

Rowan, R. L., and Howley, T. F. Ejaculatory sterility. *Fertil. Steril.* 16:768–770, 1965.

Rowan, R. L., and Howley, T. F. The electric pain response in impotency. *J. Urol.* 94:92–93, 1965.

Rowan, R. L., and Howley, T. F. Postoperative impotence. *J. Urol.* 95:68–69, 1966.

Rowan, R. L., Howley, T. F., and Nova, H. R. Electro-ejaculation. *J. Urol.* 87:726–729, 1962.

Rubin, A. Studies in human reproduction. II. The influence of diabetes mellitus in men upon reproduction. *Amer. J. Obstet. Gynec.* 76:25–29, 1958.

Rubin, A. The role of the physician as a sex counselor. *N. Carolina Med. J.* 27: 432–438, 1966.

Rubin, A., and Babbott, D. Impotence and diabetes mellitus. *J.A.M.A.* 168:498–500, 1958.

Rubin, I. Sex over 65. *Sexology* 28:622, 1962.

Rubin, I. Sex over 65. In *Advances in Sex Research* (H. G. Beigel, Ed.). New York: Hoeber-Harper, 1963.

Rubin, I. Climax without ejaculation. *Sexology* 30:694–696, 1964.

Rubin, I. Marital sex behavior: New insights and findings. *Med. Times* 92:228–237, 1964.

Rubin, I. *Sexual Life After Sixty.* New York: Basic Books, 1965.

Rubinstein, E. A., and Parloff, M. B. (Eds.). *Research in Psychotherapy.* Washington, D. C.: American Psychological Association, 1959.

Ruesch, J., and Bateson, G. *Communication: The Social Matrix of Psychiatry.* New York: W. W. Norton, 1951.

Ruesch, K., and Kees, W. *Nonverbal Communication.* Berkeley: University of California Press, 1956.

Rusakov, V. I. Treatment of impotence by transplantation of costal cartilage into the penis. *Urologiia* 29:54–56, 1964.

Russel, G. L. Impotence treated by mechanotherapy. *Proc. Roy. Soc. Med.* 52:872–874, 1959.

Russell, B. *Marriage and Morals.* New York: Bantam Books, 1959.

Russo, A. Vaginismo quale causa di impotenza funzionale nella donna. *G. Med.* 3:242–245, 1946.

Rutherford, R. N., Banks, A. L., Davidson, S. H., Coburn, W. A., and Williams, J. Frigidity in women with special reference to postpartum frigidity: Some clinical observations and study programs. *J. Postgrad. Med.* 26:76–84, 1959.

Rutledge, A. L. Sexual failure in the male. *Sexology* 29:804–807, 1963.

Ryan, M. *Lectures on Impotence and Sterility.* Baltimore: W. R. Lucas, 1835.

Sachse, H. Sexual disorders following prostate surgery. *München. Med. Wschr.* 108:1362–1364, 1966.

Salmon, U. J. Rationale for androgen therapy in gynecology. *J. Clin. Endocr.* 1:162–179, 1941.

Salmon, U. J., and Geist, S. H.   Effect of androgens upon libido in women. *J. Clin. Endocr.* 3:235–238, 1943.

Salzman, L.   Psychology of the female: A new look. *Arch. Gen. Psychiat.* (Chicago) 17:195–203, 1967.

Salzman, L.   Relationship of coital frequency to sexual satisfaction. *Med. Asp. Human Sexuality* 3(9):6–17, 1969.

Salzman, L., Fogel, J., Wenner, N., Granatir, W., and Eckardt, M. Roundtable: Female orgasm. *Med. Asp. Human Sexuality* 2(4):37–47, 1968.

Sarlin, C. N.   The feminine identity. *J. Amer. Psychoanal. Ass.* 11:790–816, 1963.

Satir, V.   *Conjoint Family Therapy.* Palo Alto, Cal.: Science and Behavior Books, 1967.

Schaefer, L. C.   Sexual experiences and reactions of a group of 30 women as told to a female psychotherapist. Ann Arbor, Mich.: University Microfilms, 1965.

Schaetzing, E.   Therapy of female impotence in gynecologic consulting-hour. *München. Med. Wschr.* 95:1226–1227, 1953.

Schaetzing, E.   The harmfulness of "coitus interruptus" as an iatrogenic suggestion. *München. Med. Wschr.* 102:1977–1979, 1960.

Schapiro, B.   Premature ejaculation: A review of 1130 cases. *J. Urol.* 50:374–379, 1943.

Schapiro, B.   Potency disorders in the male: A review of 1960 cases of premature ejaculation. *Harefuah* 45:40–41, 1953.

Scheer, A.   Impotence as a symptom of arterial vascular disorders in the pelvic region. *München. Med. Wschr.* 102:1713–1715, 1960.

Schilliro, R., Guiot, and Pes.   Chirurgie de l'impuissance. Prosthèse d'érection des corps caverneux en polyéthylène. *J. Urol. Nephrol.* (Paris) 71:683–685, 1965.

Schlessinger, N.   Supervision of psychotherapy: A critical review of the literature. *Arch. Gen. Psychiat.* (Chicago) 15:129–134, 1966.

Schnabe, S.   Sexual counseling in anorgasmy of the woman and impotence of the man. *Z. Aerztl. Fortbild.* (Jena) 60:815–824, 1966.

Schöffling, K., Federlin, K., Ditschuneit, H., and Pfeiffer, E. F.   Disorders of sexual function in male diabetics. *Diabetes* 12:519–527, 1963.

Schon, M., and Sutherland, A. M.   The role of hormones in human behavior. III. Changes in female sexuality after hypophysectomy. *J. Clin. Endocr.* 20:833–841, 1960.

Schon, M., and Sutherland, A. M.   The relationship of pituitary hormones to sexual behavior in women. In *Advances in Sex Research* (H. G. Beigel, Ed.). New York: Hoeber-Harper, 1963.

Schwartz, H. B. Prostatic-hemorrhoidal-impotence syndrome. *J. Med. Soc. New Jersey* 44:371–373, 1947.

Schwartz, N. H., and Robinson, B. D. Impotence due to methantheline bromide. *New York J. Med.* 52:1530, 1952.

Schwarz, O. *The Psychology of Love.* Baltimore: Penguin, 1949.

Seid, B. Gonadotropic (HCG) treatment of impotence: Results of therapy in fifty-five cases. *Virginia Med. Monthly* 89:178–181, 1962.

Seitz, L. Differences in concepts of reproduction and sexuality. *Deutsch. Med. Wschr.* 75:605–607, 1950.

Selmi, G., et al. Study of female sexual impotence from antiquity to today. *Clinica* (Bologna) 24:38–58, 1964.

Selye, H. *The Stress of Life.* New York: McGraw-Hill, 1956.

Semans, J. H. Premature ejaculation: A new approach. *Southern Med. J.* 49:353–357, 1956.

Semans, J. H. Premature ejaculation (ejaculatio praecox): A new method of therapy. *Z. Urol.* 52:381–389, 1959.

Sevringhaus, E. L. *The Management of the Climacteric, Male or Female.* Springfield, Ill.: Charles C Thomas, 1948.

Seward, G. H. *Sex and the Social Order.* New York: McGraw-Hill, 1946.

Sexual activity after prostatectomy. *Brit. Med. J.* 1:422–423, 1966.

Sexual impotence. *Med. Times* 83:855–864, 1955.

Shader, R. Sexual dysfunction associated with thioridazine hydrochloride. *J.A.M.A.* 188:1007–1009, 1964.

Shader, R. I., and DiMascio, A. Endocrine effects of psychotropic drugs. VI. Male sexual function. *Conn. Med.* 32:847–848, 1968.

Shainess, N. A re-evaluation of some aspects of femininity through a study of menstruation: A preliminary report. *Compr. Psychiat.* 2:20–26, 1961.

Sheffield, F. D., Wulff, J. J., and Backer, R. Reward value of copulation without sex drive reduction. *J. Comp. Physiol. Psychol.* 44:3–8, 1951.

Sherfey, M. J. The evolution and nature of female sexuality in relation to psychoanalytic theory. *J. Amer. Psychoanal. Ass.* 14:28–128, 1966.

Shope, D. F. A comparison of selected college females on sexual responsiveness and nonresponsiveness. Abstract of thesis in Counselor Education, The Pennsylvania State University, The Graduate School, Department of Educational Services, 1966.

Shor, J. Female sexuality: Aspects and prospects. *Psychoanalysis* 2:47–76, 1954.

Shuttleworth, F. K. A biosocial and developmental theory of male and female sexuality. *Marr. Fam. Living* 21:163–176, 1959.

Silló-Seidl, G. Guidelines for the treatment of impotentia coeundi. *Landarzt* 40:225–229, 1964.

Silva, L. M. de. Treatment of the manifestations of psychiatric impotentia 'coeundi' in psychiatric clinic patients. *Rev. Brasil. Med.* 23: 31–33, 1966.

Simon, W., and Gagnon, J. Psychosexual development. *Trans-Action* 6:9–17, 1969.

Simpson, G., Blair, M., and Amuso, D. Effects of antidepressants on genito-urinary function. *Dis. Nerv. Syst.* 26:787–789, 1965.

Simpson, S. L. Impotence. *Brit. Med. J.* 1:692–696, 1950.

Singh, H. A case of inhibition of ejaculation as a side effect of Mellaril. *Amer. J. Psychiat.* 117:1041–1042, 1961.

Singh, H. Therapeutic use of thioridazine in premature ejaculation. *Amer. J. Psychiat.* 119:891, 1963.

Sklansky, M. A., Isaacs, K. S., Levitov, E. S., and Haggard, E. A. Verbal interaction and levels of meaning in psychotherapy. *Arch. Gen. Psychiat.* (Chicago) 14:158–170, 1966.

Slater, E., and Woodside, M. *Patterns of Marriage.* London: Cassell, 1951.

Slikerman, I. Some experiences with phosphate of iproniazid in the treatment of premature ejaculation: Preliminary note. *Rev. Argent. Urol.* 27:448–451, 1958.

Smith, D. R. *General Urology.* Los Altos, Cal.: Lange Medical Publications, 1963.

Smith, J. A. Psychogenic factors in infertility and frigidity. *Southern Med. J.* 49:358–362, 1956.

Sonne, J. C., and Lincoln, G. Heterosexual co-therapy team experience during family therapy. *Family Process* 4:177, 1965.

Speisman, J. C. Depth of interpretation and verbal resistance in psychotherapy. *J. Consult. Psychol.* 23:93–99, 1959.

Spence, A. W. Testosterone propionate in functional impotence. *Brit. Med. J.* 2:411–413, 1940.

Spence, A. W. The male climacteric: Is it an entity? *Brit. Med. J.* 1: 1353–1355, 1954.

Spence, A. W. Sexual adjustment at the climacteric. *Practitioner* 172:427–430, 1954.

Spiegel, H. Is symptom removal dangerous? *Amer. J. Psychiat.* 123: 1279–1283, 1967.

Spiegel, H. The "ripple effect" following adjunct hypnosis in analytic psychotherapy. *Amer. J. Psychiat.* 126:53–58, 1969.

Spiegel, S.   Mechanische Therapie der Impotenz. *Ost Arzteztg.* 9:342–358, 1912.

Spitz, R.   Hospitalization. *Psychoanal. Stud. Child* 1:53, 1945.

Spitz, R. A., and Wolf, K. M.   Autoeroticism: Some empirical findings and hypotheses on three of its manifestations in the first year of life. *Psychoanal. Stud. Child* 314:85–120, 1949.

Stafford-Clark, D.   The etiology and treatment of impotence. *Practitioner* 172:397–404, 1954.

Stearns, H. C., and Sneeden, V. D.   Observations on the clinical and pathological aspects of the pelvic congestion syndrome. *Amer. J. Obstet. Gynec.* 94:718–732, 1966.

Stekel, W.   *Frigidity in Woman in Relation to Her Love Life* (J. S. Van Teslaar, Trans.). New York: Boni & Liveright, 1926. Vols. I, II.

Stekel, W.   *Impotence in the Male: The Psychic Disorders of Sexual Function in the Male.* New York: Grove Press, 1959. Vols. I, II.

Stevenson, I.   *The Psychiatric Examination.* Boston: Little, Brown, 1969.

Stewart, B. L.   Impotence in the male. *J. Lancet* 83:2–15, 1963.

Stewart, C. W.   *The Minister as Marriage Counselor.* New York: Abingdon Press, 1961.

Stokes, W. R.   Inadequate sexual function in the male. *Med. Ann. D.C.* 2:50–53, 1933.

Stokes, W. R.   Sexual frigidity in women. *Med. Ann. D.C.* 2:264–271, 1933.

Stokes, W. R.   Family counseling. *Med. Ann. D.C* 20:150–154, 1951.

Stokes, W. R.   A marriage counseling case: The married virgin. *Marr. Fam. Living* 13:29–34, 1951.

Stokes, W. R.   Sexual function in the aging male. *Geriatrics* 6:304–308, 1951.

Stokes, W. R.   Modern view of masturbation. *Sexology* 27:586–590, 1961.

Stokes, W. R.   *Married Love in Today's World.* New York: Citadel Press, 1962.

Stokes, W. R.   Inadequacy of female orgasm as a problem in marriage counseling. *J. Sex Res.* 4:225–233, 1968.

Stokes, W. R., and Harper, R. H.   The doctor as marriage counselor. *Med. Ann. D. C.* 23:670–672, 1954.

Stoller, R. J.   The sense of femaleness. *Psychoanal. Quart.* 37:42–55, 1968.

Stoller, R. J.   *Sex and Gender.* New York: Science House, 1968.

Stone, A.   The Kinsey studies and marriage counseling. In *Sexual Behavior in American Society* (J. Himelhoch and S. Fava, Eds.). New York: W. W. Norton, 1955.

Stone, A., and Levine, L.   Group therapy in sexual maladjustment. *Amer. J. Psychiat.* 107:195–202, 1950.

Stone, H. M., and Stone, A.   A *Marriage Manual*, rev. ed. New York: Simon and Schuster, 1952.

Stourzh, H.   Hormonale Therapie des Vaginismus. *Wien. Klin. Wschr.* 61:502–505, 1949.

Strauss, E. B.   Impotence from the psychiatric standpoint. *Brit. Med. J.* 1:697–699, 1950.

Street, R.   *Modern Sex Techniques.* New York: Archer House, 1959.

Strosberg, I., and Damrau, F.   Impotence and male climacteric. Evaluation of fortified chorionic gonadotropin. *Exp. Med. Surg.* 18:371–374, 1960.

Strupp, H. H.   A multidimensional system for analyzing psychotherapeutic techniques. *Psychiatry* 20:293–306, 1957.

Strupp, H. H.   Toward a specification of teaching and learning in psychotherapy. *Arch. Gen. Psychiat.* (Chicago) 21:203–212, 1969.

Sturgis, S. H.   Oral contraceptives and their effect on sex behavior. *Med. Asp. Human Sexuality* 2(1):4–9, 1968.

Sturgis, S. H.   Hormone therapy in the menopause: Indications and contraindications. *Med. Asp. Human Sexuality* 3(5):69–75, 1969.

Swartz, D.   Sexual difficulties after 50: The urologist's view. *Canad. Med. Ass. J.* 94:208–210, 1966.

Talbot, H. S.   Report on sexual function in paraplegics. *J. Urol.* 61:265–270, 1949.

Talbot, H. S.   The sexual function in paraplegia. *J. Urol.* 73:91–100, 1955.

Tapis, F., Werboff, J., and Winokur, G.   Recall of some phenomena of sleep. *J. Nerv. Ment. Dis.* 127:119–123, 1958.

Tarail, M.   Sex over sixty-five. *Sexology* 28:440–445, 1962.

Tatum, B. P.   The phallic in man and woman: A reappreciation of their erotic image. *J. Sex Res.* 2:133–140, 1966.

Taubel, D. E.   Mellaril: Ejaculation disorders. *Amer. J. Psychiat.* 119:87, 1962.

Tauber, E. S.   Effects of castration upon the sexuality of the adult male: A review of relevant literature. *Psychosom. Med.* 2:74–87, 1940.

Taylor, D. L.   *Marriage Counseling: New Dimensions in the Art of Helping People.* Springfield, Ill.: Charles C Thomas, 1965.

Taylor, G. R.   *Sex in History.* New York: Vanguard Press, 1954.

Taylor, H. C., Jr.   Vascular congestion and hyperemia: Their effect on structure and function in the female reproductive system. I. Physiologic basis and history of the concept. *Amer. J. Obstet. Gynec.* 57: 211–227, 1949.

Taylor, H. C., Jr.   Vascular congestion and hyperemia: Their effect on structure and function in the female reproductive system. II. The clinical aspects of the congestion-fibrosis syndrome. *Amer. J. Obstet. Gynec.* 57:637–652, 1949.

Taylor, H. C., Jr.   Vascular congestion and hyperemia: Their effect on structure and function in the female reproductive system. III. Etiology and therapy. *Amer. J. Obstet. Gynec.* 57:654–668, 1949.

Teilhard De Chardin, P.   *The Phenomenon of Man.* New York: Harper & Row, 1961.

Terman, L. M.   *Psychological Factors in Marital Happiness.* New York: McGraw-Hill, 1938.

Terman, L. M.   Correlates of orgasm adequacy in a group of 556 wives. *J. Psychol.* 32:115–172, 1951.

Terman, L. M., and Miles, C. C.   *Sex and Personality: Studies in Masculinity and Femininity.* New York: McGraw-Hill, 1936.

Theimer, E. T., and Davies, J. T.   Olfaction, musk odor, and molecular properties. *Agricultural & Food Chemistry* 15:6–14, 1967.

Thielicke, H.   *The Ethics of Sex* (J. W. Doberstein, Trans.). New York: Harper & Row, 1964.

Thomas, A.   Simultaneous psychotherapy with marital partners. *Amer. J. Psychother.* 10:716–727, 1956.

Thomason, B.   Marital sexual behavior and total marital adjustment: A research report. In *Sexual Behavior in American Society* (J. Himelhoch and S. Fava, Eds.). New York: W. W. Norton, 1950.

Thompson, C.   *Psychoanalysis: Evolution and Development.* New York: Hermitage, 1950.

Thompson, C. M.   Cultural pressures in the psychology of women. *Psychiatry* 5:331–339, 1942.

Thompson, C. M.   Some effects of the derogatory attitude toward female sexuality. *Psychiatry* 13:349–354, 1950.

Thompson, C. M.   Femininity. In *The Encyclopedia of Sexual Behavior* (A. Ellis and A. Abarbanel, Eds.). New York: Hawthorn Books, 1961.

Thorne, F. C.   Ejaculata praecox: Cause and treatment. *Dis. Nerv. Syst.* 4:273–275, 1943.

Thornton, H., and Thornton, F.   *How to Achieve Sex Happiness in Marriage.* New York: Vanguard Press, 1939.

Tinbergen, N.   *The Study of Instinct.* Oxford: Clarendon Press, 1951.

Tinklepaugh, O. L.   The nature of periods of sex desire in women and their relation to ovulation. *Amer. J. Obstet. Gynec.* 26:335–345, 1933.

Torrie, A.   Pre-marital chastity. *Practitioner* 172:415–419, 1954.

Trainer, J. B.   *Physiologic Foundations for Marriage Counseling.* Saint Louis: C. V. Mosby, 1965.

Trethowan, W. H.   The demonopathology of impotence. *Brit. J. Psychiat.* 109:341–347, 1963.

Turner, C. E. H.   Psycho-somatic sexual life of the family: A psycho-somatic study of suckling and coitus. *J. Ment. Sci.* 93:522–547, 1947.

Tushnet, L.   Impotence and diabetes mellitus. *J. Med. Soc. New Jersey* 57:256–257, 1960.

Tuthill, J. F.   Impotence. *Lancet* 1:124–128, 1955.

Tuttle, W. B., Cook, W. L., Jr., and Fitch, E.   Sexual behavior in postmyocardial infarction patients. *Amer. J. Cardiol.* 13:140, 1964.

Van Der Kloot, W. G.   *Behavior.* New York: Holt, Rinehart and Winston, 1968.

Van De Velde, T. H.   *Sex Hostility in Marriage: Its Origin, Prevention, and Treatment* (H. Marr, Trans.). New York: Covici-Friede Publishers, 1931.

Van De Velde, T. H.   *Ideal Marriage: Its Physiology and Technique* (S. Browne, Trans.). New York: Random House, 1965.

Van Emde Boas, C.   Group therapy of anorgastic women. *Int. J. Sexology* 4:1–6, 1950.

Vatsyayana.   *Kama Sutra* (R. Burton and F. F. Arbuthnot, Trans.). London: Luxor Press, 1967.

Vecki, V. G.   Sexual activity in old age. In *Encyclopaedia Sexualis* (V. Robinson, Ed.). New York: Dingwall-Rock, 1936.

Vermeulen, A., and Verplancke, J. C. M.   A simple method for the determination of urinary testosterone excretion in human urine. *Steroids* 2:453–463, 1963.

Verwoerdt, A., Pfeiffer, E., and Wang, H. S.   Sexual behavior in senescence. II. Patterns of change in sexual activity and interest. *Geriatrics* 24:137–154, 1969.

Vincent, C. E.   Social and interpersonal sources of symptomatic frigidity. *Marr. Fam. Living* 18:355–360, 1956.

Vincent, C. E. (Ed.).   *Human Sexuality in Medical Education and Practice.* Springfield, Ill.: Charles C Thomas, 1968.

Waelder, R.   Problems of transference and countertransference. *Bull. Amer. Psychoanal. Ass.* 6:24–27, 1950.

Waggoner, R. W.   Communication with a patient. *Int. Psychiat. Clin.* 1:3–18, 1964.

Wahl, C. W. (Ed.). *Sexual Problems: Diagnosis and Treatment in Medical Practice.* New York: Free Press of Glencoe, 1967.

Walker, K. The celibate male. *Practitioner* 172:411–414, 1954.

Walker, K. Diabetes and marriage problems. *Sexology* 27:548–552, 1961.

Walker, K. The critical age in men. *Sexology* 30:705–707, 1964.

Walker, K., and Strauss, E. B. *Sexual Disorders in the Male.* London: Cassell, 1954.

Wallin, P. A study of orgasm as a condition of women's enjoyment of intercourse. *J. Soc. Psychol.* 51:191–198, 1960.

Wallin, P., and Clark, A. L. A study of orgasm as a condition of women's enjoyment of coitus in the middle years of marriage. *Hum. Biol.* 35:131–139, 1963.

Wallis, J. H., and Booker, H. S. *Marriage Counselling.* London: Routledge & Kegan Paul, 1958.

Wassiltschenko, G. Some physiologic rules as a basis for the rational psychotherapy of impotence. *Psychiat. Neurol. Med. Psychol.* (Leipzig) 20:22–23, 1968.

Waxenberg, S. E. Some biological correlatives of sexual behavior. In *Determinants of Human Sexual Behavior* (G. Winokur, Ed.). Springfield, Ill.: Charles C Thomas, 1963.

Waxenberg, S. E., Drellich, M. G., and Sutherland, A. M. The role of hormones in human behavior. I. Changes in female sexuality after adrenalectomy. *J. Clin. Endocr.* 19:193–202, 1959.

Waxenberg, S. E., Finkbeiner, J. A., Drellich, M. G., and Sutherland, A. M. The role of hormones in human behavior. II. Changes in sexual behavior in relation to vaginal smears of breast-cancer patients after oophorectomy and adrenalectomy. *Psychosom. Med.* 22:435–442, 1960.

Weber, L. M. *On Marriage, Sex and Virginity* (R. Brennan, Trans.). New York: Herder & Herder, 1966.

Weiss, E., and English, O. S. *Psychosomatic Medicine.* Philadelphia: W. B. Saunders, 1949.

Wellman, M. Specific impotence in the married male. *Canad. Psychiat. Ass. J.* 3:87–93, 1958.

Werner, A. A. The male climacteric: Report of 54 cases. *J.A.M.A.* 127:705–710, 1945.

Werner, A. A. The male climacteric: Report of 273 cases. *J.A.M.A.* 132:188–194, 1946.

Werner, H., and Wapner, S. (Eds.). *The Body Percept.* New York: Random House, 1965.

Wershub, L. P. *Sexual Impotence in the Male*. Springfield, Ill.: Charles C Thomas, 1959.

Wessler, M. F. *Christian View of Sex Education: A Manual for Church Leaders*. Saint Louis: Concordia Publishing House, 1967.

Wesson, M. B. The value of testosterone to men past middle age. *J. Amer. Geriat. Soc.* 12:1149–1153, 1964.

Westermarck, E. *The Origin and Development of the Moral Ideas*. London: Macmillan, 1917.

Westermarck, E. *The History of Human Marriage*. New York: Macmillan, 1922.

Whalen, R. E. Sexual motivation. *Psychol. Rev.* 73:151–163, 1966.

Whitaker, C. A. A philosophical basis for brief psychotherapy. *Psychiat. Quart.* 23:425, 1949.

Whitaker, C. A. Psychotherapy with couples. *Amer. J. Psychother.* 12: 18–23, 1958.

Whitehouse, F. W. Two minutes with diabetes. *Med. Times* 96:661–662, 1968.

Whitelow, G. P., and Smithwick, R. H. Some secondary effects of sympathectomy: With particular reference to disturbance of sexual function. *New Eng. J. Med.* 245:121–130, 1951.

Williams, E. L. Frigidity. *Amer. Practitioner* 4:6–8, 1949.

Williams, R. H. (Ed.). *Textbook of Endocrinology*, 4th ed. Philadelphia: W. B. Saunders, 1968.

Winokur, G. Sexual behavior: Its relationship to certain affects and psychiatric diseases. In *Determinants of Human Sexual Behavior* (G. Winokur, Ed.). Springfield, Ill.: Charles C Thomas, 1963.

Winokur, G., and Gaston, W. R. Sex, anger and anxiety: Intrapersonal interaction in married couples. *Dis. Nerv. Syst.* 22:1–5, 1961.

Winokur, G., Guze, S. B., and Pfeiffer, E. Nocturnal orgasm in women. *Arch. Gen. Psychiat.* (Chicago) 1:180–184, 1959.

Witt, E. N. *Life Can Be Sexual*. Saint Louis: Concordia Publishing House, 1967.

Witton, K. Sexual dysfunction secondary to Mellaril. *Dis. Nerv. Syst.* 23:175, 1962.

Wolbarst, A. L. Urologic aspects of sexual impotence. *J. Urol.* 29:77–94, 1933.

Wolbarst, A. L. Gynetic factor in causation of male impotence. *New York J. Med.* 47:1252–1255, 1947.

Wolfman, C., and Friedman, J. A symptom and its symbolic representation in earliest memories. *J. Clin. Psychol.* 20:442–444, 1964.

Wolpe, J. *Psychotherapy by Reciprocal Inhibition.* Stanford: Stanford University Press, 1958.

Wolpe, J., and Lazarus, A. A. *Behavior Therapy Techniques.* New York: Pergamon Press, 1966.

Wolsing, J. von, and Langhof, H. Zur Genese und Psychotherapie einer aus intendierter Retentio seminis entstandenen Impotentia ejaculandi. *Hautarzt* 16:170–172, 1965.

Wolstenholme, G. (Ed.). *Man and His Future.* Boston: Little, Brown, 1963.

Woodside, M. Orgasm capacity among two hundred English working-class wives. *Marriage Hygiene* 1:133–137, 1948.

Wortis, S. B. Unsuccessful sex adjustment in marriage. *Amer. J. Psychiat.* 96:1413–1427, 1940.

Wrage, K. *Man and Woman: The Basics of Sex and Marriage* (S. S. B. Gilder, Trans.). Philadelphia: Fortress Press, 1969.

Wright, H. *Sex Factors in Marriage.* London: Williams & Norgate, 1930.

Wright, H. A contribution to the orgasm problem in women. In *Sex, Society, and the Individual* (A. P. Pillay and A. Ellis, Eds.). London: Delisle, 1953.

Wynn, J. C. *Sex, Family, and Society in Theological Focus.* New York: Association Press, 1966.

Yamauchi, S. Clinical studies on impaired male sexual function in diabetes mellitus. *Jap. J. Urol.* 56:715–732, 1965.

Yates, S. L. An investigation of the psychological factors in virginity and ritual defloration. *Int. J. Psychoanal.* 11:167–184, 1930.

Yoel, C. A. Impotentia coeundi. *Harefuah* 53:144–147, 1957.

Young, J. Lower abdominal pains of cervical origin: Their genesis and treatment. *Brit. Med. J.* 1:105–111, 1938.

Young, W. C. The hormones and mating behavior. In *Sex and Internal Secretions* (W. C. Young, Ed.). Baltimore: Williams & Wilkins, 1961.

Young, W. C., Goy, R. W., and Phoenix, C. H. Hormones and sexual behavior. In *Sex Research: New Developments* (J. Money, Ed.). New York: Holt, Rinehart and Winston, 1965.

Youssef, A. F. (Ed.). *Gynecological Urology.* Springfield, Ill.: Charles C Thomas, 1960.

Zeitlin, A. B., Cottrell, T. L., and Lloyd, F. A. Sexology of the para-plegic male. *Fertil. Steril.* 8:337–344, 1957.

Ziegler, F. J., and Rodgers, D. A. Vasectomy, ovulation suppressors, and sexual behavior. *J. Sex Res.* 4:169–193, 1968.

Ziesche, H. W.   Vasoresection and prostatic surgery and their effect on the sexual sphere. Z. *Urol.* 60:535–539, 1967.

Zilboorg, G.   Masculine and feminine. *Psychiatry* 7:257–296, 1944.

Zilstorff, K.   Parosmia. *J. Laryng.* 80:1102–1104, 1966.

INDEX

Abortion, criminal, trauma from, 268, 278, 280
Abstinence from sexual activity, during therapy, 18, 31, 56, 72, 74–75, 85, 87, 201, 310
Acidity, vaginal, 270–271
  male sensitivity to, 290
Acromegaly, and secondary impotence, 185
Adhesions
  in pelvic inflammatory disease, 285
  penile, 293
Adolescence
  history of, 40–41
  sexual activity in, 94
Aging population, 316–350
  bilateral sexual dysfunction in, 331
  failures in therapy of, 333–334, 360–361
  females, 335–350
    dyspareunia in, 269, 274–275, 339
    educational techniques for, 344, 346, 347, 349
    excitement phase in, 336
    failures in therapy of, 333–334, 360–361
    lubrication in, vaginal, 276, 336
    masturbatory rate in, 342
    orgasmic phase in, 338
    physiological changes in, 335–339
    plateau phase in, 337
    sex-steroid replacement in, 337, 339–349
    sexual dysfunction in, 339–350

statistical considerations, 330–334
  vaginal outlet pain in, 269
  vaginismus in, 259–260
  vaginitis in, 274–275, 276, 277
history-taking in, 49–51
males, 316–334
  educational techniques for, 322, 324, 329
  ejaculatory control in, 318, 323, 326
  ejaculatory demand in 322–324, 347
  ejaculatory inevitability in, 319
  erective responses in, 317, 325–326
  excitement phase in, 317
  failures in therapy of, 333–334, 360–361
  fears of performance in, 316, 321, 329, 348
  impotence in, secondary, 326–330, 347
  orgasmic experience in, 318–320
  physiological changes in, 319–320, 326
  plateau phase in, 317–318
  resolution phase in, 321
  sex-steroid replacement in, 324–325, 329
  sexual dysfunction in, 326–330
  statistical considerations, 330–334
  wives of, 322, 347
  See also Sex-steroids
Alcoholism, and impotence, 160, 163–168

451

Anatomy, pelvic
  female, 89, 262
  male, 88
Anxiety, as therapeutic problem, 374–376
Auditory sense, investigation of, 49
Authoritative control by therapists, 31, 61–62, 71–75, 86, 200, 296–299, 344
  alienation of, 64
  and avoidance of goal-oriented performance, 13–14, 72, 201, 205, 209
  instructions for sensate focus. *See* Sensate focus sessions
  reactions to, 68–69
  sequential steps in directions, 7, 14, 205–206, 304–306
Authoritative sources
  negative experiences with, 118, 178, 188–192, 345, 346, 384
  See also Professionals
Automanipulation. *See* Masturbation

Bacterial infections
  pelvic, and dyspareunia, 269–273, 284–285
  vaginitis from, 271
Behavior changes
  desirability of, 25, 68
  symptom reversal as therapeutic objective, 19, 21–22
Bias, in history-taking, 27–28
Bilateral sexual inadequacy, 354, 362, 363
  in aging population, 331
  with ejaculatory incompetence, 127
  with impotence in males, 238–240, 252
  with premature ejaculation, 108, 228, 229, 253
Biophysical and psychosocial systems, 66–67, 75–76, 202
  adjustment of, 225, 240, 298

in female sexual responses, 67, 214, 219–222, 224–226, 228, 241
in male sexual responses, 139, 145, 160, 198, 202
maximum interdigitation of, 313
negative psychosocial dominance in, 235–237
potential of, 295
varying levels of dominance in, 241
Body contact, attitudes toward, 46–47
Broad ligaments, laceration of, 258–259, 277–283

Changes in behavior, desirability of, 19–21, 22, 25, 68
Childhood events, history of, 37–40
Chordee, penile, and dyspareunia, 291
Clergymen, 188–189
Climacteric, 324, 329, 336–339
Clitoris
  aging affecting, 337–338, 340
  manipulation of, 302–303
  pain in, 269
  sexual tension affecting, 220
Clothing, removal of, 71–72
Coital positions. *See* Positions recommended
Coliform vaginitis, 271–272
Communication, 73, 74, 105, 298, 299
  in aging marital units, 344
  encouragement of, 86, 199, 204
  importance of, 14–15, 19, 27, 32, 66, 85, 133, 202, 298, 344, 380–381
  lack of, and secondary impotence, 163, 168, 203
  between parents and children, 216–217
  sensory, 76, 77
  and signal systems for sensual in-

terests, 86, 87, 203–204, 300–301
verbalization in, 90
Concepts
of history-taking, 24–28
of orgasmic dysfunction in women, 214–218
of roundtable discussion, 60–67
sensual, 46–49, 75–83
of therapy, 1–23
Conditioning. *See* Imprinting
Confidential information, treatment of, 62–63, 376–381, 389
Conjoint marital-unit therapy, 2–3
See also Mutual involvement in sexual problems
Contraception
sensitivity to materials in, 273–274, 293
withdrawal technique for, effects of, 95
Contractions
of prostate, 293, 319, 325, 329
rectal, in physical examination, 272
of uterus, 220, 338–339, 342
of vaginal outlet, in vaginismus, 252, 262
Counseling
negative experiences with, 118, 178, 188–192, 345, 346, 384
See also Professionals
Countertransference, management of, 29
Cultural factors, 12, 67, 69, 75, 331
double standards in, 93, 95, 155, 215–216, 229, 331
family patterns in. *See* Maternal dominance, effects of
in impotence, 139, 159–160
in orgasmic dysfunction in women, 214–218
in premature ejaculation, 93–96, 101

religious aspects. *See* Religious factors
See also Biophysical and psychosocial systems

Daily conferences, need for, 17, 19, 310
Diabetes, and secondary impotence, 186–187
Dilators, in vaginismus, 260, 263
Direction, authoritative. *See* Authoritative control by therapists
Distraction techniques, to prevent ejaculation, 98, 162
Divorce incidence, after therapy, 135, 368, 374, 385
Double standards, in sexual functioning, 93, 95, 155, 215–216, 229, 331
Douches
affecting vaginal pH, 274
male sensitivity to, 293
Drugs, effects of, 184, 374
See also Alcoholism, and impotence
Dual-sex therapy teams, 4–5, 355
advantages of, 5–8, 391
See also Therapists
Dyspareunia, 266–294
in females, 266–288
clitoral pain, 269
from endometriosis, 285–286
from infections of vagina, 269–273
from insufficient vaginal lubrication, 275–277
from laceration of uterine ligaments, 277–283
from pelvic infection, 284–285
postmenopausal, 269, 274–275, 339
postsurgical, 286–288, 348
after rape experiences, 268, 278, 280–281

Dyspareunia, in females—*Continued*
from sensitivity reactions in vagina, 273–274
and somatic sources of pain, 277–286
vaginal barrel factors in, 269–277
vaginal outlet pain, 268–269
and vaginismus, 258–260
in males, 288–294
and penile chordee, 291
in Peyronie's disease, 291
in phimosis, 290
from prostatitis, 293–294
testicular pain, 292
from trauma of penis, 291–292

Educational levels
of partner surrogates, 149
of research group, 356, 357
Educational techniques, 5, 10, 11, 16, 19, 53, 62, 65, 77, 83–84, 86, 352
for aging females, 344, 346, 347, 349
for aging males, 322, 324, 329
for orgasmic dysfunction, 302
and physical rewards, 200
for vaginismus, 264
Ejaculation, premature, 92–115
See also Premature ejaculation
Ejaculatory control
acquiring of, 103–113, 308, 344
lack of. *See* Premature ejaculation
in older man, 318, 323, 326
Ejaculatory demand, in aging male, 322–324, 347
Ejaculatory incompetence, 116–136
factors in development of, 117–126
failures in therapy of, 134–135, 359, 366, 367
female response to, 127, 130, 132
and homosexuality, 117, 120–121, 126, 135

and impotence, 116, 133
comparison of, 158
and male fear of pregnancy, 122–123
and masturbatory practices, 122, 124, 130
maternal factors in, 123–124
and multiorgasmic responses of wives, 120, 127, 132
and premature ejaculation, comparison of, 127–129, 133, 158
religious factors in, 117–120, 133, 135
results of therapy, 134–136
from specific traumatic event, 125–126, 134
treatment of, 129–134
Ejaculatory inevitability, 102, 131, 318
delay of, 105
in older man, 319
spastic reaction of prostate in, 293
Endocrine conditions
impotence from, 184
laboratory evaluations of, 60
See also Sex-steroids
Endometriosis
and dyspareunia, 285–286
and vaginismus, 259
Environmental influences. *See* Cultural factors
Erection
inadequacy of. *See* Impotence
lack of voluntary control of, 11, 166, 196, 202, 205, 317
Eunuchoidism, and secondary impotence, 185
Examination, physical, 58–59
See also Physical examination
Excitement phase
in aging male, 317
in female, 220
in aging female, 336

Failure, sexual, fear of. *See* Fears of performance
Failures in therapy, 370–391
  in aging population, 333–334, 360–361
  and antipathy toward therapists, 383–385
  and anxieties of patients, 374–376
  and early discharge from therapy, 63, 135, 381–383
  evaluation of, 370–391
  in females, 361, 366, 367
    nonorgasmic women, 314–315
    in primary orgasmic dysfunction, 314, 359, 366, 367, 383–385
    in random orgasmic inadequacy, 314–315, 360
    in situational orgasmic dysfunction, 314, 360, 366, 367
    in vaginismus, 359
  follow-up failure rates, 353, 361–362, 364–367
  initial failure rates, 352–353
  in males, 361, 366, 367
    in ejaculatory incompetence, 134–135, 359, 366, 367
    in impotence, 211–213, 358–359, 366, 367, 368
    with partner surrogates, 153
    in premature ejaculation, 113–114, 359, 366, 367
  in original population, 362–364
  overall failure rate, 367–369
  and psychotherapeutic malpractice, 385–391
  and rejection of moisturizing lotions, 81, 235
  and restricted information, 376–381
  screening process difficulties, 370–374
  See also Negative reactions
Fallacies and myths of sexual activity, 26, 84, 87, 325, 335, 350
Family patterns
  maternal factors. *See* Maternal dominance, effects of
  paternal dominance, and secondary impotence, 171–174
Fantasies
  to prevent ejaculation, 98, 99–100
  of sexual episodes with therapists, 390
Fear, affecting vaginal lubrication, 276
Fears of performance, 10, 11–14, 65, 84, 134, 151, 375
  in aging male, 316, 321, 329, 348
  effects of, 99, 238
  in female, 12, 167, 228
  and impotence, 11, 142, 143, 160, 167, 168, 173, 175, 196, 200, 203, 206, 208
  in male, 11, 122
  and premature ejaculation, 99, 102
  prevention of, 19, 200–201, 206–210
  sources of, 159, 160
Feel and touch exercises, 71–75, 201–202, 297–299, 303
Feeling and thinking sexually, 73, 109, 110, 202, 210, 229, 298–299, 303, 307, 309
  difficulties with, 358
Female population, 214–315
  aging, 335–350
    See also Aging population
  anatomy, pelvic, 89, 262
  dyspareunia in, 266–288
  failures in therapy, 361, 366, 367
  fears of performance, 12, 167, 228
  feeling and thinking sexually, 73, 109, 110, 202, 210, 229, 298–299, 303, 307, 309, 358

Female population—*Continued*
  husbands of wives with orgasmic
    dysfunction, 3, 13, 313–314
    See also Bilateral sexual inade-
    quacy
  masturbation in, 372
    See also Masturbation
  orgasmic dysfunction in, 214–315
    See also Orgasmic dysfunction
    in females
  orgasmic response in, 220, 297
    in aging females, 338
  orientation to partner, 235, 241–
    244, 275, 277
  as partner surrogates, 124, 135,
    146–154, 354
  primary orgasmic dysfunction in,
    227–240
  psychophysiological factors in sex-
    ual responses, 214–222
    See also Biophysical and psy-
    chosocial systems
  as replacement partners, 122,
    146–150, 154–156, 354
  role in therapy of males, 107,
    113, 130, 209, 210–211
  sexual tension release in. *See* Sex-
    ual tension
  situational orgasmic dysfunction
    in, 240–249
  vaginismus in, 250–265
  wives
    of aging males, 322, 347
    of ejaculatory incompetent hus-
    bands, 127, 130, 132
    of homosexual husbands, 182–
    183
    of impotent males, 2, 12, 140,
    167, 183, 194–195, 210–211,
    238–240, 252
    of premature ejaculators, 93,
    94, 95, 96–99, 110, 162,
    228, 371–374
  See also Sexual value systems
Female-superior coital position, 106–

    108, 110, 111, 131, 207–
    208, 306–310
  conversion to lateral position,
    311–312
Follow-up procedures, 22–23
  failure rates, 353, 361–362, 364–
    369
Fragrances, use of. *See* Olfaction
Frustration, from sexual tension, 93,
    94, 95, 97, 162
Fungal vaginitis, 273

Genital manipulation, 86–91, 203–
    205
  for female stimulation, 203, 299–
    306
  for male stimulation, 102–106,
    131, 204
  moisturizing lotions in, 78–82,
    129, 235
    rejection of, 81, 235
  mutual signal systems in, 86–87,
    203–204, 300–301
Geographic distribution for research
    population, 355–356
Geriatrics. *See* Aging population
Give-to-get principle, 72–75, 109,
    131, 147, 198, 298, 301
Glucose tolerance test, for impotent
    males, 60, 186–187
Goal-oriented performance, avoid-
    ance of, 13–14, 72, 201, 205,
    209
Goals of roundtable discussions, 83–
    84
Gonococcal infection, and dyspareu-
    nia in males, 293
Guilt, and acceptance of pleasure,
    75

Hegar dilators, in vaginismus, 260,
    263
History-taking
  adolescence, 40–41

aging population, 49–51
bias in, 27–28
changes considered desirable, 25
childhood, 37–40
concept of, 24–28
confidential material, 62–63
contrasex patient and cotherapist, 7, 32, 53–54
Day 1, 33, 34–53
Day 2, 53–56
Day 3, 57–84
and dual-sex team approach, 7, 29
format of, 29–34
general material, 51
laboratory evaluation, 59–60
life-cycle events, 37–45
marriage data, 43–45
medical history, 57–58
misinterpretation of material, 52, 61
perception of self, 45
physical examination, 58–59
preliminary baselines, 34–36
premarital adulthood, 42–43
repression of material, 54, 376–381, 389
role of interrogator, 28–29
same-sex patient and cotherapist, 7, 32
sensual concepts, 46–49
and sexual value systems, 25–26
specific successful sexual events, 26–28
statistics of present marriage, 36–37
teenage years, 41–42
Homosexuality
as confidential information, 377, 378, 379–380
and ejaculatory incompetence, 117, 120–121, 126, 135
and impotence
primary, 140–142, 144, 213, 377
secondary, 169, 179–183, 213

and insufficient vaginal lubrication, 276, 277
masturbatory patterns in, 180
and orgasmic dysfunction in women, 244–247
reaction of wives to, 182–183
in relatives of partner surrogates, 150
and responses to rectal examination in males, 272
between therapists and patients, 141, 390
and vaginismus, 252, 260–261
in wives of impotent males, 183
in wives of premature ejaculators, 98
Hormones. See Endocrine conditions
Husbands. See Male population
Hysterectomy, dyspareunia after, 286–287

Iatrogenic causes of dysfunction. See Counseling, negative experiences with
Identification with partner. See Orientation to partner, effects of
Identity, sexual. See Sexual identity, acceptance or rejection of
Impotence
compared with ejaculatory incompetence, 158
compared with premature ejaculation, 158
failures in therapy, 211–213, 358–359, 366, 367, 368
and fears of performance, 11, 142, 143, 160, 167, 168, 173, 175, 196, 200, 203, 206, 208
and orgasmic dysfunction in females, 140, 238–240, 252
primary, 137–156, 157, 169
factors in development of, 137–146

Impotence, primary—*Continued*
failures in therapy, 358, 366, 367
and homosexuality, 140–142, 144, 213, 377
maternal factors in, 138, 144
and prostitute experiences, 142–143
religious factors in, 139–140, 144, 213, 253
and vaginismus in wives, 140, 252
and prostitute experiences, 142–143, 171, 177
from psychic trauma, 142–143, 144, 164
reactions of wives to, 2, 12, 140, 167, 183, 194–195, 210–211, 238–240, 252
secondary, 157–192
in aging males, 326–330, 347
and alcoholism, 160, 163–168
cultural factors in, 139, 159–160
and ejaculatory incompetence, 116, 133
factors in development of, 159–183
and homosexuality, 169, 179–183, 213
inadequate counseling in, 178, 188–192
from maternal dominance, 169–171, 174
from paternal dominance, 171–174
physiological causes of, 183–188
and premature ejaculation, 99, 100, 114, 133, 160, 161–163
and prostitute experiences, 171, 177
religious factors in, 175–176, 177–179, 189, 213
as transitory state, 114, 382

spectator role in, 65
treatment of, 193–213
cooperation of wives in, 210–211
results of, 211–213
Imprinting
effects of, 94, 95, 101, 222, 225, 295
orthodoxy-influenced, 230
See also Religious factors
See also Sexual value systems
Incest, as confidential information, 377, 378–379
Incompetence, ejaculatory, 116–136
See also Ejaculatory incompetence
Inevitability, ejaculatory. *See* Ejaculatory inevitability
Infections
pelvic, and dyspareunia,, 269–273, 284–285
vaginitis from, 271
Inhibitions, and physical communication, 76, 79
Instructions from therapists. *See* Authoritative control by therapists
Interviews
introductory session, 30–31
need for daily conferences, 17, 19, 310
roundtable discussions. *See* Roundtable discussions
See also History-taking
Introductory session with therapists, 30–31
Isolation, social, therapeutic advantages of, 17–20, 355–356

Klinefelter's syndrome, and secondary impotence, 185, 193

Laboratory studies, 59–60
glucose tolerance test, 60, 186–187
See also Sex-steroids

Laceration of broad ligaments, 258–259, 277–283

Lateral coital position, 110–111, 310–313

Ligaments, uterine, laceration of, 258–259, 277–283

Lotions, moisturizing, 78–82, 129
negative reactions to, 81, 235

Low sexual tension, as clinical entity, 247–248

Lubrication, vaginal
in aging female, 276, 336
insufficiency of, 275–277
mechanisms in production of, 199, 220
use of, 303

Male population, 92–213
aging males, 316–334
See also Aging population
dyspareunia in, 288–294
ejaculatory incompetence in, 116–136
See also Ejaculatory incompetence
failures in therapy, 361, 366, 367
fear of performance in, 11, 122
See also Fears of performance
fear of pregnancy in, 122
husbands of wives with orgasmic dysfunction, 3, 13, 313–314
See also Bilateral sexual inadequacy
impotence in, 137–213
primary, 137–156, 157, 169
secondary, 157–192
treatment of, 193–213
See also Impotence
orientation to partners, 120–121, 134–135, 142
partner surrogates for, 124, 135, 146–154, 354
premature ejaculation in, 92–115
See also Premature ejaculation
replacement partners for, 122, 146–150, 154–156, 354

role in therapy of women, 302, 303–304, 307–308, 313–314
sexual response cycle in, 317–318
See also Sexual value systems

Malpractice, psychotherapeutic, 141, 385–391

Manipulation
automanipulation. See Masturbation
mutual. See Genital manipulation

Marital history, statistics of, 36–37, 43–45

Marital-unit therapy, conjoint. See Mutual involvement in sexual problems

Marriage counseling
negative experiences with, 118, 178, 188–192, 345, 346, 384
See also Professionals

Masturbation
in females, 372
in aging female, 329, 342
nonorgasmic response to, 227, 236, 238, 240, 248–249, 314, 360
in males
effects of, 95–96
and ejaculatory incompetence, 122, 124, 130
and homosexuality, 180

Maternal dominance, effects of, 123, 138, 144, 169–171, 174, 345

Medical history of patients, 57–58

Medications, effects of, 184, 374

Menopause, changes after. See Aging population, females

Menstruation
negative reactions to, 117, 134, 231
and sexual tensions, 221
vaginal acidity in, 270–271

Mistakes, value of, 18–19, 84, 86, 201, 385

Moisturizing lotions, 78–82, 129
negative reactions to, 81, 235

Motivation of patients referred, 357

Multiorgasmic wives, and ejaculatory incompetence in husbands, 120, 127, 132
Music, attitudes toward, 49
Mutual exchange, sensory. *See* Sensate focus sessions
Mutual involvement in sexual problems, 2–3, 18, 31, 69, 113, 148, 195, 200, 228, 238, 251–252
Myotonia, in females, 220
Myths and fallacies in sexual activity, 26, 84, 87, 325, 335, 350
Myxedema, and secondary impotence, 185

Negative input, in sexual value systems, 77, 79, 143, 144, 178, 179, 216, 222–223, 241
   See also Imprinting
Negative reactions
   and failure rates. *See* Failures in therapy
   to menstruation, 117, 134, 231
   to moisturizing lotions, 81, 235
   to sensate-focus sessions, 77
   to sexual dysfunction. *See* Bilateral sexual inadequacy
   to therapists, 383–385
Neurologic disorders, and secondary impotence, 185
Nondemanding activities. *See* Sensate focus sessions
Nonorgasmic women. *See* Orgasmic dysfunction in females

Objectivity, professional, importance of, 10, 62, 67, 83
Odors, awareness of, 47–49, 77–79, 82–83
Olfaction, 47–49, 77–79, 82–83
Orgasm
   in females, 220, 297
      in aging females, 338

in males, 102
   in aging males, 318–320
Orgasmic dysfunction in females, 214–315
   background of, 222–226
   concepts of, 214–218
   educational techniques in, 302
   and fear of performance, 12, 167, 228
   homosexual influence on, 244–247
   and impotence in males, 238–240, 252
   male reactions to, 3, 13, 313–314
      See also Bilateral sexual inadequacy
   masturbatory inadequacy, 277, 236, 238, 240, 248–249, 314, 360
   and orientation to partner, 235, 241–244, 275, 277
   and premature ejaculation in husbands, 108, 228, 229, 253
   primary, 227–240
      absence of dominant influence in, 233–235
      failures in therapy, 314, 359, 366, 367, 383–385
      and negative psychosocial dominance, 235–237
   psychophysiological factors in, 67, 218–222, 224–226
      See also Biophysical and psychosocial systems
   random orgasmic inadequacy, 240, 247–248
      failures in therapy, 314–315, 360
   religious factors in, 229–233, 252, 253–256
   situational, 240–249
      failures in therapy, 360, 366, 367
   and vaginismus, 230
   treatment of, 295–315

authoritative direction in, 296–
299
failures in, 314–315, 359, 360,
366, 367, 383–385
pitfalls in, 309–310
positions recommended for,
300–302, 310–313
role of husband in, 302, 303–
304, 307–308, 313–314
sensate focus exercises in, 237,
299–306
sequential steps in, 304–306
teasing techniques in, 303, 309
Orgasmic platform, vaginal, 220
Orientation to partner, effects of,
120–121, 134–135, 142, 235,
241–244, 275, 277

Painful intercourse. *See* Dyspareunia
Partner surrogates, 124, 135, 146–
154, 354
Paternal dominance, and secondary
impotence, 171–174
Pelvic anatomy
female, 89, 262
male, 88
Pelvic examination. *See* Physical examination
Pelvic inflammatory disease, and
dyspareunia, 284–285
Pelvic movements, constrained, 110,
209–210, 307–308
Penile conditions, with dyspareunia,
289–293
Penile containment, nondemanding,
107, 109, 110, 307, 309
Penile insertion, mechanics of, 207–
208
Performance fears. *See* Fears of performance
Peyronie's disease, and dyspareunia,
291
pH, vaginal, 270–271
douches affecting, 274

male sensitivity to, 290
Phimosis, dyspareunia from, 290
Physical examination, 58–59
in broad-ligament laceration, 279
in dyspareunia, 267–268
importance of, 225, 259, 329
rectal responses in, 272
in vaginismus, 250–251, 262–263
Physical instructions, specific. *See*
Authoritative control by therapists
Physiological changes in aging
in females, 335–359
in males, 319–320, 326
Physiological factors
in dyspareunia, 269–288, 339, 348
in impotence, 183–188
in vaginismus, 258–260
Plateau phase
in aging male, 317–318
in female, 220
in aging female, 337
Pleasure
and give-to-get principle, 72–75,
109, 131, 147, 198, 298, 301
and guilt feelings, 75
mutual discovery of, 70–75
Population for research studies, 353–
354
See also Statistical considerations
Positions recommended
for female stimulation, 300–302
female-superior coital position,
106–108, 110, 111, 131,
207–208, 306–310
lateral coital position, 110–111,
310–313
for male stimulation, 102–103
Postmenopausal women. *See* Aging
population, females
Pregnancy, fear of, in males, 122
Premarital adulthood, history of,
42–43
Premature ejaculation, 92–115
cultural factors in, 93–96, 101

Premature ejaculation—*Continued*
distraction techniques in, 98–99, 162
and ejaculatory incompetence, comparison of, 128, 133, 158
failures in therapy, 113–114, 359, 366, 367
and fears of performance, 99, 102
female responses to, 93, 94, 95, 96–99, 110, 162, 228, 371–374
female-superior position in, 106–108, 110, 111
and impotence
comparison of, 158
secondary, 99, 100, 114, 133, 160, 161–163
lateral position in, 110–111
no-touching concept in, 98, 102
and orgasmic dysfunction in women, 108, 228, 229, 253
results of therapy in, 113–115
squeeze technique in, 102–106
therapy affecting sexual responsivity of wife, 108–110
and transitory secondary impotence, 114, 382
treatment of, 101–115
and vaginismus in partner, 253
and withdrawal from sexual contact, 99
Professionals
negative experiences with, 118, 178, 188–192, 345, 346, 384
as referral sources. *See* Referral sources
in religious fields, 178, 188–189
for research program, 16
seduction of patients by, 141, 388–391
self-referrals by, 356, 357
Prostate, spastic contractions in, 293, 319, 325, 329
Prostatitis, and dyspareunia, 293–294

Prostitute experiences
and impotence, 142–143, 171, 177
and premature ejaculation, 93–94
Psychic trauma
and ejaculatory incompetence, 125–126, 134
and female sexual response, 226
and impotence, 142–143, 144, 164
in relatives of partner surrogates, 150
and vaginismus, 252, 256–258
Psychosocial systems. *See* Biophysical and psychosocial systems
Psychotherapy
malpractice in, 141, 385–391
prior to treatment, 2–3, 7, 21, 64, 97, 141, 142, 372, 383
value of, 357–358

Qualifications of cotherapists, 15–17, 28

Radiation, vaginitis from, 275
Random orgasmic inadequacy, 240, 247–248
failures in therapy, 314–315, 360
Rape experiences
dyspareunia after, 268, 278, 280–281
reaction of husband to, 121
in relatives of partner surrogates, 150
vaginismus after, 256–257
Recording of interview sessions, 30
Rectal examination, responses to, 271–272
Rectal intercourse
homosexual, 141
vaginitis from, 271–272
Referral sources, 20–22, 29, 356
influence of, 388
self-referrals, 356, 357
See also Professionals; Screening procedures

Reflective techniques in therapy, 10, 62, 67, 73, 77, 83
Religious factors
in patients' attitudes toward sexual functioning, 10, 24, 70
in ejaculatory incompetence, 117–120, 133, 135
in impotence, 139, 144, 175–176, 177–179, 189, 213, 253
in orgasmic dysfunction in females, 229–233, 252, 253–256
in vaginismus, 252, 253–256
Replacement partners, 122, 146–150, 154–156, 354
Repression, and orgasmic dysfunction, 223–224
Research population, 353–354
See also Statistical considerations
Reserpine, secondary impotence from, 185
Resolution phase
in aging male, 321
in females, 220–221
in aging females, 339
Roundtable discussions, 7, 15, 31, 53, 60–84, 101, 200–201, 299, 306
concepts in, 60–67
goals of, 83–84
of sensate focus, 67–75
special-sense discussion, 75–83

Screening procedures, 20–22, 29, 68, 135, 356
difficulties in, 370–374
for partner surrogates, 149
Seduction of patients, by psychotherapists and other professionals, 141, 388–391
Self, perception of, 45
Self-referrals, by professionals, 356, 357

Seminal fluid
expulsion of, 102, 318, 319
volume of, 320
Sensate focus sessions
constrained pelvic movements in, 110, 209–210, 307–308
duration of, 71, 90–91, 308
for female stimulation, 203, 299–306
first day of, 71–75
genital manipulation in, 86–91, 102–106, 131, 203–205, 299–306
and give-to-get principle, 72–75, 109, 131, 147, 198, 298, 301
in impotence, 201–205
for male stimulation, 102–106, 131, 204
moisturizing lotions in, 78–82, 129, 235
negative reactions to, 81, 235
mutual signal systems in, 86–87, 203–204, 300–301
negative reactions to, 77
nondemanding penile containment, 107, 109, 110, 307, 309
in orgasmic dysfunction, 237, 299–306
in premature ejaculation, 108–109
roundtable discussion of, 67–75
second day of, 85–91
teasing approaches in, 206, 303, 309
touch and feel exercises, 71–75, 201–202, 297–299, 303
Sensitivity reactions
penile, 290
vaginal, 273–274
Sensual concepts, 46–49, 75–83
audition, 49
olfaction, 47–49, 77–79, 82–83
touch, 46–47
vision, 47

Sex-steroids
low levels of
in females, 269, 274, 319, 336
in males, 319
replacement therapy
in females, 337, 339–349
in males, 319, 324–325, 329
need for, 259–260, 275, 276, 277
Sexual dysfunction
in aging population, 316–350
bilateral. *See* Bilateral sexual inadequacy
female, 214–315
See also Female population
male, 92–213
See also Male population
Sexual functioning
in aging female, 335–339
in aging male, 319–320, 326
denial or inhibition of, 10, 70, 218, 219, 226
double standards for, 93, 95, 155, 215–216, 229, 331
fear of failures in. *See* Fears of performance
taken from natural context, 10, 11, 12, 13, 24, 65, 70, 175, 196–197, 219, 224, 298, 315
Sexual identity, acceptance or rejection of, 27, 74, 77, 219, 223, 225, 299
Sexual response cycle
in females, 220, 335
in males, 317–318
Sexual tension
in females
elevation of, in sensate focus sessions, 109
levels in aging women, 340
low, as clinical entity. *See* Random orgasmic inadequacy
physiologic reactions to, 220–221

unresolved, frustration from, 93, 94, 95, 97, 162
release for cooperative partners, 108–110, 132, 309
Sexual thoughts and feelings, role of, 73, 109, 110, 202, 210, 229, 298–299, 303, 307, 309, 358
Sexual value systems, 25–26, 52, 68, 76, 84, 90, 155
as basis for therapy, 25, 295–296
cultural aspects of. *See* Cultural factors
in females, 215, 219, 223
imprinting affecting, 94, 95, 101, 222, 225, 230, 295
in males, 159
multiple influences on, 241
negative input for, 77, 79, 143, 144, 178, 179, 216, 222–223, 241
restructuring of, 225, 237, 239–240, 298
See also Biophysical and psychosocial systems
Signal systems, mutual, 86, 87, 203–204, 300–301
Single men and women, 122, 124, 135, 146–156
statistical considerations, 148, 354, 364
Skepticism, healthy, toward therapy, 68, 105, 108, 206
Smell, sense of, 47–49, 77–79, 82–83
Social activities, arrangements for, 18, 56
with partner surrogates, 152
Social isolation, therapeutic advantages of, 17–20, 355–356
Social structure of research group, 356
Societal influences. *See* Cultural factors

Spastic contractions. *See* Contractions

Spectator roles in sexual activity, 11, 84, 100, 151, 196, 198, 200, 203, 209
  in aging males, 348
  identification of 65–66
  in impotence, 65
  in nonorgasmic women, 302

Squeeze technique, in premature ejaculation, 102–106

Statistical considerations, 351–369
  age range in therapy, 353
  aging populations, 330–334
  bilateral sexual inadequacy, 228–229, 354, 362, 363
  divorce incidence, 368
  educational levels, 356, 357
  ejaculatory incompetence, 116–117
  failure rates. *See* Failures in therapy
  geographic distribution, 355–356
  homosexuality and secondary impotence, 179
  impotence, 137, 211–213
  inadequate counseling, 188–189
  motivation of patients, 357
  number of people treated, 353–354
  original population, 362–364
  overall failure rate, 367–369
  partner surrogates, 147–149, 153–154
  premature ejaculation, 113
  prior psychotherapy, 357–358
  rejection of moisturizing lotions, 81
  religious backgrounds, 175, 213, 230, 252, 253
  replacement partners, 147
  self-referrals, 356, 357
  single men and women, 148, 354, 364

social structure, 356
therapy teams, 355
unilateral sexual inadequacy, 353–354
vaginismus, 252–253, 264

Steroids. *See* Sex-steroids

Stimulative techniques. *See* Sensate focus sessions

Sublimation. *See* Sexual functioning, denial or inhibition of

Surgery
  in broad-ligament lacerations, 281
  dyspareunia after, 286–288, 348
  impotence from, 186

Surrogate partners. *See* Partner surrogates

Symptom reversal, as therapeutic objective, 19, 21–22

Tampons, vaginal, affecting vaginal acidity, 271

Tape recordings, of interview sessions, 30

Teasing approaches
  for female stimulation, 303, 309
  for male stimulation, 206

Teenage years, history of, 41–42

Tension, sexual. *See* Sexual tension

Termination of therapy
  effects of early discharge, 381–383
  indications for, 63, 135

Testicular pain, 292

Testosterone replacement therapy, 319, 324–325, 329

Therapists
  antipathy toward, 383–385
  authoritative directions of. *See* Authoritative control by therapists
  changing roles of, 9
  dual-sex teams of, 4–8, 355, 391
  history-taking techniques of, 7, 28–29, 32, 53–54

Therapists—*Continued*
  psychotherapeutic. *See* Psycho-
    therapy
  qualifications of, 15–17, 28
  roles of, 5–8, 11, 14, 32
  silent cotherapist role, 9
Therapy concepts, 1–23
  communication in, 14–15, 19
  and conjoint marital-unit therapy,
    2–3
    See also Mutual involvement in
    sexual problems
  dual-sex therapy teams, 4–8
    See also Therapists
  and fears of performance, 11–14
  follow-up commitment, 22–23
  healthy skepticism toward, 68,
    105, 108, 206
  procedures in therapy, 9–11
  progressive steps in, 7, 14, 205–
    206, 304–306
  qualifications of cotherapists, 15–
    17, 28
  and referral sources, 20–22, 29
  social isolation as advantage in,
    17–20, 355–356
  time commitment in, 16, 17, 29,
    355–356
Therapy format, 24–91
  Day 1 and Day 2, 24–56
  Day 3, 57–84
  Day 4, 85–91
Thinking and feeling sexually, importance of, 73, 109, 110,
  202, 210, 229, 298–299, 303,
  307, 309, 358
Time commitment, for therapy, 16,
  17, 29, 355–356
Touch and feel exercises, 71–75,
  201–202, 297–299, 303
Touch, sense of, 46–47
Tranquilizers, effects of, 184, 374
Transference, management of, 7–8,
  29
Trauma

from criminal abortion, 268, 278,
  280
  laceration of uterine ligaments,
    258–259, 277–283
  of penis, 291–292
  psychosexual. *See* Psychic trauma
  from rape experiences, 256–257,
    268, 278, 280–281
Treatment. *See* Therapy concepts
Trichomonal vaginitis, 272–273

Unmarried men and women, 122,
  124, 135, 146–156
  statistical considerations, 148, 354,
    364
Uterine ligaments, laceration of,
  258–259, 277–283
Uterus
  infections of, 284
  sexual tension affecting, 220
  spastic contractions of, 220, 338–
    339, 342

Vaginal barrel
  in aging female, 336
  infections of, and dyspareunia,
    269–273
  insufficient lubrication in, 275–
    277, 336
  sensitivity reactions in, 273–274
  sexual tension affecting, 220
Vaginal lubrication. *See* Lubrication, vaginal
Vaginal outlet
  manipulation of, 303
  pain in, causes of, 268–269
Vaginal pH, 270–271
  douches affecting, 274
  male sensitivity to, 290
Vaginismus, 190, 250–265
  demonstration of, 262–263
  dilators in, 260, 263
  and dyspareunia, 258–260
  educational techniques in, 264
  from endometriosis, 259

failures in therapy of, 359
and homosexuality, 252, 260–261
and impotence in partner, 140,
    252
from laceration of broad liga-
    ments, 258–259
postmenopausal, 259–260
and premature ejaculation in
    partner, 253
from psychosexual trauma, 252,
    256–258
after rape experiences, 256–257
religious factors in, 252, 253–256
results of treatment, 264
and situational orgasmic dysfunc-
    tion, 230
treatment of, 262–265
Vaginitis
    coliform, 271–272

    fungal, 273
    from radiation, 275
    senile, 274–275, 276
        treatment of, 277
    trichomonal, 272–273
Value systems. *See* Sexual value sys-
    tems
Vasocongestion
    in females, 220
    testicular, 292
Verbalization, during sexual activity,
    90
Visual sense, 47

Withdrawal technique for contra-
    ception, effects of, 95
Wives of patients. *See* Female pop-
    ulation